T0381508

# DADDY'S LITTLE GIRL & MOMMY'S LITTLE BOY

## AMERICA'S MORAL CRISIS IN LOVE AND MARRIAGE AND WHAT WE MUST DO ABOUT IT

## BOOKS BY ZESTER HATFIELD

*Job Security In a High-tech World*

*Knights In Shining Armor*
*A book about father/daughter relationships*

*Daddy's Little Girl &*
*Mommy's Little Boy*
*America's Moral Crisis*
*In Love and Marriage and What*
*We Must Do About It*

# DADDY'S LITTLE GIRL & MOMMY'S LITTLE BOY

## AMERICA'S MORAL CRISIS IN LOVE and MARRIAGE and WHAT WE MUST DO ABOUT IT

ZESTER HATFIELD

*Zester Hatfield, Daddy's Little Girl & Mommy's Little Boy: Amercia's Moral Crisis In Love and Marriage and What We Must Do About It.*

Order this book online at www.trafford.com
or email orders@trafford.com

Most Trafford titles are also available at major online book retailers.

© Copyright 2005 Zester Hatfield.
All rights reserved. No part of this publication may be reproduced, stored in a retrieval system, or transmitted, in any form or by any means, electronic, mechanical, photocopying, recording, or otherwise, without the written prior permission of the author.

Print information available on the last page.

**ISBN**: 978-1-4120-5856-8 (sc)
**ISBN**: 978-1-4122-3616-4 (e)

Because of the dynamic nature of the Internet, any web addresses or links contained in this book may have changed since publication and may no longer be valid. The views expressed in this work are solely those of the author and do not necessarily reflect the views of the publisher, and the publisher hereby disclaims any responsibility for them.

Any people depicted in stock imagery provided by Getty Images are models, and
such images are being used for illustrative purposes only.
Certain stock imagery © Getty Images.

Front Cover Photo by Melissa Otto with Shawn and Jessica Otto, two grandchildren of the Hatfi elds.

Cover design by Reformation Ministries International, Corp.
www.ReformationInAction.org

*Trafford rev. 09/14/2020*

Trafford PUBLISHING www.trafford.com
**North America & international**
toll-free: 844-688-6899 (USA & Canada)
fax: 812 355 4082

# Dedication

Dedicated to my Proverbs Thirty One Wife of faith and grace:

**Marilyn Jean**

Without whose loving attention and co-partnership with me in life, our outrageous success in Christ's gift of Love and Marriage and our ministry to families of the Kingdom would not be possible.

# The Author

Zester Hatfield was born in Kirksville, Missouri to Zester and Ruth Hatfield on December 11, 1936. His teenage years were spent on his parent's farm in Grovesprings, Missouri and he was honorably discharged from the US Naval Air Force in 1954. He and Marilyn Jean Jones were married in the spring of 1959 and one year after the birth of their first child, Jennifer Lynn, they moved to Mexico as missionaries. In May of 1974 they left the mission field and entered the financial services industry in northern California. They returned to the southwest and to their first love—missions and the El Paso, Juarez, Mexico frontier—in the fall of 1989. In the spring of 1991 they started their accounting company, Hatfield & Company, Inc. which is now run exclusively by Marilyn. In February, 2002, they moved to the Philadelphia area to be closer to most of their many grandchildren. In the spring of 2004 they founded the non-profit family and missions outreach ministry: *Reformation Ministries International, Corp.* to bring God's revealed Law-Word and His uncommon common sense applications of wisdom, for the success of romance, love, sex and marriage to the Christian family.

---

*"Zester and Marilyn Hatfield have been married for over 45 years, have six children—five girls and one son—have raised an additional nine foster daughters while serving as missionaries in Mexico and now have twenty grand children from their own six. This would only be a statement of numbers if it were not for the fact that God has given them great insight and success in overcoming the challenges faced by all, in the contest between the spirit and the flesh. Through God's gift of faith and grace their love not only continues to be firm but passionate and growing more so—even now as they enter their senior years. What they share with us in these pages is a rare look at how the battle is won, for all who would believe, at the point of where the rubber hits the pavement. Their applications of God's revealed Law-Word and His uncommon common sense in their lives and especially the duplication of these successes for love and marriage in their children, is exciting and challenging to the point of precedent setting magnitudes. The reader will experience riveting and exciting challenges to the status quo of our present day Christian culture."* Breck Landry, Director-Crisis Pregnancy Center, El Paso, Texas

# Acknowledgements

A book such as Daddy's Little Girl & Mommy's Little Boy cannot be born of merely a creative imaginative carnal mind—it must come from a higher source—as God's providence working through the lives of many others to influence and inspire the life of the author. I am so very grateful and honored that through the instrumentality of so many others, God has and is working His good pleasure in me and my wife, Marilyn. As the author I bring to the public only my name, but as the person behind the name I am forever—only a part—of that one flesh that God has made of me and my wife Marilyn. We mention only those that are most central in all that God has brought into our lives. We will only know the complete list when they are revealed to us in the resurrection.

My father and mother Zester and Ruth Hatfield married for seventy years and three months, who never gave up on their challenges of love and marriage! Especially my mother, Ruth who was God's instrument to focus me towards Him; Karl Ketcherside, late editor of the *Mission Messenger,* author and minister who married us and who assisted us in accepting God's gift of faith without works, Pastor Josue Lopez, our co-laborer in Mexico, Pastor Loran Biggs our great encourager in Christ, Howard Watrous and Orv Owens, two minds in the art of love and marriage, Capt. Karl Duff, personal prayer partner, Pastor Dennis Peacock, pioneer in applying God's uncommon common sense; missionary pioneer, Hudson Taylor, Church historian Eusebius; St. Augustine, a key bridge element of God in bringing to life the Reformation, Martin Luther and John Calvin the two giants of the Reformation; Cornelius VanTil, David Chilton, Greg Banson, Ray Sutton, Gary DeMar, Kenneth Gentry, Gary North, R. Rushdooney, Douglas Wilson, God's servants all and some of His most brilliant modern day theologians. Most important of all: God's revealed Law-Word and the gracious work of His Holy Spirit to enlighten, encourage, strengthen and to do His good pleasure in us!

We are especially grateful for the physical and emotional support of all our wonderful children and their spouses. Stephanie and Jennifer our two oldest daughters have been great to help with editing and personal feedback. Not only have they been a great help, but they have been challenged to do so, while keeping up with the day-to-day responsibilities of being—wife and mother—to two very large and active families of faith and grace. We appreciate so very much, Keith Avellino, Stephanie's husband for his computer knowledge and programming support. We are also grateful for our local pastor Adam Brice and for the many acts of kindness and personal encouragement from our local church family.

# Special Acknowledgments

Many individuals have given us helpful comments and suggestions, however two of these standout as examples of going the second mile in their efforts to assist us in the editing and content critique of the book.

Roger O'Dell, President and founder of Model Cities-El Paso, a strong ministry against pornography, making significant headway in a difficult international border area. www.elpasofamily.org

Greg Williams, Marriage Seminar/Workshop Presenter and Deacon at the Southland Christian Church in Lexington, Kentucky; has offered superb content critique that has sharpened several difficult topical issues. Greg Williams is also a very effective character based abstinence director.

# Table of Contents

# DADDY'S LITTLE GIRL & MOMMY'S LITTLE BOY

## America's Moral Crisis In Love and Marriage *and*

## What We Must Do About It

## Introduction

"Based on interviews with more than 1000 adults nationwide, the survey discovered that less than one out of every five adults believes that children under the age of 13 are being "superbly" or "pretty well" prepared for life emotionally, physically, spiritually, intellectually or physically. Fewer than one out of every twenty adults believes that America's youngsters are receiving above average preparation in all five of those areas of life." Americans Agree: Kids Are Not Being Prepared for Life," The Barna Group-October 26, 2004

**Purpose and vision:**

The objective of this book is to provide Christian husbands and wives, fathers and mothers of faith and grace with a new sense of God's—uncommon common sense—in all matters concerning love, sex and marriage. These are God's elements for overcoming our post modern moral crisis of love and marriage in America today and for generations to come! Saying we are Christians is an over simplification—we must be recipients of His gift of faith and grace—and live by the principles of His revealed Law-Word before the name Christian will mean anything to this lost, depraved and misguided generation![1]

**Husbands and Wives, Fathers and Mothers of faith and grace:**

These are those married couples—read one man and one woman—who have received God's gift of faith and who have committed their lives and their roles as parents to the grace of God. These couples are those who know that the future of their children is in jeopardy and that we are in a war for the control of that future! Sadly, the statistics of broken homes, divorces, adultery, domestic violence, drugs and promiscuity—to mention only some of the ills of our culture—are almost equally divided between "Christian" families and non-Christian families. This is unacceptable as a comparison and must change. Consequently, fathers and mothers of faith and grace are those—who are and or who will experience—God's promise of victory over these fruits of our fallen nature and live a marriage experience that captures the best of God's gifts of love, sex and romance in marriage. Daddy's Little Girl and Mommy's Little Boy brings us clear evidence of just how America's Christian couples can have this victory in their marriage and how to duplicate this success in their sons and daughters.

**American families under attack:**

American families are under attack by a coalition of determined foes, left-wing liberal secularist all! These socialist atheists have taken over all of the old main-line denominations, the public education system, the media, the theatre,

[1] "For by grace you have been saved through faith, and that not of yourselves; it is the gift of God, not of works, lest anyone should boast. For we are His workmanship; created in Christ Jesus for good works, which God prepared beforehand that we should walk in them." Eph. 2:8-10.

most of our civil service agencies and now they want our families as well. Awaken Fathers! Awaken Mothers! This is a mind-filling challenge that can't be made to disappear! On the contrary this is a cultural war, publicly and officially declared by the Humanist Manifesto II, which embraces many repugnant ant Biblical and anti God doctrines, that have led to easy inclusion and promotion of the Kinseyan "safe or free sex" doctrine in all of these systems (education, government and media), thus leading to our current moral morass.

> "Most Americans consider no-fault divorce a done-deal: feminists have effectively trashed the dreaded 1950's when divorce was considered a scandal. Few public opinion leaders are willing to link divorce to the arguments for heterosexual marriage. But we can't win the fight for heterosexual marriage without confronting the issue of divorce. Far from being a losing strategy, we can only win if we bring the divorce issue out of the closet." National Catholic Register: Jennifer Roback Morse, Ph.D., is the author of 101 Tips for a Happier Marriage, which you can find on her website. *www.jointhemarriagerevolution.com*

During the last several decades; church elders, pastors, radio and television evangelists have been sending out a constant call for growth of strong Christian families with moral fiber and character, reflecting the faith and grace of our Lord. All American Christians over the age of 50 have passed through most of the various "movements" that have come and gone during these formative decades. There was the Charismatic Movement, still there—but not the panacea it was proclaimed to be. There was the Shepherding Movement that left a lot of disappointed and bruised congregations and families in its wake. There was the Laughter Movement now only a whimper having left many disillusioned. Now in more recent times we have the Home Church Movement, the Home School Movement, the Betrothal Movement, the Servant Husband Movement, and the Theophostic Ministry Movement. All of this and yet our statistics continue to show us failing at the same rate as the unbelievers. No doubt some aspects of these and other movements have had a positive purpose in our modern Christian culture, especially the Christian home school movement. What is so outrageous about all of our—let's get excited—let's have another revival—let's move more in the Spirit—let's—find another "movement" to revitalize our families, ad nauseam is that it has done nothing to execute the dramatic change that is needed! Father and mothers of God—we need a dramatic change—a knock down drag out back to basics full bore no nonsense—tell it like it is—change of direction. A new paradigm of understanding and wisdom of God for sex, love and marriage kind of change! If you don't want this—QUICK—put this book down and don't look back!

**Understanding our focus:**

This book does not judge the value or efficacy of any of these movements. What this book does—is it reveals the one common element—that is consistently absent from these movements. We don't need another "modern movement" but rather a return to God's revealed wisdom and knowledge of—sex, love and marriage—for Fathers and Mothers of faith and grace. This is the consistently missing element of all of our so called—movements—they are so called because had they been true movements of God—as was the Reformation—we would now be enjoying a victorious Christian culture. We would not—as we most certainly have—sunk yet deeper into our miry pit of broken Christian homes, divorced, abused wives, abandoned children, aborted babies, adulterous relationships in church leaders and ministries, incest, pornography, all overflowing with life decisions based on misinformation, misunderstanding, biblical illiteracy, visionless, politically inept and now fearful for our very cultural existence. In stark contrast, this book brings a clear and concise focus to God's revealed wisdom and knowledge for God's married lovers—Fathers and Mothers of faith and grace—to overcome and to be personally victorious, and equally if not more important—that their children—will also be victorious!

This is not written to win the unbeliever or to change the purely religious, although it is possible that God can and in some cases will use it to reveal Himself to some and to change others. Most importantly, this is for those who have the gift of faith and who know in whom they have believed.

This is not a call to more fleshly works of better moral rectitude—although through the Spirit—such fruits must and will come from this. This is an exploration of the deeper understanding of Apostle Paul's effort to reveal his—mystery—of the gospel, hidden from the world before it was given to him, for the Kingdom. Down through the ages—from Paul to the present—many have understood this wisdom and knowledge and have been richly blessed. But for reasons that only our sovereign Lord can explain, they have never become—common practice—not in any Christian culture since the first century. Although simple in concept, these truths so challenge our fleshly egos and preconceived secular cultural biases that they are easily rejected. Were this not the case these truths would have been consistently embraced early in the history of God's Kingdom. My personal opinion is that we are more overtaken by our own natural state of sin and our pride as men and as women than we have ever thought possible and this has blinded us to the truth. Our sins have kept our minds closed to God's revealed answers. Poverty of spirit and our present condition is the result.

This book is a call—perhaps the last one for this generation—for men and women of faith and grace to accept His Lordship and His guidance in all things, especially in the matter of embracing God's gifts of—outrageously successful sexual fulfillment, in love over-flowing marriages—morality and the rearing of our sons and daughters to imitate the same! Failing this—all we have is certain personal and national discipline of enormous proportions. Have you noticed those dark clouds coming from the—Middle Eastern—skyline? It is never a question of whether or not God is sovereign or victorious. Sovereignty is never in question—victory on the other hand—is always only a question of when and with whom, He chooses to share it. I believe and am praying; that He will choose us, fathers and mothers of faith and grace, of this generation—now in our times, because of His animation and inspiration—to bring us to embrace Him through His power to change us, finally to do things His way, with His wisdom and for His glory![2]

**As you read this introduction you have only two choices:**

1. As we have said, you may put the book down and consider yourself fortunate not to be bothered by such a trivial—and most likely in your opinion—a self-righteous diatribe.

---

[2] "We have a strong city; God will appoint salvation for walls and bulwarks. Pen the gates that the righteous nation which keeps the truth may enter in. You will keep him in perfect peace, whose mind is stayed on You, because he trusts in You. Trust in the LORD forever, for in Yah, the LORD, is everlasting strength. For He brings down those who dwell on high, the lofty city; 'He lays it low, He lays it low to the ground, He brings it down to the dust. The foot shall tread it down—The feet of the poor and the steps of the needy.' The way of the just is uprightness; O Most Upright, You weigh the path of the just. Yes, in the way of Your judgments, O LORD, we have waited for You; The desire of our soul is for Your name and for the remembrance of You. With my soul I have desired You in the night, Yes, by my spirit within me I will seek You early; for when Your judgments are in the earth, the inhabitants of the world will learn righteousness. Let grace be shown to the wicked, yet he will not learn righteousness; In the land of uprightness he will deal unjustly, and will not behold the majesty of the LORD. LORD, when Your hand is lifted up, they will not see. But they will see and be ashamed for their envy of people; yes, the fire of Your enemies shall devour them." Isaiah 26:1-11.

2. You may also decide that you too are moved by our present state of moral decay and spiritual morass and although you can't say as yet whether this book contains anything that will—make a difference—you will at least take a serious look, to see if this is a clear choice of—old truth brought to new light—or an echo of yet another doomed movement.

"Tomorrow will resemble today if we continue today what we did yesterday." Star Parker, Black female author and Columnist.

**Ministry Leaders and Sexual Promiscuity:**

At the beginning of this introduction I quoted Jennifer Roback Morse: "Far from being a losing strategy, we can only win if we bring the divorce issue out of the closet."

Yes, we must bring the issue of divorce out of the closet. I only wish that divorce were the—only thing—we had locked up in our closets! To our great disgrace as a culture and especially as Christian people, our closets are overflowing with hidden sins that we—as a Christian culture—have not been willing to discuss, much less to admit and certainly from which we have yet to repent and seek God's healing. By saying this I run the risk of your disdain—"Here we go again, just another diatribe against the church." I know—I'm sorry it looks that way—but nothing could be farther from the truth! Before you pass judgment, let me share with you the results of a little known poll, taken by a well known and highly respected Christian leader and minister, Chuck Swindoll—of Dallas Theological Seminary fame. The time was July, 1994—the place was Colorado State University at Boulder Colorado—I was there. I participated and I am a personal witness of this poll.

We Americans are very familiar with polls—all kinds of polls—from what we like to eat, to whom we are most likely to vote for. Before experiencing this poll that I am about to describe, I had never heard of a poll to measure the moral health of our nations ministry leaders. This was a public—on the spot—poll, not your typical phone survey or mass mailing. I don't think that Pastor Swindoll was thinking in terms of a poll. We were all gathered together in a small indoor stadium of approximately 5,000 seating capacity. We numbered between 3,500—4,000 men, ministry leaders all. There were pastors, assistant pastors, youth pastors, elders, deacons, Sunday school teaches, evangelists and missionaries, representing every ethnic and social strata from all of the lower 48 states. Polls taken from a broad geographic section with ethnic and social diversity and in numbers exceeding 1,200 participants are considered to have an error factor of no more than three percent. This poll was truly a representation of a major cross section of American Christian leadership.

**Personal witness:**

We were in the last night of a three day leadership training conference sponsored by *Promise Keepers* of Colorado Springs, Colorado. Chuck Swindoll was the featured speaker for our last gathering before departure the following morning. Excitement and a sense of expectation filled the air. We had heard many speakers during the previous three days and had participated in many study groups to share problems unique to men and their roles as leaders in church, family and business. This last meeting would be the pinnacle of our experience. Chuck Swindoll's message would be the hot iron to—cauterize—our open wounds and to bring a measure of final healing to this group of men.

Pastor Swindoll held forth in his delivery for almost an hour. He began by giving an over-view of the general problems of men in ministry; work-a-holism, family and spousal isolation, self importance, insensitivity to spousal needs for tenderness and romance and last but not least—ministry leadership tendencies for blindness to our own sexual misdeeds. Pastor Swindoll was very transparent and graciously shared his own experiences with many of these problems, especially his past failings with regard to his having isolated his loving wife from his ministry life and his failings to appropriately cultivate her personal needs for tenderness and romance. He shared his failings and his victories through the grace of God and praised Him for giving him back his wife and his ministry, during this difficult time. We all were on the edge of our seats, hanging onto each word, expecting a testimony of victory and overcoming of evil—we were not disappointed!

Then came our moment of truth; Pastor Swindoll changed from his personal experience and challenges and began to focus—on our personal—potential for problems and challenges. He reviewed the need for all men in leadership to accept ownership for their actions and to be committed to face their problems and to seek God in honest repentance and commitment to positive change. Only through personal ownership of our problems and frank admission of our errors—could we gain God's blessing—of healing and over-coming.

Pastor Swindoll was very clear on his subsequent request for a personal declaration of guilt and an honest request for God to forgive and to heal. Not just twice did he clarify to whom he was speaking and from whom he was asking a decision for repentance—but many times—he clearly stated that he was addressing this challenge only to those who were now—present tense—involved in and guilty of sexual misdeeds for which they knew they were wrong and for which they desperately needed to repent and ask God for forgiveness. He was very clear on just what he felt constituted such sexual misdeeds: adultery, fornication, pornography, incest and homosexuality. He introduced his challenge with a qualifying statement, which I will paraphrase:

**Pastor Swindoll:**

> "Men and brothers I have spoken to many men concerning the problems we are about to discuss. I am aware that although this is a group of ministry leaders from all over the country, there are those among us who suffer from these very problems. In a group of this size it would be impossible for there not to be such men who are even right now involved in sexual misconduct with secretaries, mistresses, pornography, adultery, fornication, incest and homosexuality. At the close of my comments I am going to ask all of you who are now involved in anyway in any of these sexual sins, to be honest and to seek God's forgiveness. I want you to stand where you are and I am going to lead you in a prayer of repentance and forgiveness. God is faithful and He will hear your prayers and lead you to victory."

After repeating this explanation and challenge many times from several different perspectives it would be impossible—or so it would seem—that any of us present did not understand what was being said and what the challenge was. It was crystal clear to me and personally very impacting and of great interest.

It was a great impact personally because I too had had a problem with sexual misconduct from 1974-1985 during which time I deluded myself into believing it was alright for me to occasionally frequent "gentlemen's" bars—the oxymoron—for topless bars. The lunacy of my ways was brought home to me through a small men's prayer group I helped to form and attended, beginning in the summer of 1985. This was my first experience of real—man to man—openness and spiritual delivery. After coming to my spiritual senses—pure intellectualism will not work—I told my wife. From that moment on, I have been blessed by a deep understanding of God's wisdom on limiting my visual focus of the feminine form and—all things sexual—to my wife, Marilyn. Amazingly, this happened during a time when I was working very close with my daughters as their champion for successful romance and marriage—how willfully blind I was!

It was also of great interest to me because I too had been involved, in the years since my own delivery, in counseling men in their struggles with sexual sins. I was very interested to get a pulse on the level of such activity within the broader scope of ministry leaders from all across America. I'm not exactly sure what I expected the response to be—but be assured of this—I did not expect what actually happened!

After doing all that is humanly possible—to make clear and unambiguous—his challenge and his request for personal action, pastor Swindoll came to a point where he said:

**Pastor Swindoll:**

> "Alright men, those of you who want to respond to this call for repentance and forgiveness on any of these matters, stand up now."

**The response shows evidence of our decaying Christian culture:**
I knew that there were certainly too many men gathered to allow for any possibility that there were none present who did not have problems with some—if not all—of these areas of sexual sin. What I was not prepared for was the impact I felt, from the public response to this very personal polling of sexual sins and misdeeds. The response impacted me then and continues to bring serious reflection to me as I see our Christian culture suffering increased attacks from without while dying from within.

The response was so over-whelming that it was hard to see—who was not—standing up! As I already had experienced my own delivery many years prior to this gathering and not because of any—superior personal holiness—I did not stand in response to this challenge. The view from a seating position was advantageous for determining who else was still seated. In this oval shaped, bleacher style arena, it was easy to look both ways, up and down the isles. I spent the whole time, listening and at the same time looking to see what percentage was standing and what percentage was still seated. My most conservative calculation is that at least 90 percent of the men present were standing and only 10 percent were still seated.

Albeit this was not announced or characterized by *Promise Keepers* to be a poll—but none-the-less—a poll it is. In the interest of not over-stating the case and given the possibility that in spite of pastor Swindoll's clear explanation of to whom he was addressing this challenge; let us say that only 75 percent were actually having personal sin problems of a sexual nature. Aside from the fact that these men were courageous in their admission of guilt and in their commitment to repent and to seek God's forgiveness—the big message here for America—is that our Christian culture is decaying and dying from within—as a church nationally—we are without moral leadership. Thank God for every pastor and ministry leader who is living the victorious life over sexual sin, and thank you pastor, ministry leader, whom ever you are! May God continue to give us the victory—for it is not by flesh and blood that we overcome—it is an unmerited gift from our Heavenly Father.

The fact that our ministry leaders are having personal problems with sexual promiscuity gives us a clear understanding that they are mere men and not gods. Also it is sobering for all men, for if those who are proclaimed leaders of spiritual and moral values are having problems what can we expect from those who are more ambivalent about their commitment? The answer is in our faith: the faith we either have or do not have. We as carnal men—although in possession of the gift of faith and grace—are no more powerful than those men who reject our Lord and Savior, if we self-consciously disregard His commands and deny His gift of wisdom and power to overcome. Remember that old saying: "You can lead a horse to water, but you can't make him drink." God can and does give us the answers and the power we need to be successful in all that He has commanded us to do—but only if we accept His Lordship and His guidance. He does not indwell the unbelievers nor does He promise them power to overcome. Their failures should be—no surprise—to us who believe. But what should be of—great surprise and concern—is our rebellion against our Heavenly Father evidenced in our lack of exercising his gift of the power to overcome.

**Teenage Girls and Promiscuity:**

What is the present state of sexual awareness and sexual moral examples now being practiced across our land in thousands of high-schools? The truth is much worse than any serious parent wants to hear. Not even an unbelieving couple wants to hear what is actually taking place—much less a Christian couple!

I have included some excerpts from a recent article published in the Milwaukee Journal Sentinel by Megan Twohey which reveal the results of several serious studies that have been made across all ethnic and social borders to answer this very question. It is hard to imagine that our culture has reached such a state of moral decay that such things could be taking place among our young girls. We don't need studies and the opinions of "experts" to tell us that such activities are extremely dangers for our families and our culture. When they take pride in promiscuity, young girls—as also with young men—face untold dangers—of losing every dream of real love and marriage that they might have ever had. Such practices can even cost them their lives—certainly they become morally desensitized—morally dead!

> "A girl going by the first name of Heather, a 16-year-old with sandy blond hair, recounts one of her promiscuous encounters as she remembers how it felt the time she had sex on the same day with two different boys. Neither was her boyfriend.
>
> 'I felt like I was in control,' said the Neenah, Wis., native, who like other teens interviewed for this story is being identified only by her first name. 'I felt like a player.'
>
> Fourteen-year-old Mia of Racine, Wis., explains with pride how she uses a calculated approach to flirting and dating to extract money from multiple boys.
>
> 'I've been pimping,' Mia said. 'I've got dudes who give me money every day.'
>
> "A lot of adults may not want to believe it, but these and other teenage girls are adopting some stereotypical "male" attitudes toward sex, according to reports from a national research firm and interviews with girls and officials who work with them.
>
> "They're not only casual about having sex or "hooking up" with multiple partners; they're proud of it, referring to themselves as "pimps" and "players" and bragging about their exploits. These girls see themselves as

using sex to assert their power over boys (and girls), while liberating their gender from the stereotypical categories of virgin and whore," says Megan Twohey.

Deborah Hoffman, a sex education teacher and author of "*Sex and Sensibility: The Thinking Parents Guide to Talking Sense about Sex,*" says "Many are stripping themselves of femininity, true happiness and the ability to have healthy relationships in the process."

This is truly a disaster, Hoffman said.

"This is in no way liberation. It's dehumanizing if you're allowing people to treat you like objects, and you're treating other people like objects."

"Female players range from girls who have casual "hook-ups" that don't necessarily involve sex to those who have multiple sexual partners whom they call on regularly. Girls who call themselves pimps have sex or simply flirt with multiple boys with the intention of getting cash, car rides or other favors from them. These girls draw satisfaction from making the boys think they are the sole recipient of their affection. They talk openly about their conquests and the importance of satisfying their physical needs.

"I guess if you heard it, you'd probably be a little shocked. It sounds like stuff boys in a locker room would say," said Dan Baran, director of Professional Services, an organization that runs youth programs in Wisconsin's Kenosha, Milwaukee and Racine Counties.

"They talk about it because they think they're better or cooler for having sex," said Angela, a 14-year-old from Milwaukee.

Perhaps most prominent is the vulgar vixen Lil' Kim, who raps in graphic detail about her male conquests. Britney Spears and Christina Aguilera are among other female performers who, on stage and off, have made sexually charged behavior acceptable in the eyes of girls and boys alike.

Alicia, a 16-year-old from Neenah, said she wants to act like the male players she sees on TV because they seem powerful and in control.

"You see it on TV," Alicia said. "Boys who are players have it made. Girls want to be just like that."

But sexual activity without intimacy has left many girls feeling hollow or emotionally damaged, said Hoffman, who works with teens across the country.

Many are depressed and have no idea how to have a healthy, romantic relationship. The same goes for boys with casual and detached attitudes toward sex, she said.

"They've given away parts of themselves before they can become secure," Hoffman said. "Some may never recover."

Teenagers themselves suspect that these aggressive girls are not what they seem. Vanity, vanity![3]

---

[3] Vanity, vanity: The price of Holland's famous "free love" lifestyle is often an unhappy sex life, according to a survey of more than 1,000 Dutch singles. The poll, conducted by the online journal *Mylife,* found that less than one-fifth of Dutch singles said they are happy with their sex lives and two thirds said married couples are happier. About half of Dutch single men and a third of Dutch single women reported having regular one night stands. (World magazine-Oct. 2004, Quick Takes, p. 11)

"Outwardly, there's this attitude of `I don't care, I'm having fun, too,'" said Bridget, 18, of Milwaukee. "But there's always a pause afterward. I think they really want more than being a player. I think they want a committed relationship."

And boys on the other end can end up feeling used by girls, said Austin, a 16-year-old from Racine.

"If you're the guy who is not her boyfriend, you don't mind," he said. "If you're dating the girl, it's not cool."

"Plus sexually active girls can still get slapped with the slut label, no matter how bold and brazen they act." Bridget, Austin and other teens said, not to mention the health risks that come with promiscuity.

The teen pregnancy rate is down across the country, but teens ages 15 to 19 who have had sex have the highest rates of sexually transmitted disease of any age group in the country. The highest rates of gonorrhea and chlamydia—diseases that can cause infertility—are found among girls ages 15 to 19, according to a report released in February by the University of North Carolina's School of Journalism and Mass Communication.

In certain cases, sexual aggressiveness is escalating into sexual harassment. School officials say they see more and more girls groping boys in the hallways and classrooms. Rangel runs workshops in middle schools throughout Racine. At each school, he asks principals and assistant principals about the issues facing students.

"One hundred percent of the schools now say that girls' sexually harassing boys is the No. 1 problem," Rangel said.

**How then must we live?**

I don't mention these promiscuous teenage girls to bruise your sensitivities but to show you what is—out there now for our Christian teenage girls to deal with—and that it will only get worse if we keep doing what we have always done before! This you can be assured of: there are many—all too many—of our precious Christian young ladies who are now, or who will be getting, trapped in this same craze of promiscuity. More importantly, all our new born little girls and boys have only a very bleak future unless a great number of fathers and mothers of faith and grace answer this call to action! Let us know assuredly—that if we do not accept this call—we Christian adults will continue in our lies and deceits and our children will reap the same. They will imitate our sins and they will add all that they learn from the street, from Internet chat rooms, from Hollywood, from MTV, from all the sit-coms, from their regular public school classes—secular origins all—and certainly they will learn all that Planned Parenthood can cram into their dear little heads!

Doug Giles wrote last fall in an article posted on the Townhall.com web site on 10-31-04 *"Evangelicals Non-Prophets"*

"It's time for courageous Christian men and women to step up to the plate and for all the little tinker pot girlie men; to retreat to the stands and sit there with Mummy until the dust clears.

"In times of crisis our area of critical need is for leaders who can think widely and deeply, who can lead courageously and bring our great nation and the Church through spiritual obfuscation and demonic debilities. We must resurrect biblical truth, and apply it even-handedly to all of society during these days of decline.

"This means Lamb Chop, Kermit and all Evangelical marionettes occupying pulpits and pews must sit down and hush because the times demand prophets. We need prophets who could care less about: Political Correctness—Style over Substance—What the Masses and Wusses are Yapping for Being Popular.

"My ClashPoint is this: I'm not a doom and gloomer. It is not as if we are approaching the end of civilization's road; it's not even the beginning of the end. Most likely, it is the end of the beginning ... who knows where we stand from an eschatological view point? However, I do know where we stand from an ecclesiastical and missiological point of view.

"We stand where we have always been supposed to stand, as the pillar of truth who proclaims it publicly and globally, applying it fully to all of life. And guess what, Church? Just as Ringo said, 'You know it don't come easy.'

"Come on—we don't need anymore nicety-nice clergy in charge of churches that don't equip us to face the real issues confronting our church and culture. We can do without spineless crowd pleasers, can't we? We really do not need narcissistic, solipsistic, pseudo saints. What we need are prophets, stalwart sons and daughters who will speak and defend truth, freedom and human rights in the face of atheism, lies and hell bent special interest groups!" Doug Giles-Clash Point[4]

**Your question:**

So—you ask: "What does ***"Daddy's Little Girl and Mommy's Little Boy"*** have to do with our crisis of Love and Marriage in America"?

That is a good question, one I will answer completely, but first I will set the stage with two quotes from unexpected quarters.

"It should be your care, therefore, and mine, to elevate the minds of our children and exalt their courage; to accelerate and animate their industry and activity; to excite in them a habitual contempt of meanness, abhorrence of injustice and inhumanity, and an ambition to excel in every capacity, faculty, and virtue. If we suffer their minds to grovel and creep in infancy, they will grovel all their lives." -John Adams

"Your love of liberty—your respect for the laws—your habits of industry—and your practice of the moral and religious obligations, are the strongest claims to national and individual happiness."—George Washington

It is indisputable that—on a national scale—our Christian leaders have failed us. Yet, there is an old German proverb that says a nation gets the leaders it deserves. There is no such exact quote from the Bible, but in principle one does not have to look far to find many that apply equally well. So, let's blame our leaders and demand our rights to better spiritual oversight and care. Yeah right. We Americans, yes—even Christian Americans—have become a culture of victims. Our Creator God did not save and deliver us from our sins to be victims—we are over-comers—"we can do all things through Christ which strengthens us." Philippians 4:13

---

[4] Doug Giles' provocative weekly one-hour radio program, 'The Clash', has re-launched with several new features. Go to clashradio.com , 'listen live.'

Those of our leaders who are unrighteous—let them be unrighteous still—those of our leaders who are righteous—let them be righteous still—and may God bless them. As for us, all fathers and mothers of faith and grace let us pick up the mantel of our own personal responsibility to repent of our sexual sins and our lack of leadership in our own homes and move forward through God's revealed Law-Word of grace and strength. There are dynamic answers and priceless rewards—now in our times—for all who will take up this challenge!

**Now to your question:**

For centuries our culture has told us that in all matters of sexual instruction our daughters are best directed by their mothers. Likewise our culture has told us that in all matters of sexual instruction our sons are best directed by their fathers. I propose to you that this is not true and that it furthermore is not taught in God's revealed Law-Word. The truth is that all matters of sexual instruction for our daughters are best directed by her father of faith and grace and likewise all matters of sexual instruction for our sons, are best directed by his mother of faith and grace.

"If so why have we not adopted this as a culture?" you ask; fair enough—but let me say this—it is more difficult to answer the "whys" of God's sovereignty than it is to trust in His revealed wisdom and knowledge for the solution. As I said in the beginning of this introduction: "My personal opinion is that we are more overtaken by our own natural state of sin and our pride as men and as women than we have ever thought possible and this has blinded us to the truth. Our sins have kept our minds closed to God's revealed answers. Poverty of spirit and our present moral condition is the result."

Certainly fathers have a strong responsibility to provide a good role model for their sons, to build character and moral fiber into their hearts and minds. Father and son personal time and interaction are of a high priority. However, mother is the one who knows more about women than does her husband. Also, mothers are very important in the same way for their daughters. Yet again, it is clear that fathers know more about men than mothers. This is not only logical it is biblical and to assign the least equipped within a team to do the same thing that the most equipped should do is a demonstration of selfishness and—sexist identity ego malfunction—of the worst sort! It can only be that Barnum & Bailey have shovels equal to such moments.

Within the pages of this book you will walk with us through forty five years of learning experiences and have the opportunity to discover with us as we discover together just how wonderful is the wisdom and knowledge of God. How correct are all His ways and the joy of knowing you have control and predictability through His wisdom and knowledge.

Each detail is presented so that the reader gets not only the facts, but also the history, experience and God's revealed Law-Word behind the facts. There are pre-designed and structured processes for each step of the way. There are illustrations and actual presentations for your use. Also in order for each reader to get the most comprehensive understanding possible the book is divided into three smaller books:

**Book I: Love and Marriage**

Our adventure starts with a journey into all of the most exciting yet often overlooked or misunderstood factors in God's plan for outrageously successful marriages with heaven designed sexual satisfaction. This builds and progresses into discovering the secrets for maintaining this romance and partnership throughout all the years of even the longest marriages. Great sex and romance for men and women even in their most advanced years of marriage are possible under God's plan of love and marriage.

Building a marriage filled with God's revealed plan for romance and sexual fulfillment is one of His key elements for establishing the kind of solid base upon which to provide a healthy spiritual and love motivated environment for children. Children need examples NOT theories!

Men and women of faith and grace must first experience success in their own relationship and fulfillment in their own personal love and romance if they are to have the wisdom and understanding that God requires for leading their children into the same.

**Book II: Daddy's Little Girl**

Now with new insight and a firm grasp on how to realize God's planned success for our own personal romance and sexual fulfillment as a couple, we will discover how to apply this success to daddy's little girl.

**Book III: Mommy's Little Boy**

Likewise, this same insight and new understanding will enable us to adventure into the development of mommy's little boy.

**Summary:**

Each book gives easy to copy methods and offers each parent the opportunity to build from these outlines and make their own personal applications that fit their set of circumstances and situations. No reader is left wondering: "How can I possibly apply this to my life?" That question is sure to come up, but it is also sure to be answered.

> "Does not wisdom cry out, and understanding lift up her voice? She takes her stand on the top of the high hill, beside the way where the paths meet. She cries out by the gates, at the entry of the city, at the entrance of the doors: To you, O men, I call, and my voice is to the sons of men. O you simple ones, understand prudence: and you fools be of an understanding heart." Proverbs 8:1-5
>
> "The hero is the one who kindles a great light in the world, who sets up blazing torches in the dark streets of life for men to see by. The saint is the man who walks through the dark paths of the world, himself a light." – Felix Adler

**More importantly from the mouth of Jesus:**

> "You are the light of the world. A city that is set on a hill cannot be hidden. Nor do they light a lamp and put it under a basket, but on a lampstand, and it gives light to all who are in the house. Let your light so shine before men, that they may see your good works, and glorify your Father in heaven." Matt. 5:14-16

# Book I
# LOVE AND MARRIAGE

## Chapter One

## The Victories of Love versus the Problems of Love

**True love and romance—gifts from God:**

It was early afternoon, the sun was shining brightly. I had the windows of our rented motor-home open and the smell of redwood trees and pine needles saturated the air. I was relaxing on the sofa, enjoying a personal moment of reading while Marilyn was out stomping around our camping area in the San Pablo state park of California. Something caught my eye in that peripheral sort of way that finally makes you look up and check it out—it was Marilyn—in a slow jog coming out of the forest and into our clearing. She had a very bright and mischievous smile on her face and I confess, my first thought was of another romantic—motor-home—interlude with this woman of my dreams.

The occasion for this little outing in the forest was our twenty fifth wedding anniversary. I very much enjoy the beauty and serenity of the forest as a whole while Marilyn revels in conquering the trees—literally—she climbs them! San Pablo state park is a beautiful redwood forest and had something special for both of us. Although an avid tree climber from her earliest tomboyish years, Marilyn had never before climbed a mature giant redwood tree and climbing one that day was the farthest thing from my mind.

I'm putting my book down as the door flies open and Marilyn shouts out in excitement:

"Come on Honey, I found something and I've just got to share it with you!"

"What is it?" I asked.

"It's a surprise—come on follow me and I'll show you."

My first thought was: "Maybe I can talk her out of this escapade into the forest." We could stay in the comfort of the motor home for an afternoon—love-in—as we like to call our best times of intimacy. But one more look into those shining eyes and that broad smile made me curious as to what she had found and a hope that it would not be a waste of our time. A practical man's first thought you know—how not to waste time—come on we're on a retreat to celebrate our twenty fifth wedding anniversary! What else is there but to waste time and to waste it together—right?

Marilyn grabs my hand and out the door we go. She is so excited she starts out at a fair clip and pulls me along behind her. At this point I'm starting to get excited myself.

"Where is it, Gorgeous? Where in the world are you taking me?"

Gorgeous is what I often call Marilyn when I am not referring her to some other person. She would not be considered gorgeous by perhaps anyone but me, but through the eyes of love that God has given me for her—she is gorgeous!

"It won't be long now."

She said, as we slowed to a walk and began to look at the beautiful redwood trees all around. The suns rays were beaming down through the tall trees at an angle, lighting the forest in a surreal sense of other-worldliness. Hand in hand we meandered through this dreamlike forest on a twisting trail just barely visible through all of the fallen pine needles. Finally we came to the top of a small slope.

"There! There it is—isn't it wonderful?"

She was pointing directly towards a huge redwood tree, eight to ten feet in diameter that soared up through the forest canopy out of sight. The tree had to be a least 125 feet high possibly as much as 150 feet. Although undeniably beautiful, to me it was just another big tree; I still had not grasped what all the excitement was about. This was soon to change.

"This is a beautiful tree but what is the surprise? I said."

Still holding my hand she pulled me down the slope and right up to the base of the tree. On closer examination this tree began to show how different it was from all of the many other giant redwood trees we had seen in our several visits to the California redwoods. There was an immediate slope upwards for some distance on the opposite side of the tree that formed a semi circle around most of the area in which the tree dominated as its center piece. For some reason this special location had made it possible for the tree to keep all of its lower branches, although dead, attached to the trunk. Anyone who has visited the redwoods of California knows that the one thing you can't do is climb a giant redwood tree. There are no signs saying that you can't—you just can't. The trunks are smooth and too large to reach around with human arms. The early limbs die and fall off leaving only the green branches that start at about 25-40 feet off of the ground, completely out of reach.

"I've always wanted to climb one of these beautiful trees and now I can—and I want you to climb it with me, Honey. See how these branches are easy to reach and even though they are dead they are thick and strong—look—(and she pulls herself up onto the first branch by grabbing onto the one just above it) see, it's just like climbing a ladder."

She was correct the limbs came right out of the trunk and extended straight out for up to twenty feet or more. Dry from many years of being without live sap, this orderly system of dead branches reached upward until it came into direct contact with all of the branches that were green, alive with sap and full of pine needles. However, climbing trees—even small ones—was not my idea of a romantic afternoon and this behemoth looked a bit intimidating.

Not to be dissuaded, my gorgeous lady takes off up the tree trunk, hands on the branch above, feet on the one below she climbed up the side of that huge tree trunk with its very own built-in ladder. Meanwhile I'm standing down below, not quite sure what to do next. My first thought was the safety of those dead branches—would they hold—and just how high should we go.

"Come on Darling—I've got another surprise for you!"

I look up and Marilyn is taking her jeans off and draping them over the branch just above and on the right so that she can keep on climbing. At the next limb—off comes the blouse. No more need for encouragement now—in a *FLASH*—I'm on the first branch and climbing to catch the beautiful lady just a few branches ahead of me. By the time we had reached so far up the tree that the trunk was only a mere one foot thick and easy to put one's arm around, Marilyn was without clothes, but she had not lost the gleam in her eyes or the smile on her face. Her surprise and her anniversary gift for us that year was a most outrageous intimate time in the top of a wonder of God's creation. We could see out onto the surrounding mountain areas, even a climbing mountain road that passed some few hundred yards—straight out—from our lofty perch in the sky. We could see all of our surroundings, but no human vision could penetrate through all of the branches and pine needles to see us—a most unusual cozy feeling. We have often wondered if our special tree was still—there with its own built in ladder—or has something happened to take away the limbs and keep its lofty top, from ever again being a place of intimate retreat for two lovers?

**Discovering the gifts:**

Eight of the first ten years of our marriage were spent on the mission field in Mexico. Those first ten years were the hardest years for us. We were both raised in Christian families and we had both been very active in the youth group at our church. We had actively supported missions and were very interested in missions the first two years of our marriage. Finally, we visited the one place we had helped the most, Juarez, Chih. Mexico. It was love at first sight and for twelve years it became our home and mission point for Mexico. We worked with Victor and Gloria Richards in their early years before they founded *Vino Nuevo.* (New Wine)

During these first ten years of our marriage we were constantly in some form of competition. We were passionately in love with each other but we were also very argumentative and often very hurtful to each other. No matter what we said to each other in our many attempts to deal with this dichotomy, we always ended up right back where we started—no where. Our breakthrough came from an unsuspecting quarter.

We came in contact with a little known family and marriage counselor, Howard Watrous. A missionary couple we knew in Durango had met him on a trip they made to L.A. and they came back with some tapes of his. From this first contact I received notice of a special men's conference that Watrous was holding at Yawahnie Lodge in the Sequoia National Park, in California. I signed up and attended.

Watrous made many impacts on my thinking during the two days of the conference but none more than his emphasis on Eph. 5:25-33 [5]

In these short nine verses the apostle Paul states three times for emphasis that men of faith and grace—he's not talking to unbelievers—must love their wives in the same way and for the same purposes that Christ loves the church. The full text is in the footnote but we will look at the three verses that specifically state God's command for husbands:

---

[5] "Husbands love your wives, even as Christ also loved the church, and gave himself for it; that he might sanctify and cleanse it with the washing of water by the word. That he might present it to himself a glorious church, not having spot, or wrinkle, or any such thing; but that it should be holy and without blemish. So ought men to love their wives as their own bodies. He that loves his wife loves himself. For no man has ever hated his own flesh; but he nourishes it and cherishes it, even as the Lord the church: For we are members of his body, of his flesh, and of his bones. For this cause shall a man leave his father and mother, and shall be joined unto his wife, and they two shall be one flesh. This is a great mystery: but I speak concerning Christ and the church. Nevertheless let every one of you in particular so love his wife even as himself; and the wife see that she reverence her husband." Eph. 5:25-33

Verse 25: "Husbands love your wives, even as Christ also loved the church..."

Verse 28: "So ought men to love their wives as their own bodies..."

Verse 33: "Nevertheless let every one of you in particular so love his wife even as himself..."

Paul's description of how and for what purpose Christ loves his church as his own body is clearly stated but hardly ever applied as part of the context of Paul's message for husbands. The message could not be clearer. For men to be successful in love and marriage they must embrace the role as God's instrument for loving, faithfully and sacrificially their wives without pointing a finger of guilt toward her. Check it out:

Christ gave himself for his church—read that to be his bride—so "...that he might sanctify and cleanse (*her*) with the washing of water by the word that he might present (*her*) to himself a glorious (*wife*), not having spot, or wrinkle, or any such thing; but that (*she*) should be holy and without blemish." (Verses: 26-27, emphasis mine.)

Never has the perspective of—one flesh—been made clearer or more distinctive from the perspective of the secular mind. A man and his wife are one flesh, the husband is the head of that one flesh and he is also very personally and particularly responsible for the sanctity, moral character, perfection, romance and overall success of that one flesh!

Having said that, how is it possible that a man can do what Paul is clearly stating must be done? Certainly this is not a job that an unregenerate man can do, an unbelieving man, a man NOT of faith and grace who has no spiritual eyes and cannot see.[6] This is a job and a responsibility that can only be done and accomplished by a man of faith and grace, and that not of himself, but rather through and by the power of God that will prepare him to do so—when he surrenders—to Him and seeks his answers in his Law-Word.[7]

A father of faith and grace is an oxymoron if there is no personal reality of experience in walking in this way. None can be a spiritual leader in his own family if he doesn't know anything about God, or doesn't have any experience of trusting in Him to be a part of his own daily life. Our descriptive term—father of faith and grace—is not a physical badge of identification. This is a term that describes not the physical man—but the inner man—a man who trusts in the revealed truth of fatherhood in God's word. A man who takes his marching orders from the—Father of fathers—from the source of all truth.

**God's love and romance is forever:**

The romance that Marilyn and I started out with in our marriage was a by-product of the world's secular culture—the pursuit of all poets, romance writers, screen writers and novelists—not the gift of God. Such love is woefully inadequate to satisfy the longing heart and will never bring deep, lasting love with tender romance that lasts forever. At best it is a thoughtful expression of lust and at its worst it is a sick excuse for abuse but it is never—true love—that lasts forever.

---

[6] "The pillar of cloud moved around behind the Israelites and it became a wall of darkness to the Egyptians but a flame of light to the Israelites..." Exodus 14:19-20

[7] "And from a child you have known the Holy Scriptures, which are able to make you wise unto salvation through faith which is in Christ Jesus. All scripture is given by inspiration of God, and is profitable for doctrine, for reproof, for correction, for instruction in righteousness: that the man of God may be perfect, thoroughly furnished unto all good works." II Tim. 3:15-17

What God gave us after my willingness to believe and to act on his revealed truth that I was responsible for Marilyn's spiritual, moral and romantic success—yes me—her husband, was the revelation of what is true love and romance for her. I could no longer point the finger of blame at her nor could I seek answers for the discord in our relationship through changes that I thought she should make. I had to look to God to strengthen me and give me the wisdom and understanding to seek change within myself. The first thing I changed about me was my perspective of how and with what I would love Marilyn. Before it was all about my will and being right—now it was all about asking God for his perfect love to overflow in me so that the love I gave her would be from him, through him and by his power, to fulfill his good pleasure in her and in me.[8]

The love and romance we experienced on that romantic afternoon in the top of a giant redwood tree is only one of many such extra special moments of intimacy that God has given us in the years since we both accepted a new paradigm in our way of loving and showing love one for the other. Over twenty some years have passed since that sunny afternoon in the San Pablo redwood forest. Soon, God willing, we will celebrate our fiftieth wedding anniversary. Time passes and the years accumulate, but love and marriage that is held in the palm of God's hand, resting on his wisdom and his Law-Word never fades. His gift of love and romance in the experience of marriage only grows brighter, deeper and more satisfying with the passage of time. And of this I am certain—in eternity—our sense of love and romance for each other will exceed everything and anything that flesh and blood could ever know! God's gift of love and romance in marriage is not for just an hour, not just a day, not just years, but forever!

There are many pages of statistics that enumerate the failures of love and marriage in our Christian culture. The references made in our introduction only scratch the surface. The pain, misery and hopelessness of love lost and hearts dashed to pieces could fill libraries to bursting. Ours was a choice: to believe how we were raised and how our Christian culture teaches—Christian in faith but secular in practice—or to simply believe God's revealed Law-Word and to act on it. We chose the latter. What choices will you make?

Recently a senior writer of World magazine featured an unusual personal experience regarding grief and faith. Andree Seu is a widow and was sent a book by Patti Broderick, also a widow. Ms. Seu writes in the Dec. 4th, 2004 issue, *Simple Faith:*

"Gnosticism is thought to be a dead church issue: A clique of second-to fourth-century guys who thought the writings of Paul were quaint, and good enough for the Christian rabble, but for themselves were superseded by a secret inside track to God through mystical channels far more sophisticated than obedience to Christ's simple commands.

> "Patti Broderick has written a very simple book about her journey. She cites verses like the following and makes much of them:
>
> 'I know that you can do all things...' (Job 42:2. 'Consider how the lilies grow...' (Luke 12:27-28). 'This happened that we might not rely on ourselves but on God...' (2 Corinthians 1:9). 'His divine power has given us everything we need for life and godliness...' (2 Peter 1:3).
>
> "Ms. Broderick figures that when the Bible says 'suffering produces character and character, hope,' it means that suffering produces character and character, hope. I, on the other hand, have interposed a baroque system of hermeneutics between the Bible and my life. I have seminary

[8] "For it is God which works in you both to will and to do his good pleasure." Philippians 2:13

training. Unlike simple people who obey the Bible because they don't realize how complicated it is, I find ambiguity in every verse. I don't obey Scripture, I discuss it.

"Patti Broderick and I, at the crossroads of our respective widowhood, evidently heard the same statistics and psychological findings regarding the 'natural' course of grief and the amount of time needed to 'process' it. I went with the statistics and gave myself permission to be as bad as I wanted to be. She, more simpleminded, files the following report: 'So I chose, instead, to bank my life on Scripture being true, and I was not going to let even well-meaning Christians talk me out of it.' In this she cites as fixed anchors for the soul such meditations as the following:

'For I know the plans I have for you,' declares the Lord,' plans to prosper you and not to harm you, plans to give you hope and a future. Then you will call upon me, and come and pray to me, and I will listen to you. You will seek me, and find me when you seek me with all your heart. I will be found by you...' (Jeremiah 29:11-14)"

Dear husband and wife, I encourage you, yes, I even implore you to exercise the new heart[9] and the new mind that God has given you through Christ and to believe his written word—not to discuss it only—but to walk in it daily. If you commit to believe His word and to act upon it: Husband, first embrace the commands given in Eph. 5:25-33 and Wife, first embrace the commands given in Eph. 5:22-24, and 33. If you think that to do so will cause you pain and grief then reread the testimony of Patti Broderick and know that He will be found of you and that you will be blessed!

---

[9] "I will give you a new heart and put a new spirit within you; I will take the heart of stone out of your flesh and give you a heart of flesh. I will put My Spirit within you and cause you to walk in My statutes, and you will keep My judgments and do them." Ezekiel 36:26-27.

# Book I
# LOVE AND MARRIAGE

## Chapter Two

## Recapturing Virtue

**For all have sinned and fall short of the glory of God, Romans 3:23:**

Statistically speaking it is quite probable that at least fifty percent or more of all individuals who read this book, whether a male or female will have fallen into the trap of secular wisdom and will be inwardly dealing with sexual sins and misconducts.

Virtue once lost becomes a secret desire of almost all young men and ladies and even older, more mature men and women when they have fallen into this trap and followed the wisdom that proceeds from the hearts of stone of the secular world. Our new hearts that God has given us know better but we believe the lie of Satan rather than the truth He has revealed to us. Virtue is so easily surrendered and lost, yet, so unimaginable to regain. Once virtue has been sacrificed on the altar of promiscuity, it is only a matter of time before all realize the benefits anticipated are not, forthcoming. This brings remorse and a sense of being used to men and women, young or old. They know it was a bad choice, but they are not sure the alternatives of today's world offer anything better. They are not sure they can recapture their virtue, or how to go about it, even if they are brave enough to try. They need new insight and new direction.

When a captain is off course at sea he must reexamine his chart and get a new perspective. He must first take stock of where he is and then decide; what are his best alternatives for correcting the error and bringing his ship back to the proper course. As men and fathers of faith and grace—captains of our families—we can do no less. Our wives, our children and most assuredly we ourselves need to make this midcourse correction in recapturing virtue.

For those who are brave enough to try, there are certain basics concerning our human makeup which need to be considered. Examining these basics will be of great interest to both men and women who realize they have taken the wrong path and want to get back on course and improve the strength of their moral character.

**Spiritual beings:**

To have real hope of being able to establish a new moral perspective and to believe a new way of life is possible, we must first understand the difference between our physical actions, or functions, and our existence as living spiritual beings![10]

---

10 "Therefore, just as through one man sin entered the world, and death through sin, and thus death spread to all men, because all sinned—(For until the law sin was in the world, but sin is not imputed when there is no law. Nevertheless death reigned from Adam to Moses, even over those who had not sinned according to the likeness of the transgression of Adam, who is a type of Him who was to come. But the free gift is not like the offense. For if by the one man's offense many died, much more the grace of God and the gift by the grace of the one Man, Jesus Christ, abounded to many. And the gift is not like that which came through the one who sinned. For the judgment which came from one offense resulted in condemnation, but the free gift which came from many offenses resulted in justification. For if by the one man's offense death reigned through the one, much more those who receive abundance of grace and of the gift of righteousness will reign in life through the One, Jesus Christ.)

"Therefore, as through one man's offense judgment came to all men, resulting in condemnation, even so through one Man's righteous act the free gift came to all men, resulting in justification of life. For as by one man's disobedience many were made sinners, so also by one Man's obedience many will be made righteous. Moreover the law

Although much more complex, we are to a great extent, like computers. If you put bad information into us, into our brains, we will produce bad output. If on the other hand you put good information into our brains, we will produce good output. Our functions will be equal to the quality of what has been put into us. Unfortunately, as children, from birth to six years of age, growing up with parents and experiencing the environment that providence provides, it is impossible for one to choose the origin or quality of the information and experiences one will have. We are limited to the information and relationship experiences that our parents have given to us.

These are our most tender and most formative years, regarding attitude and moral perspective. In this first impression of life, although parental and environmental qualities are not things that we as individuals can choose, the effects are enormous. It seems as though Providence has a large deck of cards from which each hand is dealt. You get a certain number of cards with which to play the game. You can discard a few and ask for a few more, but basically, you have whatever you have. No one ever gets what could be considered a perfect hand. So, effort and energy must be put forth by all, if the game is to have any hope of being won.

What is encouraging amidst all of the seemingly unfair aspects of life and its apparently fickle ways of—appearing to bless some much more than others—is our ability to change our perspective and thus our circumstances at will. I'm referring to our God-given opportunity through the gift of faith to decide that we must seek more of His word and accept His perspective of truth. In this sense, we are very dissimilar to a computer; in as much as we have more control over the kind of information we allow to be put into our brains. We can also alter the effects of this input, should we later decide that is was not what we really wanted. Our great advantage as Christians is the fact of our gift of faith. Through this unmerited favor of God our inner man is able to connect with His word and thus to receive wisdom and understanding. Whereas contrast this with the unbelieving natural man—armed only with a secular mind—that is incapable of understanding God's wisdom.[11]

**Secular liberalism versus God's revealed Law-Word:**

Some famous words from our pop-culture are: "When life throws you a lemon, don't cry, make lemonade!"

God's revealed Law-Word says: "Come unto me, all you that labor and are heavy burdened, and I will give you rest. Take my yoke upon you, and learn of me; for I am meek and lowly in heart: and you shall find rest unto your souls. For my yoke is easy, and my burden is light."[12] Matt. 11:28-30

For those with lost virtue, bruised and battered moral fiber, values and principles, it might seem too much to overcome. Believe me, it is only appearances! Once you and I understand who we are—created beings with a living soul and spirit, we will then be able to perceive how positive change is within our grasp. The

---

entered that the offense might abound. But where sin abounded, grace abounded much more, so that as sin reigned in death, even so grace might reign through righteousness to eternal life through Jesus Christ our Lord." Romans 5:12-21.

[11] "But the natural man does not receive the things of the Spirit of God, for they are foolishness to him; nor can he know them, because they are spiritually discerned." I Cor. 2:14. For to be carnally minded is death, but to be spiritually minded is life and peace, because the carnal mind is enmity against God; for it is not subject to the law of God, nor indeed can be." Romans 8:6-7.

[12] "Come to Me, all you who labor and are heavy laden, and I will give you rest. Take My yoke upon you and learn from Me, for I am gentle and lowly in heart, and you will find rest for your souls for My yoke is easy and My burden is light." Matt. 11:28-30.

key element here is personal, it is you. You have to understand who you are, and you, only you, can make the decision for change. Once this is realized, anything is possible!

C. S. Lewis, once an atheist, was drawn by God to Himself through a personal quest for truth and had this to say about it in his book, "Mere Christianity".

> "My argument against God was that the universe seemed so cruel and unjust. But how had I got this idea of just and unjust? A man does not call a line crooked unless be has some idea of a straight line. What was I comparing this universe with when I called it unjust? If the whole show was bad and senseless from A to Z, so to speak, why did I, who was supposed to be part of the show, find myself in such violent reaction against it? A man feels wet when he falls into water, because man is not a water animal: a fish does not feel wet. Of course I could have given up my idea of justice by saying it was nothing but a private idea of my own. But if I did that, then my argument against God collapsed too—for the argument depended on saying that the world was really unjust, not simply that it did not happen to please my private fancies. Thus, in the very act of trying to prove that God did not exist—in other words, that the whole of reality was senseless—I found I was forced to assume that one part of reality—namely my idea of justice—was full of sense. Consequently atheism turns out to be too simple. If the whole universe has no meaning, we should never have found out that it has no meaning: just as, if there were no light in the universe and therefore no creatures with eyes, we should never know it was dark. Dark would be without meaning."

These are words of insight which C. S. Lewis could make only after he had received God's gift of faith. Remember, as an atheist Lewis could only argue with God and rationalize his condition on things about which he knew nothing. We can say emphatically that C. S. Lewis—as an atheist—could not live his life of order and peace as a college professor under the principles of his atheism. All atheists are forced to steal the bare skeleton of God's revealed Law-Word just to survive. Living strictly by the tenants of atheism is an oxymoron! All truth and law for them is mere convention—the agreement of the majority. Therefore, being lost without God—they cannot choose life and are left with death only. By robbing pieces of the Christian worldview of God as the origin of all truth they can escape death for awhile. They do this by denying that God exists and at the same time accepting His law that "You shall not commit murder." And "You shall not steal" and "You shall not covet your neighbor's wife." They translate that to read: Don't kill me, don't steal from me, and don't covet my wife because they love to kill, steal and covet their neighbor's wife![13]

**The power to change:**

Are we getting the point? We as husbands and wives, father and mothers of faith and grace—because of Christ—can change our actions, our physical expression of who we are by changing our perspective of who we really are! You are the one who is now in control of what goes into your brain, not your parents, not your friends, not your circumstances, but you. You can blame your parents for your lack of early training as a child, but after you are old enough to have experienced some of life's harsh realities, you must decide to take over the training

[13] "For whoever finds me finds life, and obtains favor from the LORD; but he who sins against me wrongs his own soul; all those who hate me love death." Proverbs 8:35-36.

yourself!

We can decide what goes into our brain, therefore, it is essential to eliminate the bad influences which cause us to be tempted to reject the responsibility for our own development. As men and women we must not allow circumstances, unfortunate or otherwise, such as bruised and irresponsible parents, race or environmental disadvantages, to control the outcome of our life experience. We have the opportunity and the power, through God's grace, to dilute the negative effects of our past. By flooding our brains with the reality of what is possible and refusing to act on the old negative information that says we can't do it, we can change the present and the future. Act positively! Positive actions bring positive feelings and perspectives. Often the only way to bring about the reality or a given quality you desire is to start behaving as if you had it already.

Although we are more than our limited ability to express who we are through our thoughts/attitudes and physical actions, it is our thoughts/attitudes and physical actions that are going to bring us either painful results or joyful results in this life.[14] We cannot escape the consequences, good or bad. If you jump off the Empire State building and half-way down realize it was a bad choice, you the person will have made a great discovery, but your body is going be splattered all over the street below.

In recapturing lost virtue, it is important to remember that former mistakes will exact a certain toll. It will not be more than you can bear, but it would be foolish and wrong for one to think such actions would not carry a residual price. Just pray for ample courage to overcome the obstacles, and don't concentrate on what you think to be fair or unfair. One of life's great discoveries is that—life is not fair—but the joy of overcoming is not dependent upon fair, it is dependent upon Christ in you.

Admittedly, we are all going to do some things better or worse than others and no matter how hard we try , we are not going to be perfect. There are no perfect men or perfect women. I do not hold myself up to be a moral giant, better than others. Nor am I using this as an opportunity to *preach* to you. On the contrary, this is in response to my gift of faith from the Father and His love for fathers and His stated claim of total sovereignty over our lives and—yet He holds us to our personal responsibility to respond and to submit willingly to His power to give us the victory. Thus, I believe in His victory over our sins and His power to lift you and me up and to give us the victory—even this victory—which as a post modern culture we have as yet not experienced! In short, I believe in Him in you, as father, as the champion for your little girl and her development as a wife, lover of her husband and successful mother of the future. I believe in Him in you, as mother, as the champion for your little boy and his development as a husband, lover of his wife and successful father of the future. I strongly believe that we cannot speak clearly and effectively about how—husbands and wives, fathers and mothers—should or should not conduct themselves, without first establishing the actuality of a Right and Wrong morality, with which to guide our discussion. If what I am sharing with you is true, then we are all in need of repentance, but we can't repent of what we don't know or understand that we did or are doing to sin. Even if we can identify a sin, in need of repentance, it is impossible to successfully do so

---

14 "Do not be deceived, God is not mocked; for whatever a man sows, that he will also reap. For he who sows to his flesh will of the flesh reap corruption, but he who sows to the Spirit will of the Spirit reap everlasting life. And let us not grow weary while doing good, for in due season we shall reap if we do not lose heart. Therefore, as we have opportunity, let us do good to all, especially to those who are of the household of faith." Galatians 6:7-10

without sufficient insight, wisdom and understanding to map a way out of the darkness and the sin, into the light that God has provided![15]

Women, young and older alike, can begin anew to build their virtue and their moral integrity, anytime they want, while there is yet time to repent. They can recapture the essence of their virtue in spite of the loss and suffering they have experienced!

Men, young and older alike, can also decide to do the same thing, anytime they want, while there is yet time to repent. They can recapture the essence of their virtue, and also the opportunity to take up the challenge of real fathers of faith and grace! Through the grace of God, His gift of faith and the inner working of the Holy Spirit, both men and women can be successful in this effort. Christ assures us that it is possible. But, He also warns us not to grieve the Spirit. Self conscious delays in taking action, only adds to our sins.

"Come now, and let us reason together," Says the LORD,
'Though your sins are like scarlet,
They shall be as white as snow;
Though they are red like crimson,
They shall be as wool.
If you are willing and obedient,
You shall eat the good of the land;
But if you refuse and rebel,
You shall be devoured by the sword;'
For the mouth of the LORD has spoken." Isaiah 1:18-20.

15 "There is no temptation that has taken you but such as is common to man: but God is faithful, who will not suffer you to be tempted above that you are able; but will with the temptation also make a way to escape, that you may be able to endure it." I Corinthians 11:13

# Book I
# Love and Marriage

## Chapter Three

## Breaking Old Habits

**Making the break:**

Change is said to be stressful, well when things really become a habit—a really old habit—establishing ourselves into new patterns of life is not easy. In order to break old habits and make a break from the incorrect perceptions which led to those habits, we must do a minimum of just two things. First we must have a change of attitude. Secondly, we must have access to what is correct. It's exactly like navigation. If we become lost or disoriented while sailing at sea, we must first admit that we are lost, and then secondly we can review our actions and understanding of our map, in order to set a new course.

Remember what Star Parker said? "Tomorrow will resemble today if we continue today what we did yesterday." It's time to challenge decades of conventional wisdom that has delivered scant positive results, and even the little positive results we can see—are in spite of the methods employed—not because of those methods. These few positive results are much more illustrative of our unmerited favor of God's grace and mercy than any evidence of the truth of our past methods!

We are familiar with such statements as "the Law of Gravity," "the Law of Aerodynamics," or "the Law of Physics." In these statements we are using the word "law" to describe what we have seen to be consistent behavior. That is, when you drop a rock off a cliff or a building or just from your hand, while standing, it always falls straight to the ground. We would be most surprised if, when we dropped a rock, it all of a sudden took off like a feather in the wind. We would say, "Well, it looked like a rock but really it was something else." We would simply not accept it as a rock if it did not "obey" our "law" of gravity. However, we do not really think the rock has any conscious understanding about what it is supposed to do when it is dropped. We call its actions a "law" simply because we know that we can depend on it to do what we have always observed it to do—hence, "the Law of Gravity." Likewise, the other statements about laws are actually our way of saying these areas have been observed and experienced to a point where we can say for certain that if you do—or do not do—certain things within these areas, it follows that certain other things will happen. The response is always the same for any given set of actions or conditions, so, we call them "laws," meaning they are predictable and consistent without fail.

Now we are all familiar with another concept called "Human Nature." We use this, more often than not, to mean that we as humans do not always do what is expected of us. For example we excuse ourselves when we forget things, because it is "human nature" to be forgetful. We pass off many personal failings as the result of human nature. If you observe someone being selfish you might very well be tempted to say, "Well, it's human nature to be a little selfish." However, do you really like the idea of people forgetting the things which they say they are going to do? Do you really appreciate a person who is selfish? I think not. So, in today's world, when we are talking about "human nature" we most often are speaking in terms of what is weak about our natures, the reality of our "Humanity" and all that we have observed about how humans act in the Wrong way has left us no alternative but to call it by some name—i.e., human nature. Having said this, one should immediately ask the questions, "Why do we assume that these acts are Wrong?" and "Why do we feel uncomfortable and embarrassed when we are the guilty party?"

Good questions, and important for our discussion about husband/wife relationships in love and marriage, because as we have seen in the previous chapter, there are a great many tendencies we men have that are not the ones we most desire to see in action. These tendencies can cause a great deal of pain and suffering for the female sex, beginning from the time they are born and continuing throughout the whole process of life. Knowing this, it is imperative we establish guidelines relative to what is proper behavior for a husband and father of faith and grace and what is not. If indeed there is any reality in the existence of a right way and a wrong way to be a husband in general and in particular as regards being a father and rearing sons, and daughters, then by all means we must clarify those standards for the benefit of all concerned.

**The law of nature:**

To do this we need to look deeper into another concept which used to be very common among men throughout the world but which in modem times has taken on a new meaning. I am referring to the concept of "the Law of Nature." In our world of today we think of "the Law of Nature" as meaning things like gravitation, chemistry or physics. However, not too many decades ago it was, considered common sense to understand that "the Law of Nature" was referring to the way in which humans were supposed to act, or in other words, really meaning "the Law of *'Human'* Nature." It was expected that humans were supposed to act in certain ways that were considered best—or Right—for the success of the individual and those with whom they lived, loved and worked. The striking difference in this "Law" is that instead of representing an area of known or observed predictability and consistency, such as we see in the way rocks fall, birds fly, or chemicals and metals react, it represents what *should be* predictable and consistent but which more often is not. This brings up the existence of a reality in which we all believe and want to see happen, the reality of God's revealed Law-Word. We all have definite ideas about what is right and wrong, and even though we may differ considerably in education, background, age and ethnic origin, it is amazing how much we can agree on what is basically right and wrong. Where do we get these notions and why are they so similar? Is it merely a coincidence or is it evidence there is indeed a law which exists that somehow communicates to us how we should act in certain ways in order to do what is right and when we don't we are wrong? For example, you cannot say a line is crooked if you have not first established what a straight line is. You cannot say something is Wrong unless you have first established what Right is.

C. S. Lewis, the late professor of Medieval and Renaissance Literature at Cambridge University, in his book *Mere Christianity* gives a vivid account of how we have come to see the concept of Right and Wrong in such similar ways.

> "When the older thinkers called the Law of Right and Wrong 'the Law of Nature,' they really meant the Law of Human Nature. The idea was that, just as all bodies are governed by the law of gravitation and organisms by biological laws, so the creature called man also has his law—with this great difference: a body could not choose to obey the law of gravitation or

not, but a man could choose either to obey the Law of Human Nature or to disobey it.

"We may put this another way—each man is at every moment subjected to several sets of laws—but there is only one of these which he is free to disobey. As a body, he is subjected to gravitation and cannot disobey it; if you leave him unsupported in mid-air, he has no more choice about falling than a stone has. As an organism, he is subjected to various biological laws which he cannot disobey any more than an animal can. That is, he cannot disobey those laws which he shares with other things; but the law which is peculiar to his human nature, the law he does not share with animals or vegetables or inorganic things, is the one he can disobey if he chooses.

"This law was called the Law of Nature because people thought that every one knew it by nature and did not need to be taught it. They did not mean, of course, that you might not find an odd individual here and there who did not know it, just as you find a few people who are colorblind or have no ear for a tune. But taking the race as a whole, they thought that the human idea of decent behavior was obvious to everyone. And I believe they were right.

"I know that some people say the idea of a Law of Nature or decent behavior known to all men is unsound, because different civilizations and different ages have had quite different moralities.

"But this is not true. There have been differences among their moralities, but these have never amounted to anything like a total difference. If anyone will take the trouble to compare the moral teaching of, say, the ancient Egyptians, Babylonians, Hindus, Chinese, Greeks and Romans, what will strike him will be how very like they are to each other and to our own—but for our present purpose I need only ask the reader to think what a totally different morality would mean. Think of a country where people were admired for running away in battle, or where a man felt proud of double-crossing all the people who had been kindest to him. You might just as well try to imagine a country where two and two made five. Men have differed regarding those people to whom you ought to be unselfish—whether it was only your own family, or your fellow countrymen, or everyone. But they have always agreed that you ought not to put yourself first. Selfishness has never been admired. Men have differed as to whether you should have one wife or four. But they have always agreed that you must not simply have any woman you liked.

"But the most remarkable thing is this. Whenever you find a man who says he does not believe in a real Right and Wrong, you will find the same man going back on this a moment later. He may break his promise to you, but if you try breaking one to him he will be complaining 'It's not fair' before you can say Jack Robinson. A nation may say treaties do not matter; but then, next minute, they spoil their case by saying that the particular treaty they want to break is an unfair one. But if treaties do not matter, and if there is no such thing as Right and Wrong—in other words, if there is no Law of Nature—what is the difference between a fair treaty and an unfair one? Have they not let the cat out of the bag and shown that, whatever they say, they really know the Law of Nature just like anyone else?"

Does this answer the questions we asked before?—"Why do we assume that these acts are Wrong?" and "Why do we feel uncomfortable and embarrassed when we are the guilty party?"

**Establishing standards:**

Not entirely. It does set us in the right direction and it does show how similarly men in general think in terms of Right and Wrong. What it does not answer is why some standards of moral conduct are viewed by us as different. I'm sure you will agree that there are people who live by a standard of moral conduct which is different from the standard used by other people, i.e., organized crime families and people with so called sexual "alternative" life styles. The latter are referred to as sexual deviates or perverts by those of us who do not believe that a real bon-a-fide alternative life style should exist. But then we must ask, deviates from what, perverted from what?

The moment we agree that there are different sets of morality; we are also saying that there is a standard of morality which is better or best. By Virtue of this very admission, whether from those we would consider perverted or Wrong in their actions or by those we would consider Right—we are all saying that somewhere there exists a standard which is absolutely correct and what we are comparing are simply variations from the absolute standard which are different. We are saying we believe certain acts and practices are better than others, thereby we in reality are admitting to comparing them both with some Real Morality.

Consequently, we are admitting there is a real Right, independent of what people think. We are in effect saying that some people have ideas about moral correctness and values which are nearer to the real Right than others.

Now we have answered our two questions. Yet, in answering these questions we now raise other questions. Having established our belief in a real Right and Wrong, in spite of the rationalization used to condone behavior which allows for the practice of so called alternative life styles—we are now confronted with the reality of an error in the use of a very popular phrase for many people today, namely, "Do your own thing, " which is obviously not a good recommendation where Right and Wrong are concerned. We are also brought face-to-face with the fact that when we rationalize our behavior, trying to seek "easier" ways of living or what we might think to be more "exciting" ways to live, we violate our conscience which firmly believes in the correctness of the Real Morality and tells us we are wrong. As a result, large numbers of people seek help for their feelings of guilt.

Knowing that we are violating what is really Right is the cause of our guilty consciences. The guilt feelings come even after we have attempted to believe with all our heart that what we want to do must be right because we like it so much, and so many others are doing it and they could not all be wrong. We can go through classes on refocusing our values, such as are taught to many of our children today in the Public School systems, and we can join groups who have established so-called alternative life styles and become one of them, but we cannot escape our conscience which will continue to tell us that it is Wrong and that we have strayed from the standard of Real Morality that is Right. Our personal circumstances of failure to perform as we would like and the guilt of our conscience when we fail this standard of morality, are all confirmations of what God is telling us in His word when He declares that He has given those who have the gift of faith a new heart—a heart of flesh to replace the heart of stone that is the old man of our old natures. Paul confirms this in eloquent and clear terms in his message in Romans 2:1-16.[16]

[16] "Therefore you are inexcusable, O man, whoever you are who judge, for in whatever you judge another you condemn yourself; for you who judge practice the same things. But we know that the judgment of God is according to truth against those who practice such things. And do you think this, O man, you who judge those practicing such things,

It is this law which is written in our hearts that also confirms the revealed law of the ten commandments, which guides us and also which chastises us immediately with our bruised conscience—our guilt—when we rebel against it.

When I say these things I know that it is easy to feel overcome with hopelessness, because we tell ourselves that no man can fully comply with these standards. Yet, this begs the question: to what "man" are you referring when you say that no "man" can fully comply with these standards?

Carnal, fallen man, man without faith in God, man of the flesh: if you are referring to this kind of man, then yes, that man cannot comply with these standards. The truth is we who have the gift of faith are not such men and women. We have the promise of God's gift of wisdom, understanding and overcoming because we now are resurrected in Him. Romans 6:1-23[17] is crystal clear on who we are and why we are no longer servants of sin and rebellion against God. It is because of His work in us. To say or to do otherwise is to deny Him and the grace of His salvation!

Our modern world has become so committed to violating the Law of Human Nature, our God-given inner sense of Right and Wrong which would otherwise guide us into more correct life styles and more correct behavior, that we have invented a variety of ways to deal with the guilty consciences which are natural by-products of such lifestyles. We have different types of psychoanalysis, family psychology, self-improvement clinics, self-improvement books, and a host of other attempts, all of which are focused basically on one goal, that of helping people to overcome their guilty consciences. There is also a trend among many to claim that since there is no "absolute truth" then it is only—your truth or my truth—when in

---

and doing the same, that you will escape the judgment of God? Or do you despise the riches of His goodness, forbearance, and longsuffering, not knowing that the goodness of God leads you to repentance? But in accordance with your hardness and your impenitent heart you are treasuring up for yourself wrath in the day of wrath and revelation of the righteous judgment of God, who 'will render to each one according to his deeds': eternal life to those who by patient continuance in doing good seek for glory, honor, and immortality; but to those who are self-seeking and do not obey the truth, but obey unrighteousness--indignation and wrath, tribulation and anguish, on every soul of man who does evil, of the Jew first and also of the Greek; but glory, honor, and peace to everyone who works what is good, to the Jew first and also to the Greek. For there is no partiality with God: for as many as have sinned without law will also perish without law, and as many as have sinned in the law will be judged by the law (for not the hearers of the law are just in the sight of God, but the doers of the law will be justified; for when Gentiles, who do not have the law, by nature do the things in the law, these, although not having the law, are a law to themselves, who show the work of the law written in their hearts, their conscience also bearing witness, and between themselves their thoughts accusing or else excusing them) in the day when God will judge the secrets of men by Jesus Christ, according to my gospel." Romans 2:1-16.

17 "What shall we say then? Shall we continue in sin that grace may abound? Certainly not! How shall we who died to sin live any longer in it? Or do you not know that as many of us as were baptized into Christ Jesus were baptized into His death? Therefore we were buried with Him through baptism into death: that just as Christ was raised from the dead by the glory of the Father; even so we also should walk in newness of life. For if we have been united together in the likeness of His death, certainly we also shall be in the likeness of His resurrection, knowing this, that our old man was crucified with Him, that the body of sin might be done away with, that we should no longer be slaves of sin. For he who has died has been freed from sin. Now if we died with Christ, we believe that we shall also live with Him, knowing that Christ, having been raised from the dead, dies no more. Death no longer has dominion over Him. For the death that He died, He died to sin once for all; but the life that He lives, He lives to God. Likewise you also, reckon yourselves to be dead indeed to sin, but alive to God in Christ Jesus our Lord. Therefore do not let sin reign in your mortal body, that you should obey it in its lusts. And do not present your members as instruments of unrighteousness to sin, but present yourselves to God as being alive from the dead, and your members as instruments of righteousness to God. For sin shall not have dominion over you, for you are not under law but under grace. What then? Shall we sin because we are not under law but under grace? Certainly not! Do you not know that to whom you present yourselves slaves to obey, you are that one's slaves whom you obey, whether of sin leading to death, or of obedience leading to righteousness? But God be thanked that though you were slaves of sin, yet you obeyed from the heart that form of doctrine to which you were delivered. And having been set free from sin, you became slaves of righteousness. I speak in human terms because of the weakness of your flesh. For just as you presented your members as slaves of uncleanness, and of lawlessness leading to more lawlessness, so now present your members as slaves of righteousness for holiness. For when you were slaves of sin, you were free in regard to righteousness. What fruit did you have then in the things of which you are now ashamed? For the end of those things is death. But now having been set free from sin, and having become slaves of God, you have your fruit to holiness, and the end, everlasting life. For the wages of sin is death: but the gift of God is eternal life in Christ Jesus our Lord." Romans 6:1-23.

**fact the only truth is God's truth, His gospel of Christ crucified and Christ resurrected and living in us. This is absolute truth.**

# Book I

# LOVE AND MARRIAGE

## Chapter Four

## Navigation

## The Key to a Successful Journey

"Let not your heart be troubled; you believe in God, believe also in Me. In My Father's house are many mansions; if it were not so, I would have told you. I go to prepare a place for you. And if I go and prepare a place for you, I will come again and receive you to Myself; that where I am, there you may be also. And where I go you know, and the way you know." Thomas said to Him, 'Lord, we do not know where You are going, and how can we know the way?' Jesus said to him, 'I am the way, the truth, and the life. No one comes to the Father except through Me.'" John 14:1-6.

**The rules of navigation:**

Life is a type of navigation. If you make a small error in your heading and do not correct it, the error will compound in its effect to take you off the course that otherwise would have taken you to your desired destination. If one does not make constant checks and course corrections the trip is doomed to disaster. As husbands/fathers and wives/mothers of faith and grace we have certain inner desires which we want to fulfill. You may not know how to describe just what it is you hope to accomplish or just exactly what is the main goal or destiny of your life, but you are conscious that there is a longing and a yearning for personal fulfillment which burns in your breast. As in navigation, life works better when we have a map. The map is admittedly only a piece of colored paper. It is not the trip, or the oceans or the sky that it represents, but a record of the experiences of the many that have made the trip before us. Consequently, it gives us a feeling of comfort and security to look at the map. We can see where the reefs and the mountains are and which ones might sink our fragile craft. We can see where the obstacles are that others have seen with their own eyes because they have been there. If you think God's revealed truth of Right and Wrong is too cumbersome and unwieldy to be practical, then you might think that it is also too cumbersome and unwieldy to use a map. It is true that you can attempt the trip without the map—maps are an option—but wisdom dictates that trips without maps are foolhardy! The most important map of life is God's map![18] Given the state of affairs of the moral decay and the loss of leadership in our families today, it is obvious that many men and women have decided to make the trip without the advantage of God's map.

[18] "A wise man will hear and increase learning, and a man of understanding will attain wise counsel, to understand a proverb and an enigma, the words of the wise and their riddles. The fear of the LORD is the beginning of knowledge, but fools despise wisdom and instruction." Proverbs 1:5-7.

"Blessed is the man who walks not in the counsel of the ungodly, nor stands in the path of sinners, nor sits in seat of the scornful; but his delight is in the law of the LORD, and in His law he meditates day and night. He shall be like a tree planted by the rivers of water that brings forth its fruit in its season, whose leaf also shall not wither; and whatever he does shall prosper. The ungodly are not so, but are like the chaff which the wind drives away. Therefore the ungodly shall not stand in the judgment, nor sinners in the congregation of the righteous. For the LORD knows the way of the righteous, but the way of the ungodly shall perish." Psalms 1:1-6.

However, embarking upon the experience of reading this book is encouragement in itself. It shows you are sensitive to your need for a map and that you are wise enough to know sailing and flying without maps is a design for disaster. Dr. James Dobson says: "The bottom line is that many men have lost their compass." See the full statement below.[19] I hope and pray that this desire leads you to the Ultimate Map, the Holy Bible; God's revealed Law-Word for your direction for the rest of life's journey!

Like the compounding effect of wrong directions in our navigation, we also experience a compound effect in the moral decisions we make, right or wrong. Small steps or decisions that are wrong when we first start out—that might seem trivial—soon become compounded into larger problems. Likewise, small corrections we make which are right—our efforts to overcome the Wrong by doing the Right—also compound and bring us more and more blessings. It is not so much the big things we do wrong or right which make the most difference in our course and the success of our trip, but the consistency with which we continue to do either. If you are wrong some of the time, but you are always quick to recognize your error and you make consistent corrections that are right, you will experience a consistently more successful trip as life goes on. However, if you consistently are wrong in what you do and in your general lifestyle, you will experience a constantly worsening condition in the quality of your life and—if you survive—you will see all your dreams destroyed.

One of the big problems of today concerns the millions of men who have decided there is no Real Map, no Real Morality of Right and Wrong; they have launched themselves on the sea of life without any maps. Simple observation reveals they are trying to make-it-up as they go. The results to themselves, to the women who become involved with them and to the millions of children born to these unions are disastrous. Yet, when these same failing men and women are interviewed by—secular liberal humanists—of the many polling agencies, devoting their full-time trying to discover sources for our moral problems in the American family: these same people can see faults only in the government, schools, social agencies or churches, never in themselves. Consequently, what men and women hear and see in the media and in all of the so called "Studies & Research" from the secular world is that if we can just get the government to do more, more money for this or for that, and now even money for "faith based" social work, things will get better. At best this is a war against the symptoms of our sinning and rebellious culture but it definitely is not a war against the causes of our sinning and rebellion. This war is a war we must wage with ourselves through repentance and a return to God and His power to enable us to overcome. Government and social agencies, not even the local organized church can change our sinful hearts and our destructive nature against each other, only God is in the heart changing business—only He can give a new heart to replace the old stony heart with which we were born!

Christ gets to the real heart of the matter in the Gospels as in Matthew 5:27-30[20] (see complete text below) here He tells us that even the thoughts of lust

---

[19] "The bottom line is that many men have lost their compass. Not only do they not know who they are, they're not sure what the culture expects them to be.' It is time that men acted like men—being respectful, thoughtful and gentlemanly to women, but reacting with confidence, strength and certainty in manner. Some have wimped out, acting like whipped puppies. Others have boldly spoken out against feminist influence, refusing to be intimidated by the advocates of political correctness. Some have lashed out, reacting with anger and frustration. Some have flamed out, resorting to alcohol, drugs, illicit sex and other avenues of escape. Some have copped out, descending into mindless TV, professional sports and obsessive recreational activities. Some have sold out, becoming advocates of the new identity. Some have simply walked out, leaving their families in a lurch. Many, however, seem placidly unaware that they have lost their places in the culture. The result is a changing view of manhood with far-reaching implications for the future of the family." --Dr. James Dobson

[20] "You have heard that it was said to those of old; 'You shall not commit adultery.' But I say to you that whoever looks at a woman to lust for her has already committed adultery with her in his heart. If your right eye causes you to sin,

in our hearts condemns us as though we had committed the act of sin! Sin is the problem—sin is a state of being—and its locus is our heart. Therefore the offending member must be cut out. Douglas Wilson says in his book: *"Fidelity—What it Means To Be a One Woman Man."*

> "What is the offending member? What brings us to sin? What produces sin in us? What must therefore be cut off? The answer is that the offending member is the human heart. The doctrine is that a man must have a new heart or he will die.
>
> "The solution is regeneration. We must get the doctrine of regeneration straight in our minds. A tremendous amount of mischief has resulted from confusion at this point. We are not born again because we have repented and believed. Rather, we have repented and believed because God has given us the new birth. If the old heart is capable of repentance and belief, then a man does not need a new heart. He simply needs to continue to improve the old one."[21] Fidelity, Canon Press, Moscow, Idaho, p. 50.

Once one has accepted the idea that there indeed is a Real Morality and a real Right and a Wrong—then it is not so hard to understand what is happening to these millions of American families. They are suffering the same problems one suffers when one has navigated for a long time on the wrong heading. They started with only a small error, yet now they are thoroughly off course, headed for dangerous reefs and certain disaster, but without a map they cannot tell where they are, and thus cannot get their bearings straight and make a major course correction. They desperately need God's map!

**In "Mere Christianity," C. S. Lewis said:**

> "No man knows how bad he is till he has tried very hard to be good. A silly idea is current that good people do not know what temptation means. This is an obvious lie. Only those who try to resist temptation know how strong it is. After all, you find out the strength of a wind by trying to walk against it, not by lying down. A man who gives in to temptation after five minutes simply does not know what it would have been like an hour later. That is why bad people, in one sense, know very little about badness. They have lived a sheltered life by always giving in. We never find out the strength of the evil impulse inside us until we try to fight it. When a man is getting worse, he understands his own badness less and less. A moderately bad man knows he is not very good: a thoroughly bad man thinks he is all right. This is common sense, really. You can see mistakes in arithmetic when your mind is working properly: while you are making them you cannot see them. You can understand the nature of drunkenness when you are sober, not when you are drunk. Good people know about both good and evil: bad people do not know about either."

---

pluck it out and cast it from you; for it is more profitable for you that one of your members perish, than for your whole body to be cast into hell. And if your right hand causes you to sin, cut it off and cast it from you; for it is more profitable for you that one of your members perish, than for your whole body to be cast into hell." Matthew 5:27-30.

[21] Douglas Wilson is pastor of Christ's Church, Moscow, Idaho and editor of Credenda/Agenda magazine. He is author of: *"Recovering the Lost Tools of Learning," "Reforming Marriage," "Federal Husband," "My Life for Yours"* and *"Future Men."* Contact: www.canonpress.org

I will give one last point on this. Whether you believe in a real Morality, a real Right and Wrong or not, whether you believe in taking a map along on the voyage of life or not, one thing you must do is accept the responsibility for your actions, good or bad. If our parents have failed to rear us in the truth of God's revealed Law-Word from the moment of our birth—we have a problem—but after the age of thirty we do not have the luxury of blaming our parents for our bad directions or our bad beginnings. By age thirty one has had many years to respond personally to the call of God's voice and to seek Him. We have no right to blame the government, social agencies, our wives or the church; we have no one to blame but ourselves. In today's milquetoast world of escapism, such a statement will make many cry out in alarm and ask why we must blame ourselves, when it is clear in many cases that our parents were wrong in many of the things they did?

Well, first of all it is nice to know such people can see there is a Wrong. To ask the question means they believe in a Real Morality, even though they are the very people who most often try to convince everyone else of the non-existence of any—absolutes—a Real Right and Wrong. Such insight they have with respect to their parents is evidence they know the law of nature as revealed through God's common grace, just like everyone else.[22]

Secondly, the answer is very clear why we must blame ourselves—because we have God's gift of faith—and His presence within us. Paul speaks to this in his letter to the Philippians 2:5, "Let this mind be in you which was also in Christ Jesus." We have the choice to choose to have the mind of Christ. Also in chapter 3:12-15, he reveals a most astounding factor of our life and being: vs. 13, "For it is God in you who works both to will and to do His good pleasure." Let us pray that He should give us the grace to receive more of His mind![23]

**Using our new hearts:**

Fathers—we are His—we can do no other; we must exercise our new hearts in repentance and commitment to change. We are in this world but we are not of this world. We can change; we are not stones that cannot change their shapes. We are new creatures in Christ with His power and mind to decide what and when we want to change. Fortunately—life in Him—unlike a voyage on the high seas or in the sky—whereas if you didn't bring the correct map or lost the one you had you can't just pull over at the next rest stop and get another one—does allow us the privilege of "waking up" to our need for a map and the privilege of rethinking our decisions about Right and Wrong before we wreck our fragile craft. We can make mid-course corrections and alter the outcome of bad and incorrect beginnings. My own role as a husband and father of faith and grace would be a disaster and my present course unsure if I had not made many mid-course corrections and many adjustments to my perceptions and efforts to understand God's revealed law in me. I'm still making mid-course corrections and I expect it will be necessary to do so for as long as I live.

**Wisdom:**

Husbands and wives, fathers and mothers of faith and grace, to make the trip of life a success and a fulfillment of the destiny which burns within our

---

22 "For when the Gentiles, which have not the law, do by nature the things contained in the law, these, having not the law, are a law unto themselves: which show the work of the law written in their hearts, their conscience also bearing witness, and their thoughts the meanwhile accusing or else excusing one another; in the day when God shall judge the secrets of men by Jesus Christ according to my gospel." Romans 2:14-16

23 "I beseech you therefore, brethren, by the mercies of God, that you present your bodies a living sacrifice, holy, acceptable to God, which is your reasonable service. And do not be conformed to this world, but be transformed by the renewing of your mind, that you may prove what is that good and acceptable and perfect will of God." Romans 12:1-2.

breasts, we must exercise wisdom. In the Bible God encourages us to seek wisdom.[24] Wisdom is the ability to know how and when to make the right decision. God has gifted us all with a measure of His uncommon common sense. It is not wisdom in and of itself, He tells us, but it is that wisdom is a doorway to him and to eternity. (Later we will look at wisdom as a representation of Christ.) Through His revealed law in us we can discover the right perspective to take concerning life's challenges and problems. Then, with this clarity of vision-like radar in a storm tossed sea—we can see clearly how we should navigate the ship. We will thus be able to exercise wisdom in knowing when to make the right course corrections and when to hold steady our course no matter the wind and the wave.

**Femininity—the practicality of the impractical:**

We men don't expect mechanical things, buildings, bridges, roads, automobiles, sports or money to come to us without effort. Yet, in our relationships, especially with the opposite sex, we seem inclined to win them over to where they like us, and then stop. We tend to see little or no need to continue the romancing process which proved so successful, in order to win them in the first place.

When was the last time you ever weaned your car from using gasoline, or your horse or dog from eating? We are often like the farmer who kept trying to wean his horses from eating. About the time he would get one weaned—it died!

Look around you; are any of your female relationships dying? How is your relationship with your wife? Is it as good as when you were courting her?

"She doesn't need such kid stuff anymore, she knows I love her," you say.

Sure she doesn't, the sun doesn't come up in the East anymore either, birds don't sing, dogs don't bark and fire doesn't burn.

Tell me, now, when was the last time you ever heard of a woman being practical when it comes to love? Some of you are probably thinking you never knew a woman to be practical about anything, much less about love! When Marilyn has a bad day my first impulse—as a "practical" man—is to analyze the details and offer my "practical" solution—whereas all she really wants is for me to hold her in my arms and tell her I love her and that it will somehow be all right. Practical, as a concept of reality, is antithetical to femininity. Femininity is emotion, feelings, an inner vision of balance and harmony that flies in the face of masculine practicality. How practical can it be to tell our wives five or six times a day that we love them? Didn't they believe it the first time? No, there is nothing "practical" about it but there is—everything wonderful about it for them—and the positive feedback is just as wonderful for us!

It is blatantly unfair to accuse women of being impractical about everything, although one thing is for sure; they are not practical about love. They love the way they love and that is it. You cannot change it, I cannot change it, and from all appearances of their actions down through the centuries, God does not intend for them to love any other way. In fact a good argument can be made that if women were practical about love, they would not want to have much to do with men. I thank God it is not it is not a matter of practicality that causes a woman to desire the love of her husband, God so decreed this reality in Genesis 3:16: "and your desire shall be for your husband and he shall rule over you." Also, "Wives, submit yourselves unto your own husbands, as unto the Lord." Eph. 5:22

---

[24] "Wisdom cries without; she utters her voice in the streets: she cries in the chief place of concourse, in the openings of the gates: in the city she utters her words, saying, how long, you simple one's, will you love simplicity and you scorners delight in your scorning and fools hate knowledge?" Proverbs 1:20-22

The first point of wisdom and understanding that we gain from these verses of God's revealed Law-Word is that his creation—woman—is to experience a much deeper than originally planned, inner desire and need for her husband. As a result of seeking to become independent from God through eating of the tree of knowledge of "good" and "evil," that is to say Satan's perception of good and evil as opposed to God's, she is now to be more dependent, in an inner and inescapable way, tied emotionally to her husband. We on the other hand, His creation—man—have had our responsibility for her increased and are now God's instrument to refine her and present her without spot or blemish back to God, even as Christ so does for the Church—His bride! To say that this is not so, is first of all to be intellectually dishonest and secondly to risk being in out-right rebellion against God's sovereign will. He said very plainly that such is so—our opinion to the contrary is only that—our opinion. The beginning of wisdom is to fear/have deep respect for God! Let us be wise! Our only response must be: "Have mercy on us our Father of fathers, teach me and empower me to do this impossible task, for without your strength and wisdom I am undone and without hope!"

**Great sex for old men and women:**

The mere idea that unregenerate man has any valid idea of what constitutes a successful sexual relationship or holds any hope for future understandings of how to have and maintain a successful family, is on its face preposterous. The term—unregenerate—says it all! I continue to be increasingly amazed at how "Christians" seek the counsel of the ungodly-unregenerate, secular sources for the solutions to their personal spiritual and relationship problems.

Proverbs 5:15-19 spells out God's basic promise of great sex for old men. The whole chapter is dedicated to this rarely discussed portion of God's revealed wisdom and understanding. However, verses 15-19 deal with the specific promise of great sex for old men. Given our modern day proclivities for sexual experimentation I find it ironic that such pointed promises of—great sex for old men—should never have made it into our everyday conversation. It could only be one of two things:

**First:**

Perhaps it's another example of a great truth going unnoticed because of its apparent simplicity.

**Second:**

It could be because the power of this great truth lies in its spiritual understanding and therefore is deliberately hidden from the minds of the unregenerate. "The natural man does not understand the things of God, they are foolish to him and he cannot know them because they are spiritually discerned." (I Cor. 2:14) I personally believe it is the latter, which also begs the question:

"Why is it of so—little notice—to the Christian men of today?"

From 1994-1996 I was actively engaged in leading men's conferences for *Promise Keepers* in the El Paso, Texas and Juarez, Mexico area. I was instrumental in leading three such conferences, one in El Paso and two in Juarez. In each instance I would ask the men present if any of them knew that God promised great sex for old men in the Bible. They would just grin and look at each other and shake their heads, "No." I never had an occurrence where a man would raise his hand and say that he knew that such was the case or that he had even so much as heard of it—strange in deed! (We're talking several hundred men here.)

After all, we are talking about a promise for satisfaction in an area where men, Christian and Pagan alike, claim to have an intense interest. I'm saying to you that the Pagan man—only thinks—he knows what constitutes good sex, while the Christian man is given certainty on the matter by God! Yet, from the statistics of today's broken homes, unresolved marital problems, unwed mothers, abortions, teenage pregnancies, venereal diseases, and single parent households, both unbelieving secularists and Christians are alike!

Whereas—by contrast—the difference should be strikingly obvious: as to which cultural group is more successful in all matters involving love, sex, marriage and the family. Among other things this should also raise our attention to the fact that not all who say Lord, Lord are of the Kingdom.[25]

Since few Christian men seem to know how to guarantee great sex for both young and old—we need not even approach the unregenerate secularist—what then is the basis for our understanding of the matter?

What is the basis for your understanding of sexual satisfaction? Do you know where to direct your attention and effort in order to insure the success of good sex? Do you know how to develop a relationship with a woman who will bring you true sexual joy and fulfillment?

If you listen to the sexual libertarians of our time, you would think sexual fulfillment and joy were limited to having a good orgasm and that with as many different people as possible.

The efforts at sexual moral values and principles of our early American forefathers were intended first and foremost to protect against single-family situations. Their response to the importance of the family unit was to teach their children about sex in the context of marriage and not as an isolated experience limited to achieving orgasm with the opposite sex. Although their methods and manner of communicating this moral perspective may have led to some sexual misunderstandings between men and women, the intent was wise. In contrast, the ways of modernity have created horrible misconceptions and misunderstandings.

You will notice that I specify American forefathers, our entire hemisphere was not settled by such men, in fact not many areas in the whole world, were ever settled by such men. By God's grace America was!

As for improving the sexual life of men and women, ask yourself the question: "Have the sexual libertarians of today raised the level of sexual satisfaction between men and women?" Or—"Have they sown the seeds of doubt and selfish rationalization against God's wisdom and understanding?"

When we, Christian men and women of faith and grace, consider the facts with our new mind of Christ and not our hormones, we come up with the truth. They have not! Unless, however, you consider divorce, broken relationships, violence against women and children, sexual deviates, incest, rape, AIDS, venereal disease, drug addiction, alcoholism, depression, suicidal tendencies and disadvantaged children as necessary for a good orgasm. This is what the moral values and principles of the libertarians have brought us. These are the results of the concept of "free love" and "open sexual relationships", designed to bring us new heights of "sexual satisfaction!" These are the results of secular sex "education" and the "free sex" Kinseyan doctrine! Like the children of Israel, we must choose this day who is God? Is God the secular humanist god of Baal, or is God the—risen Christ—our Lord and Savior?

[25] "Not everyone that says to me, 'Lord, Lord,' shall enter into the kingdom of heaven; but he that does the will of my Father which is in heaven." Matt. 7:21

"All that is necessary for the triumph of evil is that good men do nothing." Edmund Burke

Our great-grandfathers and our great-grandmothers; might have been a little prudish and strait-laced, when it came to their methods and manners of communicating sexual specifics, but they weren't stupid, nor were they ignorant of God's Law-Word. Although criticized without mercy by today's liberal media and the leaders of Secular Reformation, the quality of the off-spring of those less "enlightened" souls was the direct result of a much deeper fear/respect for God and for His revealed truth. What we might think they did not know about sexual matters is not important. What is important is the commitment they had—to use all that they did know—for the honor and glory of God! We claim to know much, yet our "commitment" pales so much in contrast to theirs as to seem almost—non-existent!

Sex without emotional and moral commitment is shallow at best. Anyone who seriously wants really good sex is going to consider first what the basis for good sex is. Having sex without emotional and moral commitment is like swimming in a cesspool. Yes, it can be done, but it's much more fun and exhilarating in clean water. Those who would opine to the contrary only expose their sinful past and show how little they really know about sex.

My own personal experience in observing and communicating with many promiscuous men and comparing what they say they experience in sex without moral and emotional commitment, with what I know otherwise, convinces me beyond a doubt; sex in a marriage with moral and emotional commitment, based on God's revealed Law-Word, provides the best emotional, physical release, joy, ravishingly fulfilled, personal satisfaction and contentment possible!

If you don't believe it just consider God's promise of good sex for old men in Proverbs 5:15-19.

**Summarizing God's promise of good sex for old men:**

The chapter begins with the teacher addressing his son, a young man. The young son is admonished to not consider the sexual advances of the promiscuous woman. That her appearance is one of—delight and joy—but that to engage in sex with her is guaranteed to bring dissatisfaction and complete loss of all he holds dear. In contrast, the young son is told that all of his amorous attentions should be focused on the wife of his youth and that her breasts will satisfy him all the days of his life, and that she will be beautiful for him and he will be ravished by her love all his life. A lesson from the Father of fathers!

Now to get the point the teacher is making, one has to notice that the teacher starts out talking to a young son and then towards the end of the chapter he changes the scene to one of an old man. A young man cannot look back on his present wife as a wife of his youth, they are both young. The promise is for the young son when he is old. The secret is to focus all of his amorous attentions onto his wife. This will bring sexual satisfaction and success for them both now while young and also later when they are both old. Also: Eph. 5:25-29 Just insert the word "wife" where there is the word "church" and you get the connection.

The miracle and the spiritual elements should be obvious to the man of faith and grace. Older women do not usually have breasts that are as beautiful as when they were young. How then shall they satisfy as much and indeed even—to ravish—the young son when he is old? Also, it is considered normal for our "enlightened" times, that many older men will be impotent and sexually inactive. Well, impotent or not, sexually active or not—the truth according to God's word is:

whatever our old men are having—if they have lived a life of sexual disobedience—they are not having the great sex promised in God's word.

I'm now in my late sixties, my wife is in her early sixties. It only takes one glance in the mirror to know that I am not the hunk that I thought I was when I was young. My wife shows her own signs of age when viewed only with the eyes of the flesh. For those who don't already know from experience—I can tell you—that God is faithful and the eyes that He has given me in honor of His promise are—eyes of love only—and my wonderful wife is more beautiful to these eyes than ever she was when she was "young!"

# Book I

# LOVE AND MARRIAGE

## Chapter Five

## Let's Talk

## Communication Between the Sexes

**Communication is more than just hearing:**

The time was 4:00 PM, the date was early May, 1957, the place was Alameda Naval Air Station, San Francisco Bay, California. I was the first radioman in a twelve man crew aboard a Naval Air force P5M-2 Martin Marlin twin engine seaplane. I was on the flight deck checking out our radio and radar equipment when our First Mechanic, 1st Class Petty Office, Karnath, came up to me and gave me the order to assist in topping off the oil tanks for our engines. Unlike engines that most would be familiar with, these 3,000 horse power radial engines had 50 gallon oil reservoirs. I had never before assisted in any of the preflight activities other than those that were directly related to my first radioman responsibilities and I felt honored that he would give me such an order. So, I said sure, I'm ready, what can I do?

"Go up on top of the wing and I will hand you up the hose from the oil pump and when you have the nozzle in the hole I will start the pump, when it shows full just signal me and I will stop pumping." He said.

I said: "Great I'm on my way."

To gain access to the top of the wing on this 40 ton sea plane it was necessary to climb up a small ladder positioned about midway in the fuselage and leading to an upper platform where our auxiliary power plant was located. Then once on this platform there was a hatch in the upper ceiling of the fuselage that led to the top of the main wings, midway of the points where they joined together. A misstep or a fall from this location would be twenty five feet straight down to the cement tarmac below. Thus, I made my way with care as I stepped out onto the main wing and proceeded to the starboard engine nacelle where I found the metal flap door of the oil compartment open and ready for service. The First Mechanic called out and said:

"Do you see the round cap at the bottom of that shaft under the open flap door?"

"Yes!" I yelled.

"Good, take it off and place it on the small shelf midway down the shaft."

"OK, I've got it off, what now?

"Catch this line and pull up the hose then put it down into the shaft and into the opening at the bottom and let me know when the oil gets to the top of that hole." He said.

I did as I was told and when the oil became visible at the top of the hole I yelled "Stop!"

"Good, now put the cap back on and go to the other engine on the portside and we will repeat the same operation."

We concluded the oil operation and I was released to go back to my radio and radar check-out. Later that same evening, sometime just before sunset we fired up our engines and took off bound for Hawaii as a first stop on our way to the Philippine Islands. We left late so we could avail ourselves of the favorable winds that came up in the evenings along the California coast blowing westward. Our plane did not have enough cruising range to make the 2,300 mile over water trip without these favorable winds.

Flying has always been a great passion with me and this particular flight was something I had looked forward to with great anticipation. We were a close net crew of twelve men and we shared many duties together in our up-keep and operation of the plane. Yet, I had never before been checked out on how to service the oil tanks or assisted with the process in anyway. It had felt especially good to help the First Mechanic, a talented level headed young man. We were all young; no one was over 30 except the Captain who was about 35. I and several of the other non-commissioned officers were still waiting for our 21st birthday.

There was a full moon that night and we were flying between scattered layers of billowy stratus clouds only a few hundred feet thick. The moon light danced off of the upper sides and down through the breaks in a way that made the clouds look phosphorescent. I could see out a porthole that was located next to the radioman's control panel. A dreamy kind of flight—the steady drone of the engines and the constantly changing light patterns dancing through the clouds. I was thinking—I really wanted to do something like this with Marilyn after we got married. I was startled out of my dream-state with a tap on my shoulder.

It was sometime around midnight and the First Mechanic was motioning for me to take off my headset so we could talk without being heard by everyone else in the crew. He looked a little disturbed and I wondered why he would want to talk to me without using our inner communication system. (We weren't flying a passenger liner and the engine drone was really loud if you didn't have your headset on.) So, in order to hear better he motioned me to follow him down below in the waste area under the flight deck where the noise levels were a little less and we could be out of the way of others.

"Did you put the dip sticks back in the oil filler neck before you put the oil cap back on?" He asked.

"What dip stick?" I replied

"The long metal dip stick standing on the shelf in the access shaft, that same shelf where I told to you put the cap while you held the hose." He further explained.

"No, I didn't see any dip stick standing there. I didn't even know there was a dip stick."

I'm very glad that our First Mechanic was a very mild mannered person. He had every reason to be very up-set with me and especially with himself for not double checking my work which was his responsibility. I felt very bad for him because I could tell by the look on his face we were having a problem that somehow had something to do with those dip sticks.

"Follow me and take a look at this." He said.

He took me back to one of the portholes in the after station fuselage wall just aft of and under the starboard engine nacelle. From this vantage point and with the moonlight reflecting on the trailing edge of the nacelle we could look up and see a small stream of something coming from somewhere off of the top of the wing and down over the engine nacelle. He put his flashlight beam on this point and it glistened like oil.

> "Hatfield it's my fault. I forgot to tell you about the dip sticks. There is a small hole about ¾" in diameter just to one side of the main oil filler hole where you put the hose. I always stand the dip sticks up on that shelf and when I am done I put them back in their holes. I think that the lift pressure that is created on the upper surface of the wing has created enough vacuum pressure in the oil shaft filler compartment that it is sucking oil out through those dip stick holes and out under the filler cap flap and down the wing. That's what I think that is. I can't tell for sure but we have only two more hours until we reach our midway point to Hawaii and if we don't have enough oil in our tanks to make it the rest of the way we will have to turn back to San Francisco."

I can't begin to tell you what a sinking feeling I had at that moment. All of my joy and the elation I was feeling only minutes before about the beautiful flight were all drained out of me in that moment of realization. How could we have made such a blunder in our communications and in our shared understanding of what we thought was going on when I was up on that wing helping to top off the oil tanks? What was the captain going to say? If we had to go back we would have to make the flight the next night and catch up with the rest of our squadron later.

Two hours later we made the decision that was best for safety's sake and we turned the big seaplane back for a return to the San Francisco bay. The following evening we made a successful flight to Hawaii after our First Mechanic made sure that I knew everything there was to know about topping off the oil tanks.

**We rarely communicate what we are thinking:**

The lack of communication between me and the First Mechanic had started early in our efforts to understand each other. He knew exactly what he wanted me to do. He had done the oil top-off procedure so many times that he could do it in his sleep. I on the other hand had never done it before. This in no way reflected any lack in my desire to do it—only the danger of my not understanding exactly what he wanted. The First Mechanic would never have missed the little detail about the dip sticks. To him that was second nature—to me it was NEWS—and I needed to know that little detail in order to perform the job correctly. He was ignorant of my ignorance and I was ignorant of his details. We are all ignorant of something and when two people are ignorant about some little details that are relevant to the success of a project or a request; the out-come will always be less than expected—sometimes even deadly.

In order to avoid such traps of miscommunication husbands and wives must quickly learn with deep respect, that one only communicates what the other actually hears and you don't really know if—real communication—has occurred until you see the results. I'm sure, because I have done it many times. My First Mechanic was thinking the words about the dip sticks but he never spoke them. Therefore, in his mind he was sure that he had told me about the dip sticks—he visualized the whole thing as he spoke to me—otherwise he would have never allowed us to take off with out checking. By definition communication says that something is transmitted from one source and received by another. Biblically it also means that if you truly receive what is communicated you will then act on that communication accordingly.[26] It doesn't matter by what means, radio, TV, computers, pictures or the lowly tongue—what leaves the source bound for the recipient is one thing—what is actually received by the recipient is hardly ever the same. The ultimate example of this is found in God's own revealed Law-Word—the transmission from God to those he chose to receive it was perfect in its original form. What we receive through our eyes and ears as we read it is often incorrect because of our interpretation. God says that with unbelief and a hard heart eyes cannot see and ears cannot hear and in some cases he even sends strong delusions to some so that they should believe a lie and never come to the truth.[27]

How many times does the husband just—KNOW—that he told his sweet wife to do this or that and really didn't? Or how many times does the wife just—KNOW—that she told her wonderful husband to do this or that and really didn't? When I make this mistake I often can remember in my mental vision just how it was with great detail—all to no avail—because I didn't do what I thought I did. Poor wife, not always was I able to see through my blindness as well as I do now. Oh yes—I'm still making the mistake—it's just that I'm quick to rethink it correctly when she says—"What did you say?" Remember it is not what we are thinking that is actually being transmitted, only God has the luxury of being perfect in the ability to say and communicate exactly what he is thinking. For us—His creation—it is a constant challenge. Imperfect—yes—almost always, but without it what hope would we have for our lives? We would be as limited as the animals. Unlike the hard wired communication of instinct, God has given us the opportunity to communicate and to experience and do so much more—to reflect Him—to be his image! Nothing is as humbling as are our efforts to communicate between the sexes.

We must also ask ourselves the very serious question of: How many times do we not hear or understand our mates because we are listening with little faith and with hard hearts? I have found that when husbands and wives are conversing about anything that is challenging to one or the other—something they are trying to understand together—it is very difficult not to miscommunicate. Whereas in contrast, both husband and wife can navigate complex communication challenges with friends, clients, business associates, employers and employees with apparent ease but are prone to stumble and misunderstand the thread of conversation when it is between each other. The intimacies of love and marriage easily provoke

---

[26] "For not the hearers of the law are just before God but the doers of the law shall be justified." Rom. 2:13 "But be doers of the word; and not hearers only, deceiving your own selves. For if any be a hearer of the word and not a doer, he is like unto a man beholding his natural face in a glass: For he beholds himself, and goes his way, and soon forgets what manner of man he was. But whoever looks into the perfect law of liberty and continues therein, he being not a forgetful hearer, but a doer of the work, this man shall be blessed in his deed." James 2:22-25

[27] "And when Jesus knew it, he said to them, why do you reason such, because you have no bread? Do you not yet perceive? Having eyes, do you not see? Having ears, do you not hear? And don't you remember?" Mk. 8:17-18. "And for this reason God shall send them strong delusion that they should believe a lie: That they all might be damned who believed not the truth, but had pleasure in unrighteousness." II Thessalonians 2:11. "He has blinded their eyes, and hardened their heart; that they should not see with their see with their eyes, not understand with their heart, and be converted, and I should heal them." John 12:40 (Also see Isaiah 6:9-10)

extraordinary glandular activity and emotional uneasiness at these times. Most couples never develop a very smooth communication style for these very important moments of communication. These are the moments where traditional couples—those using secular understanding and assumptions—are most likely to attack one another at the first sign of misunderstanding. Such moments are the test of all that makes men and women of faith and grace more successful in the art of love and marriage than any others.

Men and women of faith and grace are equipped with wisdom sufficient to allow them to recognize their need to back off and to not press the issue to a real fight. Yes, this is often the beginning of those arguments that occur between husbands and wives we all have experienced. Yet, as we grow in our understanding of the principles of marital communication between the sexes our ability to discuss difficult issues without submitting to emotional haranguing or disorder will also increase. We will explore the basic principles and the tools of successful marital communication in this chapter.

**Garbage in garbage out:**

We've all either read or heard of "*Men are From Mars and Women are From Venus*" one of the more recent pop-psychology blurbs to entertain the secular mind. Regardless of just how one might view such a book the truth is far more dramatic and exciting. The first man Adam is a creation of God from the dust[28] of the ground and woman, Eve—his wife—is a creation of God cloned from Adam's rib.[29] The truth could pass for science fiction in the secular world if one were to just change the word God for some lesser offensive word for them—try the "force"—that will grab them.

Books, university and government studies that end with the mind shattering surprise that there is a difference between the sexes is not exactly news. What would be interesting would be the discovery of how best to develop communication skills between the sexes. One of the key blessings of our journey together in this book is to make just such a discovery! Communication between the sexes is both the cause and the solution of all relationship difficulties and successes. True communication brings success while false communication brings failure.

Conferences, shrinks, studies, journals, articles, books, movies—all are prime tools—of the secular professionals who have carved out their exclusive claim to the science of communication and relationship problems between the sexes. So far their batting less than 50% or that is to say; more than half of secular couples end their marriages in divorce the first time around and over 65% the second time around. Guess what? The Christian community is not doing any better. How much do you want to bet that almost all of the Christian community is using the—same sources—for their understanding of communication and relationship between the sexes?

*Christianity Today* posted an editorial in August, 2003 that focuses on this and other problems within the Christian community in America. The following is from the article: *A Laboratory for Marriage:*

---

28 "And the Lord God formed man of the dust of the ground, and breathed into his nostrils the breath of life; and man became a living soul." Gen. 2:7

29 "And the Lord God caused a deep sleep to fall upon Adam, and he slept: and he took one of his ribs, and closed up the flesh instead thereof; and the rib which the Lord God had taken from man, made he a woman, and brought her unto the man, and Adam said. This is bone of my bone and flesh of my flesh: she shall be call Woman, because she was taken out of Man. Therefore shall a man leave his father and his mother, and shall cleave unto his wife: and they shall be one flesh, and they were both naked, the man and his wife, and were not ashamed." Gen. 2:21-25

"Still, the local church has a key role in recreating a biblical understanding of marriage in our society.

"First, we must admit that the church's current record is dismal. Divorce statistics inside the church are indistinguishable from those outside.

"Second, we need to repent for allowing the Zeitgeist of expressive individualism to permeate the way many of our churches relate to marriage, divorce, and remarriage.

"Third, we need to restore the community context of marriage. A married couple is more than the sum of its parts. It is a thread in a community fabric. Societies are built out of people who are loyal to one another and who work and sacrifice for the common good. Expressive individualism is a poor foundation for a society, and marriages so conceived do not build loyalties or give us practice in sacrificial service. Marriages and families are schools for service.

"Fourth, we need to recover the sense of human limitation inherent in marriage and family life. This is the beautiful biblical picture: a two-gendered, complementary couple improving on and channeling nature, but neither conquering it nor twisting it."

This article is just one of a myriad of efforts to bring attention to the moral crisis we are suffering within the American Christian community. From all the reports I receive from my contacts in other countries—especially the Americas and China—the whole of Christendom is going through the same moral decay and rot.

I applaud their efforts to sound the alarm but I don't agree with their editorial position on the value of individualism; nor their stand on "improving on and channeling nature." We will deal with these issues a little later but just take note that these conclusions by *Christianity Today's* editorial writer—no name was given—are evidences of some of the same secular thinking I have been talking about. For now let it suffice to say that individualism is most assuredly biblical[30] and it does not take a village to raise a child—it takes a man and a woman of faith and grace with much personal sacrifice.

Sex, love and marriage; with all of its many facets and accessories—children, how many, home-making, where to live, how to pay for it, how to make a living, meaningful goals, conflicting goals, how much income, how to spend it, continuing education, for whom, how much, in what, where do we go to church, do we go to church, what do we believe, what are our politics, how will we relate to our parents, etc., etc., and so forth and so on—all are decided and understood through communication!

**What are the most powerful words in communication?**

The secular unbelieving mind will automatically think of something like Elizabeth Barrett Browning's poem: *How do I love you? Let me count the ways.* Or something of equal romantic construct. There is nothing wrong with romantic poems, songs or love stories with plots that are descriptive of sound relationships built on integrity—do not read—Hollywood movies of the last 40 years or any of the last 30 years of 99% of what you see on television and nothing from MTV. For all that is good about much love and romance literature and the arts, it is all just an attempt to communicate. The proof is in eating the pudding. If the ideals of such

[30] "Who are you that judge another man's servant? To his own master he stands or falls. Yes, he shall be upheld, for his God is able to make him stand....So then every one of us shall give an account of himself to God. Let us not therefore judge one another any more: but judge this rather, that no man put a stumbling block or an occasion to fall in his brother's way." Rom. 14:4, 12-13.

literature were actually communicated—let's say—from the husband to the wife, then the results would be seen in our society. No results mean that there was no communication—at least not the idealism that was intended. So, if there is no real communication between the sexes through what we would consider acceptable idealistic love and romance literary works imagine how empty all that we consider unacceptable is!

My wife Marilyn and I love poems and stories about love and romance. During our first ten years of marriage we put our hearts and souls into using all these means to communicate our love and devotion for each other—but we were never able to experience anything close to what God has given us—since I came to more fully understand my role as a husband, lover, partner and friend for my wife. Not surprising—for men and women of faith and grace—that is, my answer came through prayer. As a result of a self conscious awareness that all that I had said and done in the past was not getting the job done and no longer willing to allow myself the indulgence of blaming Marilyn for the problem, I was forced to pray for answers. My fleshly man hates it when that happens—but my spiritual man says: "It's about time!" Things get done when I listen to my spiritual man—the new me—and not the old man of flesh.

Much to my surprise I was reminded of something that we had done on several occasions while we were dating and during our engagement period—we had prayed together. I don't mean the prayers at the table that we are all so familiar with, I'm referring to prayers about us, our love and our future together. After we got married; those prayer times together seemed to get farther and farther apart.

I approached Marilyn with this and we immediately began to pray together again. Over time we developed what is now our daily habit—we pray together in the morning and then again just before we go to bed. The time we invest in our prayers is strictly a matter of the needs we feel in ourselves and our perceived needs as a couple. If we are separated by schedules or travels we still keep our appointed time together and through the miracle of telephones we are able to pray together at our usual times.

At first when our troubles were painful, in our face and immediate we were cautious and then bold to pray about these and to ask for wisdom on the details and to confess our faults and our desires for change. As we both began to address our relationship from a perspective of changing from within ourselves and not any longer through the attempts to change the other, God began to give us a new depth of love and romance. There were evidences that things were not the same!

The words of our prayers are powerful means by which to communicate with one another. At first blush, most who have read the foregoing are probably thinking that this is very over simplified. I agree—on the surface—it does look over simplified. Our most powerful science often comes from the simplest of formulas. Likewise, many of God's secrets of power and success for this life come packaged in simple terms. What is lacking is not complexity but FAITH![31]

Our prayer words—Marilyn's and mine—are words that have more credibility and more weight than just words of regular conversation. Yes, prayer itself is powerful, but I am speaking here of our communication to each other. When I say to God in a prayer that I am sharing with Marilyn that I am sorry for a given action that I have committed against her, some slight or perhaps a weightier

[31] "But Naaman was angry, and went away, and said, Behold, I thought, He will surely come out to me, and stand, and call on the name of the Lord his God, and strike his hand over the place, and recover the leper. Are not Abana and Pharpar, rivers of Damascus, better than all the waters of Israel? So he turned and went away in a rage. And his servants came near, and spoke to him, and said, My father, if the prophet had asked you to do some great thing, would you not have done it? How much rather then, when he says to you, Wash and be clean? Then he went down, and dipped himself seven times in the river Jordan, according to the saying of the man of God: and his flesh came again like unto the flesh of a little child, and he was clean." II Kings 5:11-14

matter, it is more powerful in her ears than when I said it to her in person. The increased credibility is in the fact that I am a lot less likely to lie to God than I am to her. Now—even if this is not so—that I would lie to her: she is human, and she is a woman who needs all of the assurances possible that what I say regarding her is the absolute truth and nothing but the truth! Saying it to God in her presence is certainly good for me in my relationship with God. But it is also wonderful for her to hear it and to have—confidence reinforced—that her man is true to her and that his desire is to be to her all that God's grace can empower him to be.

Now you know what I meant when I said: "At first when our troubles were painful, in our face and immediate we were cautious and then bold to pray about these and to ask for wisdom on the details and to confess our faults and our desires for change." These words—the words of our prayers—are for us. God already knows our needs the question is—do we know what our needs are?

**Powerful words bring powerful results:**

Our kisses were sweeter, our caresses more tender and our intimacies deeper and more satisfying. We could tell the differences—what we could not tell was why. We didn't kiss any differently, our caresses were the same and our sexual intimacy patterns were the same—why then the difference? The difference is that little six inches between your ears—inside your brain—inside of the center of you—your heart and all of the other mysteries of feelings and awareness that God has given us. At first we wondered if it was just another cycle of renewed interest in each other—we had experienced that kind of thing before—so we half expected it to not last. The truth is even stranger for our carnal minds to understand. Instead of lessening and fading as all of our other attempts at renewal had done we have continued to gain in this love and romance sensitivity to this day. I have no doubt that it will continue until we are taken from this earth and reunited again later in eternity. What happens after that—God has not said—but I'm sure it will exceed human comprehension or else He would have told us about it. No need to tell us if we would never understand it anyway, right?[32]

When I say that God began to give us a new depth of love and romance I don't mean that in a poetic way, I mean that God actually does give us more of his love and romance that we can use towards each other. Make no mistake—we would never have lasted on the strength of our own brand of love and romance! We would have long ago joined the ranks of the divorced and shattered Christian family group. Through His sovereign will and providence of grace we have survived the valleys, the storms and all that Satan could throw at us—and his gift of love remains supreme and victorious.

Many years have passed since the bulk of our prayers were for guidance and details on how to deal with our needs for change from within. Since then and to the present our prayers are mostly of thanks giving and of a great peace in the assurance and the success for our lives in all of His sovereign will for us—no matter the circumstances—He is Lord of the circumstances of all carnal life, for He is Life and the Resurrection.[33]

Do not allow yourself to fall into the secular trap of—mind over matter—that they preach for life's success over the challenges of love and marriage. It is just that and no more—your mind—and what we need, and what we must have is not—OUR mind—but His mind and his love and romance, his wisdom! "For who has

[32] "Oh the depth of the riches both of the wisdom and knowledge of God!—how unsearchable are his judgments, and his ways past finding out." Romans 11:33.

[33] "Jesus said to her, I am the resurrection, and the life: he that believes in me, though he were dead, yet shall he live; and whosoever lives and believes in me shall never die. Do you believe this?" John 11:25-26

known the mind of the Lord, that he may instruct him but we have the mind of Christ." I Cor. 2:16. Christ has called us friends and has sacrificed all for us! His standards must become our standards. [34] Our prayers are also for you to be blessed by this writing and the ministry associated with it for your personal victories in love and marriage.

**The mind of Christ and our worldview:**

Often we hear a statement such as: "We must have a Christian worldview." The problem is we don't all agree on what a "Christian" worldview is. The fact is, most who claim to have faith in Christ actually have a worldview that is neither SECULAR nor of the MIND of Christ. I can't use the word Christian in this context because of the confusion and disagreement within the universal church as to what such a view is. For this reason I refer us back to the basics—Christ's worldview! If we have the mind of Christ then we—by his grace—can also understand his worldview. It is the worldview of Christ that is important to adopt and to understand, not the one fostered upon us by secularists, nor one of our own private interpretation. It is Christ's worldview that is so essential for our successful communication in love and marriage. In deed, the course and success of our very lives depends upon it![35]

Our Christian culture is rife with false teachers and false prophets that have poisoned the minds of millions of people over the last two generations. We are now at the point where instead of reading God's revealed Law-Word we find that most Christians depend on the latest new doctrine on rapture, healing, naming and claiming, prophecy and politics and a host of other claims; all provided by so called Christian pop psychologists, pop prophets and pop theologians to teach them what to believe. This practice has led to a variety of worldviews among believers but not according to the mind of Christ—his worldview. His worldview is the *vowel and alphabet system* of our new language in Christ. Without this new language, derived from His worldview, we are left with only incorrect presuppositions. We all have fundamental presuppositions upon which all of our subsequent decisions are based. Our presuppositions will guide us into a life based on truth or a life based on the fables of atheistic secularism—neutrality—is not an option![36] If my wife and I communicate in a language that we cannot understand or that tells us things that are false, have we really communicated? We may speak lies but we cannot effectively communicate with lies. When I am flying I must trust my navigational instruments to tell me the truth. Junk information will only get me and my passengers lost or possibly killed—not the object of our purpose for flying—right? Well, neither is it the object of marital communication to crash and burn but rather that it should lead to continual success in all areas of love, romance and successful family life.

Our worldview is ultimately made up of all our presuppositions—we either learn these from our Lord Jesus Christ through his revealed Law-Word—or we

---

[34] "Greater love has no man than this that a man lay down his life for his friends. You are my friends, if you do whatsoever I command you. From now on I will not call you servants; for the servant does not know what his lord does: but I have called you friends; for all things that I have heard from my Father I have made known to you. You have not chosen me, but I have chosen you, and ordained you, that you should go and bring forth fruit, and that your fruit should remain: that whatsoever you shall ask of the Father in my name, he may give it you. These things I command you, that you love one another." John 15:13-17

[35] "And be not conformed to this world: but be transformed by the renewing of your mind: that you may prove what is that good and acceptable and perfect will of God." Romans 12:2.

[36] "Then spoke Jesus again unto them, saying, I am the light of the world: he that follows me shall not walk in darkness, but shall have the light of life." John 8:12. "Then said Jesus to those Jews which believed on him, If you continue in my word, then are you my disciples indeed; and you shall know the truth, and the truth shall make you free." John 8:31-32.

adopt some other source of reference to guide us. Understand this: there is no neutrality—everyone has a worldview—all constructed of presuppositions!

> "The results of (Rapture addiction) are predictable: an initial high followed by a debilitating let down, followed by painful withdrawal symptoms (mentally re-entering the hum-drum world), followed by another injection. Again and again millions of emotionally vulnerable Christians return to their 'pushers' for another 'fix.'"[37] Gary North
>
> "These pessimistic peddlers of the gospel-according-to-Van Gogh see all major shifts in the jet stream, every new STD, every elevation of a corrupt, homunculus-horn-dog politician, all R-rated movies and every animated series by Michael Judge as 'proof' that Jesus is getting ready to ride back into town to rescue the Church from this naughty place and just let the monkeys run the jungle.—
>
> "When are these guys going to stop? I mean, how many failed prophecies regarding when Jesus is going to return do these guys get to rattle off before we blow them off and stop buying their books? How many anti-Christs have to come and go before we unplug their laptops, take the TV clicker out of their hands and cancel their subscription to *Paranoid Weekly*? The thing that I don't get about these supposed experts is how in the world did they miss the profuse texts in scripture which state that Christ triumphs in time over evil and that He accomplishes this domination through His Church?
>
> "The last time I checked, the scripture said:
>
> 1. History is the working out of Christ's purposes, not the anti-Christ's.[38] To hell with the anti-Christ and the horse he rides in on.
>
> 2. God is Lord of history, even turning evil into His and the Church's ultimate good.[39]
>
> 3. The kingdom is coming—it has come—and is growing by leaps and bounds over the forces of darkness.[40]

---

[37] Many incorrect presuppositions such as the "rapture" myth, dispensational theology and many false prophesies and opinions come from a radical misunderstanding of the very nature and purpose of the book of Revelations. Much of this misunderstanding and misapprehension is traceable to confusion regarding its original date of writing. Kenneth L. Gentry, Jr.: brings us the most thorough scholarly study of the true dating of Revelations ever accomplished. For those who are still wandering in the myth of the rapture his book: *Before Jerusalem Fell,* International Scholars Publications, is a must read! Also, for those still mired in the mud of dispensationalism and its inevitable links to the "rapture" myth, Gary North offers one of the best resources for understanding why these two heresies are so popular and why they are so dangerous to a victorious Christian life, now in our present history and in our present times! *Rapture Fever,* ICE Publications. This and many other great works by outstanding theologians may be accessed free of charge by going to: Freebooks.com. Books may be selected by title, subject or author. ZH

[38] In Matt. 22:44, Jesus quotes a passage from the Psalm's of David concerning himself: "The Lord said unto my Lord, Sit at my right hand, until I make your enemies your footstool. The Lord shall send the rod of your strength out of Zion: you will rule in the midst of your enemies. Your people shall be willing in the day of your power, in the beauties of holiness from the womb of the morning: you have the dew of your youth. The Lord has sworn, and will not repent; You are a priest for ever after the order of Melchizedek." Psalm 110:1-4. Also: "And Jesus came and spoke to them saying, all power is given unto me in heaven and in earth." Matt. 28:18. Also, Daniel prophesied of Jesus the Son of man: "I saw in the night visions, and, behold, one like the Son of man came with the clouds of heaven, and came to the Ancient of days, and they brought him near before him. And there was given him dominion, and glory, and a kingdom, that all people, nations, and languages, should serve him: his dominion is an everlasting dominion, which shall not pass away, and his kingdom that which shall not be destroyed."

[39] "And Joseph said unto them, Fear not: for am I in the place of God? But as for you, you thought evil against me; but God meant it unto good, to bring to pass, as it is this day, to save much people alive." Genesis 50:19-20.

[40] "And I heard a loud voice saying in heaven: Now is come salvation, and strength, and the kingdom of our God, and the power of his Christ: for the accuser of our brethren is cast down, which accused them before our God day and night. And they overcame him by the blood of the Lamb and by the word of their testimony; and they loved not their lives unto the death." Rev. 11:10-11.

4. And lastly, the Church is not going to have to be rescued from some haggard existence within a demon-dominated *terra firma*, but rather will deliver up to the Father, by the Holy Spirit, the kingdoms of this world, which have become the kingdom of our Lord and of His Christ.[41]

"My ClashPoint is this: Quit smoking these nickel bags of bad weed. This defeatist, pessimistic, *there's-nothing-we-can-do-to-right-this-nasty-world* stuff is crap, pure and simple.

"Now—Clear your lungs and inhale the biblical victory entailed within the pages of holy writ. Feel better?

"Okay, now put on some clothes—go back to school—raise a good family—get involved in politics, education, entertainment, business, the arts—and watch the beast, the anti-Christ, ant-pasta, anti-freeze, the auntie Em's and the whores of Babylon and Broadway begin to melt away through your righteous influence upon this godless environment." Doug Giles[42]

If you haven't heard from men like Gary North or Doug Giles before—stand-by—you haven't heard or seen anything yet! There is much more to come: Douglas Wilson, R. C. Sproul, Kenneth Gentry, Greg Banson and David Chilton to mention only a few. These are men, some still alive and some recently departed, that are God's current warriors and wild men. In the fifth century it was Augustine, in the sixteenth century it was Martin Luther and John Calvin, John Knox, Tyndal and others too numerous to mention. These were God's elements to bring into focus what became known as the *Reformation* and a term much in use at that time; *Evangelical.*

The points of doctrine that you will learn in this writing will reflect the most important aspects of these historical Reformation understandings of God's revealed Law-Word. To believe and understand what Giles says in his four points of Christ's Kingdom, history and the Church plus the terms *Reformation* and *Evangelical,* is a great step forward in bringing into focus a true Christ or Christian worldview.

**Confusion in the Church:**

"The Reformation has been eclipsed in the evangelical church. Theology is either considered a necessary evil or something that is, practically speaking, irrelevant to the concerns of ministry and church growth. Lip service is often paid to the Reformation but it is rarely more than that." Gary L. W. Johnson

"Historically speaking, the term evangelical came into vogue during the Reformation when it was virtually a synonym for protestant. But today, evangelicalism/Protestantism (by and large) has lost its clear identity together with its protest. In less than a century, evangelicalism has gone, according to Os Guinness, from 'a confessionally defined body, to a frat house of institutions, to a coalition of causes, to a movement in disarray.'

---

41 "And the seventh angel sounded: and there were great voices in heaven, saying: The kingdoms of this world are become the kingdoms of our Lord and of his Christ; and he shall reign for ever and ever." Rev. 11:15.

42 Doug Giles, Political Twerps, Cultural Jerks, Church Quirks, p 163, 164, 165-166 Also, Doug Giles' provocative weekly one-hour radio program, 'The Clash', has re-launched with several new features. Go to clashradio.com and hit 'listen live.'

"The Protestant church, no longer moored to its historical biblical landings, is currently floating around on the flotsam and jetsam of postmodernism's whimsically ridiculous views. It doesn't matter what you believe—truth is relative—doctrine is unimportant—there are many roads to God—unity is more important than creeds.—

"The Church, having bought these satanic narcotics, now no longer looks to Scripture to proclaim God's word, but as Dave Wells states:

'The church borrows strategies from the psychiatric and business communities in hopes this will make up for the supposed irrelevancy and insufficiency of the scriptures. I can't turn on Christian TV or radio without feeling like I'm listening to Oprah, or sitting in on a marketing roundtable for Nike, or watching Mr. Rogers try to calm Liza Minelli's nerves."'

**"Seldom do we hear the great truths of the scripture, truths like:**

Justification by faith alone;
The Bible as ultimate and final authority for all people, at all times and in all places;
Salvation through Christ alone;
The necessity of the new birth;
Radical corruption and the depravity of man;
The reality of the judgment of God and of an eternal hell;
Recognizing God's lordship, and no rule but His rule;
Living solely unto God's glory.—

"We need to reform Protestantism back to the Reformation. I can't think of a greater need for the Church than the need to turn back the clock to the Reformation, to revisit this great epoch moment in evangelical history and get the message, the motive and the courage that coursed through our forefathers' veins. We must quit seeking to be liked and cool, and once again reject truth-denying and the truth-reconstructing culture, so full of lies, hype and spin.

"Let us follow anew the word of God that will brutally slay the idolatrous notions of atheistic men. We must once again lurch the Church—and the planet—back into the blessing of and obedience to the word of God." Doug Giles

**Christianity Today's Editorial Article on marriage:**

Context is important, and this is a good place to bring up what I said earlier that we would address regarding the editorial published in August of 2003 by Christianity Today.

The second point of their editorial made light of personal individualism of the Zeitgeist form: I agree, but this is a radical perspective that is narcissistic, selfish and overbearing. This is not the individualism of a man and a woman of faith and grace who commit to be responsible under God for their decisions and actions in love, marriage and rearing their family to His honor and glory. Any time one chooses to speak negatively about such an important thing as individualism it must be clarified that there is a correct perspective of individualism—without such clarification you are left with a sense more of communism than anything Christian.

Further more, their third point continues to bash individualism under the term of—expressive individualism—just what other kind there could be I can not imagine. They offered no further in-depth explanation other than to mix this statement with their thoughts that such individualism somehow keeps one from being a team player in marriage. Common sense would tell you that they either did not research the subject or they are again parroting secular academia's watered down pabulum—or maybe they just want to give credence to Hillary Clinton's book "*It takes a village*," without actually quoting her. Christianity Today can and often does do a better job than this. But like so much of what we have become used to calling fundamentalism and evangelicalism really isn't—it's just the same old secular academia—with a different dress on.

They also say that marriage is more than the sum of its parts. This is true, it is not two parts, it is ONE FLESH and this is a mystery of God—"For this cause shall a man leave his father and mother, and shall be joined unto his wife, and they two shall be one flesh. This is a great mystery: but I speak concerning Christ and the church." Ephesians 5:31-32. The synergism that this creates is a gift of God and not because they have sacrificed their individuality. The greatest service in marriage and in all of God's ordained systems of organizations from the—simple to the most complex—are one and all, performed best, when each individual within those systems takes expressed personal—individual ownership—for their responsibilities.

When married couples accept the watered down pabulum of secular academia's drool as a truth they can live by, they reduce themselves to victim status. Each time the other appears to be too individual—read attempts to fulfill his/her God ordained role in the relationship—the other cries foul and claims to be—you guessed it—a VICTIM!

**Understanding our new language:**

Learning how to use our new vowel and alphabet system is one of the great privileges and joys of our Christian heritage, we are citizens of a new Kingdom, we have been adopted into the Family of God, we speak a New Language and we are free in Him to do all things well!

As a first radio operator in the Naval Airforce aboard the P5M2 seaplane, I was trained to use Morse Code. The pilots had microphones and could use voice communication to talk to towers on land or ship based facilities. However, as our missions were classified we were obligated to make all of our position reports and any pertinent information via Morse Code transmission. In order to do this it was necessary to attend classes and study the code and the tools needed to send and receive the dots and dashes that make up one's message. Our equipment consisted of low frequency transmitters and a keying device. Before each message was sent the officer in charge—usually the designated navigator—would prepare the message by using a code book and then giving me the finished product—a series of five digit numbers made up in columns, that when decoded on the other end would reveal the contents of the message. Thus, I learned my first—second—language through secular means of simple functional education.

Later, in Mexico where I served as a missionary for 20 years—12 full-time and 8 part-time—I was challenged to learn Spanish. In both instances I was successful and was proficient for the task at hand. Unfortunately I am not able to send and receive the Code today as I did then—although it is still used today to identify navigational aid stations for airplanes—and this allows me some continued use of the skill. Spanish, however, became a true second language which Marilyn and I use currently in our accounting business as we have many clients who speak Spanish. Also, I continue to promote and do mission work within Mexico and Spanish speaking churches in the USA. The key to continued proficiency in any learned skill is practice. I stopped using the code as a means of communication after my discharge and thus I lost the proficiency to use it as a communication tool. Likewise if I should cease to speak Spanish I would ultimately lose the ability to converse or to read and write it as I do today.

Our new language in Christ is not something you can go to school, seminary or otherwise to learn. The language that we learn as Christians comes to us by virtue of our new birth into Christ and because he comes to live in us in the form of his other self the Paraclete—or Holy Spirit—as was prophesied by Joel. This language is made possible for us through the gift of faith we have received from the Father. With this gift of faith we can see with spiritual eyes and hear with spiritual ears and understand spiritual works. In other words—we see and believe His works after him—we hear and think His words after him—we speak His words after him—know and do His works after him. We should always remember that we do nothing in and of ourselves but sin. All that we do that is good and acceptable to Him are all that we do after Him—we are his image—and doing all that we do after him is our reflection of Him. Without this gift of faith the unbeliever has eyes that cannot see spiritual truth, cannot hear spiritual truth and cannot see spiritual works. All men and women of faith and grace know what I am talking about, even if you have not heard it presented in this way. A few examples will verify what I am saying:

1. When our Lord says that he is the Christ—the Savior of the world—our King and our Redeemer, our hearts ring with joy and visions of all the promises of his word come alive in our minds. Thus, we can both hear and see spiritual truth. For all those without the Father's gift of faith, for all of those who are not drawn to Christ by the Father—what is joy and confidence to us—is confusion and enmity for them!

2. When we who have the Father's gift of faith contemplate our natural depravity and our lost condition before we heard His voice and knew who he was—we see the miracle of our salvation. We are blessed with the revelation that what was once dead is now alive—behold all things are new—we can do all things through Christ who loves and strengthens us! We experience in time and space the reality of a new birth—our resurrection from the dead—is confirmed with every passing day! We no longer fear the second death, for we have passed from death unto life—life everlasting! Our goals and our reality are no longer confined to this present life or to this current planet. We serve and seek to follow all of our Savior's leading that we might experience and fulfill all that He has prepared for us—not to win His favor—but as befits our duty and as an expression of love, gratitude and appreciation for being called and adopted into His family.

We know in whom we have believed and we are confident that He is able to do all that He has promised and more—MORE—because even with our gift of faith we cannot comprehend the magnitude of what He has prepared for us![43] Whereas,

[43] "However we speak wisdom among them that are mature: yet not the philosophy of this world, nor of the leading men of this world, that come to nothing: but we speak the truth of God in a hidden form, even the hidden wisdom, which God ordained before the world unto our glory: which none of the leading men of this world knew: for had they known it, they would not have crucified the Lord of glory. But as it is written: *Eye has not seen, nor ear heard, neither have entered into the heart of man, the things which God has prepared for them that love him.* But God has revealed them unto us by his Spirit: for the Spirit searches all things, yes, the deep things of God. For what man appreciates the things of a man, save the spirit of man which is in him? Even so the things of God no man knows, but the Spirit of God. Which things also we speak, not in the words which man's wisdom teaches, but which the Holy Spirit teaches; comparing spiritual things with spiritual. But the natural man does not receive the things of the Spirit of God; for they are foolishness unto him: neither can he know them, because they are spiritually discerned. But he that is spiritual

while we are blessed by this revelation, it creates anger and fear in those to whom God has not yet revealed himself. Their fears are expressed in many ways: politically, academically, vocationally, socially, and often—in your face—angry and personal, using all available derogatory language to decry and demean God's elect. They do not speak the language of our Father; they speak the language of their father.[44]

I could be tempted as many are, to digress and make an attempt to answer the unanswerable—why and how does God choose the Elect? While those who would be so brave—read *foolish*—as to attempt such a thing, might just as well explain why God exists. For the secular humanist this is no challenge, for his answer is simply that God does not exist. Yet, I am referring here to Christians. We Christians who speak and understand the language must learn to accept with humility the truths that God is pleased to express and to explain to us. While those things that He has chosen to keep secret for this time—He does promise to tell us later[45]—we must not disrespect with our puny, self righteous speculations.

**Using our new language:**

Common sense tells us all that if we do not use a talent or ability regularly we lose proficiency in that talent or ability. Even such basic tools as our arms and legs: if we do not use them for extended periods of time, they become atrophied and we lose the use of them entirely. We can expect no less reality from God's gift of our new language—if we refuse to speak it—but rather allow secular academia and humanist liberalism to dictate the terms and meanings of our conversation—then we stand mute to both ourselves and to the world at large.

We become mute—sterile—in our conversation within our own inner self, for we lose the understanding of Christ's worldview. We have no—salt or word—with which to impregnate our world around us.[46] We become mute—sterile and incoherent—in our conversation with our wives and children. We are impotent and we cannot hope to speak to them of God's truth and lead them with God's wisdom if we have refused to honor and speak His language. We have our new language as a GIFT—we do not earn it—and we show great disrespect and actually a rebellious heart, when we insist that the secular world of unbelief has the correct understanding of God, his plans, his promises and his creation.[47] Much—much

---

understands all things, yet he himself is not understood by any mere man. For who has known the mind of the Lord, that he may instruct him? But we have the mind of Christ." I Cor. 2:6-16.

44 "Jesus said unto them, if God were your Father, you would love me: for I proceeded from and came from God; neither did I come of myself, but he sent me. Why do you not understand my speech? even because you cannot hear my word. *(Understand my message.)* You are of your father the devil, and the lusts of your father you will do. He was a murderer from the beginning, and lived not in the truth, because there is no truth in him. When he speaks a lie, he speaks of his own: for he is a liar, and the father of it. And because I tell you the truth, you do not believe me. Which of you convinces me of sin? And if I say the truth, why do you not believe me? He that is of God hears god's words: you therefore to do not hear them because you are not of God." John 8:42-47.

45 "When I was a child, I spoke as a child; I understood as a child, I thought as a child: but when I became a man, I put away childish things. For now we see through a glass, darkly; but then face to face: now I know in part; but then I shall know even as I am known. And now there is faith, hope and love, but the greatest of these is love." I Cor. 13:11-13.

46 "You are the salt of the earth: but if the salt has its strength with what shall it be salted? It is from then on good for nothing except to be cast out, and to be trodden under foot of men. You are the light of the world. A city that is set on a hill cannot be hid. Neither do men light a candle and put it under a basket but on a candlestick and it gives light unto all that are in the house. Let your light so shine before men, that they may see your good works, and glorify your Father which is in heaven." Matt. 5:13-16.

47 "This I say therefore, and testify in the Lord, that you henceforth walk not as other Gentiles walk, in the vanity of their mind, having the understanding darkened, being alienated from the life of God through the ignorance that is in them, because of the blindness of their heart: Who being past feeling have given themselves over unto lasciviousness, to work all uncleanness with greediness. But you have not so learned Christ; If so be that you have heard him, and have been taught by him, as the truth is in Jesus: That you put off concerning the former conversation the old man, which is corrupt according to the deceitful lusts; and be renewed in the spirit of your mind; and that you put on the

more—important to me than the WHY and HOW of God's reasons and methods of election is the WHY and HOW of our failure to respect this great new language that we have been freely given. With this language we have understanding and we can embrace the wisdom of God for all things that he has purposed for us to do and for his Kingdom.[48] Without this language we become deaf, dumb and blind children of the King seeking who will take us by the hand and lead us around the rooms of our own inherited royal palace.

Imagine—if you can—adopted children, blessed with all the riches of their Father the King, living in the palace—Kingdom—of their great Father and they are all blind seeking servants from without the palace—illegitimate children not of the Kingdom—to lead them about! WHAT is WRONG with this picture?

May our hearts be filled with remorse and may we have a renewed and inflamed desire to repent of such rebellion to our wonderful, gracious, caring Father who has given us all things. Our Father is faithful and when we repent He hears our cry of remorse. He knows our hearts—we cannot—fool Him. He is always ready to forgive us and to lift us up again and again. May we not grieve the Holy Spirit by our spiritual adultery in seeking out those NOT of the Kingdom to give us sight, hearing and understanding. It is to us that they must come to get such things. We borrow not from them—but it is written that they will indeed borrow from us![49]

**Prayer is a powerful part of our new language:**

When I spoke earlier of the weight of prayer being greater and of more credibility than normal speech, I was speaking of prayer as a function of this new language.

Some of my Pentecostal friends will want to take issue with me on this: it is their common practice to teach that what they call "tongues" is their spiritual prayer language. This is true when presented as Paul the Apostle taught it and as Romans speaks of the unutterable groaning of the Spirit to assist us in our times of stress and anguish when we do not know what to say. But, you will note that the Pentecostals and Charismatics did not gain notoriety because of speaking in tongues and groaning in the spirit while praying in the privacy of their prayer closet—as instructed by Paul—but rather for doing exactly what he said not to do. As the Corinthians before them, they most often have been guilty of using tongues as a demonstration of superior spirituality—pride. Rare are the occasion—almost nonexistent—where a genuine interpretation is given to a public message in tongues. I count genuine any interpretation that would be revealing of some message of—significant depth and of purpose—for the time and place not easily attainable by other means and in full agreement with His Truth already revealed. I certainly do not count as genuine the oft repeated drivel that is served up over and over again in the public worship of many such congregations.

It is so bad in the modern Pentecostal church and those Charismatics who practice the same; that the worship leader or pastor knows who to call on for a prayer in tongues for any given "interpretation" that he wants. Sister "Ruby" gives

---

new man, which after God is created in righteousness and true holiness. Wherefore putting away lying, speak every man truth with his neighbor: for we are members one of another.

[48] "But you are a chosen generation, a royal priesthood, a holy nation, a peculiar people; that you should show forth the praises of him who has called you out of darkness into his marvelous light: which in time past were not a people, but are now the people of God: which had not obtained mercy, but now have obtained mercy." I Peter 2:9-10.

[49] The Lord prophesied concerning his elect and their standing in the world. "For the Lord thy God blesses you as he promised you: and you shall lend unto many nations, but you shall not borrow; and you shall reign over many nations, but they shall not reign over you." Deut. 15:6

this kind of interpretation, Bro. Jones gives another, generalizations, platitudes, claims of blessings, warnings of general types all, nothing of real—significant weight—that a thousand other believers without this "gift" could not give.

For those who believe in tongues—I also believe in tongues—just as Paul believed and taught.[50] My point is that what is practiced and what is taught in God's revealed Law-Word is not the same thing in 99% of the cases. Get it right or abstain as Paul suggested.

The prayer language that I am talking about for men and women of faith and grace is that prayer offered in what ever language you speak that is understood by your mate and your children. This is the language that Paul said he would rather speak just FIVE words of, rather than TEN THOUSAND words in a tongue that is not understood.

**Reading is a powerful part of our new language:**

Unbelievers and believers—those without and those with—the gift of faith; can all read in their own native languages, if they have received reading instruction in those languages. This is no mystery. The mystery and yet another proof of our new language—if you need proof—is that those with the gift of faith may read the Law-Word of God and receive knowledge, wisdom and faith. That is they will understand the relevance and application of the message and their faith will be increased. Whereas, those who do NOT have the gift of faith will only find argument against anything they think that they have found that could possibly bring shame and ridicule against all who do HAVE the gift of faith. God's Law-Word is foolishness and anathema to them. Again—all such are not of our Kingdom, they do not have our Father, they are not part of our FAMILY and they DO NOT speak our language!

None of what I have just said is strange to those men and women of faith and grace who are reading this. To others—yes—it might seem, probably will seem—strange. Stranger yet to me is why the Christian community is so lacking in their reading, study and meditation of God's revealed Law-Word? Most pastors do not read the Bible on a daily basis, few have read it cover to cover, very, very few read it once a year. If this is normal among pastors—pray tell me what is happening within the membership. Personally, I know that there are many believers who read the Law-Word of God at least once a year, I say—many—only because it is a respectable number in the thousands, but is not—many—if you count the tens of millions of those who say they are Christian.

Therein lays our problem. Pastors more often than not are poor examples of how to faithfully feed on God's revealed Law-Word! As a direct result of this bad example, only an extremely small percentage of the overall membership, actually accept the challenge, to read it once a year. The truth is that—without some spiritual input from the Word—a Christian cannot grow into a mature servant: one who knows who they are in Christ and what the overall plan of God is. Such who do not feed at all from God's revealed Law-Word are left to the crumbs of pastors—poor in spirit—bad authors, false prophets aplenty, radio and TV evangelists, most who are also poor in spirit—misguided, wrong headedness and just plain ignorant of God's revealed Law-Word.

---

50 "I thank my God; I speak with tongues more than you all: yet in the church I had rather speak five words with my understanding, that by my voice I might teach others also, than ten thousand words in an unknown tongue. Brethren, be not children in understanding: however in malice be like children, but in understanding be men. In the law it is written: *With men of other tongues and other lips will I speak unto this people; and for all that will they not hear me, says the Lord.* Wherefore tongues are for a sign, not to them that believe, but to them that believe not: but prophesying serves nothing for them that do not believe, but for them which believe." I Cor. 14:18-22.

**Spiritual anorexia and our rebellious carnal nature:**

Anorexics have been proven to be individuals who seek total control over their bodies. The act of not eating or of gorging and then evacuating the stomach by induced vomiting and thus maintaining an artificially low body to fat ratio for purely misguided and yes—evil purposes—gives them a sense of independence and power. They actually pride themselves on their independence to choose—to eat or not to eat. It is a defiant attitude of rebellion against God's common grace to provide us with health through proper eating habits. Where these individuals are able to continue this practice for prolonged periods of time, they reach a point where there is no turning back. There is an Autonomic Nervous System shutdown mode, and in extreme cases all attempts to reverse this self destruct mode is met with failure and the person dies. Karen Carpenter, the famous singer was one of these sad examples.

Spiritual anorexia is the name I have chosen to describe the present spiritual condition of so much of our "Christian" culture, with respect to our resistance to wholeheartedly feed on God's revealed Law-Word. I use the word in parenthesis because it is inconceivable that God's true children, His elect and adopted family, bought and paid for by the blood of Christ, would be His—that is Christian—and at the same time refuse to eat at His table of daily nourishment for our spiritual and character development! Our tendencies to assume that we can live by receiving a few morsels of spiritual food once a week—if even that much—from the pulpit is stark evidence that we are rebellious children at best and outright apostates at worst! And the fact is quite evident, that this is just one of the many ways, we demonstrate our desire to be in control and to know good and evil on our own terms and not God's.

However as men and women of faith and grace we want the truth. We want the wisdom of God and we want the knowledge of God to bring us into the fullness of Christ that we might know the riches of his blessings! Therefore, we must consider God's Law-Word to be a necessary food for our spiritual health and wellbeing. A priceless tool to unlock all of life's mysteries that God has foreordained that we should know! Who among us does not know that without nutritious food and water our physical bodies will soon wither and die? How then can we hope to flourish in our understanding of love, sex, marriage, rearing God's children and fulfilling the destiny of His sovereign will for our lives, if we starve ourselves from the very source of our nourishment?

**Feeding on the word:**

On average, depending on the page size and the fonts that are chosen, the Bible has about a thousand pages of text not including such things as a concordance, and other study material. Almost everyone who does not read the Bible has the same excuse—ready and primed—like: "I just can't understand all of those begots and begets it's just so confusing." Okay, if you don't want to read the begots and begets just skip them, they make up less than one percent of God's revealed Law-Word. So now you can read it—right? Also, you might find other passages that just don't make sense to you—I'm thinking of some of the chapters in Leviticus regarding the purification rights and temple worship. If any such passages give you more of a challenge than you want to wade through, fine, don't read them, move on to the next chapter. If you do this and set a goal for yourself that you will read an average of only—THREE PAGES—per day, you will read the Bible from cover to cover in one year.

It would be very embarrassing for you to claim that you do not have enough time—you see—our President, George Bush is a man who gets up at 4:30 AM and before he meets with his advisors and begins his very hectic day—guess what? He reads a few pages in the Bible—his goal is to read it once every year. He is Commander and Chief of our military forces world-wide and sets the pace, style and substance of our government, for the service of every American. Don't you wish your pastor would read the Bible once every year like your President does? Don't you wish that you did too? Tell me, friend—husband or wife—how can you be spiritually nourished if you do not read God's revealed Law-Word? How can you pray intelligently if you don't even know what your heavenly Father has said that he wants you to do? How can you hear with understanding what your pastor or any other Christian leader says is true if you don't know and understand what God says in his revealed Law-Word? How can you possibly know that what I am writing in this book is—correct and good—for you and your spouse, if you don't read and prayerfully seek God's message for you in his revealed Law-Word?[51]

**There are great riches in using our new language:**

Love and marriage are the crown jewels of his richest blessings for all men and women of faith and grace—now in this time—not later—NOW in our history—in our time. It has been so for all who came before us, it is so for us and it will be so for our children and for all who follow after us![52] We seek not the abnormal; on the contrary this is the—normal—Christian life. Our salvation, our resurrection from our dead sins and dead lives is the greatest miracle of all for us. So much so in fact: that we will not know the full extent of just how great until we have passed from this life. But for us here and now; men and women of faith and grace, we have the hope and the promise of God to receive—uncommon common sense, uncommon love—from him for use in our relationships with each other and with our children. Even our enemies benefit. Does anyone who is a believer not know that we are to pray for our enemies? Does anyone who believes actually think that they—in and of themselves—have the power to offer such prayers? I think not—I know they don't! Whatever real love we give to our mates we give only that which we have already received from Him who is LOVE![53]

Lest those who are single and who have no knowledge of whether or not they will ever marry, should think that there are no blessings for them—let us say

---

[51] "It is a faithful saying: For if we be dead with him, we shall also live with him: If we suffer, we shall also reign with him: if we deny him, he also will deny us: If we believe not, yet he abides faithful: he cannot deny himself. Of these things put them in remembrance, charging them before the Lord that they strive not about words to no profit, but to the subverting of the hearers.

Study to show yourself approved unto God: a workman that needs not to be ashamed, rightly dividing the word of truth. But shun profane and vain babblings: for they will increase unto more ungodliness. And their word will eat as doth a canker: of whom is Hymenaeus and Philetus; Who concerning the truth have erred, saying that the resurrection is past already; and overthrow the faith of some. Nevertheless the foundation of God stands sure, having this seal; The Lord knows them that are his. And, Let every one that names the name of Christ depart from iniquity." II Timothy 2:11-19.

[52] "He who finds a wife finds a good thing, and obtains favor from the Lord." Proverb 18:22. "Houses and riches are an inheritance from fathers, but a prudent wife is from the LORD." Proverbs 19:14. "Who can find a virtuous[c] wife? For her worth is far above rubies. The heart of her husband safely trusts her; so he will have no lack of gain. She does him good and not evil all the days of her life." Proverbs.31:10-12. "Her husband is known in the gates, when he sits among the elders of the land." Prov. 31:25. "Her children rise up and call her blessed; her husband also, and he praises her: Many daughters have done well, but you excel them all. Charm is deceitful and beauty is passing, but a woman who fears the LORD, she shall be praised. Give her of the fruit of her hands, and let her own works praise her in the gates." Prov. 31:28-31.

[53] "Yours, O LORD, is the greatness, the power and the glory, the victory and the majesty; for all that is in heaven and in earth is Yours; Yours is the kingdom, O LORD, and You are exalted as head over all. Both riches and honor come from You, and You reign over all. In Your hand is power and might; in Your hand it is to make great and to give strength to all. "Now therefore, our God, we thank You and praise Your glorious name. But who am I, and who are my people, that we should be able to offer so willingly as this? For all things come from You, and of Your own we have given You." I Cronicles 29:11-14.

very clearly—yes, there are blessings promised for you, now in this time. However, although there are rich blessings for the single man or woman of faith and grace they pale in comparison to those promised blessings for those who marry in the Lord. Both the single and the married will suffer many problems and challenges. But it is the mysteries of the ONE FLESH—the melting together—of two beings into one over-riding expression of God's gift of love, tenderness and passion that fuels the blessings of marriage and family!

# Book I

# LOVE AND MARRIAGE

## Chapter Six

## Reigning With Christ

"Now when He had taken the scroll, the four living creatures and the twenty-four elders fell down before the Lamb, each having a harp, and golden bowls full of incense, which are the prayers of the saints. And they sang a new song, saying: 'You are worthy to take the scroll, and to open its seals; for You were slain, and have redeemed us to God by Your blood out of every tribe and tongue and people and nation, and have made us kings and priests to our God; and we shall reign on the earth.'" Revelations 5:8-10

**Christ's worldview of men of faith and grace:**

As we have seen repeatedly—God's revealed Law-Word—states clearly the many facets and the complete scope of Christ's worldview. I have collected the most pointed and important verses relevant to Christ's world view of MALES in general and MEN of faith and grace in particular. Rarely heard from the today's pulpits but clearly stated in the Word is the fact that from God's perspective there are—TWO ADAMS! The first failed because of—SIN—the second was successful because of—OBEDIENCE!

**The first man of faith and grace was Adam; of the flesh, natural and from the ground:**

"Then God said, 'Let Us make man in Our image, according to Our likeness; let them have dominion over the fish of the sea, over the birds of the air, and over the cattle, over all the earth and over every creeping thing that creeps on the earth.' So God created man in His own image; in the image of God He created him; male and female He created them. Then God blessed them, and God said to them, 'Be fruitful and multiply; fill the earth and subdue it; have dominion over the fish of the sea, over the birds of the air, and over every living thing that moves on the earth.'

"And God said, 'See, I have given you every herb that yields seed which is on the face of all the earth, and every tree whose fruit yields seed; to you it shall be for food. Also, to every beast of the earth, to every bird of the air, and to everything that creeps on the earth, in which there is life, I have given every green herb for food'; and it was so. Then God saw everything that He had made, and indeed it was very good. So the evening and the morning were the sixth day. Genesis 1:26-28.

"And Adam said: 'This is now bone of my bones and flesh of my flesh; she shall be called Woman, because she was taken out of Man.'

"Therefore a man shall leave his father and mother and be joined to his wife, and they shall become one flesh. And they were both naked, the man and his wife, and were not ashamed. Genesis 2:23-25.

"Then the serpent said to the woman, 'You will not surely die. For God knows that in the day you eat of it your eyes will be opened and you will be like God, knowing good and evil.'

"So when the woman saw that the tree was good for food, that it was pleasant to the eyes, and a tree desirable to make one wise, she took of its fruit and ate. She also gave to her husband with her, and he ate. Then the eyes of both of them were opened, and they knew that they were naked; and they sewed fig leaves together and made themselves coverings.

"And they heard the sound of the LORD God walking in the garden in the cool of the day, and Adam and his wife hid themselves from the presence of the LORD God among the trees of the garden. Genesis 3:4-8.

"And He said, 'Who told you that you were naked? Have you eaten from the tree of which I commanded you that you should not eat?'

"Then the man said, 'The woman whom you gave to be with me, she gave me of the tree, and I ate.'

"And the LORD God said to the woman, 'What is this you have done?' Genesis 3:11-13.

"To the woman He said: 'I will greatly multiply your sorrow and your conception; in pain you shall bring forth children; your desire shall be for your husband, and he shall rule over you.'

"Then to Adam He said, 'Because you have heeded the voice of your wife, and have eaten from the tree of which I commanded you, saying, 'You shall not eat of it': Cursed is the ground for your sake; in toil you shall eat of it all the days of your life. Both thorns and thistles it shall bring forth for you, and you shall eat the herb of the field. In the sweat of your face you shall eat bread till you return to the ground, for out of it you were taken; for dust you are, and to dust you shall return.'" Genesis 3:16-19.

**The second man Christ; of the flesh, Spiritual and from heaven above:**

"But now Christ is risen from the dead, and has become the first fruits of those who have fallen asleep. For since by man came death, by Man also came the resurrection of the dead. For as in Adam all die, even so in Christ all shall be made alive. But each one in his own order: Christ the first fruits, afterward those who are Christ's at His coming. Then comes the end, when He delivers the kingdom to God the Father, when He puts an end to all rule and all authority and power. For He must reign: till He has put all enemies under His feet. The last enemy that will be destroyed is death. For: 'He has put all things under His feet.' But when He says 'all things are put under Him,' it is evident that He who put all things under Him is excepted. Now when all things are made subject to Him, then the Son Himself will also be subject to Him who put all things under Him that God may be all in all. I Cor. 15:20-28.

"So also is the resurrection of the dead. The body is sown in corruption, it is raised in incorruption. It is sown in dishonor, it is raised in glory. It is sown in weakness, it is raised in power. It is sown a natural body, it is raised a spiritual body. There is a natural body, and there is a spiritual body. And so it is written, 'The first man Adam became a living being.' The last Adam became a life-giving spirit.

> "However, the spiritual is not first, but the natural, and afterward the spiritual. The first man was of the earth, made of dust; the second Man is the Lord from heaven. As was the man of dust, so also are those who are made of dust; and as is the heavenly Man, so also are those who are heavenly. And as we have borne the image of the man of dust, we shall also bear the image of the heavenly Man. I Cor. 15:42-49.

> "I desire therefore that the men pray everywhere, lifting up holy hands, without wrath and doubting; in like manner also, that the women adorn themselves in modest apparel, with propriety and moderation, not with braided hair or gold or pearls or costly clothing, but, which is proper for women professing godliness, with good works. Let a woman learn in silence with all submission. And I do not permit a woman to teach or to have authority over a man, but to be in silence. For Adam was formed first, then Eve. And Adam was not deceived, but the woman being deceived, fell into transgression. Nevertheless she will be saved in childbearing if they continue in faith, love, and holiness, with self-control." I Tim. 2:8-15.

**All other men of faith and grace:**

All others are those of the Royal Priesthood of Christ—all who have come before us—and all who will come after us.

> "Coming to Him as to a living stone, rejected indeed by men, but chosen by God and precious, you also, as living stones, are being built up a spiritual house, a holy priesthood, to offer up spiritual sacrifices acceptable to God through Jesus Christ. Therefore it is also contained in the Scripture, 'Behold, I lay in Zion a chief cornerstone, elect, precious, and he who believes on Him will by no means be put to shame.' Therefore, to you who believe, He is precious; but to those who are disobedient, 'the stone which the builders rejected has become the chief cornerstone,' and 'a stone of stumbling and a rock of offense.' They stumble, being disobedient to the word, to which they also were appointed. But you are a chosen generation, a **royal priesthood**, a holy nation, His own special people, that you may proclaim the praises of Him, who called you out of darkness into His marvelous light; who once were not a people but are now the people of God, who had not obtained mercy but now have obtained mercy." I Peter 2:4-10

**God's revealed Law-Word is especially revealed and written for men:**

All of God's revealed Law-Word is for all of his creation but not all have the gift of faith to understand it. All of His created men are under—common—grace[54] but some are also called to be under—special—grace.[55] It is these who are called to be under special grace to which He gives the gift of faith that we might know Him, believe on Him and be saved, called according to His calling and for His purposes.

---

[54] "But I say to you, love your enemies, bless those who curse you, do good to those who hate you, and pray for those who spitefully use you and persecute you, that you may be sons of your Father in heaven; for He makes His sun rise on the evil and on the good, and sends rain on the just and on the unjust." Matt. 5:44-45.

[55] "And we know that all things work together for good to those who love God, to those who are the called according to His purpose. For whom He foreknew, He also predestined to be conformed to the image of His Son, that He might be the firstborn among many brethren. Moreover whom He predestined, these He also called; whom He called, these He also justified; and whom He justified, these He also glorified." Romans 8:28-30.

God's revealed Law-Word is received and written by men and for men. There are only three recorded exceptions to God's preference for spiritual leadership: Deborah, Ruth, and Esther.

Deborah was chosen by default because the men in leadership refused to take up the mantel of leadership and it fell to her. She even warned them that by so doing it would bring shame to them[56], but they would not take the lead. Ruth was chosen to be an example of a woman of faith and grace and also to highlight God's use of other races in the lineage of Jesus Christ[57]. Esther was chosen for a specific role of intervention that only a woman of faith and grace could have done. She was God's elected contact with her husband the King of Persia, and her adopted country and only she had entrance with the King, to speak to him in such a way as only a—wife of faith and grace—could have done[58]. Her successful intervention brought about the deliverance of God's people in the country. Each of these occasions was allowed because of a specific need within the history of God's providence in working out his will for his promised Savior: Jesus Christ.

However, these instances did not and do not change God's original position for men. In every other instance the Word is clear: God has foreordained that his creation—MAN—read male men, is to have prominence in all matters of leadership in two of his institutions: the Family Institution and the Church Institution.

Only one of His institutions is reserved as a potential place of prominence in leadership for women of faith and grace, and that is the State Institution. Of the three institutions, the State Institution is the least important in God's hierarchy of principles and institutions, although it gets the—most press—from the secular humanist persuasion. The State depends for its—moral values, character and integrity—on the Family and the Church. Moral values, character and integrity are not created by government, they are—implemented and protected—by government![59] Therefore, the woman of faith and grace is never allowed—in God's

---

56 "Now Deborah, a prophetess, the wife of Lapidoth; was judging Israel at that time. And she would sit under the palm tree of Deborah between Ramah and Bethel in the mountains of Ephraim. And the children of Israel came up to her for judgment. Then she sent and called for Barak the son of Abinoam from Kedesh in Naphtali, and said to him, "Has not the LORD God of Israel commanded, 'Go and deploy troops at Mount Tabor; take with you ten thousand men of the sons of Naphtali and of the sons of Zebulun; and against you I will deploy Sisera, the commander of Jabin's army, with his chariots and his multitude at the River Kishon; and I will deliver him into your hand'? And Barak said to her, "If you will go with me, then I will go; but if you will not go with me, I will not go!" So she said, "I will surely go with you; nevertheless there will be no glory for you in the journey you are taking, for the LORD will sell Sisera into the hand of a woman." Then Deborah arose and went with Barak to Kedesh. 10And Barak called Zebulun and Naphtali to Kedesh; he went up with ten thousand men under his command,[a] and Deborah went up with him." Judges 10:4-10.

57 "So Boaz took Ruth and she became his wife; and when he went in to her, the LORD gave her conception, and she bore a son. Then the women said to Naomi, "Blessed be the LORD, who has not left you this day without a close relative; and may his name be famous in Israel! And may he be to you a restorer of life and a nourisher of your old age; for your daughter-in-law, who loves you, who is better to you than seven sons, has borne him." Then Naomi took the child and laid him on her bosom, and became a nurse to him. Also the neighbor women gave him a name, saying, "There is a son born to Naomi." And they called his name Obed. He is the father of Jesse, the father of David." Ruth 4:13-17.

58 "And Mordecai told them to answer Esther: 'Do not think in your heart that you will escape in the king's palace any more than all the other Jews. For if you remain completely silent at this time, relief and deliverance will arise for the Jews from another place, but you and your father's house will perish. Yet who knows whether you have come to the kingdom for such a time as this?' Then Esther told them to reply to Mordecai: 'Go, gather all the Jews who are present in Shushan, and fast for me; neither eat nor drink for three days, night or day. My maids and I will fast likewise. And so I will go to the king, which is against the law; and if I perish, I perish!' So Mordecai went his way and did according to all that Esther commanded him." Esther 4:13-17.

59 "Let us therefore rely upon the goodness of the Cause, and the aid of the supreme Being, in whose hands Victory is, to animate and encourage us to great and noble Actions. Let it simply be asked where is the security for property, for reputation, for life, if the sense, of religious obligation desert the oaths, which are the instruments of investigation in the Courts of Justice? And let us with caution indulge the opposition, that morality can be maintained without religion. Whatever may be conceded to the influence of refined education on minds of peculiar structure, reason and experience both forbid us to expect that National morality can prevail in exclusion of religious principle." George Washington

revealed Law-Word to have the highest positions of authority for leadership in moral values, character and integrity. These are reserved for MEN of faith and grace who are specifically under orders to assume the position of responsibility for such leadership and authority as fathers of His Families and elders, deacons and pastors of His Church.

The Family Institution originally encompassed all that was considered economical as well as all that was considered educational. Over time God's development of the division of labor and the revelation of technology has made it necessary to have sub-sets of society under the family such as, business and education. These are all areas of opportunity for female leadership. However, in the family of faith and grace these and all positions of authority—in and outside—of the family unit are approved and delegated responsibilities from the husband to the wife.

It is said of Margaret Thatcher that her husband approved of her being the Prime Minister of England.

**God's uncommon—common sense about His Chain of Command:**

Now that we know more about Christ's worldview and about the most important aspects of God's master chain of command for families of faith and grace, let's look at how this understanding of God's wisdom can bless us in ways we never could have imagined.

We have seen where God has ordained—positions and authority—for men of faith and grace over His family institution and how such husbands can delegate authority roles to their wife and children. If we have understood this clearly—without confusion—then the next step in how to use such wisdom in uncommon ways will be easy.

To make this discovery more interesting we will first look at how the unbelieving, rebellious Atheist rationalizes his—position, authority and freedom—from God.

**The Atheist:**

The Atheist says in his heart: "If there were a God he would not let little children suffer. He would not allow wars. He would never permit disease and famine among His people. He would provide perfect environments for all of us and we would never know want. Therefore, since there are little children who suffer and who go hungry, there are wars, famine and disease and there are many people who do not have everything they want, I then conclude that based on my premise there is no God. Since there is no God—it is necessary for me, the enlightened one—to take the place of this non-existent God and do for the world what He should do if He did exist."

Does any of this sound familiar? Well, before we are done with this portion of our discoveries, you will have recognized a few other things as well. To do this we must now move to the men and women of faith and grace—the elect of God—the husbands and wives of His families. Oh, how easy it is for us to fall into the same trap as the Atheist.

**The husband:**

The misguided husband of faith and grace says in his heart: "My wife does not respect me; she criticizes everything I do—even when I am trying so hard to please her. My wife will not let me lead—she says that no man will ever lord it over her. My wife won't allow me to touch her in intimate ways—she says the children are watching—or she has a headache—or she is busy—or, well you get the picture. My wife never forgets anything I do wrong—every time I come up with a new idea or

I think I know how to do something—she always reminds me of how my last idea didn't work and how I am always thinking I know so much when she knows that I don't. My wife doesn't take care of herself like I think she should—she's too fat—too skinny—too this or too that. I am really frustrated and disappointed with her. Therefore, since my wife is all of these things that—I know she should be—and she is not, I think it would not be so bad if I took a little more interest in that cute little thing down at work—or in the choir—or in our bowling club—after all a man has got to do what a man has got to do, right?"

You say to me: "Is this is a man of faith and grace? If so; what in the world is he doing?"

Candidly, yes, he is a man of faith and grace, a badly misguided one for sure—he is also a fool—for he has fallen for the same trap that Eve fell for in the Garden. I can say that he is a fool because I too have played the part of the fool—poor little me—Marilyn had treated me so mean and cruel, surely I was justified in my thoughts? Well, NO I was not and would never be justified in such thoughts. I thank God that by his unmerited favor He kept me from ever consummating that other woman part—and I feel very deeply for those men who have not been so blessed, and who have consummated their thoughts with that other woman! Only God knows why they were not delivered—surely none of us—deserve to be delivered. Make no mistake—we are all guilty of unfaithfulness—just by the very thought of it. However, there is worse to pay when there is consummation—much worse!

This is the same trap of Satan's lies that is used everyday in millions of places and situations around the country to justify the usurpation of—POSITION and AUTHORITY—not ordained or delegated! This deluded and self serving man is about to destroy some of the most precious opportunities God has ever given him. Instead of seeking God's wisdom on how to better understand, love and provide for all of his wife's needs, he seeks to justify a position of JUDGE and the authority of EXECUTION that he does not legitimately have. He is violating his wedding vows and his commitment to love and cherish her for better or for worse. He is rebelling against his God and his Lord who has told him what is expected—has offered him assistance—promises him success[60]—if he will trust and believe—but no: our poor little man—our poor little wimp—our poor misguided ignorant soul—a prodigal son, a miserable example of a husband of faith and grace. He can only see relief in the arms of—you guessed it—ANOTHER woman! See anything familiar here?

**God's instructions and promises are clear:**

> "My son, pay attention to my wisdom; lend your ear to my understanding, that you may preserve discretion, and your lips may keep knowledge. For the lips of an immoral woman drip honey, and her mouth

---

[60] "Now these things became our examples, to the intent that we should not lust after evil things as they also lusted. And do not become idolaters as were some of them. As it is written, 'The people sat down to eat and drink, and rose up to play.' Nor let us commit sexual immorality, as some of them did, and in one day twenty-three thousand fell; nor let us tempt Christ, as some of them also tempted, and were destroyed by serpents; nor complain, as some of them also complained, and were destroyed by the destroyer. Now all[b] these things happened to them as examples, and they were written for our admonition, upon whom the ends of the ages have come. Therefore let him who thinks he stands take heed lest he fall. No temptation has overtaken you except such as is common to man; but God is faithful, who will not allow you to be tempted beyond what you are able, but with the temptation will also make the way of escape, that you may be able to bear it." I Cor.10:6-13.

is smoother than oil; but in the end she is bitter as wormwood, sharp as a two-edged sword. Her feet go down to death, her steps lay hold of hell. Lest you ponder her path of life—her ways are unstable; you do not know them. Therefore hear me now, my children, and do not depart from the words of my mouth. Remove your way far from her, and do not go near the door of her house, lest you give your honor to others, and your years to the cruel one; lest aliens be filled with your wealth, and your labors go to the house of a foreigner; and you mourn at last, when your flesh and your body are consumed, (*sexually transmitted diseases*) and say: 'How I have hated instruction, and my heart despised correction! I have not obeyed the voice of my teachers, nor inclined my ear to those who instructed me! I was on the verge of total ruin, in the midst of the assembly and congregation.'

"Drink water from your own cistern, and running water from your own well. (*Have sex with your own wife, partake of her vagina.*) Should your fountains be dispersed abroad, streams of water in the streets? (*Should your penis be spread abroad, should your sperm flow in the streets?*) Let them be only your own, and not for strangers with you. (*Reserve them for your wife not for strangers.*)Let your fountain be blessed, (*Let your penis be blessed.*) and rejoice with the wife of your youth. As a loving deer and a graceful doe, let her breasts satisfy you at all times; and always be enraptured with her love. For why should you, my son, be enraptured by an immoral woman, and be embraced in the arms of a seductress? For the ways of man are before the eyes of the LORD; and He ponders all his paths. His own iniquities entrap the wicked man, and he is caught in the cords of his sin. He shall die for lack of instruction, and in the greatness of his folly he shall go astray." Proverbs 5:1-23. The *italicized comments* are mine.

**The wife:**

The misguided wife of faith and grace says in her heart: "My husband does not respect me; he criticizes everything I do—even when I am trying so hard to please him. My husband never trusts me with anything—he criticizes my every move—he makes me feel so worthless. My husband has forgotten how to court me, he takes me for granted, when he wants sex it's always on his terms, his way—I don't count anymore. He never treats me nice and tender—never says he loves me—never does the little things that I like so much. He never takes me out on a date anymore. He says that I'm cold and that I've changed from when he first knew me. My husband never keeps his promises—he promised me so many things when we were dating—I'm still waiting. He will never amount to anything. He thinks he is so smart and is always talking about what we are going to do when he does this or that—yeah right! My husband never forgets anything I do wrong, I keep telling him that I will do better—but he always says that he doesn't believe me. My husband is so lazy, if he really cared for me and the kids he would take us places and take better care of us! He is always saying that things will get better between us—they never do. I don't feel like doing anything anymore—I just want someone who will listen to me and care about me. My husband doesn't take care of himself—he's too fat—too skinny—too this or too that. I am really frustrated and disappointed with him. Therefore, since my husband is all of these things that—I know he should be—and he is not, I think it would not be so bad if I took a little more interest in that nice guy who keeps looking at me down at work—or in the choir—or in our bowling club—after all if my own man isn't interested in me, what's wrong with hooking up with one that does, right?" See anything familiar here?

**Informational authority—the JUDGE ROLE:**

What is going on here? What is going on is informational authority, the oldest game in town. It is the most popular tool of the secular humanist propaganda machine—a tool of Satan—straight out of hell. Meet the--JUDGE ROLE—the slight of mind rationalization that we use to usurp position and or authority of which we have no legitimate claim! The logic is as simple as it is old—Eve being its first victim[61]—simply requires that one find enough wrong, imagined or real—in any individual or position of authority to whom you want to do damage, and use this list as proof that you—not them—now have the authority. Informational authority is just that, it is authority assumed—based on information—not on position or delegation, such as the wife who rebels against her husband. It is also used to abdicate from a position of authority by abusing the delegated authority for purposes not authorized, such as the husband against his wife. It should come as no surprise that this is the same type of rationalization—judge role—used by children to disobey and rebel against their "undeserving" parents or any other authority figure.

**Positional authority:**

True authority is through—POSITION—not through the person who occupies the position. First there is the position, then when someone is ordained—voted—selected—delegated—into the position, then that person has the authority that goes with the position. Accumulating information against a person does not remove them from the position it only serves as a means to "justify"—read rationalize—one's actions against the person in authority. There is no justification for rebelling against the person in authority without due process to determine if those who put them into authority want to remove them. This is a lot easier in business or politics because these are much lesser offices than the office of husband or wife. The office of husband and wife are committed to each other in unique ways of service and loyalty until death—in fact their vows are more to God—than they are to each other. It is God who said: "Let not man put asunder what God has joined together." We will deal with the relevance of all this as it relates to divorce later, for now we will continue with God's uncommon—common sense about His Chain of Command.

**Informational authority:**

When we engage in the use of informational "authority" against God's ordained positions of leadership we are playing the harlot against God—we are pulling a judge role on God. The most egregious sins of the children of Israel were their whoredoms of deceit and desire to serve other gods—gods that they thought were better than Jehovah. God used the prophet Jeremiah to bring His divine suit against Judah, his last hope among the children of Israel.

> "The LORD said also to me in the days of Josiah the king: 'Have you seen what backsliding Israel has done? She has gone up on every high mountain and under every green tree, and there played the harlot. And I

---

[61] "Now the serpent was more cunning than any beast of the field which the LORD God had made. And he said to the woman, 'Has God indeed said, 'You shall not eat of every tree of the garden'? And the woman said to the serpent, 'We may eat the fruit of the trees of the garden; [3]but of the fruit of the tree which is in the midst of the garden, God has said, 'You shall not eat it, nor shall you touch it, lest you die.' Then the serpent said to the woman, 'You will not surely die. For God knows that in the day you eat of it your eyes will be opened, and you will be like God, knowing good and evil.' So when the woman saw that the tree was good for food, that it was pleasant to the eyes, and a tree desirable to make one wise, she took of its fruit and ate. She also gave to her husband with her, and he ate. Then the eyes of both of them were opened, and they knew that they were naked; and they sewed fig leaves together and made themselves coverings." Genesis 3:1-7.

said, after she had done all these things, 'Return to Me.' But she did not return. And her treacherous sister Judah saw it. Then I saw that for all the causes for which backsliding Israel had committed adultery, I had put her away and given her a certificate of divorce; yet her treacherous sister Judah did not fear, but went and played the harlot also. So it came to pass, through her casual harlotry, that she defiled the land and committed adultery with stones and trees. And yet for all this her treacherous sister Judah has not turned to Me with her whole heart, but in pretense,' says the LORD." Jeremiah 3:6-10.

The Hebrew was keen to criticize and to bring a judge role against Jehovah for not measuring up to their concept of what they thought He should be, politically, economically and in freedoms to commit sin. The pagan gods in contrast were considered to be more liberal, they promised material blessings and also sexual freedoms without fear of reprisals—they resembled our post modern secular humanist religion. They promised what Jehovah called sin, but without consequence.

Our present day post modernism is pulling out all the stops to preach their doctrines of amoral life styles filled with every imaginable sexual perversion. Theatre, news print, radio, TV, movies, academia at all levels, now even in the primary grades, political correctness, political in-fighting, corrupt trial lawyers and the ACLU—all preach their brand of sin without consequence. Their end goal is to drive Christ and his Church out of the public square, out of media, out of government, out of education and if indeed possible—out of the family—as well! There is a great irony in all of this because they are using—informational authority—to argue their case and to usurp authority over the American family! They have pulled the ultimate JUDGE ROLE against God and they have concluded—He is NOT—so now they think they reign as kings and gods over all others!

I ask you: "From where do we Christian husbands and wives get our devilish tactics to rebel against our spouses and against our God if not from the secular mind and secular humanist religion to which we have all been exposed for decades. How is it that we can attend church—I'm assuming we are attending church somewhere—on Sunday and sing praises to our God and our Lord Jesus Christ, and then all during the rest of the time play the harlot with the secular humanist religion?

**Victory over informational authority:**

There is victory and life after the bruises, the broken hearts and all of the tears and frustrations brought on by playing the harlot with informational authority. Victory and life, not as the world gives but as Christ gives[62], begins with faith and repentance. Faith that you believe Christ is in you and that He will give you the victory—repentance from accepting informational authority as a valid means by which to get your way. We must all accept God's sovereign will over our lives—this we will demonstrate by embracing His ordained order—His master chain of command—for husbands and wives. We will demonstrate our commitment to

---

62 "These things I have spoken to you, that My joy may remain in you, and that your joy may be full. This is My commandment, that you love one another as I have loved you. Greater love has no one than this, than to lay down one's life for his friends. You are My friends if you do whatever I command you. No longer do I call you servants, for a servant does not know what his master is doing; but I have called you friends, for all things that I heard from My Father I have made known to you. You did not choose Me, but I chose you and appointed you that you should go and bear fruit, and that your fruit should remain, that whatever you ask the Father in My name He may give you. These things I command you, that you love one another." John 15-11-17.

Him by destroying all of our long lists of informational authority that we have stored up against each other.

I strongly suggest that the husband and wife write down all of the things that they have been holding against each other and then after reading the list—each to the other—asking each other for forgiveness. Solemnly offer a prayer of thanksgiving for His forgiveness and commit to Him in your prayer that you are repentant of this heinous act of rebellion against Him and against each other—then tear them up and flush them down the toilet!

Our struggle against this most common of our many sins will never cease so long as we live. Yet, Christ is faithful and will give us the victory over each and every battle that we must encounter with ourselves—as we witness our flesh time and time again fight back—with its attempts to reinstate its most favorite tool of rebellion.

Once we are faithful to obey Him and to embrace His worldview of how husbands and wives are to relate to each other and thus how they are to present themselves to their children, we are given new wisdom, new insight and a new attitude in how we can be the husband and the wife that Christ has foreordained that we should be. Then we get the blessings of increased mutual understanding, increased commitment to each other and increased joy in our sexual intimacies. It is amazing how a godly ordered relationship between a man and a woman in marriage, can increase their joy and success in sexual expressions of love and passion, for each other!

**Time and experience is our investment in overcoming:**

If we were not still living in human biological bodies—prone to sin, selfishness, and pride—our healing process from the whoredoms of informational authority would be swift and painless. I wish I could tell you that such will be your experience. Alas, I cannot do that. However, I can promise you that like all real treasures it will take an investment of time and experience. Although I know that is not what we want to hear—it is the truth—and it is also not so hard to understand given our circumstances of life. We have all practiced our different little games of playing the harlot with our rebellion through informational authority to the point that it became second nature. Our responses were all—on autopilot—every time we needed to justify our position of rebellion we didn't even have to think about it—the list just came popping into our heads in full color—and we were off and running! Our recovery and our victory will come—it is assured through the promises of Christ—we need only to maintain our commitment and submit to His principles.

**Five Important Changes**

1. **The first change you will notice;** is that you feel so much freer and cleaner inside. All of those—JUDGE ROLES—you have had cluttering your mind were like barnacles on the bottom of a ship. No matter how much effort you put into your attempts to move forward you could never get up any real speed. Now that we have repented and embraced Christ's worldview of the matter with His master chain of command for our lives as husbands and wives, we can really make some meaningful progress!

2. **The second change you will notice;** is that you can talk to each other without having to justify your position through accusations of each others failures or inconsistencies.

3. **The third change you will notice;** is that there will be flashbacks of the old ways—you will be tempted—but with your new perspective of reality and because of Christs' blessing you with new wisdom and understanding you will successfully recognize it for what it is and choose not to go there.

4. **The fourth change you will notice;** is that over time your mind will refuse to catalog the old or the new mistakes of your spouse. You will notice that although neither of you have reached any new level of perfection—the old tendency to catalog each others mistakes and misdeeds will fade away. Eventually, as in the case with Marilyn and me it will become second nature—completely automatic—to let them fall by the wayside as they happen, never to pick them up to store for future use. Yes, we continue to make mistakes and to mistreat each other on occasion, but we deal with it—then and there—then we let it go. There is no need to store it—we have rejected informational authority—as a way of life! Likewise, you will learn to deal with your mistakes and misdeeds as they happen—transparently, without malice—and then move on, never looking back!

   There will be many new positive and wonderful experiences that you will have because of your rejection of informational authority as a way of life. I will not attempt to relate all of them, but there is one more that is very important—so important—that I must mention it.

5. **The fifth and the most important of all the changes that you will notice;** is the way your prayer life will change.[63] You will soon discover that you have many more things for which to be thankful than you ever had before. Your list of needs and wants will diminish and your list of things for which you are grateful, appreciative and thankful will increase! One of these things will be your spouse!!

I pray that your time lines will be shorter than were ours. Marilyn and I struggled with our old natures in this process for five years before there was real peace and healing from the wounds and scars we had inflicted upon each other. It took fifteen years for us to reach the point where our rejection of informational authority was automatic. The GOOD NEWS is that our sense of new freedom and cleansing was almost immediate. Also, our increased joys of romance and sexual expression were almost immediate. God will give you first blessings such as these and many others to encourage you to keep trusting in His promises for you and your family.

**Love and marriage is an institution of teamwork:**

Working as a team with your wife in developing family structure and being able to fulfill your destiny as moral role model, family leader, disciplinarian, teacher and counselor, is of the highest priority. In today's world of—church going male drop-outs—who refuse to take seriously the high calling of fatherhood, and who so easily abdicate their roles as family leaders make it hard for a woman to have the confidence in her husband that God wants her to have and that they both need. This is no excuse for the husband to abdicate the role of family leader, but it does recognize that when a husband abdicates God's command to lead, this creates pressures on the wife that are not good for her. This abdication is evidence of the poor family leadership in which such husbands are reared. "Like father like son."

[63] "Husbands, likewise, dwell with them with understanding, giving honor to the wife, as to the weaker vessel, and as being heirs together of the grace of life, that your prayers may not be hindered." I Peter 3:7.

In my own experience, I have found it is wise and absolutely necessary to seek and respect the input that my wife, Marilyn, has to offer in any given situation. At first I was threatened by her and looked on her as competition, but as I grew in my understanding of God's revealed Law-Word, I began to also grow in my understanding of her. I began to understand that all of her gifts of functional and relationship quality were meant by God to be part of her role as my help meet. How can a wife be a help meet to her husband if all she ever does is take orders without ever giving him the benefit of her perspective? She is not my—competition—she is my greatest physical and emotional asset—a precious gift—from my heavenly father, for this very undeserving husband. I have been greatly impressed with the depth of her wisdom.

Marilyn, on the other hand, has determined as a matter of faith, through God's grace[64], that the best overall results for both of us and our family are ensured by my taking the reigns of leading the family and after counsel, making the final decisions. We do this not because we are—perfect examples—but because we trust in God's principles and his promises to strengthen us to do things His way. Many is the time that we both react according to the "old man" and strike off in the wrong direction only to catch ourselves—back up and say I'm sorry—then pick up where we left off, but now in the right direction. We never do it perfectly—but it is always our upper most goals—to be perfect and by God's grace we are successful in this most every time.

Once accepted as the family head and leader, the husband can delegate authority in many areas of family life to the wife and support her in ways that give her—more authority and success—than if she usurped those roles independently. Eve's very first sin was to decide that it would be better for her if she took charge of learning about—good and evil—as Satan told her she should. It is clear that God would have taught both Adam and Eve about all things, including good and evil—His way and in His good time—not Satan's way. Satan promised her that if she did it his way she would be like—God—and to this day it is still the most tempting thing for a woman to do. Secular feminism only serves as a tool of Satan to sow discord into God's family charter and to deceive a sinful and rebellious generation!

A man who will not or who cannot lead, because of a wife who is so afraid of his mistakes, and so intimidated by the thought of a man—any man—leading her, is never able to develop his God-given abilities to be a husband and father of faith and grace. Such a man must be content with attempting to find expressions for fulfilling his inner longings for—fathering, leading and being in control—outside the family structure: i.e., business, sports, politics, hobbies, and also very tempted towards pornography, promiscuous acts and affairs with other women. Admittedly, the first four of these activities are normal in and of themselves. However, when the—normal—is engaged in as an answer to a deeper frustration—it is no longer normal. The rest speak for them selves, porn—on-line or in person—is never a solution for anything, and it only numbs the senses and takes away the joy God intended for the man of faith and grace to have with his own wife.[65] Promiscuity or

---

[64] "Wives, likewise, be submissive to your own husbands, that even if some do not obey the word, they, without a word, may be won by the conduct of their wives, when they observe your chaste conduct accompanied by fear. Do not let your adornment be merely outward--arranging the hair, wearing gold, or putting on fine apparel—rather let it be the hidden person of the heart, with the incorruptible beauty of a gentle and quiet spirit, which is very precious in the sight of God. For in this manner, in former times, the holy women who trusted in God also adorned themselves, being submissive to their own husbands, as Sarah obeyed Abraham, calling him lord, whose daughters you are if you do good and are not afraid with any terror." I Peter 3:1-6.

[65] The most recent survey, of all divorce counselors in 2004, has revealed that Internet porn and infidelities through "chat rooms" is now the single greatest cause for divorce in America. Wives, remember, it takes a woman on the other end of the chat room conversation and follow-up to bring your man or some other man into this trap. ZH

any flirtations with other women spell death for the man of faith and grace, while bringing disgrace and destruction to the family for which God has given him charge![66] Such foolishness although destructive; has become all too familiar and a regular occurrence in the Christian family of today.

The women who feel this way and who cannot come to grips with the different roles for which each of the sexes is uniquely prepared and ordained of God, are self-destructive to themselves and to their families. They are forced to settle for emasculated men, who are impotent in their desire and ability to be—husbands, lovers, fathers of faith and grace—to them and to their children. Consequently, such men are unable to be the—Knights in Shining Armor—their wives envisioned them to be in the beginning. Also, men who are unsuccessful in over coming this problem are unable to develop the level of sexual fulfillment for their wives or themselves, which otherwise would have been possible. The woman, who refuses to allow her husband opportunity to fulfill his destiny as her head, her lover, father of faith and grace for her children, fails on all counts. She fails to achieve the most desirable development for her children, and she fails in her romantic relationship with the man of her dreams.[67] Such an attitude creates an environment filled with circumstances which make a mockery of team leadership, and forces the woman into a role for which she is not emotionally or naturally prepared.

We men are, to a great extent, our own worst enemies when it comes to our relationships with the opposite sex. In general, we have certain fears of any woman knowing a great deal about us, even our wives. We feel compelled to silence, perhaps by our own bad self-image, no doubt fostered in great part by our shame and embarrassment of many fantasies, thoughts, and deeds regarding women of which we are not proud. This will be further compounded when it comes to meeting the development needs of our daughters and our sons.

This kind of fear and bad self-image—read as ignorance of who we are in Christ—often creates a wall of self protection which assumes an air of aloofness and separation from members of the female sex as real persons. Thus, male preconditioning begins at a very young age, beginning with the manner in which their fathers teach them by example. By example they witness the verbal battles between their parents and they clearly see when the father seems to be without the answers his mother is demanding of him. He cannot help but notice the times when father blurts out some high decibel incoherent response and storms out of the room—sometimes out of the house—and sometimes out of his life. As young boys mature, and as their fathers have more opportunities for expressing themselves in their son's presence, the sons pick up on father's inconsistent perspectives of femininity.

On the one hand, the son assumes that father loves mother—but what evidences does he have? On the other hand he hears how his father talks about women in general. It is not uncommon for many young men to hear the term "bitch" in a derogatory statement from his father long before he hears it from a another young boy on the street, not of his own family. We will never be able to

---

[66] "Do not be deceived: "Evil company corrupts good habits." [34]Awake to righteousness, and do not sin; for some do not have the knowledge of God. I speak this to your shame." I Cor. 15:33.

[67] "Better to dwell in the wilderness, than with a contentious and angry woman." Proverbs 21:19.

"A continual dripping on a very rainy day and a contentious woman are alike; whoever restrains her restrains the wind, and grasps oil with his right hand. Proverb 27:15-16."

hide our true feelings about women from our sons, they will learn—the question is—what will they learn?

# Book I

# Love and Marriage

## Chapter Seven

## Structuring our Love and Sexual Relationship

"There are three things which are too wonderful for me, yes, four which I do not understand:

1. The way of an eagle in the air:
2. The way of a serpent on a rock:
3. The way of a ship in the midst of the sea:
4. And the way of a man with a virgin." Proverbs 30:18.

### *The wedding reception and the Honeymoon*

1. The Bride—his Queen of the Universe speaks: (Chp. 1:1-4)
   Let him kiss me with the kisses of his mouth--
   For your love is better than wine.
   Because of the fragrance of your good ointments,
   *Your name is ointment poured forth;*
   *Therefore the virgins love you.*
   Draw me away! ....

2. The Bride—his Queen speaks: (Chp. 1:12-14)
   *While the king is at his table,*
   My spikenard sends forth its fragrance.
   A bundle of myrrh is my beloved to me,
   That lies all night between my breasts.
   My beloved is to me a cluster of henna blooms
   In the vineyards of En Gedi.

3. The Husband—her King responds: (Chp. 1:15)
   *Behold, you are fair, my love!*
   Behold, you are fair!
   You have dove's eyes.

4. The Bride—his Queen speaks: (Chp. 1:16-17 & Chp. 2:1)
   *Behold, you are handsome, my beloved!*
   Yes, pleasant!
   Also our bed is green.
   The beams of our houses are cedar,
   And our rafters of fir.
   I am the rose of Sharon,
   *And the lily of the valleys.*

5. The Husband—her King responds: (Chp. 2:2)
   *Like a lily among thorns,*

So is my love among the daughters.

6. The Bride—his Queen speaks: (Chp. 2:3-7)
*Like an apple tree among the trees of the woods,*
*So is my beloved among the sons.*
*I sat down in his shade with great delight,*
*And his fruit was sweet to my taste.*
*He brought me to the banqueting house,*
*And his banner over me was love.*
*Sustain me with cakes of raisins;*
*Refresh me with apples,*
For I am lovesick.
His left hand is under my head,
And his right hand embraces me.
I charge you, O daughters of Jerusalem,
By the gazelles or by the does of the field,
Do not stir up nor awaken love
Until it pleases. ...

7. The Bride—his Queen speaks: (Chp. 2:16-17)
*My beloved is mine, and I am his.*
*He feeds his flock among the lilies.*
Until the day breaks
And the shadows flee away,
Turn, my beloved,
And be like a gazelle
Or a young stag
Upon the mountains of Bether. ...

8. The Husband—her King speaks: (Chp. 4:1-15)
Behold, you are fair, my love!
Behold, you are fair!
You have dove's eyes behind your veil.
Your hair is like a flock of goats,
Going down from Mount Gilead.
Your teeth are like a flock of shorn sheep
Which have come up from the washing,
Every one of which bears twins,
And none is barren among them.
Your lips are like a strand of scarlet,
And your mouth is lovely.
Your temples behind your veil
Are like a piece of pomegranate.
Your neck is like the tower of David,
Built for an armory,
On which hang a thousand bucklers,
All shields of mighty men.
Your two breasts are like two fawns,
Twins of a gazelle,
Which feed among the lilies.
Until the day breaks
And the shadows flee away,
I will go my way to the mountain of myrrh

And to the hill of frankincense.
*You are all fair, my love,*
*And there is no spot in you.*
Come with me from Lebanon, my spouse,
With me from Lebanon.
Look from the top of Amana,
From the top of Senir and Hermon,
From the lions' dens,
From the mountains of the leopards.
*You have ravished my heart,*
*My sister, my spouse;*
You have ravished my heart
With one look of your eyes,
With one link of your necklace.
*How fair is your love,*
*My sister, my spouse!*
How much better than wine is your love,
And the scent of your perfumes
Than all spices!
Your lips, O my spouse,
Drip as the honeycomb;
Honey and milk are under your tongue;
And the fragrance of your garments
Is like the fragrance of Lebanon.
*A garden enclosed*
*Is my sister, my spouse,*
*A spring shut up,*
*A fountain sealed.*
Your plants are an orchard of pomegranates
With pleasant fruits,
Fragrant henna with spikenard,
Spikenard and saffron,
Calamus and cinnamon,
With all trees of frankincense,
Myrrh and aloes,
With all the chief spices--
A fountain of gardens,
*A well of living waters,*
And streams from Lebanon.

9. The Bride, his Queen responds: (Chp. 4:16)
*Awake, O north wind,*
*And come, O south!*
Blow upon my garden,
That its spices may flow out.
Let my beloved come to his garden
And eat its pleasant fruits.

10. The Husband—her King speaks: (Chp. 5:1)
*I have come to my garden, my sister, my spouse;*
I have gathered my myrrh with my spice;
I have eaten my honeycomb with my honey;
I have drunk my wine with my milk.

The poetry, music, loves and passion described in these verses is from God's revealed Law-Word as expressed in the Song of Solomon. All emphasis and structural layout are mine.

**Submissive and dominant roles:**

In this chapter we will learn much about structuring our sexual and love relationship from these few verses. Unfortunately it will come as a surprise to those who do not read their Bible regularly from cover to cover, that SEX and PASSION between a wife and her husband is the only subject in the entire Bible to which a complete book is dedicated! If you have been taught that—sex and passion—was a subject to be treated with less respect and honor than say the subject of—faith and grace—you do the math. I say it is unfortunate because if we Christians had been giving the same respect and honor to the subject of sex and passion as—we say—that we give to faith and grace, our walk in both—as a Christian culture—would have been much superior in quality than it obviously has been![68]

If we are faithful to this text in our study of the complete Bible, then we will know that sex and passion within marriage should be a good work. The fact that secular liberalism strives evermore to debase and degrade sex and passion should alert us to the fact, that such efforts are no more than a demonstration of yet another working out, of Satan's lies within unbelievers. Christ's worldview on sex and passion could not be clearer. These verses describe the beauty of sex and passion between a wife and her husband; they also describe the love relationship between Christ and his bride—the Church—that cannot be ignored. Thus, revealing His worldview on sex and passion.

Rarely mentioned—but very clear—is the message of God's chain of command in his ordained marriage of respect, friendship, love, sex and passion. The two partners in this beautiful marriage are also sharing in the exercise of two distinct roles: One role is the masculine—*dominant*—role the other role is the feminine—*submissive*—role. Our journey into God's chain of command will also reveal how these two distinct roles work and also how they are not limited to either of the sexes.

**The Song of Solomon and God's chain of command for family:**

I divided our texts from the Song of Solomon into ten numbered sections for ease of reference and to better identify the words and flow of the Bride and her Husband. The *italicized* highlighting will help us focus on certain important words as we discover the family chain of command as well as how this contributes to their sexual expression of passion and satisfaction.

(1) The Bride says: *"Your name is ointment poured forth; therefore the virgins love you."*

In these words we see the bride exclaiming it is her husband's quality of name and reputation that forms the basis for his attraction among the virgins. She is obviously very proud of the fact that her husband has such a name and such a reputation as to make him desirable to the others, who undoubtedly also desire to

[68] "All Scripture is given by inspiration of God, and is profitable for doctrine, for reproof, for correction, for instruction in righteousness, that the man of God may be complete, thoroughly equipped for every good work." II Timothy 3:16-17

have such a husband. These are not temptresses; they are just admiring the virtues of a man of character and integrity.

(2) The Bride says: *"While the king is at his table,..."*

Clearly the Bride recognizes her spouse as her king. He is the head of her and their family. The facts that her spouse is her king and head does not in anyway lesson her desire or passion for him as the following lines reveal: "My spikenard sends forth its fragrance. A bundle of myrrh is my beloved to me that lies all night between my breasts." On the contrary; his name and status as her king and head heightens her desire for him.

(3) Her king responds: *"Behold you are fair my love, behold you are fair!"*

Her spouse, her king; responds to her words of intimacy with his declaration of her fairness. He repeats the words for emphasis; she is very fair—very feminine—to him, and obviously very pleasing. He does not lord his kingship and headship over her, he is gentle and charming.

(4) His queen speaks: *"I am the rose of Sharon and the lily of the valleys."*

His queen continues her praise of his person and position. First she says that he is "handsome and pleasant," then she praises his provision for them. Their bed is green (productive) their house is well built with cedar and fir, choice high quality products for any culture. He has provided their foundations and provision but she is the glamour and the beauty that adorns the whole: the rose of Sharon the lily of the valleys!

(5) Her king responds as should every husband: *"Like a lily among thorns, so is my love among the daughters."*

Here the husband declares that she is so much more beautiful to him than all of the other daughters—that they are as thorns—in comparison to her. This is an example of—focusing—that is so important in the fulfillment of marital love, sex and romance. So long as the eyes of married couples seek out beauty and attraction in the person of others, they will never develop the complete transformation from fleshly eyes to—eyes of love—that see each other in the highest levels of quality and beauty. Only such eyes as those given by God, to a husband and wife of faith and grace, can see the unique quality and beauty of each other—it is God's gift to them and is reserved for no other!

(6) His queen speaks: *"Like an apple tree among the trees of the woods, so is my beloved among the sons. I sat down in his shade with great delight, and his fruit was sweet to my taste. He brought me to the banqueting house, and his banner over me was love. Sustain me with cakes of raisins, refresh me with apples. For I am lovesick."*

The queen is so thrilled with her husband's productivity and his position of honor among the other men. She revels in his protection—his shade—and rejoices that he supplies all her needs. It is though they live continually in a banquet and she begs that he might sustain and refresh her so that she can continue in this state of bliss. There is obviously both provision of food and provision of satisfied passion in this scene, for she declares: "I am love sick." A malady from which I am sure she does not want to recover.

(7) His bride and queen speak again: *"My beloved is mine, and I am his. He feeds his flock among the lilies. Until the day breaks and the shadows flee away."*

This is a night time scene. His queen declares their mutual possession of each other, as Paul states clearly in I Cor. 7:3-5, "Let the husband render to his wife the affection due her, and likewise also the wife to her husband. The wife does not have authority over her own body, but the husband does. And likewise the husband does not have authority over his own body, but the wife does. Do not deprive one another except with consent for a time..."

She knows that she is his Rose of Sharon and his lilies, beautiful above all others in his eyes and she invites his affections, his feeding of his flock among her lilies, like a gazelle or a young stag upon her mountains. So here we see that a husband's queen can be very overt in her approach to their sexual expressions—something most men find very exciting.

(8) Her king declares: *"You are all fair, my love, and there is no spot in you. ...you have ravished my heart, my sister, my spouse; ...how fair is your love, my sister, my spouse! Your lips, O my spouse, drip as the honeycomb; honey and milk are under your tongue; and the fragrance of your garments is like the fragrance of Lebanon. A garden enclosed is my sister, my spouse, a spring shut up, a fountain sealed. ...a well of living waters, and streams from Lebanon."*

Here her king increases his claim of her perfection in femininity; he declares that there is—no spot—in her. Also, his description of her lips and mouth is not only sensuous but also prophetic in his declaration of her being as a fountain—sealed for him only—but yet also as a well of living waters and streams from Lebanon; Christ says: "But whoever drinks of the water that I shall give him will never thirst. But the water that I shall give him will become in him a fountain of water springing up into everlasting life."..."He who believes in Me, as the Scripture has said, out of his heart will flow rivers of living water." John 4:14, 7:38

Wisdom and virtue are also characteristics of the mouth of a person of faith and grace: "The words of a man's mouth are deep waters; the wellspring of wisdom is a flowing brook." Proverbs 18:4

Here we discover a great contrast between the lips of a woman of faith and grace and the lips of an immoral woman! Whereas the lips of the woman of faith and grace is depicted in the glowing terms of God's gift of sensuality, passion and wisdom for her husband of faith and grace; the lips of the immoral woman—although attractive and sensuous—they in actuality are a deep pit into which the Lord throws those that he abhors.[69]

(9) His queen rejoins: *"Awake, O north wind, and come O south! Blow upon my garden, that its spices may flow out."*

---

[69] "My son, pay attention to my wisdom; lend your ear to my understanding, that you may preserve discretion, and your lips may keep knowledge. For the lips of an immoral woman drip honey, and her mouth is smoother than oil; but in the end she is bitter as wormwood, sharp as a two-edged sword. Her feet go down to death, her steps lay hold of hell. Lest you ponder her path of life—Her ways are unstable; You do not know them."..."The mouth of an immoral woman is a deep pit; he who is abhorred by the LORD will fall there." Proverbs 5:1-6, 22:14

The queen hears her king speak of her most intimate charms as spices and of her as of a garden. The queen is very aware that he refers not only to her overall feminine charms but most specifically of her vagina—the garden—where he will sow his seed. She exclaims in answer to his words that—"Yes I am your garden—and I appeal to the heavens, both north and south to send wind to blow upon my garden to bless it that its spices may flow out." She also asks that he come to his garden and that he eat of its spices. Clearly she is inviting him to have oral sex with her along with intercourse as part of their sexual delights.[70]

(10) Her king speaks: *"I have come to my garden, my sister, my spouse; I have gathered my myrrh with my spice; I have eaten my honeycomb with my honey; I have drunk my wine with my milk."*

The king accepts her offer, comes to his garden and delights in all of her feminine charms of sex and passion.

How wonderful is the language we are given through Christ who loved us first, called us, gave us the gift of faith and has raised us up to sit in heavenly places with Him.[71] The secular, unbelieving world tries so hard to imitate the wisdom of God, but they cannot so much as speak or understand His language, much less imitate him in any way.

**Discovering God's chain of command with *dominant* & *submissive* roles:**

In Chapter One-subheading-**Discovering the gifts**: we discovered the verses in Ephesians 5:25-33 are one of the clearest descriptions of God's commands to husbands as to—how and why—they are to be the head of His institution—the Family. When God deals with families his priority is to start with the husband.[72] Now we will discover in that same chapter of Ephesians God's ordained chain of command for His first[73] institution, the family: Chapter 5: 17-24 gives the clear breakdown for most of this chain of command. The second part involving the children is found in chapter 6:1-4.

We have already read in the footnotes, Genesis 2:24-25, that God established man as the head of the family and thereby revealing the first family chain of command. The subject of a chain of command will be touched on several times during the course of this book. Such a chain of command is immediately discounted as invalid by the secular, humanistic academia and all those modernists who lay claim to knowing the truth—outside—of God's revealed Law-

70 "Marriage is honorable among all, and the bed undefiled; but fornicators and adulterers God will judge." Hebrews 13:4

71 "And you He made alive, who were dead in trespasses and sins, in which you once walked according to the course of this world, according to the prince of the power of the air, the spirit who now works in the sons of disobedience, among whom also we all once conducted ourselves in the lusts of our flesh, fulfilling the desires of the flesh and of the mind, and were by nature children of wrath, just as the others. But God, who is rich in mercy, because of His great love with which He loved us, even when we were dead in trespasses, made us alive together with Christ (by grace you have been saved), and raised us up together, and made us sit together in the heavenly places in Christ Jesus, that in the ages to come He might show the exceeding riches of His grace in His kindness toward us in Christ Jesus." Ephesians 2:1-7

72 "And the following day they entered Caesarea. Now Cornelius was waiting for them, and had called together his relatives and close friends. As Peter was coming in, Cornelius met him and fell down at his feet and worshiped him. But Peter lifted him up, saying, 'Stand up; I myself am also a man.' And as he talked with him, he went in and found many who had come together." Acts 10:24-27.

"Then Crispus, the ruler of the synagogue, believed on the Lord with all his household. And many of the Corinthians, hearing, believed and were baptized." Acts 18:8.

73 "Therefore a man shall leave his father and mother and be joined to his wife, and they shall become one flesh. And they were both naked, the man and his wife, and were not ashamed." Genesis 2:24-25.

Word. However, this is another example of how such unbelievers cannot live by their principles of rebellion. They must steal from the principles of the believers to establish—meaning and order—in those areas they deem important. Know assuredly that all such unbelieving individuals who have accepted leadership positions and roles of responsibility within an organization or group also establish a—chain of command—within that organization or group.

No sane normal human being—a creation of the Creator—knowingly agrees to go to sea, fly in an airplane, send an army to war or invest in a company that does not have a chain of command. Not only does common sense tell us that to do otherwise is to guarantee failure, it also tells us that there needs to be good communication and loyalty throughout the ranks of said chain of command. In the best of all chain of commands there is also—cross and reverse chains of commands within the same master chain of command. God's revealed wisdom accounts for all of these and the world at large spends much time and energy to attempt to duplicate that in their government, business and military—in spite—of the secularist claims that there should be no real clear lines of authority or chain of command in the family! Pray tell me, what plane, ship, army or company is more important than the family. Nations who lose the family as—God intended it—one husband and one wife—living by faith in grace, lose everything!

The direct—master—chain of command is from the top down; the—cross—chain of command is that sub group or division that has a master chain of command within it, but its head reports to and is responsible to the master chain of command. The—reverse—chain of command is when there is a need to change roles within a command—temporarily or permanently—and thus, an individual who was originally in charge under another may now become the one in the dominant role while the original person in that role takes the submission role.

**Some basic examples**

**The Master family chain of command:**

Father is the head of the family.

Mother is the second in command.

Children rank in descending order by age and maturity.

**The Cross family chain of command:**

Father or Mother may be delegated authority of an area or project to lead. As the authorized leader of this area or project they have the freedom and responsibility—if necessary—to gather under them all the necessary assistance they need to successfully carry out the job.

**Financial support as an example of the cross family chain of command:**

Father is God's delegated primary element for procuring the financial support of the family unit. There are many tools and services that he may employ, including individuals to assist him in this matter. He may also find it necessary to delegate his wife to assist him. Such action on the part of the husband was common for thousands of years—but the wife rarely had to leave the family home to do it—not so in our modern world of working away from the home. Consequently, in our modern times of centralized industries, often located miles from where we live, a husband has to be very cautious about how his wife assists him in this responsibility. In the case of many families who do not have the training or skills to demand enough income from only one person—the husband in this case—to be the sole provider, both father and mother are called upon to accomplish this task. As we have indicated this is not the best arrangement, especially if the wife and husband must both work away from the house and thus leave the children—under supervised—and alone in the care of others.[74] (*Home-Alone America—The Hidden Toll of Day Care, Behavioral Drugs, and Other Parent Substitutes:* as quoted in the footnote below, is a radical challenge to the way America's kids are being raised today—and a clarion defense of the traditional family and the values cherished by our forefathers.)

**Women in leadership as an example of the cross chain of command:**

Mother is God's delegated primary element for child care and home economics. There are many tools and services that she may employ in her execution of these duties: outside services, mechanical devices, children, and requests to her husband for his personal assistance. While working under her direction she is due the respect and loyalty of the authorized leader. She occupies—the POSITION—and the position is very important and must be respected. If family members, husband, wives and children alike do not respect these different departments and their authorized leaders—who occupy the position—chaos and discord are sure to prevail.

The problem we face in our post modern society today regarding the concept of women in the home and in business is much more a political agenda of the radical left and secularist feminist movement, for political, cultural and media dominance—NOT—the revelation of any—NEW—truth! Truth is not part of their agenda—destroying faith—is their real agenda. Nothing in the world upsets unbelievers like believers. All who are not foreordained to receive the gift of faith—in God's own time and choosing—are not of God, they are of their father the devil and they hate those who are of the family of God.[75]

There is great confusion in our present post modern society about what constitutes equality between the sexes. In light of what I have said thus far, raising the fathers of faith and grace to a level not normally considered by the majority of our Christian culture, I must not exclude women—as leaders—especially women of faith and grace, that Christian counterpart to men of faith and grace.

First of all, the general leadership qualities of women are a record of historic fact. As early as four thousand years ago God's revealed Law-Word declared a virtuous woman was of great value, and included such virtues as the capability to buy and sell real estate, to manage a girdle factory and to run and operate a textile mill. This early history records her ability to also run and operate wineries. The biblical version is truly our first glimpse of what we would call a "Super Mom," because she could do all of this in addition to being able to manage all of the

---

74 "It never used to be this way: so many kids today are troubled. Huge numbers are diagnosed with learning disabilities or behavioral problems. Childhood obesity is epidemic. Teenagers are contracting herpes and other sexually transmitted diseases at unprecedented rates. In Home-Alone America, scholar Mary Eberstadt explains why, offering an answer that's too politically incorrect to say out loud—but factually irrefutable.

"Eberstadt points out that it wasn't too many years ago that most children came home from school to a mother who monitored their diets, prevented sexual activity or delinquency by her mere presence, and provided a basic emotional safety net. Most children also lived with their biological fathers.

"But those days are gone, and that, Eberstadt demonstrates here, is the heart of the problem with kids these days. Today, most mothers work outside the home. Many fathers are divorced and living far away because society promotes adult fulfillment at the expense of our children. In this book, Eberstadt offers hard data proving that these developments have been anything but positive for our nation's children: too many kids now feel like just another chore to be juggled - dropped off at day care; handed over to a nanny; left in front of a television or a computer; and often simply home alone, with easy access to all kinds of trouble." *Home Alone America,* Mary Eberstadt, Author, Dec. 2004

75 "And we know that all things work together for good to those who love God, to those who are the called according to His purpose. For whom He foreknew, He also predestined to be conformed to the image of His Son, that He might be the firstborn among many brethren. Moreover whom He predestined, these He also called; whom He called, these He also justified; and whom He justified, these He also glorified. What then shall we say to these things? If God is for us; who can be against us?" Romans 8:28-31.

household chores and domestic responsibilities. Such realities also must include her ability to delegate and manage a work force of some considerable complexity.

So much for the—Door Mat—accusations of the secular feminists: who claim that women in ancient times were treated as mere chattel. The truth is that the women in ancient times who lived under the rule of ancient men of—NO faith and NO grace from God, just like our post modern secular feminists—suffered exactly that and more! They did not suffer such treatment at the hands of men of faith and grace.

Meanwhile, her husband—a man of faith and grace—was the head of the family, a counselor and teacher, and held in highest respect among the city leaders. Such are the women of faith and grace. Thus, in Proverbs 31:11-31, we discover the worldview of Christ as he describes the role of a virtuous wife, a woman of faith and grace.

Women of faith and grace: please take note that our Lord brings this beautiful report through the lips of—NOT of a man—but of a woman!

**The Words of King Lemuel's Mother**

"Who can find a virtuous wife? For her worth is far above rubies.
The heart of her husband safely trusts her;
So he will have no lack of gain.
She does him good and not evil
All the days of her life.
She seeks wool and flax,
And willingly works with her hands.
She is like the merchant ships,
She brings her food from afar.
She also rises while it is yet night,
And provides food for her household,
And a portion for her maidservants.
She considers a field and buys it;
From her profits she plants a vineyard.
She girds herself with strength,
And strengthens her arms.
She perceives that her merchandise is good,
And her lamp does not go out by night.
She stretches out her hands to the distaff,
And her hand holds the spindle.
She extends her hand to the poor,
Yes, she reaches out her hands to the needy.
She is not afraid of snow for her household,

"Her husband is known in the gates,
When he sits among the elders of the land.
She makes linen garments and sells them,

For all her household is clothed with scarlet.
She makes tapestry for herself;
Her clothing is fine linen and purple.

"And supplies sashes for the merchants.
Strength and honor are her clothing;

"She shall rejoice in time to come.
She opens her mouth with wisdom,
And on her tongue is the law of kindness.
She watches over the ways of her household,
And does not eat the bread of idleness.
Her children rise up and call her blessed;
Her husband also, and he praises her:
"Many daughters have done well,
But you excel them all."
Charm is deceitful and beauty is passing,
But a woman who fears the LORD, she shall be praised.
Give her of the fruit of her hands,
And let her own works praise her in the gates."

**The Reverse chain of command:**

In our modern world where two income families have become more the rule than the exception, little attention is given to the wife who brings home an income. However, it is also becoming more and more common for the wife to be not just an additional income but the only income. The father stays home and assumes most of the roles that were originally assumed to be those of the wife. Therefore, when it is necessary for any of the individuals—who are God's primary element for the family institution in some area—to assume the role of what was considered the dominant role and the other spouse to take on what was considered the submission role—then this is reverse chain of command. Also, it must be realized that cultures do not always have the same understanding of what is dominant and submissive, do not confuse this with—positional authority. For our modern world it is assumed that the man is still the main financial provider yet in the ancient world a thousand years before Christ it is clear from Proverbs 31, that the woman was considered the most ideal element for assuming the management responsibilities for the economical strength of the family unit. However, Proverbs also reveals that this in no way reduced the—position, the headship or authority—of the father. So, as God's primary element for the income of the family—the father—may delegate this responsibility when he feels that this is the best route for his family to take. Proverbs says very clearly that such abilities on the part of the wife are part of Christ's worldview concerning a virtuous woman of faith and grace. A most startling and frightening discovery for today's secular feminists!

**Our personal experience:**

Our family has experienced both—the master chain of command and the reverse chain of command realities—of the financial dominance roles. In the first thirty two years of our marriage I was the primary income provider, with back-up support from Marilyn in the form of secretarial and public relations work. Then in 1991 this pattern began to change. I began a return to further education, at first to bridge the ignorance gap we suffered in computers, for our new accounting business. Then in 1994 I moved on to further studies in theology and political science, finishing in the spring of 1998. We shared the business responsibilities again, until early 2004. Finally in Feb. of 2004 I made the decision to dedicate full time to the pursuit of our ministry goals—writing and missions—this completed the transition. Marilyn as our chief accountant and most gifted in the accounting, tax work and IRS tax remediation services of our business, has been our primary source of income since 1991 and she is now our sole income provider. This is tremendously important in our lives at this time! In addition to our joys of being the grandparents of twenty grandchildren, we both long for more action in ministry and for the first time since our early years on the mission field I am now able to concentrate completely on that effort. God, in his marvelous sovereignty, providence and grace has developed Marilyn into a most remarkable—virtuous woman—of faith and grace: praise to His name!

As you might expect—now that I am the one spending more time in the home—I am busy with little things that I would never have thought of doing before. I fix Marilyn's lunch, do the dishes and do most of the shopping, especially groceries. I accept her—honey do—list with joy and pride. I am honored to be able to serve such a wonderful woman when the occasion permits.

When the main work portion of the day is over we delight in taking a few minutes to caress and pet each other, as we unwind and relate our personal experiences of the day to each other. Serving each other in—little things—as well as the big things—means a lot. Remember that old song—*Little Things Mean a Lot*—well they do. In fact, doing little things with an attitude of love and joy coupled with tender touches and words of intimacy as often as possible, creates an atmosphere of—tender sexual foreplay—that prepares both the husband and the wife for their most intimate times of sexual expression. Without such moments and ongoing foreplay sex and marital intimacy can slip into the trap of—slam, bang thank you mamma. Sex is much too central and much too important to the harmony, emotional flow, and example for the children and general success of marriage to allow such irresponsible actions.

**A word of caution:**

God's ordained position for the woman of faith and grace as a help meet, a second in command, life time partner, friend and love companion for her husband, brings with it certain feminine characteristics.

It's important for husbands and wives to remember that in God's—Master Chain of Command—for His family of faith and grace, the position of authority never changes. God's husband of faith and grace cannot—delegate away—his position and responsibility. We men of faith and grace are held accountable for all that God has given us to do as His leaders. Therefore, when we delegate authorities to our spouse or our children to assist us in our fatherly tasks and responsibilities it in no way changes our position or responsibility as the head of our wife and of our family. The buck stops with us! God judges us on the quality of our leadership as His appointed representatives in these positions that He has given us. He never judges our wives or our children on the quality of our leadership—only us.

So what is the word of caution? It is this: "For Adam was formed first, then Eve. And Adam was not deceived, but the woman being deceived, fell into transgression. Nevertheless she will be saved in childbearing if they continue in faith, love, and holiness, with self-control." I Tim. 2:13-15.

The certain feminine characteristic to which I refer above, is that a woman—yes, even a woman of faith and grace—has a tendency to assume that when a man accepts a role within the family structure to further the success of his position as the head of the family—it has now become his duty. Meaning, a wife will ask a favor of her husband and he will accept—then she has a tendency to turn what he has accepted to do for her as a favor—into a new duty that is now his to do. Wrong, it is still hers to do as part of her responsibility and is done only as a favor—thank you—is the proper response—NOT—OK now it's your job!

Likewise, when the wife is accepting in love and faith the delegated authorities that will come to her from time to time from her husband, the husband's proper response is—thank you my love—I appreciate what you are doing!

**Men must assume their roles as God's head of the family:**

In order to turn the tide on our family moral decline and disintegration, we must accept our gift of being supernaturally and uniquely equipped through the Spirit for family leadership. Thus, a man of faith and grace is especially equipped and prepared by God and even our wives have been prepared to accept us. We men—this element of God—have been given a new mind and a very new nature—in Christ—which cries out from inside to take charge. Our glands and hormones are all working to motivate us to action. Our very soul and spirit are yearning to take up the challenge!

The fact that our wife may be president of a company, a successful actress, executive, or even president of the country itself, does not change the absolute need for our place and role as the family leader. Of all the leadership possibilities for women in the world, heading the family is the role for which a woman is least suited! Contrary to what you would ever hear from the left wing secular atheistic liberals and their feminist minions—the more successful the professional woman—the more she needs a man of strong faith and grace!

The sadness, grief, pain and sorrow wrought on the world of today because of men who have abdicated their God-given role and talent for being the head and leader of the family, cannot be over emphasized, but it can be overcome! Embracing fatherhood as a top priority for our lives is transforming and motivates us to rise above personal greed, warped egos, and miserly selfishness, all of which are built on a foundation of rebellion against God and sexual immorality—robbing the family of the opportunity for real success. Fatherhood as expressed by men of faith and grace refuses to allow thoughts of rebellion against God, wandering eyes, promiscuous acts, pornographic thoughts, business, sports, and politics to dominate or replace the family as a man's first priority.

**The great commission for husbands:**

In the gospels we read of the instructions given by Christ to his disciples to go into the entire world to disciple the nations and baptize believers. This is referred to by theologians as the—Great Commission—and presented to the church as God's great call upon us to evangelize the world. I agree: it is God's call—read command—to go into all of the world and disciple the nations and baptize the believers—however—the interpretation that this is God's greatest command is one of theological opinion and not of revealed knowledge through God's Law-Word. It is never referred to by God as the—GREAT—commission. I contend that it is a very important command of God that must be obeyed but that the truly—GREATEST—commission and commandment of God-given to man is this:

The greatest commission and commandment to the husband of faith and grace; is to be the head of his wife and his family, to be charged with her spiritual, moral, emotional and personal development to the point of returning her to God as one without spot—just like the queen we discovered in the Song of Solomon. To be charged with the responsibility to rear his children in the Lord and to not be a discouragement to them. This is the truly GREAT commission and commandment. Failure to complete this commission and commandment guarantees our failure in the commission to go into all the world and disciple the nations and baptize the believers; which is exactly the state of affairs in which we find ourselves, with respect to missions. Failure to complete this commission and commandment also guarantees our failure to provide character, moral values, integrity or righteous judgment in the market square or in God's civil institutions.

Furthermore, I charge that the church as expressed in today's culture has failed in the GREAT commission and commandment of God to teach—by word and by example—that a man of faith and grace is the head of his wife and his family and that he is charged by God to minister to them and to deliver them all to God through Christ. By putting second things first the church leadership has for decades—if not centuries—sinned against God—weakening and in many cases alienating—the effectiveness of his greatest tool for the Kingdom here on earth, second only to the Holy Spirit. That tool He has placed here on earth to sojourn and serve Him as head of all of His daughters of faith and grace and His family units until He returns is—THE HUSBAND—of one wife and the father of the Lord's institution The Family! God has ordained only three institutions on the earth: His *Family Institution,*[76] His *Church Institution*[77] and His *State Institution.*[78] All three of these institutions are part of His Kingdom here on earth and are dependent upon His theocratic rule; The Lord of Lords and King of Kings—His Son Jesus Christ. All the leaders of the State Institution and all the leaders of the Church Institution come from the success or failure of the quality of His Family Institution. Thus, is it any wonder that God's Family Institution is the—number one target—of Satan and all his minions in secular atheistic humanism?

**The true locus of the battle:**

Speaking of Satan: You will notice that I highlighted a portion of text in the footnotes below: "On this rock I will build My church, and the gates of Hades shall not prevail against it." Because ignorance of Scriptural understanding is so rampant in today's post modern Church, most who claim the name of Christian—and have heard of or read this text—think that Christ is saying in this phrase that the Church will barely withstand the onslaughts of Satan. By their attitudes and lifestyles their thoughts must be something like this: "Oh, me, oh my, the Church is being attacked by Satan and his minions but somehow it will survive—barely—but it will survive." Consider the series on: Left Behind and all the other books and articles afloat in most Christian homes today that deal with end time issues. A large majority of our post modern Christian culture embraces some or all of these end time doctrines. The very fact that we have such a large number of authors and books on this subject is striking; especially given the fact that Christ gave specific instructions that the whole matter of the time of the resurrection and when it

[76] "Therefore a man shall leave his father and mother and be joined to his wife, and they shall become one flesh." Genesis 2:24

[77] "When Jesus came into the region of Caesarea Philippi, He asked His disciples, saying, 'Who do men say that I, the Son of Man, am?' So they said, 'Some say John the Baptist, some Elijah, and others Jeremiah or one of the prophets.' He said to them, 'But who do you say that I am?' Simon Peter answered and said, 'You are the Christ, the Son of the living God.' Jesus answered and said to him, 'Blessed are you, Simon Bar-Jonah, for flesh and blood has not revealed this to you, but My Father who is in heaven. And I also say to you that you are Peter, and **on this rock I will build My church, and the gates of Hades shall not prevail against it.** And I will give you the keys of the kingdom of heaven, and whatever you bind on earth will be bound in heaven, and whatever you loose on earth will be loosed in heaven.'" Matt. 16:13-19.

[78] "Let every soul be subject to the governing authorities. For there is no authority except from God, and the authorities that exist are appointed by God. Therefore whoever resists the authority resists the ordinance of God, and those who resist will bring judgment on themselves. For, rulers are not a terror to good works, but to evil. Do you want to be unafraid of the authority? Do what is good, and you will have praise from the same, for he is God's minister to you for good. But if you do evil, be afraid; for he does not bear the sword in vain; for he is God's minister, an avenger to execute wrath on him who practices evil. Therefore you must be subject, not only because of wrath but also for conscience' sake. For because of this you also pay taxes, for they are God's ministers attending continually to this very thing. Render therefore to all their due: taxes to whom taxes are due, customs to whom customs, fear to whom fear, honor to whom honor." Romans 13:1-7.

"Therefore submit yourselves to every ordinance of man for the Lord's sake, whether to the king as supreme, or to governors, as to those who are sent by him for the punishment of evildoers and for the praise of those who do good. For this is the will of God, that by doing good you may put to silence the ignorance of foolish men—as free, yet not using liberty as a cloak for vice, but as bondservants of God. Honor all people. Love the brotherhood. Fear God. Honor the king." I Peter 2:13-17.

would take place was not a subject that we were to be concerned about.[79] However, contrary to the often negative impact that such literature has had on our post modern Christian culture, if our reading time were consistently focused on God's revealed Law/Word on a daily I am confident that such doctrines and literature would not only be less popular but they would also have little or no negative effect on our day to day walk in the Lord. You have all seen the cartoon where the cat is hanging by its claws from the clothes line rope and the caption says: "Hang in there baby!" This is the image that most have in their mind about Christ's Church—"hang in there baby—you aren't meant for true—in your face—victory; you're just a wimp, a pimple, no more than an—irritation—on the hind end of world affairs, but hang in there, somehow you will survive—and please God—please don't leave me behind!" (sic)

**Christ's world view on the end times:**

Whatever our thoughts may be regarding the many theories and postulations of end time theories and doctrines, we must conclude that Christ's world view on the matter is of priority. The Scripture texts in the footnotes below clearly set forth four very important points of truth that directly affect all of us.

1. The end time comes without warning and this is bad for the unbelievers.
2. The elect are of the light not of darkness therefore we see and are not afraid.
3. The end time will not be a surprise to the elect because we are always ready.
4. The end time will find all of the elect in peace without spot or blemish.

We are lifted up on the wings of eagles and we sit with Him in heavenly places even now in this time, in our generation. Our focus is to be on the victory over all things through Christ who strengthens us, not on the end of days. The end of days for me and for you; comes when we leave these bodies to go and be with our Lord, until such time as He will call us forth to inherit the mansions and the riches of His Kingdom that it pleases Him to have prepared for us!

**Who is defeating whom?**

Men of faith and grace—PLEASE—let me clear it up for you! In the ancient world when—walls and city gates—were a major source of protection and survival,

---

79 "But of that day and hour no one knows, not even the angels of heaven,[e] but My Father only." Matt. 24:36

'Therefore, when they had come together, they asked Him, saying, 'Lord, will You at this time restore the kingdom to Israel?' And He said to them, 'It is not for you to know times or seasons which the Father has put in His own authority. But you shall receive power when the Holy Spirit has come upon you; and you shall be witnesses to Me in Jerusalem, and in all Judea and Samaria, and to the end of the earth."' Acts 1:6-8.

"But concerning the times and the seasons, brethren, you have no need that I should write to you. For you yourselves know perfectly that the day of the Lord so comes as a thief in the night. For when they say, 'Peace and safety!' then sudden destruction comes upon them, as labor pains upon a pregnant woman. And they shall not escape. But you, brethren, are not in darkness, so that this Day should overtake you as a thief. You are all sons of light and sons of the day. We are not of the night nor of darkness." I Thessalonians 5:1-5.

'But the day of the Lord will come as a thief in the night, in which the heavens will pass away with a great noise, and the elements will melt with fervent heat; both the earth and the works that are in it will be burned up. Therefore, since all these things will be dissolved, what manner of persons ought you to be in holy conduct and godliness, looking for and hastening the coming of the day of God, because of which the heavens will be dissolved, being on fire, and the elements will melt with fervent heat? Nevertheless we, according to His promise, look for new heavens and a new earth in which righteousness dwells. Therefore, beloved, looking forward to these things, be diligent to be found by Him in peace, without spot and blameless;" II Peter 3:10-14.

the most important element and the most fiercely guarded were the gates! To lose the gates was to lose the city, your power and your freedom. These words of Christ do not mean—SURRENDER—they are instead a—CHALLENGE—to war! In this verse Christ is putting Satan on notice.

In these few words Christ paints a picture of siege and warfare. The Royal Priesthood of Christ—his men of faith and grace have brought the battle to the city walls of Hell itself and the gates of Hell will not prevail! In this picture Satan and his minions are desperately trying to hold their position—the battle is fierce—the gates are trembling under our onslaught. Christ is in the forefront of the battle[80]—His banner is waving brilliantly in the light of His sword of truth and power, the enemy is reeling back screaming for mercy—but no quarter is given. The age old enemy of God's creation is doomed! The very gates of his lair—his hiding place—are coming DOWN!

Christ is saying to Satan: You think you are real tough and you think you are going to lord it over my elect, my redeemed: I have a message for you Satan, my elect, my redeemed men of faith and grace—with me their Messiah at the forefront—through my name and by my power are going to KICK your GATES DOWN!!! Your gates, your protection, your security is no match for what I have in store for you and your minions and false ministers of evil!

Men, do you get the point? We are the winning team in this battle; it is Satan who fears Christ and his Church, his Royal Priesthood. We are that Royal Priesthood men[81], we are the elect, we are His Church. Never—I say NEVER—take the position that you are weak because you are a Christian. On the contrary all who are NOT Christians are the weak ones and not only weak but they are to be pitied. No amount of worldly power, riches or fame[82] can compare with the riches that we share in Christ Jesus.[83]

**False prophets, apostles and teachers:**

Never in the history of God's creation has the Church had more false prophets, false apostles and false teachers than she has today.[84] Albeit, this does

---

80 "This hope we have as an anchor of the soul, both sure and steadfast, and which enters the Presence behind the veil, where the forerunner has entered for us, even Jesus, having become High Priest forever according to the order of Melchizedek. ...

"For it is evident that our Lord arose from Judah, of which tribe Moses spoke nothing concerning priesthood, and it is yet far more evident if, in the likeness of Melchizedek, there arises another priest who has come, not according to the law of a fleshly commandment, but according to the power of an endless life. For He testifies: 'You are a priest forever according to the order of Melchizedek.'" Hebrews 6:19-20, 7:14-17. Christ is our High Priest and we men are His Priesthood—a Royal Priesthood—because He is King of Kings and Lord of Lords!

81 "But you are a chosen generation, a royal priesthood, a holy nation, His own special people, that you may proclaim the praises of Him who called you out of darkness into His marvelous light; who once were not a people but are now the people of God, who had not obtained mercy but now have obtained mercy." I Peter 2:9-10

82 "For what will it profit a man if he gains the whole world, and loses his own soul? Or what will a man give in exchange for his soul?" Mark 8:36-37.

83 "What then shall we say to these things? If God is for us, who can be against us? He who did not spare His own Son, but delivered Him up for us all, how shall He not with Him also freely give us all things? Who shall bring a charge against God's elect? It is God who justifies. Who is he who condemns? It is Christ who died, and furthermore is also risen, who is even at the right hand of God, who also makes intercession for us. Who shall separate us from the love of Christ? Shall tribulation, or distress, or persecution, or famine, or nakedness, or peril, or sword? As it is written: 'For Your sake we are killed all day long: we are accounted as sheep for the slaughter.' Yet in all these things we are more than conquerors through Him who loved us. For I am persuaded that neither death nor life, nor angels nor principalities nor powers, nor things present nor things to come, nor height nor depth, nor any other created thing, shall be able to separate us from the love of God which is in Christ Jesus our Lord." Romans 8:31-39.

84 "But what I do, I will also continue to do, that I may cut off the opportunity from those who desire an opportunity to be regarded just as we are in the things of which they boast. For such are false apostles, deceitful workers, transforming themselves into apostles of Christ. And no wonder! For Satan himself transforms himself into an angel of light. Therefore it is no great thing if his ministers also transform themselves into ministers of righteousness, whose end will be according to their works." II Cor. 11:12-15.

not relieve—MEN and HUSBANDS—of faith and grace from their responsibilities to answer to God for the spiritual, moral, character and educational success of His families! Arise men and husbands, we must all repent of our sins and rebellion against our God and his Christ who has redeemed us and sanctified us and set us up as His ordained heads of his most precious institution the family. The most precious—not because it is the most holy—we are sanctified through Christ[85]—or the most important—but because it is the crucible from which all else proceed.[86] The corrupt leaders of our nation, our churches and our educational systems, all come from unbelieving, rebellious, leaders of families—or more correctly—what passes for families in our post modern world. These corruptions do not fall from the sky. They are allowed to dominate and to rule because MEN and HUSBANDS of faith and grace have abdicated our role as God's elements as spiritual, moral, character and educational leaders of our families![87] When enough men and husbands of faith and grace repent and embrace God's sovereign will over their position in His creation,[88] we will—by His grace and power—rid this country of these wimpy, corrupt, false prophets and rebellious God hating leaders, from their positions of power and influence. Then His will—expressed through His Kingdom—shall prevail!

**Understand what the will of the Lord is:**

> "Therefore **(1) do not be unwise, but understand what the will of the Lord is.** And do not be drunk with wine, in which is dissipation; but **(2) be filled with the Spirit,** speaking to one another in psalms and hymns and spiritual songs, singing and making melody in your heart to the Lord, **(3) giving thanks always for all things** to God the Father in the name of our Lord Jesus Christ, **(4) submitting to one another in the fear of God. (5) Wives, submit to your own husbands, as to the Lord.** For the **(6) husband is head of the wife**, as also **(7) Christ is head of the church**; and He is the Savior of the body. Therefore, **(8) just as the church is subject to Christ, so let the wives be to their own husbands in everything. ...**
>
> (9) Children, obey your parents in the Lord, for this is right. (10) 'Honor your father and mother', which is the first commandment with promise: (11) 'that it may be well with you and you may live long on the earth.' And you, (12) fathers, do not provoke your children to wrath, but

---

[85] "Now may the God of peace Himself sanctify you completely; and may your whole spirit, soul, and body be preserved blameless at the coming of our Lord Jesus Christ. [24]He who calls you is faithful, who also will do it." I Thessalonians 5:23.

[86] "Coming to Him as to a living stone, rejected indeed by men, but chosen by God and precious, you also, as living stones, are being built up a spiritual house, a holy priesthood, to offer up spiritual sacrifices acceptable to God through Jesus Christ." I Peter 2:4-5.

[87] "Now I'm not real high on 'New Years Resolutions.' Most of these are done in the soul and are doomed to fail. But I am FOR examining myself before communion or any other time to see what's really there. Then I must decide how much pruning I am willing to let Him do in order to see abundantly improved fruit at harvest time. So when you reflect on your life for the past year, as I intend too to do, ask yourself, am I willing to give up my pride, arrogance, selfishness, gossip and greed so that His love, joy and kindness may flow through me?" Is it worth giving up rebellion and stress for His peace? Are any of us willing to prune the over indulgence of donuts, ice cream, brownies and snicker bars for the healthy body He wants? (Now I've stopped preaching and gone to medaling.) It's your choice and mine. We can continue to carry all of that dead wood or we can let Him do some major pruning. The question is simple, how much quality fruit do we want to bear for the Master Harvester?" James G. Dunham, Christian Columnist, Excerpts from the Blackberry Patch-12-29-04:

[88] "As iron sharpens iron, so a man sharpens the countenance of his friend." Proverbs 27:17.

bring them up in the training and admonition of the Lord. Emphasis mine:

## God's Family Charter

1. Do not be unwise, but understand what the will of the Lord is.
2. Be filled with the Spirit.
3. Giving thanks always for all things.
4. Submitting to one another in the fear of God.
5. Wives, submit to your own husbands as unto the Lord.
6. Husbands, live with your wife in understanding and honor her.
7. The husband is head of the wife.
8. Christ is head of the church.
9. Just as the church is subject to Christ, so let the wives be to their own husbands in everything.
10. Children, obey your parents in the Lord.
11. Honor your father and mother; that it may be well with you and you may live long on the earth.
12. Fathers, do not provoke your children to wrath, but bring them up in the training and admonition of the Lord.

**The world looks at men and women, but —especially at men—and it asks these questions:**

1. Who are his parents?
2. Where did he go to school?
3. How much education does he have?
4. What is his profession?
5. What is his net financial worth?
6. Whom did he marry?
7. Is he famous?

**God looks at men and women—very, very especially at men—and He asks these questions:**

1. Is he one of Mine?
2. Does he hear My voice?
3. Does he obey My voice?
4. Does he seek My understanding?
5. Does he seek My wisdom?
6. Does he love his wife?
7. Does he execute the leadership role of his wife and family?

Men of faith and grace, we indeed want to be great and successful—truly great and successful—so let us be in the eyes of Christ, our Lord and King as he wants to see us—clothed in His righteousness—and not in our own righteousness![89] He is faithful who has called us and he knows our needs for the things of this life—even before—we ask Him![90]

---

[89] "And He Himself gave some to be apostles, some prophets, some evangelists, and some pastors and teachers, for the equipping of the saints for the work of ministry, for the edifying of the body of Christ, (Remember, men, the family is the basic unit of the body of Christ.) till we all come to the unity of the faith and of the knowledge of the Son of God, to a perfect man, to the measure of the stature of the fullness of Christ; that we should no longer be children, tossed to and fro and carried about with every wind of doctrine, by the trickery of men, in the cunning craftiness of deceitful plotting, but, speaking the truth in love, may grow up in all things into Him who is the head—Christ—from whom the

**God's great commission for the wife of faith and grace:**

The Church has also failed the women of faith and grace by allowing the secular atheistic humanist world of academia to set the terms and standards for their relationship with men. True, the Church cannot keep such individuals or man made institutions from establishing such terms and standards for themselves—after all—they have refused to accept God's terms and standards so it is only logical that they would establish their own. My contention is that the Church—as represented in our current American culture—has adopted these same terms and standards for its own women of faith and grace. For sure there are some few congregations in America who reject these godless terms—but much to our shame, the majority of Christian women adopt these terms for their own and adjust their life-styles in keeping with the lies put forth by these left liberal atheistic feminist, anti-Christian organizations. Now we must face the facts that most of our men of faith and grace have abdicated their God ordained leadership roles in the family and our women of faith and grace are now living lifestyles that are based on the terms and standards of unbelievers. If it's not so—show me the statistics—that will prove it's not so!

In stark contrast to our present disgraceful status quo, God's women of faith and grace have also been given a—GREAT COMMISSION—and commandment for their roles as wives:

> "Wives, likewise, be submissive to your own husbands, that even if some do not obey the word, they, without a word, may be won by the conduct of their wives, when they observe your chaste conduct accompanied by fear. Do not let your adornment be merely outward—arranging the hair, wearing gold, or putting on fine apparel—rather let it be the hidden person of the heart, with the incorruptible beauty of a gentle and quiet spirit, which is very precious in the sight of God. For in this manner, in former times, the holy women who trusted in God also adorned themselves, being submissive to their own husbands, as Sarah obeyed Abraham, calling him lord, whose daughters you are if you do good and are not afraid with any terror. Husbands, likewise, dwell with them with understanding, giving honor to the wife, as to the weaker vessel, and as being heirs together of the grace of life, that your prayers may not be hindered." I Peter 3:1-7.

> "This is a great mystery, but I speak concerning Christ and the church. Nevertheless let each one of you in particular so love his own wife as himself, and let the wife see that she respects her husband." Ephesians 5:32-33.

**The prayers of the husband:**

We have mentioned before, in chapter five, how important prayer is as a means of communication. However, in context with the great commission to wives of faith and grace it is important to illustrate just how much power God can withhold from the man who will not love his wife as He intended. It is clear that God can and does choose to—NOT—hear a husband's prayers as punishment for

---

whole body, joined and knit together by what every joint supplies, according to the effective working by which every part does its share, causes growth of the body for the edifying of itself in love." Ephesians 4:11-16.

90 "Therefore do not worry, saying, "What shall we eat?' or "What shall we drink?' or "What shall we wear?' For after all these things the Gentiles seek. For your heavenly Father knows that you need all these things. But seek first the kingdom of God and His righteousness, and all these things shall be added to you. Therefore do not worry about tomorrow, for tomorrow will worry about its own things. Sufficient for the day is its own trouble." Matt. 6:31-34.

such disobedience. A husband of faith and grace must realize that God is serious and that the husbands prayers can be hindered—read, won't make it past the ceiling—if his attitude toward his wife is lacking in understanding and honor. Wives are not door mats, they are not sex objects, they are not chattel—they are WIVES—precious in God's sight! Let us also consider the blessings implied for all husbands of faith and grace who are faithful to dwell with their wives in understanding, and who give them honor as unto the weaker vessel!

**Husbands let us read again and solemnly consider His words!**

> "Husbands, likewise, dwell with them with understanding, giving honor to the wife, as to the weaker vessel, and as being heirs together of the grace of life, that your prayers may not be hindered." I Peter 3:7.

# Book I
# LOVE AND MARRIAGE

## Chapter Eight-Part I

## Structuring Our Children's Environment

### Establishing the Origins of our Moral Fiber, Values and Principles

#### The Origins

"If you endure chastening, God deals with you as with sons: for what son is there whom a father does not chasten? But if you are without chastening, of which all have become partakers, then you are illegitimate and not sons. Furthermore, we have had human fathers who corrected us, and we paid them respect. Shall we not much more readily be in subjection to the Father of spirits and live? For they indeed for a few days chastened us as seemed best to them, but He for our profit, that we may be partakers of His holiness. Now no chastening seems to be joyful for the present, but painful; nevertheless, afterward it yields the peaceable fruit of righteousness to those who have been trained by it." Hebrews 12:7-11.

**The locus of moral fiber, values and principles for the family:**

Establishing moral fiber, values and principles is very important in our role as father! Much to the chagrin of the radical left there are origins to moral fiber, values and principles—absolute origins—not by concession among men but from God. We will direct our discovery of these absolutes into two sections: Part I, The Origins and Part II Discipline.

Contrary to a wide segment of popular belief, it is not the mother who should set the standards of how a family measures up to God's revealed Law-Word, the real source—the true locus for Right and wrong within the family—it is the father. For those who doubt this—and won't believe God's many examples in his Law-Word as the verses from Hebrew quoted above illustrate—just look at all the results of the matriarchal cultures in the world. In these cultures the majority of men have abdicated their family and cultural leadership roles. Thus, the families which make up such a society are considered to be predominantly headed by women and not by men.

Cultures where the majority of the families are recognized to be headed by men are referred to as patriarchal cultures. Although America has within its borders, ethnic cultures that are considered to be patriarchal, the country as a whole is moving more and more in the direction of matriarchal.

**Matriarchal societies:**

Consider for a moment two highly matriarchal societies and their cultures: American Black African societies and American Hispanic societies. These two societal groups are very different in many of their cultural traditions. However, both are considered matriarchal in their family structure.

The mothers in these families are for the most part strict moralists attempting—as though it were, to appease God for their own sins and mistakes—and in many cases literally smothering their children with concern for their moral development. These mothers have suffered greatly because of the lack of husband of faith and grace, real father leadership and responsibility. Many have been completely abandoned by their husbands or "boyfriends," for they often never officially marry—a by-product—of our sexually enlightened post modern culture. Many of the men in these matriarchal centered cultures maintain a "boyfriend" relationship with several women—or what could be called an unofficial "husband"—all at the same time throughout their lifetimes. In more literal terms, they practice bigamy.

By default, this leaves many women to fend for themselves and their children. They attempt to assume the role of disciplinarian and try—many valiantly—to establish the family moral fiber, values and principles. Unfortunately, their efforts are never successful in establishing a basis for moral and character development. I say never because the feminine source cannot produce such a result. This does not mean that all children reared by a single mother will have no moral fiber or sound character development—what I am saying is that such outcome is never the direct result of the mother's solo efforts, especially where an official wedding never took place! To say that a single mother who was never officially married—one without God's gift of faith and grace—can teach moral fiber and sound character development is an oxymoron. The many whippings and the endless words chiding and cajoling her off-spring to adhere to a life-style that she has already abandoned, falls on deaf ears and—is pure folly—at its best!

When moral fiber and sound character development is achieved, it is because of the other positive influences that were available to these children: a grandfather, coach, Sunday school teacher, Bible studies or other male source that complimented the mother much as would have happened, if she had had the support and direct involvement from a husband—a man of faith and grace—fulfilling his call as gifted by God to her and to their children. The facts of life have amply shown that this unusual arrangement is rarely entered into and even more rarely continued with enough successful input to make a dramatic change in a child's life

This is so important that I must say it again! The children from these "families" who go on in life to excel in spite of their acute disadvantages from the lack of any biological father leadership or responsibility do so because of some alternative father figure in their lives. A teacher, a coach, a minister, or a friend, often supplies the only hope of fatherhood for these developing children. Excellence of character, moral fiber, values and principles have nothing to do with race, skin color or ethnic origin. Such excellence is the result of teaching God's revealed Law-Word and His operation of grace and providence.[91]

The differences between the sexes are unique. God has made a woman to be a mother and in so doing, he has established—a barrier beyond which we men cannot climb over—and experience what it is to be a mother. Being a mother is a unique role with unique experiences. And being the family role model and disciplinarian is not one of them[92]. She can be a supporter of the structure and does play—a very important role—in giving this support to her husband.[93] Yet, if

---

[91] "Children's children are the crown of old men, and the glory of children is their father. ...Train up a child in the way he should go, and when he is old he will not depart from it." Proverbs 17:6, 22:6.

[92] "My son, hear the instruction of your father, and do not forsake the law of your mother; for they will be a graceful ornament on your head, and chains about your neck." Proverbs 1:8-9.

[93] "My son, keep your father's command, and do not forsake the law of your mother. Bind them continually upon your heart; Tie them around your neck. When you roam, they will lead you; when you sleep, they will keep you; and when you awake, they will speak with you. For the commandment is a lamp, and the law a light; reproofs of instruction are the way of life, to keep you from the evil woman, from the flattering tongue of a seductress." Proverbs 6:20-24.

she tries to assume the full responsibility as family role model and disciplinarian, she will fail to accomplish what the father could have accomplished; if he had not abdicated his God-given role.

In like fashion, God has gifted men with special insight and strength of character distinctively appropriate for establishing moral fiber, values and principles for his family. In spite of their arduous efforts to the contrary, women are not gifted in the same way. There is a barrier over which they cannot climb and assume the role of father, anymore than we men can assume successfully the role of mother. However, we men can very successfully delegate many aspects of our role as disciplinarian to our wife. We will talk more about this later, but I want women to know that they can be effective in discipline when they do it with and according to their husband's delegated authority.[94]

You don't have to be a Harvard graduate in social science to know which cultural groups have the lowest success rates in teaching moral fiber, values and principles. If you read your daily newspaper or watch the news on TV, simply ask yourself the following questions:

**Two examples of matriarchal fallout:**

Which cultural groups have the highest percentage of broken homes? Which cultural groups have the highest percentage of drug use? Which cultural groups have the highest percentage of gang members? Which cultural groups have the highest percentage of unwed mothers? Which cultural groups have the highest percentage of alcohol abuse? Which cultural groups make up the highest percentage of our criminal population in our prison system?

The answer is clear; they are those who are matriarchal, relative to family leadership. These matriarchal ethnic groups suffer tremendously because of the lack of real father leadership and responsibility in the family.

It is interesting to hear the comments most often made by the many special interest groups who say they represent these cultural groups in America. They tell us racial prejudice and poverty is the cause of these high percentage problems. They tell us their people are a "disadvantaged" people. Granted, there is still some racial prejudice around which would lend it self to some social disadvantages for some people. However, when considered from the perspective of the most important social and cultural institution in the whole world—the family—these factors are small!

The disadvantage the African American and Hispanic American are suffering is the reality of having a majority of their men abdicating their roles as real fathers of faith and grace in the family. When you remove the issue from the political and macro environmental influences and you directly approach the mothers of these two ethnic groups, you get a different perspective. Ask any Black mother or any Hispanic mother only one question to find out the answer.

"Do you believe that the average adult man in your ethnic group provides good family leadership and responsibility?"

The majority will answer candidly that he does not. These mothers all demonstrate common sense; they know it is fathers who make the most striking difference between these ethnic groups. Being matriarchal, as opposed to patriarchal is not a fact of color, race or ethnic origin. These women know the

94 "The eye that mocks his father, and scorns obedience to his mother, the ravens of the valley will pick it out, and the young eagles will eat it." Proverbs 30:17.

primary difference—where true difference exists—is in the lack of a biological father of faith and grace!

**Black men speak out:**

Listen to these very recent commentaries by two black professionals. Haki Madhubuti said in his book, "Black Men, Obsolete, Single, Dangerous?"

> "Black men as a collective body have not been able to get our act together, and it is not accurate or in our best interest to blame Black women for our current condition."
>
> DeWayne Wickham, a black writer for Gannett News Service in Washington, D.C., says: "The black family structure is being badly ruptured.
>
> "Today, more than half of all black children live in female-headed households. Divorce among blacks is on the increase, remarriages on the decline.
>
> "Add to this the most recent finding: 25 percent of black women may never marry and the socially conscious among us should hear the harsh sound of alarm bells ringing in our ears.
>
> "Left unchanged, this widening gap between black men and women will bring about a great disruption of American society.
>
> "Interracial marriages, now still something of a novelty, will rise sharply as black women-unable to find black husbands—cross over the racial divide to marry.
>
> "An increasing number of black men will join the ranks of those for whom marriage—and constructive male—female relations—is becoming less and less of an option. And in the process, the disintegration of the black family will continue."

**It's not a matter of color:**

In October of 1991, the national Education Goals Panel reported, "Currently, one of every four children in U.S. schools comes from a single-parent family. Among black Americans the number of single-parent families runs over 60 percent."

The problem of Hispanic and black men is not their ethnic origin or color; it is the high percentage of their numbers who will not accept the challenges of manhood and fatherhood. There is either a warning or an encouragement here for each one of us. If you are a man, regardless of your color or ethnic origin, embracing or willing to embrace the challenges of God to be a father of faith and grace, then you are to be commended. If you are a man who will not accept the challenge of Christian fatherhood, regardless of ethnic origins or color, then you are part of the problem.[95]

If you check the background record of all the individuals who make up the statistics on our society's problems, you will see a law broken and a law at work. The law broken is God's revealed Law-Word; the law at work is God's curse of passing the effects of the disobedient father's sins on to the third and fourth generations[96]. God is not mocked—whether the persons involved are Black, Latin,

---

[95] "The rod and rebuke give wisdom, but a child left to himself brings shame to his mother." Proverbs 29:15.

[96] "You shall not make for yourself a carved image—any likeness of anything that is in heaven above, or that is in the earth beneath, or that is in the water under the earth; you shall not bow down to them nor serve them. For I, the LORD your God, am a jealous God, visiting the iniquity of the fathers upon the children to the third and fourth generations of those who hate Me, but showing mercy to thousands, to those who love Me and keep My commandments." Duet. 5:8-10.

Asian, Italian, and Anglo or—of any other ethnic origin—the majority has biological fathers who exercised little or no family leadership or responsibility. In fact, you will see the pattern—of God's promised transference—has developed before our very eyes! The majority of these same men received the bulk of their instructions on moral fiber, values and principles from—you guessed it—their mothers! Consequently, women who accept a life-style that refuses God's plan for her to have a husband, attracts the faithless and disobedient man and creates in her son another one to take his place and a daughter just like herself![97] They choose to fend for themselves and later will be left with children, often from different men, for whom they cannot adequately provide—spiritually—emotionally—morally—or financially. They are like ships without rudders; they proceed forward in life's struggles for success and happiness with great ambition and energy, only to end up in a vicious cycle of transgenerational sin and repeating history. Sure, at first they all think that all they need is—a chance—to prove them selves. They swear that they will not make the same mistakes of their mothers—and as for father—well he was just a necessary evil in order for them to be born.

They soon find themselves enmeshed in a life with no real direction. They have no real sense of where they have come from, where they are going or how to get there. They end up as mothers themselves and even though it is 5, 10 or 20 years later, they must face the fact, they are in the same mess their mothers found themselves in, or worse!

As young girls, these mothers all start out with no map, no compass, no direction, and end up a shipwreck on the shores of life's problems. They are valiant in many ways. God has given them a natural desire to be mothers, to love and protect their babies. He also gave to them a natural desire for a husband the fathers of their children, to whom He gave the responsibility to ensure their safe and successful journey. Where are these fathers?

However, the factor of motherhood, carrying the unborn child for nine months, the act of actually giving birth to her babies, breast-feeding them, and responding to their every need during their first months and years, has a unique effect upon a young woman. Whether such a mother is protected or not she will want to protect her child. Whether or not she has had a good moral structure, she will want to provide a moral structure for her child. Whether or not she has had a good family structure and good moral role models, she will want to provide a good family structure and be a role model for her child.

Ironically, her desires are going to be greatly, if not entirely, frustrated if she has not had a good father who taught her how these things are accomplished. The mere fact of being naturally gifted by God to feel sensitive to all of these needs has been proven—in the laboratory of life—to be insufficient to pull it off. If it were sufficient, then all of the millions of young mothers who have NOT had biological fathers of faith and grace to teach them the way these things are accomplished, would be turning out wonderful, well-balanced and morally responsible children, right? Where are the successes of the doctrines of the liberal left atheistic secular humanists—where?

---

97 "A foolish woman is clamorous; she is simple, and knows nothing. For she sits at the door of her house, on a seat by the highest places of the city, to call to those who pass by, who go straight on their way: 'Whoever is simple, let him turn in here'; and as for him who lacks understanding, she says to him, 'Stolen water is sweet, and bread eaten in secret is pleasant..' But he does not know that the dead are there, that her guests are in the depths of hell." Proverbs 9:13-18.

**Where do we find the children of these women in America today?**

They are comprised in basically two groups, separated by only a fine line. The first group looks normal, but in reality is confused and frustrated to the point of distraction. They are the young couples living together, who believe marriage is a lost institution and free love is emotionally safer. They move in and out of intimate love affairs, looking for the perfect romance and love that will satisfy. Single parent families are also part of the first group. Those from this group who marry are just as confused as those who don't. They fill our divorce courts and our child custody courts with claims and counter claims. They have no real hope of experiencing a strong loving family, they are bruised and lost. Unfortunately, they make lawyers and psychologists a lucrative income and get little or nothing in return.

The second group does not look or act normal. They are angry at life in general, but more to the point, their parents never, took them seriously, they're missing something and they know it. What is it they are missing? They don't know. If you told them their problems and hurt stemmed from their lack of having a father of faith and grace—one who would accept his role as family leader and provide for them the structure and discipline it takes to become a mature successful adult—they would just as likely burst out laughing as to take you serious. The girls would suspect that you were correct but they would not know why, the boys would just simply shrug and say that the old man was never there.

Their confusion and frustration are more acute than in the first group. They resort to drastic responses. As we said earlier, they're in the gangs, on the streets as prostitutes, using and pushing drugs, into sexual alternative life styles. When they have children, they most often abuse them. Many find their place in the criminal world, seeking love and financial rewards in a life of crime and violence!

It is the children of these women, from both groups, which are so hard to teach in our public schools. These are the children most likely to receive some form of detention or expulsion from school as punishment for their uncontrolled actions and attitudes. Most are likely to drop out and never go on to finish high-school or go to college! These are the children who fill our prisons and who sit on death row. Saddest of all, these are the future parents who will rear millions more just like themselves!

In other words, the natural inner sensitivity of a young girl regarding her own need for protection and moral structure, does prepare her for being open and willing to learn. Yet—without a biological father of faith and grace and the family structure within which to learn interpersonal relationship skills, moral fiber, values and principles—it is little more than frustrated inner yearnings. The reality of her life will always be a contradiction to her inner sense of what should be. She has a desire to do right by her children—given to her by God, her Creator—but not the slightest notion of how to pull it off. God also created a man that could have provided the missing pieces to her needs—but alas—she thought him unnecessary!

What awesome pain and frustration such women must go through. No wonder they lash out at the school system, the government, the church, men in general and any they have been intimate with in particular! The despair they feel and live with, day in and day out, is harsh reaping for a life sown without the wisdom of God's revealed Law-Word![98] When life is sown to the wind those who sow reap the whirlwind and a barren crop. Hosea 8:7 For them—there can be no other.

Besides their own personal losses, most have seen the same trend and destruction of personal lives in their own mothers, their own brothers and sisters

[98] "They sow the wind, and reap the whirlwind. The stalk has no bud; it shall never produce meal. If it should produce, Aliens would swallow it up." Hosea 8:7.

and in family members for several generations. The more they do to be all things to their children, the more they seem to fail in their efforts.

Don't kid yourself into thinking this pattern is limited to women born into welfare. This scenario is played out in millions of families with long standing educational and business achievements. The pathway of their family fore-fathers and mothers is strewn with the debris of divorce, unfaithfulness, chemical substance abuse, sexual abuse and moral ambivalence. The fact of being educated or having money in no way reduces or changes the absolute need for men to be real fathers of faith and grace!

**Someone is to blame, right? Is their a victim here?**

These women have put forth great effort and they have strong feelings about how life should turn out for their children, but all they see is more and more hopelessness. Someone or something has to carry the blame besides them, or so they think.

Truthfully, they are both right and wrong. They are right that something is wrong. However, they are the immediate cause of their children's most severe problems. They are not capable, nor were they ever intended to be, of providing the leadership required for strong family moral fiber, values and principles. Behind the scenes, the blame lies squarely at the feet of their biological fathers—a male whom most have never met—for never having accepted their roles as real fathers of faith and grace. Unfortunately, these women are left with no hope of—love and marriage—as God intended it to be. They have no respect for men. Thus, they have no hope of ever finding anyone who will prove worthy—in their eyes—to be a real family leader. So, they turn to governments and other outside entities to seek both sources for blame and for help. In reality, what they desire and are seeking for their children comes not from governments or social infrastructures, not even from churches. It is a phenomenon of moral and personal character, uniquely reserved for the—TWO-PARENT family structure—in which the father is the guiding spiritual strength, moral role model, disciplinarian, counselor and teacher.

**Black women speak out:**

A word from Ms. Star Parker, a one time welfare mother, a woman of faith and grace, a black American columnist, best selling author and founder of CURE had this to say in a posting on the www.townhall.com web site, September 24, 2004:

> "Several weeks ago, black pastors from around the nation, under the sponsorship of my organization, CURE, gathered for a press conference at the Lincoln Memorial in Washington to express support for President Bush's proposal for a constitutional marriage amendment. The amendment would define marriage as between a man and a woman.
>
> "The date and place for the event were selected to mark the 41st anniversary of Dr. Martin Luther King, Jr.'s *'I Have a Dream'* speech. The congregations of the pastors who participated in this event have a combined total of well over 40,000 members.
>
> "The gay marriage issue has struck a nerve in the black community and may well mark the beginning of a sea change in black voting behavior. Pastors who have voted Democratic all their lives have told me and others that this issue has lead them out of the Democratic Party.
>
> "A CBS/NY Times poll on the marriage amendment done last March shows blacks more aligned with Republicans than with Democrats. The poll showed 59 percent overall in favor of the marriage amendment.

However, 77 percent of Republicans, 52 percent of Democrats, and 67 percent of African Americans were in favor.

"These pastors are worked up over this issue because it touches fundamentally the core concerns they have for their communities. They know that the bedrock on which human lives and communities are constructed is made of spiritual and moral fiber. And they know that the profound social problems in their communities stem from the shattered state of that bedrock."[99]

Billy Graham once said: "When wealth is lost, nothing is lost; when health is lost, something is lost; when character is lost, all is lost."

**False prophets and failed politics:**

Unfortunately for the black community of America, the last twenty five years or more has seen little more than—black political leaders such as Jesse Jackson,[100] Al Sharpton and the NAACP—encouraging black pastors and black people in general to identify themselves as VICTIMS, who's only recourse in life is to look to government to solve their problems. These are false prophets of the worst kind. These are the kind—who selfishly use—a whole generation to satisfy their own ambitions for power and money!

Leaders of the black church are beginning to grasp that the welfare state and the politics of the liberal left only—rape the black community sending them on a mindless merry-go-round—like a dog chasing its tail! They know that the first order of business in these communities is the reconstituting of its spiritual and moral base, specifically as it relates to husbands and fathers. In this context of repeated failures and diminished black cultural values, these pastors view as—preposterous and outrageous—the idea, of our society formally abandoning traditional standards of sexual behavioral and traditional concepts of love and marriage for the family!

The proof of this change can be seen in the many black pastors that no longer believe the lies of the false prophets or their political hacks. Our 2004 Presidential election just completed demonstrated a 22 % increase (An increase from 9% of all black voters to 11% of the black vote.) in the black vote for President Bush over the 2000 election. That does not represent a victory for black understanding of the total enormity of their plight but it does show progress. Although we have gone from 9% of the total black vote to 11% of blacks who have publicly declared themselves aware of the traitors in their midst, it will not be a victory for the black family until—we can see over 50 % who are aware—then we can begin to talk about victory.

Simultaneous with the Washington press conference, CURE released a policy report titled "*The Impact of Gay Marriage on the Black Community.*" The report shows that study after study documents the coincidence of promiscuity, disease, and family breakdown with homosexual behavior. Regardless of whether

---

[99] Star Parker is president of CURE, Coalition for Urban Renewal and Education, (www.urbancure.org ). She is the author of "Uncle Sam's Plantation: How Big Government Enslaves America's Poor and What You Can Do About It."

[100] "The politics of deflection and blame, for which Jackson can claim significant responsibility, has rooted itself deep in black consciousness and has made our problems many times worse. John McWhorter discussed in his book "Losing the Race" the cultural resistance in black kids to education because learning and studying is "white" behavior.

This week we remember and commemorate the Rev. Martin Luther King Jr. We must remember that King's message was that eternal truths and values transcend race.

Love, family, responsibility and education are values toward which every human being must aspire."

Star Parker, The credibility of black conservatism ; posted on Townhall.com January 18, 2005

one chooses to identify homosexual behavior as the chicken or the egg of social and moral breakdown, it without question is coincident with it.

The last thing that the black community, which has the nation's highest incidence of new AIDS cases, out of wedlock births, and abortions, needs is formal institutionalization of our nation's moral degeneration.

Government's role is to provide a safe and peaceful country in which men and women can exercise freely the responsibilities of fatherhood and motherhood. The church, when it is functioning properly, serves as a third party influence to confirm and support fathers in their role as family leaders. Neither of these institutions provides an adequate substitute for the role of a father of faith and grace.

**Christian men of faith and grace have the answer:**

If just the Christian male population of our country were to decide to accept their true roles as fathers and family leaders of faith and grace that God has provided, we could turn the moral decay of our country around in one short generation. However, without such action by Christian men in—ALL ethnic groups—our country will continue its moral decline. Fathers, I say again—we can do no other—we CANNOT escape our calling! Ultimately we must abandon any idea of escape from our roles, as genuinely effective fathers and family leaders, and submit to God's foreordained plan for our purpose in His creation.

Rest assured, with our present approach, all the political programs and ethnic activist movements you can put on the streets of America will not change the direction of our moral decay. Yes, we should all vote for all of the men and women of faith and grace that God will—providentially provide—as candidates. More importantly, if we are to be successful in changing the transgenerational migration of the American family from its present course of structural disintegration and moral decay, then our efforts must—start by returning fathers—to their God ordained position of family leadership and responsibilities!

No one person or organization can force this to happen. It requires the decision of each Christian man—of all ethnic origins—to accept his role as a true father of faith and grace, family leader and role model for his children. Male leaders from every walk of life, ethnic and cultural origin in America who value the quality of life of their people, must first commit—to lead by example—and to also speak out for fatherhood in the family! The efforts and money we are putting forth in other areas that do not focus on rebuilding fatherhood, is like using teaspoons to bail out a sinking ocean liner. We must WAKE UP—repent of our half hearted wimpy ways—and engage the fight on all fronts! We must hook up the main pumps—God's gift of faith and grace to FATHERS—if we don't want our ship to sink!

Marvin Olasky, Editor for World magazine posted this personal testimony of how important love and marriage is to him and how it forms the heart of his annual New Year's resolution.

**Wanting both: Looking for love in all the right places**

Marvin Olasky, Editorial in World magazine, Dec. 31, 2004

"Reprinted from World; the weekly news magazine from a Christian perspective. For subscription information, go to www.worldmag.com or call 800-951-NEWS."

"Since both my wife and I formally became Christians (through baptism) in the same year we were married, 1976, our love for each other in some loopy way is tied up with our love for Christ's church. Our

Christian beliefs, growing even before we were fully aware of them, pushed us to church membership.

"Wonderfully, we've never had any significant frustrations in our marriage, providentially but not so happily, we've had some in church relationships. Yet Christianity is true and churches are God's major vehicles for growing believers, so despite all that goes wrong in them they're still the only true game in town.

"My favorite 20th century writer of fiction, Walker Percy, poured on the criticism in his next-to-last novel, '*The Second Coming*' (1980). He complained that the contemporary Christian is 'nominal, lukewarm, hypocritical, sinful or, if fervent, generally offensive and fanatical. But he is not crazy.' The unbeliever is, because of the 'fatuity, blandness, incoherence, fakery and fat-headedness of his unbelief. He is in fact an insane person.'

"Percy continued, 'The present-day unbeliever is crazy because he finds himself born into a world of endless wonders, having no notion how he got here, a world in which he eats, sleeps—works, grows old, gets sick, and dies—takes his comfort and ease, plays along with the game, watches TV, drinks his drink, laughs—for all the world as if his prostate were not growing cancerous, his arteries turning to chalk, his brain cells dying off by the millions, as if the worms were not going to have him in no time at all.'

"Percy's describes the typical academic: 'The more intelligent he is, the crazier he is—He reads Dante for its mythic structure. He joins the ACLU and concerns himself with the freedom of the individual and does not once exercise his own freedom to inquire into how in God's name he should find himself in such a ludicrous situation.'

"The international news of 2004 once again showed how far from sanity this world resides. Iraq. Sudan. Israel. Afghanistan. Holland. China. Chechenia. Cuba. Nagorno Karabakh. On the surface, our domestic news is better. No terrorist attacks. No mass murders in schools or churches. But Percy's quiet terror continues: arteries to chalk, brain cells to mush, dust to dust.

"This was a year in which many people sought the love of another. I feel extraordinarily blessed in my marriage, but hit television shows like '*Sex and the City*' and '*Desperate Housewives*,' as well as Tom Wolfe's fine novel '*I Am Charlotte Simmons*,' display the desperate desire for love that some sadly reduce to a desperate search for sex—as if momentary excitement can substitute for years of contentment.

"Some of the gays and lesbians who lined up for 'marriage licenses' in San Francisco early this year merely wanted to poke their fingers in the eyes of straights, but others were there because they thought they suddenly had an antidote to loneliness. They deserve not hatred, but pity.

"What's more striking is how the desperate search for horizontal love, person-to-person, is not matched by what should be an even more desperate search for vertical love, person-and-God. Here's Walker Percy again: 'I am surrounded by two classes of maniacs. The first are the believers, who think they know the reason why we find ourselves in this ludicrous predicament yet act for all the world as if they don't. The second are the unbelievers, who don't know the reason and don't care if they don't.'

"Confession: I often act for all the world as if I'm clueless. So do most Christians I know—and those who don't act clueless often act as if they know everything, which is even more obnoxious. But here's my continuing New Year's resolution, now 24 years old, taken from the end of the '*The Second Coming*,' after protagonist Will Barrett has fallen in love and also come to understand a little about God: 'Am I crazy to want both, her and Him? No, not want, must have. And will have.'"[101]

If you are of the male gender, and you have had the interest and courage to read this far, you are one of the potential answers for rekindling a spirit of God ordained fatherhood in our country. More importantly, you are the answer to your own requirement to accept God's claim on you for fatherhood and to be that all-important—guiding force and light—for your family! Every family was intended by God to have such guidance and light. Again—congratulations—on caring enough and for being moved enough at least to read a book such as this! Invite other men in your area of contact to also read it. Make it a gift to some young man or middle aged father with more than his share of family struggles—we must all work together—to get the message to the millions of American men and women who are in great need to know these things and to be encouraged to join the battle. Obviously I also invite women of faith and grace to do likewise, but the very core of the problem is the lack of male initiative. If only women are concerned—all is lost! Also, see the appendix for more contact information.

**A monumental challenge:**

The challenge for single parent families is monumental. Each partner in the sexual union which brings forth a new child into the world is so important; it is pure folly to think of single parent families as normal. Yet, because there is so little appreciation for the differences between the roles of motherhood and fatherhood, a significant portion of our society are attempting to accept single parent families as the "new family" structure for the future.

If it's "new," it is so only by reason of being freakish, abnormal—it is no design of God. The product of these single parent families, the children who are being asked to mature and take their places in the social world around them, are in fact the—truly disadvantaged—of the future. The design that works—and is—intended for all time to produce the environment in which newborn babies can become mature, productive, well-adjusted and happy adults, is the two parent family. It takes "two to tango" in bed to make a child and it takes "two to tango" in the challenge of life, to establish a solid family structure environment, in which to rear the child. The notion of anything less being acceptable or desirable is purely the result of either selfish and irresponsible thinking or ignorance of the facts. I might suggest rebellion against God! Indeed, the single parent family can and does happen, but these are tragic anomalies, not norms to be accepted as just another alternative method of having and raising children! With so many single-parent families and the tragedy of having individuals who support the idea as normal, or as a viable alternative, is evidence that such people are self consciously ignorant and rebellious. They are without excuse, and stand condemned before our God, we must challenge them on every occasion possible.

Single parents of today need to be aware of the great challenges they face. It is an enormous task to do a good job of rearing children, even with all of God's spiritual and enabling support. The only real hope for our country—long term—is

---

[101] Dr. Marvin Olasky is considered the father of compassionate conservatism and was an informal advisor to Texas Gov. George W. Bush during his presidential campaign. Olasky has been a professor of journalism at the University of Texas at Austin since 1983, a senior fellow at the Acton Institute for the Study of Religion and Liberty, and the editor of *World*, a national weekly news magazine from a biblical perspective with a circulation over 335,000.

the success of committed fathers of faith and grace working side by side with their equally committed wives! When you have the full understanding and loving cooperation of two mature adults of the opposite sex, you have the bare bones basics of the tools you need. To attempt to be successful as single parent should only occur as a result of extreme circumstances, never by virtue of a predisposed attitude that single parent status is—desirable—as an alternative life style.

The sexual libertarians, with their prevailing attitudes have an agenda to establish our moral perspectives on sexual values and principles of their own invention—void of any input—from God. Their concepts of man/woman relationships and their total lack of understanding of God's plan for fatherhood, challenge the thinking of our fore-fathers and what we learn in the Bible. They call our fore-fathers prudish and Victorian and sexually unfulfilled. Since self-discipline for any male must certainly include, if not start with, his perspective on sexual morals, values and principles, such a challenge cannot go unanswered.

Those who pursue and promote sexual promiscuity as a normal way of life—for the so-called successful enlightened person—are incapable of knowing the truth without God. These secularists believe in one-dimensional sex (solely a factor of biological orgasm), and in getting as many varieties as they can. For them, this is the hallmark of great sex and a great life. In reality all you get is sexual frustration, broken hearts, sick bodies, sick minds, and single-parent families!

**God's revealed Law-Word rings loud and clear in our ears:**

"Hear, my children, the instruction of a father, and give attention to know understanding; for I give you good doctrine: Do not forsake my law. When I was my father's son, tender and the only one in the sight of my mother, he also taught me, and said to me: 'Let your heart retain my words; keep my commands, and live. Get wisdom! Get understanding!'" Proverbs 4:1-5.

Let us pray fervently that we will be doers and not only hearers of the Word![102]

---

[102] "Therefore lay aside all filthiness and overflow of wickedness, and receive with meekness the implanted word, which is able to save your souls. But be doers of the word, and not hearers only, deceiving yourselves. For if anyone is a hearer of the word and not a doer, he is like a man observing his natural face in a mirror; for he observes himself, goes away, and immediately forgets what kind of man he was. But he who looks into the perfect law of liberty and continues in it, and is not a forgetful hearer but a doer of the work, this one will be blessed in what he does. If anyone among you thinks he is religious, and does not bridle his tongue but deceives his own heart, this one's religion is useless. Pure and undefiled religion before God and the Father is this: to visit orphans and widows in their trouble, and to keep oneself unspotted from the world." James 1:21-27.

# Book I
# Love and Marriage

## Chapter Eight-Part II

## Structuring Our Children's Environment

## Discipline

"Thorns and snares are in the way of the perverse; he who guards his soul will be far from them. Train up a child in the way he should go, and when he is old he will not depart from it." Proverbs 22:5-6.

**True love and discipline are inseparable:**

Discipline is a gift from God. Discipline is the deciding factor in creating a good, healthy, supportive and emotionally stable environment for our family. Moral fiber, values, principles and a good self-image are as impossible without structure and discipline, as trying to pour concrete without forms. Fathers are gifted with natural abilities to be good disciplinarians, but we need some good counsel from those who have proven abilities. How a father goes about establishing his role as disciplinarian will have a great effect on his image as Hero and Knight in shining armor.

Discipline is a bad word for many, but in reality it is quite a good word. The word discipline comes from the word "disciple" or "student". In other words one who learns is a "disciple" and therefore one who is in the process of learning is being "discipled" or "disciplined". It is impossible to learn anything without discipline. Discipline is a fundamental part of our expression of love and protection for each family member. We discipline because we love. Those fathers who won't or don't accept their proper role as the one in charge of family discipline and its structure, are abdicating their role in one of the most important expressions of love.

The Bible says that God disciplines us because He loves us and because we are His children. He says that if He does not discipline us, then we are illegitimate and no children of His. Can we say or do any less[103]?

Children expect discipline. Even though discipline can be unpleasant, everyone who has experienced good discipline knows not only that he needed it, but also appreciates, and loves those who had the courage to give it to him! To attempt to raise a child without discipline is like trying to build a complex building without a blueprint, or like leaving the rebar out of concrete when it is poured, or deciding not to install the steel beams and girders into a sky scraper—you steal its spine—you create a disaster. It would mean there were no measures of Right and Wrong or standards. To ignore discipline is to be irresponsible and grossly insensitive to reality and the true meaning of love. Christ the Word says in the book

103 "If you endure chastening, God deals with you as with sons: for what son is there whom a father does not chasten? But if you are without chastening, of which all have become partakers, then you are illegitimate and not sons. Furthermore, we have had human fathers who corrected us, and we paid them respect. Shall we not much more readily be in subjection to the Father of spirits and live? For they indeed for a few days chastened us as seemed best to them, but He for our profit, that we may be partakers of His holiness. Now no chastening seems to be joyful for the present, but painful; nevertheless, afterward it yields the peaceable fruit of righteousness to those who have been trained by it." Hebrews 12:7-11.

of Hebrews, that discipline and love are inseparable. Agape love—the pure love from God the Father—is as much discipline as it is blessing, for you cannot separate what the human mind considers to be a blessing from what Christ says is discipline! One without the other does not exist.

**Christ's worldview on love and discipline:**

Therefore, we see clearly that Christ's worldview on love and discipline is that to say you have—one without the other—is to say you have nothing. What we would call an oxymoron. We cannot change the situation of family deterioration by simply criticizing men as a group. Change is not a group function. We can only make changes in ourselves, and one by one we will turn the American Christian family into the proper center of love, structure and discipline which every child and family member deserves. Discipline is like the helm of a ship; it gives direction. It makes little or no sense to have a Map on board our vessel if we refuse to man the helm. Our vessel will not go where the Map says it should go unless we take the helm in our hands and steer on course through wind and waves. Discipline is to the family what the helm is to a vessel. We begin to take command of our vessel when we apply discipline to keep ourselves and our families on course.

**Many small corrections are better than a few big ones:**

As a certified instrument flight instructor for general aviation I have had many hours of flight training and have taught others the finer points of flying, especially flying under instrument conditions. For those who don't know, this is flight—without visual references outside of the airplane—all flight maneuvers and navigation are done strictly by reference to the instrument panel, i.e. "instrument flight." One of the most important and yet more difficult things to learn about this process is that control is absolutely essential but that—over control—is absolutely devastating. Learning the light "two finger" thumb and forefinger touch on the yoke and very light touch with the feet on the rudders must be achieved if the pilot is to master the intricacies of instrument flight. Once learned the pilot comes to realize, in retrospect, that he was actually over-controlling the plane even when he could fly visually by looking out the window!

As husbands and fathers, let's learn to maintain a control that requires only light touches and not heavy handedness. In my experience as a flight instructor I find that over controlling with a heavy hand on the controls is so unconscious that even experienced pilots don't know when they are doing it. One technique I have learned from other instructors is to have the pilot hold a pen in his left hand—the hand that is on the yoke—and limit the hand use to just the thumb and forefinger. By reducing the number of available fingers for gripping the yoke, the pilot is better able to limit the control inputs to small two finger motions.

Another very important parallel analogy from instrument instruction is the concept of following up the small inputs with a—pause—between inputs to analyze the results. In other words, once a change—no matter how small—has been put into the control system it is very important to wait a few seconds for the plane to respond to that input. Otherwise, the pilot continues to put in more change, or continued input of the same change, which soon develops into the same result as the heavy handed, over controlling would have given.

**Over control creates unnecessary problems:**

Our post modern culture has taught us to expect results and outcomes to be almost immediate. When we as husbands and as fathers of faith and grace mimic this expectancy with regards to our expectations of results from what we think our wife or our children should do in response to our inputs—we create unnecessary—self induced negative feedback. Negative feed back is good and desired—but self induced negative feed back—is one of the clear indications that we are over controlling. No two husbands or fathers will get the same reaction from their inputs, but all will have the tendency to over control. This is because we are human and we must learn from our mistakes. The good news is the husband and father of faith and grace—those who are committed to seek and implement God's principles—will find the correct touch that is best for his wife and children.

Discipline—as an expression of love—is expressed through a man or a woman's personality make-up. Some men and women have strong personalities, short tempers and intense expression of emotions. Conversely, there are many who are more in the middle—not too strong and not too weak; and there are those who are very mild mannered, soft spoken and who show little or no emotion.

When it comes to our personal application of discipline, parents tend to fall in either the strong or the mild personality approach. They either over-control or they under-control. The emotional ideal is to be more moderate—but consistency—is the most important element of all. To discipline spasmodically and inconsistently with our approach is almost, if not worse, than not disciplining at all!

Over-control creates self induced negative feedback. The plane will actually reflect these large inputs of correction as a bumpy—almost chaotic ride—one that feels like your flying through turbulence. This is not a good ride! Sometimes I will say to a student: "Lighten-up, you are putting in more turbulence than the wind." Then I remind him of the two fingers—sometimes it works just by holding up two fingers so the student can see them—no words are necessary.

**The family meeting:**

The family meeting is a great way to make these small inputs and allow for enough time to review the results before making further inputs. Like the pencil in the left hand of the student pilot—learning to overcome the tendency to over-control the family meeting—serves as a great leveling tool for discipline. This is true whether the meeting is with just the husband and wife who have no children or for those couples with children.

The family meeting affords us the opportunity to review our team successes and weaknesses. Like the instrument pilot who must wait a few seconds after each new input, we husbands and fathers of faith and grace must track the results of our instructions. Correcting small oversights on the part of all of the members and praising the successes of all, creates the positive atmosphere and attitudes necessary to keep progress moving forward.

**Small and frequent inputs are hardly noticed:**

My aviation experiences have taught me yet another analogy that is also confirmed in the husband/father experience. A good instrument pilot can fly along for hours—without an autopilot—changing altitudes and directions so smoothly that it is hard to detect how and when he makes corrections. The secret is that although it looks—like no correction is being made at all—the reality is that such a pilot is constantly making corrections. Conversely, when a pilot waits too long to correct for the little mistakes in navigation and then finally realizes that the plane is way off course—read the family life-style—the correcting maneuver must be more drastic. The very fact that a more drastic maneuver is required also presents the pilot with the possibility of making yet more mistakes—more over controlling—and then more drastic maneuvers until finally a series of small easy to correct oversights have now become a BIG problem!

Now we're flying in real turbulence—but notice—it is not from outside of our ship, it is being self induced, it's coming from us! We are getting a lot of negative feedback for nothing!!

**Recognizing and correcting our navigational and life-style input errors:**

**The Five Points of Smooth Parenting**

1. Make small inputs.
2. Wait for evidence of the effects of your last change.
3. Recognize small errors as soon as possible.
4. Make small directional and discipline corrections as often as necessary.
5. Don't wait to make changes until it requires a BIG change.

**Self discipline; turbulence and the death spiral:**

Learning control and discipline from God starts first with self discipline—of ourselves—and then of our families. Our general lack in self discipline has created the worst self induced turbulence possible for our Christian culture—THE ABDICATION—of our roles as guardians and protectors of the family. As men of faith and grace, God's chosen pilots for His families, our sloppy, inattentive, lousy navigation—read lack of attention to our own self discipline in personal moral development—has accumulated so many off-course and lousy mistakes in our journey of life that we have reduced our course correction to only one strong maneuver—you guessed it—ABDICATION!! Not to sound tough just to be tough, but in all too many instances we have reduced our role with women to the shallow standard of a mere sex partner, an additional income check and with our children as mere means to carry on our name. As a Christian culture, we have become so pathetic in our own mismanagement of our personal self discipline that the majority of our individual personal ships are in a death spiral. Most of the rest are just bouncing along, barely able to stay airborne—while only a few—really show signs of a steady hand on the controls and blessings for all on board!

A death spiral is an uncontrolled spin that occurs due to improper control inputs by the pilot. These can be control inputs that are either conscious or unconscious. The plane will react to the input regardless of the origin of their motivation. Turbulence—the outside forces of wind and weather—or that which we as ignorant husbands and fathers induce into the course of our lives, can cause these improper control inputs.

From the pilots point of view the airplane is in what appears to be a steep dive, either left or right, and the earth below is circling around and around. Everyone on board feels a sinking in the pit of their stomach and there is a sense of increasing anxiety.

**How did we get here?**

Remember the first man Adam and how he failed because of disobedience? (Disobedience is death, a curse and a great turbulence causing factor.) The second Adam, Jesus Christ, and how he succeeded because of obedience? (Obedience is life, a blessing and a great calming factor.) The answer is not difficult to figure out:

we are here because of disobedience. Our Christian culture is—upside down and in a turbulence induced spiral—because of disobedience. Although we are God's elect and we have received the gift of faith and grace, yet we can and do sin. Sin has consequences—not just for the unbelievers—but also for us, those who are called and who believe. What does God say?

"If you endure chastening, God deals with you as with sons: for what son is there whom a father does not chasten? But if you are without chastening, of which all have become partakers, then you are illegitimate and not sons." Hebrews 12:7-8.

**Curses on Disobedience:**

"But it shall come to pass, if you do not obey the voice of the LORD your God, to observe carefully all His commandments and His statutes which I command you today, that all these curses will come upon you and overtake you:

"Cursed shall you be in the city, and cursed shall you be in the country.

"Cursed shall be your basket and your kneading bowl.

"Cursed shall be the fruit of your body and the produce of your land, the increase of your cattle and the offspring of your flocks.

"Cursed shall you be when you come in, and cursed shall you be when you go out.

"The LORD will send on you cursing, confusion, and rebuke in all that you set your hand to do, until you are destroyed and until you perish quickly, because of the wickedness of your doings in which you have forsaken Me. ..."

"You shall betroth a wife, but another man shall lie with her; you shall build a house, but you shall not dwell in it; you shall plant a vineyard, but shall not gather its grapes. Your ox shall be slaughtered before your eyes, but you shall not eat of it; your donkey shall be violently taken away from before you, and shall not be restored to you; your sheep shall be given to your enemies, and you shall have no one to rescue them. Your sons and your daughters shall be given to another people, and your eyes shall look and fail with longing for them all day long; and there shall be no strength in your hand. A nation whom you have not known shall eat the fruit of your land and the produce of your labor, and you shall be only oppressed and crushed continually. So you shall be driven mad because of the sight which your eyes see. The LORD will strike you in the knees and on the legs with severe boils which cannot be healed, and from the sole of your foot to the top of your head." Deuteronomy 28:15-20, 28:30-35.

**Blessings on Obedience:**

"Now it shall come to pass, if you diligently obey the voice of the LORD your God, to observe carefully all His commandments which I command you today, that the LORD your God will set you high above all nations of the earth. And all these blessings shall come upon you and overtake you, because you obey the voice of the LORD your God:

'Blessed shall you be in the city, and blessed shall you be in the country.

'Blessed shall be the fruit of your body, the produce of your ground and the increase of your herds, the increase of your cattle and the offspring of your flocks.

'Blessed shall be your basket and your kneading bowl.

'Blessed shall you be when you come in, and blessed shall you be when you go out.

'The LORD will cause your enemies who rise against you to be defeated before your face; they shall come out against you one way and flee before you seven ways.

'The LORD will command the blessing on you in your storehouses and in all to which you set your hand, and He will bless you in the land which the LORD your God is giving you.

'The LORD will establish you as a holy people to Himself, just as He has sworn to you, if you keep the commandments of the LORD your God and walk in His ways. Then all peoples of the earth shall see that you are called by the name of the LORD, and they shall be afraid of you. And the LORD will grant you plenty of goods, in the fruit of your body, in the increase of your livestock, and in the produce of your ground, in the land of which the LORD swore to your fathers to give you. The LORD will open to you His good treasure, the heavens, to give the rain to your land in its season, and to bless all the work of your hand. You shall lend to many nations, but you shall not borrow. And the LORD will make you the head and not the tail; you shall be above only, and not be beneath, if you heed the commandments of the LORD your God, which I command you today, and are careful to observe them. So you shall not turn aside from any of the words which I command you this day, to the right or the left, to go after other gods to serve them." Deut. 28:1-13.

My dear brothers and sisters in Christ, there are consequences in the decisions of our lives: we can sow either the seeds of—construction—or we can sow the seeds of—destruction—the choice is ours.

**Three basic factors for our recovery:**

If, in our roles as fathers, we cannot be serious about our own rules, then discipline is very unlikely to have much of an effect. In fact, almost any kind of discipline with respect to family rules or structure is of little consequence if at least three basic factors are not in strong evidence.

**First:** we as the father must be under our own self discipline. Your rules cannot be just a matter of convenience for keeping your child in order while you allow yourself the privilege of breaking the rules as you please. Your child will see through such shallowness so fast it will make your head swim. Be forewarned, you are human and you will break your own rules. When such a mistake on your part does occur and your child should notice and bring it to your attention, do not deny it.

**Second**: you must be ready to admit very frankly and candidly that you did break the rule. Tell what it has cost or will cost you, and promise to do all you can not to break it again. This is exactly what you expect from him or her and anything less from you will only give reason to your child to disrespect you.

**Third:** you must be the main guardian and disciplinarian. Mothers can and should be involved in the disciplining and teaching of the children, absolutely they should! However, authority comes from the head, and she needs your delegated authority to perform this role successfully. If you as father do not supply the main support for this structure, that is, outline the structure and methods for discipline—teach by example in the family for her support and use—the mother's influence is limited. Without the husbands support and example the children very quickly learn to play both of you against each other. This can reach advanced levels, and they will play you like a fine instrument.

Families without the father of faith and grace leadership are families where you see—children running the family—while the whole of God's ordained family structure disappears. These kinds of families vary to the degree the children are allowed to set the standards and to run the family. Yet, to whatever extent they are allowed to do so, to that extent they will grow up unprepared for successful relationships in the world outside the family. If they have no structure or basis for successful relationships and no experience of being held responsible or accountable to each other as a family, there is no reason to expect them to function any differently outside the family.

**Defying the obvious:**

If this God-given role as father of faith and grace, as moral role model, teacher and disciplinarian, is threatening to you—you are not alone—join the "club" of all of us who are God's men. We are not just any group of men, but God's men, who pray to God to gift them with a greater sense and purpose in their call of fatherhood—men who are concerned that they might tuck their tails, but pray God for strength not to do so—not to run. Men, who know they need all the help they can get. In fact we need so much help it is unthinkable not to approach the whole matter, in humble prayer for help and guidance from our Creator. If, indeed, He has created us and called us to the role of fatherhood, then it seems only natural for Him to willingly enable and strengthen us for the task. In spite of all my weaknesses and mistakes, I have personally found it to be so! He teaches us both with the written Law-Word and with discoveries in his natural laws.

**How God's natural laws can teach us uncommon common sense:**

In the early years of aviation history the rules of flight said that if you were in a dive and you wanted to pull out you must—PULL—on the controls so as to deflect your elevators up pushing the tail of the plane down and thus pointing the nose up and back to normal straight and level flight. It sounds good and it even works most every time. In fact there is only one instance when it—will not work—and that's when your plane is in a death spiral! What a lousy deal—Right? Why when you need it most doesn't it work?

Many early pilots must have screamed that question into the howling wind as they plummeted toward the earth below—their fragile open cockpit airplanes—

spinning down and down out of control as they helplessly pulled on the controls with all of their might! Down and down they spiraled, hands locked onto the controls, every muscle straining to pull harder, until they crashed and burned on the ground below. It is sad, but true.

God's aerodynamic laws are just like His spiritual and moral laws—you break it—you pay. In the case of the death spiral it is simply a matter of God's aerodynamics. His law of aerodynamics says that if you don't have air flowing over the wings of your airplane—it might as well be a car—because it won't fly. How can an airplane be in the air and not have air flowing over its wings. That's a good question, one that many others were asking long before they found the answer. Which begs the question: How long will it take us to find the answer to our death spiraling Christian culture?

Through His gift of faith He is the wind under our wings, He is the one who makes us soar upon wings as Eagles. "But those who wait on the LORD shall renew their strength; they shall mount up with wings like eagles, they shall run and not be weary, they shall walk and not faint." Isaiah 40:31.

The answer for the pilot is this: The plane enters a slow turning motion, left or right, because of incorrect control inputs from the pilot. This is because of sloppy, inattentive, lousy control habits. Once these control inputs or—the lack of the proper inputs—are ignored sufficiently the plane enters a spiral and stalls the wing. A stalled wing is a wing that no longer is moving forward through the air fast enough to create lift—without lift—the plane no longer is flying and the controls no longer will respond. When we are in a spiral our problem is not the DIVE or the CIRCLING scary descent, our problem is we are no longer flying!!

**In order to fly again we must do what common logic tells us not to do:**

**First:** we decide that we are not going to keep doing the same thing. We are going to STOP what we were doing and we are going to take DECISIVE STEPS to correct this death dealing problem.

**Second:** we are going to slam our foot down on the rudder pedal that is opposite to the direction in which we are spiraling and at the same we are going to—PUSH—forward on the controls and point our nose even more directly toward the ground than before.

Trust me men and women, husbands and wives of faith and grace, when I say that this is an act of FAITH and COURAGE. Faith because it is against what appears to be normal and courage because if you are wrong you are going to die.

**Third:** we are going to pull the throttle all the way back and let the engine only idle.

Wait—hold it right there—we are going to crash for sure! We are using our feet on controls that no longer have air over their surfaces, thus they can't work. We are pointing the nose down in an ever steeper dive—and now—we cut the engine back to idle. Pleeeease—give me a break!

Strange as it might seem—just like the laws of God's revealed Law-Word and the testimony of Jesus Christ that he will be with us always and sustain us even until death—it really, really, really works!!!

No sooner have we done these three things—all at the same time mind you—than our faithful craft makes amazing changes in what it is doing. Instead of screaming out of control ever faster and faster towards the earth—as you might think with the nose down and all—there is feeling in the controls again, the ground is no longer going around in circles and we can now hear the swiiish of the air as in once again flows rapidly over the wings. Hallelujah! Our plane is flying again:

1. NOW—we can pull on the controls, lift the nose of our craft once again towards the heavens—we have control once again!
2. NOW—we can push the throttle back in and feel the surge of power as the engine roars to life and the propeller spools up to the proper RPM—we have power, correctly applied once again!
3. NOW—life is beautiful again; faith, hope and love surge once again in our veins—our ship has returned to normal flight!

Wow—what a heart stopper—that was! Been there—done that—both in the plane and in my personal life.

How much do you suppose those early pilots would have paid to know what we pilots of today take for granted? I have thought about that many times. I have also thought about the pilot who first decided that he thought he knew the answer and had the courage, to go up in his plane and deliberately put his plane into a death spiral, to prove that he could get it out. Remember, in those days they didn't use wind tunnels to ground test every new design and maneuver before they tried it in the air. If you wanted to prove it—you had to do it.

Fortunately for husbands and fathers of faith and grace God has given us a proven model—kept from the unbelievers—but freely given to us! Thus, the answer for fathers of faith and grace is this: we must first repent—I've said it before—but maybe now you understand better just how important it is. Repentance means we change. We stop doing as a culture what we have always been doing that has gotten us into this death spiral. We believe God's Law-Word and we decide to act on it.

What we have been discovering together in this book has—NOT—been a repeat of our historical cultural sloppy, insensitive misguided and misdirected sameness. We are discovering a radical change that defies what the unbeliever calls the obvious—that which the secular humanists tell us is the truth—our discovery insists on God's answers in His revealed Law-Word. How sad that for those called of God and gifted with faith and grace we should experience the sound of God's truth in our ears—as radical. When in fact for Christians of faith and grace it is NOT radical—it is NORMAL!

Like the death spiral of the airplane—once you have learned its cause and its cure—it is hard to believe people actually died for lack of understanding it. Once learned, it seems so simple and straight forward. Be humble and remember always that we have it as a gift and not because we are intellectually superior.

**Father as the main teacher:**

Fatherhood must be taken seriously, by every man. The concept of father as the primary teacher, counselor and disciplinarian in the family is not by accident. This is our God-given role. When approached and executed with wisdom, this role gives the father the most respect and opportunity to influence his children in a positive and productive way. After several fits and starts I discovered the best way to get my points across was at a time when I was not trying to discipline anyone. Little private talks with my wife turned into family meetings. The little private talks with Marilyn continued but the family meeting became the focal point for teaching as a family unit. I will never forget the first such "meeting" I held with my family. I was afraid of looking silly, the children were so young. I thought I would have difficulty communicating on a level they could understand. Much to my surprise, they understood more than I thought possible—they especially were able to sense my openness and concern. It made them feel important to be accepted as part of a team. From that moment forward the family meeting became my main tool for communication and team building. In retrospect, I am sure that twice as many meetings were in order. If I could do it over again—the area of greatest change—would be the family meeting. I would hold at least one family meeting each week. Ironically—to this day—Marilyn and I do exactly that.

**Depersonalizing the problem:**

Emotions and personal defenses tend to be one of the greatest problems that impede good discipline. I debated with myself as to where and when to bring this up in our process of discoveries. I finally decided that although it would have fit in chapter five: "Let's Talk—Communication Between The Sexes," it would be more effective in this section on discipline.

As fallen carnal beings we have an enormous capacity to misapply every challenge or need for change as a direct personal attack. We even display this fallen nature when we experience disappointments in the function of our mechanical and the other non-living things in our life. How many times have we had the sad experience of a flat tire on the way to an important engagement and immediately felt animosity to the car and to the tire? How about when we trip over something? It's the fault of the object, right? The stick, the chair, the rock; they just jump up and trip us. If our sensitivities to our own egos and selfish natures can be so easily upset by such things outside of the realm of the living—and they are—perhaps we can better appreciate our difficulty to accept discipline and deal with it. There are no perfect ways to solve the dilemma of our fallen nature but we can certainly recognize our propensity to over-react and adopt methods that will allow us to develop with less stress and more success. The best method that I have ever learned or employed for our family and even for myself when I am alone, is the following:

**Remove All Topics for Discussion From Personal Identification**

1. Define what the topic is going to be:
2. Agree that the topic is not part of our personal being:
3. Visualize the topic as an item for discussion that is not in our possession:
4. Visualize the topic as inanimate and place it on the floor before the group:
5. Discuss the topic and arrive at conclusions without personal blame:
6. All members of the group must accept the conclusions of the discussion:
7. Applications must be applied according to the need of each individual:

**Transparency as a tool for teaching:**

While children are still quite young, it is important for the father to introduce some revolutionary thinking. How many of you ever saw faults in your parents? How old were you when you began to notice their inconsistencies and their faults? Amazing isn't it, how young we can be, when we see right through our parents and all their efforts at putting forth an image of Mr. and Mrs. Perfect? It's time to face reality.

Our children see—or most likely—have already seen through our best efforts to hide our faults from them. I knew that mine knew plenty; but I admit that I was humbled by how much they really did know.[104]

"Ouch!" I know you don't want to hear such things, we didn't like it either, but we must face it, it's the truth. Not only do they see right through us, they lose respect for us when we continue to act as though we were perfect and never do anything wrong. Children are disarmingly simple in the way they view things. They are honest to a fault with what they see and feel, much more so than adults. As adults we mirror what we have been taught by our parents and by others who play at the game of self-righteousness—namely, avoiding being transparent with others at all costs. This is a type of denial on a par with the "king has no clothes." Transparency is very important and equally private. Certainly, it is not to be exercised with everyone, but with your family—yes—especially your wife and children.

Since God gave them all the ability to see right through us anyway, we might as well take the road of greatest wisdom, which is to take the initiative. This is not hard and it will bring you and your wife great positive results with your children.

At the earliest opportunity, from as early as three years and up, children will understand you when you tell them you are not perfect. How do you do this and not lose face or respect? Through the consistent use of the family meeting, it becomes your time and place to make announcements, to talk things over and to share family "insider" information.[105]

Children are very sensitive to the way we express ourselves—our emotional expression—of our own self-image. When we are sad or unhappy they become stressed also. When we are happy and outgoing they are relieved and relaxed. Being honest about our own mistakes and not feeling the need to cover-up and play like we don't have any, helps improve the quality our own self-image. This is good for us and also for the children. It is natural for our children to want to love and respect us. Yet, they don't like us to be imperfect; remember we men are the Heroes, and the Knights in shining armor and mothers are the Queens of the Universe. But—even more so—they don't need us to fake it. We present a more real and loving personality when we are sincerely open with them. So, a simple explanation is in order. We simply tell the truth. Truth that they can receive and assimilate, not all our "dirty laundry."

In the family meeting fathers should take the initiative. Now don't—wimp out—on me here, this is very important!

> "Children, Daddy has some things he wants to tell you that are very important! You know how we have rules in the family and how we all want to show our love and respect for each other? You also know how difficult it can be sometimes to obey the rules or to show the love we would like to, correct?"

Here is where you might get that oblique look out of the side of the eyes to each other or a denial that such is true, especially when they are very young. You

---

104 "Confess your trespasses to one another, and pray for one another, that you may be healed. The effective, fervent prayer of a righteous man avails much." James 5:16.

105 "Brethren, if a man is overtaken in any trespass, you who are spiritual restore such a one in a spirit of gentleness, considering yourself lest you also be tempted. Bear one another's burdens, and so fulfill the law of Christ. For if anyone thinks himself to be something: when he is nothing, he deceives himself. But let each one examine his own work, and then he will have rejoicing in himself alone, and not in another. For each one shall bear his own load" Galatians 6:1-5.

will hear the little ones say: "Not me Daddy." The little ones are always the most transparent. Do you suppose that was what Jesus had in mind when he said?

> "Then Jesus called a little child to Him, set him in the midst of them, and said, 'Assuredly, I say to you, unless you are converted and become as little children, you will by no means enter the kingdom of heaven. Therefore whoever humbles himself as this little child is the greatest in the kingdom of heaven. Whoever receives one little child like this in My name receives Me.'" Matthew 28:2-5

After all they might not want to admit faults. It is just the weak side of our human nature to deny guilt. We are just the grown up version of them, remember? "I didn't do it, Johnny did it," or "It wasn't my fault, she pushed me and made me do it," are common responses when facing the problem of who's guilty. So, in our family meetings it is wise to present being transparent and admitting our mistakes as something good. As each child comes to the moment of truth when he has to admit he broke a rule, he will be prepared for being honest.

**Now comes the big moment, the big revelation:**

"Well, children, Daddy and Mommy started to learn good family rules when we were your age, and we have been working on them ever since we were children. Would you like to know a secret? Mommy and Daddy are still learning how to love and to follow God's good family rules. I know you have seen or heard Mommy and Daddy do things or say things you have felt were wrong, and we wanted to let you know we understand it makes you feel sad. Well, Daddy has some very good news to tell you. As a family we can all help each other to do better. Daddy wants you to tell Mommy and Daddy when you see us break a rule or when you think we are unkind to you or to each other. This way we can all work together to make our family the best family ever."

If you are a man who thinks that you cannot honestly say that you were learning good family rules when you were young, you might want to rethink your premise. You were learning rules, some bad some good; the bad rules are those you are ashamed of and that give you this feeling of inadequacy and brings doubt into your mind when it comes to setting good standards for your family—higher standards—than you had as a child. Don't worry; this is the dirty laundry you don't have to share. There are always some good family rules experienced in even the worst of families—you were taught to use the bathroom and not the kitchen floor—right? OK, stuff the guilt and suck it up! You can do this—write it down—use cheat notes—a black board or anything else you want to—just DO it!

Now that wasn't so hard, was it? Be prepared for looks of surprise and awe-struck wonderment.

Believe me, done sincerely, and with intent to follow through as a good team leader and team captain with fairness and tenderness mixed with firm commitment, you will never regret revealing this seldom shared truth in today's families. With this simple confession you have just established the greatest foundation there is for love, respect, and honesty. Your children will never be able to say their parents are fakes and liars. On the contrary, you have just grown immensely in their sight, and they will never forget it.

**Reliving our past through our children:**

As children get older and are able to understand more complex aspects of this same reality, it is important to keep reinforcing their understanding of what they are up against. There is another big revelation they need to know. When they see you and Mommy do things they think are bad or wrong, they also are telling themselves they will never do those things when they grow up. Remember how you used to tell yourself you would never do the things which your father or mother had done, and you were never going to be like them? You guessed it, your children will say the same thing, and they won't be anymore successful at it than you were.

That's another "ouch!" But you handle it the same way you did the other one. You simply let them know the truth of the matter. The reality of these child reactions to parental imperfection is not the problem; it is the tendency for parents to insist they don't exist which is the problem. Dr. Stella Chess, a leading child psychiatry expert and a professor at New York University School of Medicine says, "If you have a hotheaded child blame Mother Nature, not mother. The fault is in the genes."

At this point you should reveal to them just how much a part of you they really are. When given the opportunity to work with parents who are not afraid of themselves, children can overcome almost anything, even hereditary tendencies.

Indeed, they are most likely to follow all of your bad habits, unless they are willing to work with you in overcoming them. None of us will ever overcome all of our bad habits completely. However, great progress is possible. Helping them understand this gives hope to the children and reduces their tendency to judge you and to feel "inferior" to the world outside the family.

Adults all know the world outside the family is not perfect, but children do not know. Everyone outside the family keeps his or her mask on and plays the game of self-righteous perfection so well; children can come to believe the only weirdos in town are Mommy and Daddy. Add our post modern public school's efforts to reinforce this attack on the family and—what do you get? Trouble at home, that's what!

What are some of your bad habits? Do you have a bad temper? Do you procrastinate about everything and find it hard to follow through with plans and ideas? Do you always leave everything to the last minute? Are you disorganized and find structure and rules confining and uncomfortable? Are you sloppy and disorderly in your dress, environment and work habits? Do you drink too much alcoholic beverage? Are you self-centered and prefer to have everything your own way? Does sharing with others leave you feeling threatened and fearful you won't get your fair share? Are you playing around with drugs and other artificial stimulants? Do you have a habit of being late for important meetings? Are you a workaholic? Do others consider you to be a neat freak? Do you put sports and your career ahead of everything else, including the family? Does responsibility give you butterflies in your stomach? Are you addicted to pornography? Do you run around on your wife and have other sexual partners besides her?

Whatever our bad habits are; rest assured—our children will soon find out what they are. In fact they may know before we do, that is before we—trying to give an impression of Mr. Perfect—realize the jig is up. The whole idea of false impressions is a sure way to fail at being a real father or mother of faith and grace. Being perfect in our function as human beings is impossible. However, to have an attitude of openness with our loved one's and a willingness to admit our faults, whatever they might be, is real wisdom. No one expects his Hero and Knight in shining armor to be perfect, but he does expect him to be honest. Being honest about his imperfections and his desire and efforts to improve is an illustration of his noble character and reinforces the image of: Hero and Knight in shining armor!

We will sum up this new attitude of transparency in seven easy-to-remember points of fact we will name: *The Confession of Transparency*. As fathers and mothers of faith and grace we need to memorize these seven basic points and teach them to our children:

**The Confession of Transparency for a Father of Faith and Grace**

1. Father is responsible for the structure and discipline of the family and its moral role model.
2. Father is still learning, but even so, he is the best the family has and what he learns he will always share with the family.
3. Father has bad days in spite of his desire for more perfection.
4. Father has bad habits that he is still working on.
5. You my children will genetically image your father and will have a tendency toward my same bad habits.
6. Father is committed to change and grow together with mommy and you children, as a team player.
7. Our family is our most important institution and personal responsibility in the world!

**The Confession of Transparency for a Mother of Faith and Grace**

1. Mother is responsible for supporting father in the structure and discipline of the family and its moral role model.
2. Mother is still learning, but even so, she is God's gift to daddy and the family and what she learns she will always share with the family.
3. Mother has bad days in spite of her desire for more perfection.
4. Mother has bad habits that I am still working on.
5. You my children will genetically image your mother and will have a tendency toward my same bad habits.
6. Mother is committed to change and to grow together daddy and you children as a team player.
7. Our family is our most important institution and personal responsibility in the world!

**Wise counsel or on-the-job-training:**

You will get great results with your children's attitude toward your counsel and discipline if you remind them often that there are really only two ways to learn life's secrets. They can either receive wise counsel[106]; or they can learn by trial and

---

[106] "Wisdom calls aloud outside; She raises her voice in the open squares. She cries out in the chief concourses, at the openings of the gates in the city She speaks her words: 'How long, you simple one's, will you love simplicity? For scorners delight in their scorning, and fools hate knowledge. Turn at my rebuke; surely I will pour out my spirit on you; I will make my words known to you. Because I have called and you refused, I have stretched out my hand and no one regarded, because you disdained all my counsel, and would have none of my rebuke, I also will laugh at your calamity; I will mock when your terror comes, when your terror comes like a storm, and your destruction comes like a whirlwind,

error, experimenting in the larger laboratory of life, outside the family structure, i.e.—on-the-job-training.

You must use every illustration and example you can think of to bring them to a clear understanding of the difference in these two methods of learning. Your structure and discipline, although it may seem hard at times, is in reality a cake walk compared to the unforgiving nature of the larger laboratory of life, outside the family structure. In that arena of experimentation, the discipline applied for making a mistake or breaking a rule is not only much more painful than your structure and discipline, it is infinitely more dangerous. It can cause pain beyond belief and even kill without warning! The more your children come to understand this, the more they will respect you personally, and also respect your structure and discipline. If you have not read it, please read the footnote at the bottom referencing wise counsel. God takes a very dim view of children who will not receive wise counsel. When appropriate read these verses to your children and any others that you have found helpful.

**Respecting the position:**

A word of caution: sometimes parents will mistake this advice as meaning they are to allow their children to criticize them and bring up their faults to them in any manner they choose. Absolutely not, respect for father and mother is of the highest priority in family discipline. Because our children know of our own faults and of our sincere desire to improve is no basis for disrespect. Husbands and wives are not perfect but the positions they hold are perfect—they are ordained and assigned by the Almighty—children disrespect them at their own peril![107]

Any and all disrespect must be dealt with immediately! In our family this is the only rule you have to break just once to get disciplined. All of the other rules depend mostly on good function; this rule, the rule of respect, depends entirely on attitude.[108] If they don't get this one, the others are going to receive less than their best.

When good discipline and family structure are in order, respect for parents is a reality for every child very early in their experience, before age two in most cases. So, by the time you are telling them these things about yourselves in a family meeting, you are basically just clearing up some of the confusion already existing in their minds. By age two you are a god and can do no wrong; by age four they've got you figured out better than you think! Thus, by being transparent you again grow in their sight beyond all proportions. You will never be real gods, but you can certainly be great Heroes and Knights in shining armor and Queens of the universe.[109]

For those who are already committed in this area—Fantastic—be encouraged to continue and to improve. For those who are indecisive and not sure, go take a long walk and review your options. You have nothing to lose and

---

when distress and anguish come upon you. Then they will call on me, but I will not answer; they will seek me diligently, but they will not find me. Because they hated knowledge and did not choose the fear of the LORD, they would have none of my counsel and despised my every rebuke. Therefore they shall eat the fruit of their own way, and be filled to the full with their own fancies. For the turning away of the simple will slay them, and the complacency of fools will destroy them; but whoever listens to me will dwell safely, and will be secure, without fear of evil." Proverbs 1:20-33.

107 "Whoever curses his father or his mother, his lamp will be put out in deep darkness." Proverbs 20:20.

108 "Whoever robs his father or his mother, and says, 'It is no transgression,' the same is companion to a destroyer." Proverbs 28:24.

"There is a generation that curses its father, and does not bless its mother." Proverbs 30:11.

109 "Let your father and your mother be glad, and let her who bore you rejoice." Proverbs 23:25.

everything to gain. Without your commitment to discipline and good family structure your present efforts, no matter how well intentioned, are down the drain.

Children constantly test the limits of the structure we establish. The most common method for children to learn the limits of the family structure is experimentation. This should not seem strange, since it is the same method we adults use to discover most of our new technology. The only major difference is that we adults call what we do "research" and what the children do, we call many different names.

We refer to the experimentation and exploration of babies as "cute" and say things like, "Look at that, isn't he (or she) smart?" or "Just a chip off the old block," Right? Then when they are two years old we change our tune. Now it's the "terrible twos." Then when they are a little older we call them "motor mouth" or some other term to illustrate their constant questions of "What is that?" or "Why, Mommy?" and "Why, Daddy?" Then, eventually, they graduate to the "terrible teens!"

**Challenging teenagers:**

When was the last time you heard a parent of a new teen-ager say, "Oh! I'm so thrilled, my son, (daughter) just turned thirteen, and I'm so excited to have a teen-ager now!" It is not impossible to hear it said, but in private most will confess that they are not so sure just how well they will be able to handle it. I too had many misgivings with my first daughter, of whom we will say more later. However, I can with great conviction say that all of the others were a joy to watch as they moved into their teen years.

What's the big deal? What is so bad about teen-agers? If we understand from the beginning the natural desire of children to want to know the limits of their structure and they're need for fathers and mothers of faith and grace to help them discover these limits, there is no problem. By the time your children are teen-agers they will have long since learned how to trust and respect your leadership, and you will not have the so called "normal" teen-age problems.

Consequently, teen-agers offer some of the most exciting and fulfilling times for parents. That is, for parents who have understood their roles and the importance each one plays, in the family structure and discipline?

However, if one waits until they are teen-agers before taking over as the family disciplinarian—look out! You are not in for a good time. In fact, it is virtually too late to do much by that time. One would need a miracle at this point. Most—at best—will simply limit the damage. The laboratory of life with its cruel and unforgiving discipline takes over, and you become more an observer than anything else. Your best opportunities to establish the kind of mutual trust and confidence needed for successful teen-age development, with your active guidance and input, has long been lost. Yet, with sincere repentance and positive action there is still hope!

If this is your present state of affairs be courageous, repent of your past short comings and pray for God to forgive you. Seek His wisdom, pray daily for His grace to have the courage to do all that you teenage son or daughter needs for successful structure and discipline. Although difficult this is no time to give up! God is faithful and merciful if we are serious!

When we men wait until our children are teen-agers to take over the role as real a father of faith and grace, moral role model and disciplinarian, we will discover a great deal of pent-up hostility. There is an important dichotomy at work here. It is natural for our teen-agers to want to be more independent, they are young adults and have an inner urge to spread their wings. At the same time they are powerless to make a peaceful transition from childhood to adulthood without our structure and guidance. When this is lacking then we see only the negative side, their rebellion. The reason is simple, we have let them down and they know it. They don't know how to put it in words, maybe, but they know. They are mad, because their only real hope of structure and true moral guidance—read father and mother of faith and grace—have left them adrift in the sea of life without a prayer as to where they are going or what to expect[110]. Fathers, if this happens to your children then you will have left them without structure or discipline!

This does not have too happen, as some of your adult friends might try to tell you. Stop whatever you are doing in life that is taking you away from your children! Start now to structure your life to include them. Start the family meetings, wipe the egg off your face, eat humble pie and make a new commitment to God, your wife and children. You might be a little late, but it's not as bad as it's going to be if you do nothing. You will be blessed more than you deserve, trust in God and take action!

**Situation awareness:**

Understanding the—lay of the land—is critical to any mission and life is no exception. In navigation of any type—whether in the air or on the sea—requires constant up-dating on our surroundings and what is coming over the horizon. The proper term for this is SA or situational awareness. Sloppy situation awareness has been the root cause of disaster for more than one trip. Life, marriage and families are no less susceptible than are other forms of navigation. Learn to be aware of your surroundings—situational awareness is critical for the success of love and marriage.

Imagine, if you can, a city that is laid out without any structure or discipline. There are no streets; you just go wherever there is room for your car or truck, across someone's lawn, or garden, wherever you can get through. No streets of course means no intersections, and no intersections means no traffic lights. No traffic lights or streets mean no policemen or traffic monitoring of any kind. What chaos, what a disaster! We would scream for structure and discipline; we could not live or function in such a disordered environment.

This scenario of chaos and destruction I have just painted is what a child experiences when we as fathers fail to provide the proper discipline and family structure needed to assure successful transition from childhood to adulthood. Is it any wonder our cities have become a spawning ground for gangs and violence? All we get when we have no structure, rules, or discipline is destruction and chaos!

**"For three things the earth is perturbed, yes, for four it cannot bear up:**

> "For a servant when he reigns, a fool when he is filled with food, a hateful woman when she is married, and a maidservant who succeeds her mistress." Proverbs 30:23.

**Corporal punishment:**

Spanking a child as a valid option is something we need to consider for a moment. Oh, wow, what a mean and dirty idea! Some of you might think it is absolutely wrong for a child to ever feel the pain and embarrassment of physical punishment—maybe so maybe no. Let's think about it and see if it has an appropriate place or not. Is there an uncommon common sense approach to physical discipline which makes for a compelling argument in its favor, or not? If you conclude that there is not, then proceed with your best alternative. Before we

---

[110] "And you, fathers, do not provoke your children to wrath, but bring them up in the training and admonition of the Lord." Ephesians 6:4.

decide let's examine a father's source for evidence that supports or disavows such action.

"He who spares his rod hates his son, but he who loves him disciplines him promptly." Proverbs 13:-24.

First consider the kind of world in which we are teaching this child to grow up in and to function in. Do we see a world without rules, one which allows you do what you please, when you please? I'm sure you agree, we do have a world full of rules, and it can be pretty serious if you continue to break them. What recourse does our world take when one continues to break the rules? Does the world we live in, and in which our children will have to function, have a priority of discipline, or is the same discipline applied to everything and everyone? Again, we must agree that there is a priority of discipline and it does vary depending on the seriousness and nature of the rules broken.

Does the world in which our children must live ever inflict pain—in the process of discipline—both emotional and even physical pain? Once again we will have to agree it does.

So, given the fact that our world is a world of rules and discipline which, when broken, can and does affect disciplinary action, both emotionally and physically painful, what choices do we have regarding our children's development? It seems pretty clear we have but two basic approaches.

We can teach our children that rules are really meant to be broken, and they are no big deal. We can adopt an informal approach, each member doing his or her own thing, with little or no structure or discipline. However, if we choose this first option we must also bear the responsibility for the consequences.

On the other hand, we can adopt a serious attitude toward structure and discipline and teach our children the importance of rules and how if ignored continually, with no effort to respect them, there can be serious consequences. These consequences can, and when necessary should, include embarrassment and physical pain. Believe it or not, physical discipline when properly executed reinforces your love and concern for a child, whether male or female.

When we consider these two options and the realities of the world for which we are preparing our children, spanking a consistently disobedient child becomes a logical and rational response.

However, just grabbing a child by the arm and starting to flail away with a spanking or other form of physical punishment is not what I am talking about. This is no more effective than simply yelling, screaming or insulting your child to achieve some form of emotional coercion. Many who, say they are against any form of physical punishment, end up venting their frustrations over the child's disobedience in tactics that are purely emotional coercion. This is also unacceptable as an effective disciplining method.

Consequently, the trick is to hold our cool. Given the creative ways and manners in which a child can be disobedient, I can personally testify it is not always an easy thing to do.[111] But, none-the-less, it is what we as fathers must endeavor to do and to teach our wives to do also. Many mothers scream and threaten their children all day long, telling them such things as: "Just you wait until your Daddy gets home; I'm going to tell him what a little monster you've been, and you're really going to get it when he comes home." Wow, what a bummer! A man works hard all day long for his family and comes home to find out he is the

---

[111] "He who mistreats his father and chases away his mother is a son who causes shame and brings reproach." Proverbs 19:26.

elected "hatchet man" for the ineffective disciplinary methods of his wife. Do you see a problem here? Our wives should be disciplining based on the instructions and guidelines we have given them. Otherwise they are left with their own methods in an effort to make up for our unwillingness to give them proper instructions and training.[112]

**The importance of consistency:**

What I am talking about is taking five minutes to address a child who is being extremely unruly or continually breaking rules, set him down and bring this to his attention. If you have properly set forth your expectations for your children concerning certain situations, functional correctness, etc., then this will open the way for physical punishment. The child should already know the rules. Children are not stupid; they know when they break the rules, especially if it has been more than once or twice. After they have admitted breaking the rule and you have reminded them of the price—a spanking—then the spanking is meaningful and gives them something to think about next time they are tempted to break the rule.[113] Just remember to be consistent. Inconsistency on your part is the worst thing in such a situation. Your inconsistency only teaches the child that sometimes it is all right to disobey, and sometimes it is not. The confusion leads to rebellion and disrespect for discipline in general and for you in particular. Whereas, when you are consistent the child learns very quickly to honor your rules and to respect your word as law. You will soon find subsequent spankings are less and less necessary. You speak out of love and conviction and they learn to obey out of love and respect. Their convictions and principles will mature as they grow older and develop understanding.[114]

Such spanking should not be overly zestful or pursued to a point of real physical harm. What is wanted, in these situations, is to make it uncomfortable enough for the child so they will consider this rule is important and should be understood and obeyed. Certainly, as the head of the family and the one who is setting the structure and discipline for the family, you must indicate just how serious you are about the rules. Basically what you accomplish with this is to establish your authority. Some children require more physical discipline to do this than others. Our children ranged from simple verbal instructions to repeated physical spanking to accomplish the same thing. A sensitive father of faith and grace will always start with a light touch but—never give an inch—until the objective is accomplished.

After such an encounter has taken place, the bonds of love and tenderness need to be reinforced. Holding the child close and reassuring him or her of your love and tenderness lets him or her distinguish between discipline and your simply getting mad. Such attention to detail may appear at first to take a lot of time and to be very frustrating. The truth is quite the opposite. Such attention and time taken to discipline a child greatly reduces the frequency and severity of disobedience. The objective of good quality disciplining is to create a desire on the part of the child to respect your rules and to be obedient, not to give you opportunity to exercise your mouth or your right arm. Most parents I have witnessed disciplining their child do

112 "A wise son makes a glad father, but a foolish son is the grief of his mother." Proverbs 10:1.

113 "Wisdom is found on the lips of him who has understanding, but a rod is for the back of him who is devoid of understanding." Proverbs 10:13.

114 "My son, if your heart is wise, my heart will rejoice--indeed, I myself; yes, my inmost being will rejoice when your lips speak right things. Do not let your heart envy sinners, but be zealous for the fear of the LORD all the day; for surely there is a hereafter, and your hope will not be cut off. Hear, my son, and be wise; and guide your heart in the way." Proverbs 23:15-19

so with such inconsistency or half-baked attempts, it is no wonder they are constantly nagging at the child to be obedient. The poor child hasn't the foggiest idea what the parent is trying to do. Perhaps with a little effort you can remember when you were confused and disoriented concerning what your parents were really trying to get you to do. If we fathers are not very, very careful and deliberate in our planning and execution of discipline, we will end up with intermittent and very disappointing results.

**Discipline examples:**

Discipline as a learning process is a real father of faith and grace's basic tool for family leadership. Now, let's use the bathroom as a training example. Everyone who has ever lived in the same house with any female knows that she can get lost in a bathroom and spend hours doing almost nothing. Daughters follow quickly in their mothers' footsteps and soon display this feminine tendency. Be courageous! This is just another opportunity for daddy to teach and discipline a daughter in good family structure.

"This is just great! How do I go about doing that?" Well—truth to tell—you probably won't ever change your wife and daughters feminine tendencies for taking too much time in the bathroom. So, if you're still working on that one, I suggest you either learn to be more patient or, if you can afford it, build another bathroom. I'll bet you thought I had an answer for that one, ha!

However, when we understand discipline as basically a learning process, we should think first of a teaching method. We men have a bad habit of wanting to discipline with the tone of our voices. It's called the "decibel method." If we are pleased, we speak softly; if we are mad or upset about something, we speak in a loud voice or even yell. The family learns if we are serious or not by the tone and pitch of our voices. Although this may result in certain desired immediate behavioral responses, it is not the best or easiest way to teach or discipline.

Strange as it might seem a little meeting, class room style or informal—even better in a semicircle like the method I use—is one of the most effective methods of delivering your message. Also, every husband needs to understand how to implement this same "meeting" environment in communicating with his wife.

We develop bad habits in discipline from the very beginning of our lives. We see how our parents do it, and most don't discipline very well, so we are left with little to draw on when it comes our turn. We follow such examples as yelling, striking out without warning, and getting mad when it isn't necessary. Some adults have even learned how to torture their children. This happens from both watching their parents discipline their brothers and sisters and from receiving such discipline themselves. These approaches seldom, if ever, teach anything desirable.

When I say torture I do mean bodily and psychological harm in some cases. Torturing children can simply be making them stand for long periods of time in a corner, or hiding them in a closet or making them do physical work until they cannot even stand up any longer. All of these methods at discipline are a form of torture.

You can lose your standing as a Hero and Knight in Shining Am1or if you don't know how to discipline well. On the other hand, when correct and consistent discipline is applied to a family structure, the Hero and Knight in shining armor image is strengthened and reinforced. When discipline is correctly applied, family members are encouraged and know they can relax and be protected at home from outsiders, from each other and most importantly—from themselves.

The discipline process is more than just rules and physical actions. Discipline is established more by an atmosphere of respect and recognition of who is in control. Remember, God has given you the delegated authority as head of the home, but you must earn the respect and recognition of that authority. Work on developing communication methods and habits with your wife that will cultivate her respect and increase your own sense of well being. (We are talking about using words of wisdom; not physical or mental coercion.) This is the atmosphere into which you will want to bring your new-born children.

Harsh words between you and your wife and a sense of scant control on your part will create an atmosphere of stress and tension for all children who witness it and especially for daddy's little girl! Our daughters are the most sensitive to these flare-ups.

Body language is important. Throwing things or hitting out with arms flailing, even in fun, can instill fear into the heart of a child, and whereas hugging, kissing, patting and laughing bring a sense of comfort, joy and happiness. A happy home is a home where discipline is more effective. Conversely, a properly disciplined home is a happy home.

Body language such as hugging can be so important as to make the difference between success and failure. We need to hug our wives more and do so in front of our children. Our children need to see our affection for each other and know that our romance is extremely important to us! Thus, when we hug our children they will know that it is also very important. There has always been a lot of hugging and kissing in both our families, but I never thought of hugging as a means of disciplining until an experience I happened to have with my daughter, Melissa.

**The secret and power of hugging:**

Being male means that the possibility of appearing to be overly intense while communicating with others—especially when we are trying to make a point—is going to be very close to the surface and could do more damage than we think. Personally, I have a very intense nature—genetically based—my own father could scare me just by voicing a highly held opinion on something as benign as the weather. I could scare my children and get a negative reaction from my wife just declaring how much I cared about an issue. My wife was the first to get me to recognize this miscommunication and in our own personal talks she was able to address this and to assist me—over time—to counter this natural tendency of mine. My personal technique is to self consciously speak softer, slower and best of all to do most of my serious communication in the family meeting. Just another example of how important the family meeting is for good and effective communication.

Melissa is my third biological daughter, she was born on May 20, 1970, and from the very first time my wife held her in her arms to nurse her we knew that we had a real challenge on our hands. Melissa displayed from birth one of the most impatient and intense spirits I have ever witnessed in a child.

When she was hungry she would get very demanding and wanted the milk to come into her mouth immediately. It was very frustrating for all of us and for my wife in particular. I can vividly remember Marilyn having an extra small bottle of milk ready to give Melissa at feeding time, while she massaged her breast to get the milk to flow. If she failed and the little "primer" bottle wasn't ready in time, Melissa would suck on her breast for about a minute or less. and then start getting upset and showing her displeasure, and within seconds we had a screaming, inconsolable child on our hands. Then the milk would come in—Marilyn would be spraying milk everywhere—at the same time trying to get Melissa to take the nipple into her mouth, all to no avail. When things get like that you don't know whether to laugh or cry. We traveled a lot with our work in Mexico in those days, and it used to be a riot to experience feeding time in the car as we drove down the road. The other children would look on in dismay, as though to say, "What is wrong with that kid?"

Well, as you might imagine, this intensity of spirit and short-fused attitude didn't limit itself to breast feeding. As Melissa grew older she matured very rapidly, much faster than our other children. Her demeanor and determination to do things right showed a maturity far beyond her years. Some of you will recognize these as characteristics common among "middle" children. It is true, she is a classic middle child—much more so than any child I have probably ever seen or read about.

At the slightest imperfection in anything you did for her or in what she expected of herself, she would begin to sob, these sobs would grow into tears, and the tears would turn into a full- blown crying scream. I'm talking eighteen months old here. As her father, I was beside myself as to what to do. Talking to her before, during or after got me nowhere. I even tried spanking her through her diaper and on her legs, all to no avail. So, ultimately we would hold her and do our best to calm her down.

Then one evening, when she was about two years old, she was going into one of her sessions over something that had happened between her and one of the other children. She was building up steam fast and I just happened to be coming into the living room where she was standing in the middle of the room letting it all out. As if from nowhere I got the idea to grab her into my arms and roll on the floor with her. I hugged her close, not in a hurting way, just snuggling her close, and I rolled back and forth with her on the floor, patting her on the back and saying all the while, "Melissa, Melissa, my Melissa, " laughing as I said it. To my great astonishment she stopped crying in a matter of seconds and starting laughing; she patted my back in time with me and said, "Daddy, Daddy, my Daddy," laughing all the while.

In the magic of the moment, a new door was opened in our life! Together we had discovered a new dimension to the art of hugging. From that day forward Melissa grew rapidly in her ability to overcome her intense spirit and impatient attitude. Every time she had a bout with her impatient and intense spirit I would hug her and roll on the floor with her. When she grew old enough she would come to me and say, "Daddy, hug me! I need your hugs right now." Shortly after she married in May of 1988, her husband thanked me for all the hugs I had given to Melissa. This experience also helped me to understand how important it was for all of my family to get regular hugs from Daddy.[115] Keep alert and expect to get your own creative new dimensions for discipline.

**Discipline priorities:**

The following is a list of discipline priorities. Adopting a plan along these lines will greatly reduce stress and disorder in the home.

1. Establish an atmosphere of respect and control with openness and joy—lots of hugging and kissing.

2. Hold regular family meetings to discuss the do's and don'ts of family functions, activities and duties as a whole, and for each member. Here is where you begin to introduce the concept of schedules and the importance of being consistent. This atmosphere eliminates the need to get mad or speak unkindly in order to get your point across. It also establishes you in the role of leader and teacher of the family.

---

[115] "Rescue me and deliver me from the hand of foreigners, whose mouth speaks lying words, and whose right hand is a right hand of falsehood—that our sons may be as plants grown up in their youth; that our daughters may be as pillars, sculptured in palace style;" Psalms 144:12.

3. In this teaching atmosphere you have an opportunity to express your deeper thoughts, concerns and experiences about life and love. You are able to teach the basics of moral fiber, values and principles. You can ask and answer questions to make sure they understand Mother can also have her meetings, especially when you are not present. However, father should always be given the respect as the main teacher, counselor and disciplinarian for the family.

4. Have several questions in mind that will help the children get into the theme of what you want to discuss. Be as creative as possible. Learning is easier when it is fun.

5. Open and close each meeting with a short prayer honoring God's place in your life and the life of your family.

A word of caution: Do not attempt to cover too many details in one meeting. Keep the meetings short, 30-45 min. an hour at most, interesting and to the point. Some fathers will have a tendency to be a bit preachy when they get up on their soap boxes.

Your next order of priority is to display the agreed-upon rules and structure of the family where everyone can see them. The front of the refrigerator, inside the bathroom door, or perhaps on the inside of each bedroom door all seem to work. Use your imagination in displaying the rules.

This same list should include the punishment for not obeying the rules. This will take a variety of forms and approaches. First the child must admit that he did indeed break the rule. Once this is understood you can begin with such things as writing the rule several times to make sure it is remembered and understood. This develops the consistency you need to emphasize from time to time in your meetings. Then move up in intensity by taking privileges away or reassigning them to others who are doing a better job. A little friendly competition can do wonders. Finally, if all other means of teaching a given child have not gotten any measurable improvement, and the child continues to break the rule, then physical discipline is in order. Sometimes a child will stare you right in the eye and do exactly what they have just been told they cannot do—this requires immediate action to apply physical discipline. This is the child's way of saying: "I'm really the boss here!"

**What results can we expect?**

After saying all of this relative to structure and good consistent discipline, is it possible for parents to do a great job of teaching and disciplining, and in spite of their—honest and best efforts, love and concern—live to see their child fail miserably in his/her personal efforts at living his/her life? Painful as it may be, parents can and sometimes do witness everything from failed marriages and small scrapes with the law to death row. In such cases there is little a parent can do. Each child eventually becomes an adult and must establish his or her own personal set of responses to their Creator, moral values and to life's requirements and responsibilities. When children refuse to accept parental structure and guidance they will most assuredly end up with a lot of problems. Children like adults, will reap what they sow!

However, a family who has the blessing of God's gift of a real father of faith and grace, willing to be the moral role model for them and establish consistent, loving discipline, will rarely have such an experience. We must put our faith in God's promise, that we will be victorious in spite of the dangers:

"Train up a child in the way he should go, and when he is old he will not depart from it." Proverbs 22:6.

No one can guarantee you a perfect solution to this problem. Nonetheless, I do know from experience that these methods of establishing yourself as a real father of faith and grace in the family, and these approaches to teaching respect and discipline to your children will have enormous positive effects.

Time and space in this book do not allow for complete coverage of the different ramifications and in-depth perspectives on the subject of discipline. For further study in this area I suggest you read some good books which focus entirely on discipline. "Dare to Discipline" by Dr. Dobson is a good example.

**Holding steady on course:**

Jesus gives us many examples of His power to multiply recourses for His ministry through His many powerful miracles:

1. Feeding the multitudes: Mathew 14:15-21[116]
2. Converting the water to wine: John 2:1-10[117]
3. The giving of Living Water, never to thirst again: John 4:10-14[118]

Our supply and our strength are in Him and we must not let our fallen state of the flesh, or our circumstances of life, to determine the depth or the scope of our commitment and vision!

**Being drawn to Christ by our Heavenly Father:**

Every promise or hope of success through the application of all that has been said or discovered in Book I on Love and Marriage—is invalid and mere

---

116 "When it was evening, His disciples came to Him, saying, "This is a deserted place, and the hour is already late. Send the multitudes away, that they may go into the villages and buy themselves food."

"But Jesus said to them, 'They do not need to go away. You give them something to eat.'

"And they said to Him, 'We have here only five loaves and two fish.'

"He said, 'Bring them here to Me.' Then He commanded the multitudes to sit down on the grass. And He took the five loaves and the two fish, and looking up to heaven, He blessed and broke and gave the loaves to the disciples; and the disciples gave to the multitudes. So they all ate and were filled, and they took up twelve baskets full of the fragments that remained. Now those who had eaten were about five thousand men, besides women and children." Matt. 14:15-21.

117 "On the third day there was a wedding in Cana of Galilee, and the mother of Jesus was there. Now both Jesus and His disciples were invited to the wedding. And when they ran out of wine, the mother of Jesus said to Him, "They have no wine."

'Jesus said to her, "Woman, what does your concern have to do with Me? My hour has not yet come.'

"His mother said to the servants, 'Whatever He says to you, do it.'

"Now there were set there six waterpots of stone, according to the manner of purification of the Jews, containing twenty or thirty gallons apiece. Jesus said to them, "Fill the waterpots with water." And they filled them up to the brim. And He said to them, 'Draw some out now, and take it to the master of the feast.' And they took it. When the master of the feast had tasted the water that was made wine, and did not know where it came from (but the servants who had drawn the water knew), the master of the feast called the bridegroom. And he said to him, 'Every man at the beginning sets out the good wine, and when the guests have well drunk, then the inferior. You have kept the good wine until now!'" John 2:1-10.

118 "Jesus answered and said to her, 'If you knew the gift of God, and who it is who says to you, Give Me a drink, you would have asked Him, and He would have given you living water.'

"The woman said to Him, 'Sir, You have nothing to draw with, and the well is deep. Where then do You get that living water? 12Are You greater than our father Jacob, who gave us the well, and drank from it himself, as well as his sons and his livestock?'

"Jesus answered and said to her, 'Whoever drinks of this water will thirst again, 14but whoever drinks of the water that I shall give him will never thirst. But the water that I shall give him will become in him a fountain of water springing up into everlasting life.'" John 4:10-14.

wishful thinking—if men and women seek such success through their own strength without God! Men and women are created to have a minimum inner sense about their need for God but only those who are called by the Father can believe and enter into the joys of His adopted family.

A young girl, when exposed to the possibility of a personal relationship with God through prayer and an awakened awareness of His presence, will respond much more quickly than will a young boy of similar age. Young boys are not spiritually insensitive. Boys simply attain strong sensitivity to their spiritual needs at a later age.

As an adolescent young boy or girl, did you respond positively to your inner sense of your own spiritual needs, or did you listen to the voice of temptation and accept the notion of God as dead and make up your own rules, that is, draw your own Map of life's Right and Wrong?

I am writing this book especially for men who have already recognized and acted on God's gift of faith in them. However, if you are reading this and you have not yet done so—then I urge you to begin by taking these first steps toward discovering your gift of faith. Many men and women resist the move of the Spirit. If you are one of those, and you have not yet dealt with your own spiritual needs honestly, openly, and with a sincere heart, you need to deal with this important area. I suggest you begin by, first of all, secluding yourself and offering a short and simple prayer. Something like:

> "Heavenly Father, I have an inner sense that you do exist, I need to know it from you. I have learned through what I have read that you alone can draw me to your Son, Jesus Christ. Forgive me for my rebellious attitudes of the past, as I have been wrong about you and your part in my life and the life of my family. Help me to understand and to know your reality and your personal involvement with your creation of men and women. Please open my heart and draw me to you that I too may receive your gift of faith and be one of your adopted children through Christ my only hope of salvation!"

This is not a prayer of confession of faith in Christ, but rather an appeal to God the Father to consider your sinful state—to draw you to Christ your Savior through His gift of faith. God's revealed Law-Word is clear, unless you be drawn to Christ by the Father you cannot believe. Some will tell you that all you have to do is "raise your hand," don't believe it! Seek the Father. He and only He is faithful to both know your heart and to give you the gift of life eternal through faith! Unfortunately, our churches are filled with individuals who raised their hands but whom the Father has never drawn. Much needs to be said and done about this but for now—seek the Father. He is faithful.

**The sincere words of a man or woman must be followed up with action:**

Follow your prayer up by including regular church attendance in your family's activities. Visit several churches and be sensitive to getting the answer to your prayer. You will get answers. You will get insight as to where you should go to church and what you should do. Only consider churches offering at least three spiritual growth basics:

1. One that consistently teaches salvation by faith only in Jesus Christ and that as a gift and act of God: Read: John 1:12-14; Eph. 2:8-10; and II Cor. 2:14-16

2. One that teaches personal responsibility for one's actions and for repentance and submission to the sovereign will of God for one's life. Read: Acts 20:22-24; Gal. 2:17-21; and Mk. 5:36, 10:30

3. One that teaches strong support for parents as the primary family leaders, and for fathers as the heads of the family leadership. Read: I Pet. 3:7; Col. 3:18-21; I Tim. 3:4-5; and Eph. 6:1-4

You cannot be a husband/father or wife/mother of faith and grace without God so—just do it—and expect Him to guide you. I have focused on this reality from several different perspectives. At the risk of over emphasizing; I continue to remind us all of our dependence upon our Heavenly Father for the source of our faith, grace, wisdom, understanding—the motivation and strength to express our love for our spouses and for our babies—our little girls and our little boys—in actions that reflect His uncommon common sense.

As I have said before: A father and mother of faith and grace is an oxymoron if there is no personal reality of experience in walking in the Way. No man can be a spiritual leader in his own family or a second in command spiritual woman if they don't know God and His revealed Law-Word, or don't have any experience of trusting in Him to be a part of their own daily life. Our descriptive term—father and mother of faith and grace—is not a physical badge of identification—not a badge of honor. This is a term that describes not the physical man and woman—but the inner man or woman—a man or woman who trusts in the revealed truth of fatherhood and motherhood in God's word. A man and woman who takes their marching orders from the—Father of fathers—from the source of all truth. Praises be to His name and to His Christ our Savior!

# Book II

# DADDY'S LITTLE GIRL

## Chapter One

## The Early Challenges

**A glimpse into the past:**

It's 6:00 AM and the sun is just coming up from a point on the horizon, about 60 miles East of El Paso, Texas. The early morning light streams over the vast desert, bounds the Rio Grand river and up the eastern slopes of the Juarez Mountains, on the Northern border of Mexico—Marilyn along with our four foster teenage daughters, was busy setting the breakfast table as I came into the kitchen and dining room area. It was the start of another busy day managing the daily needs of over 150 homeless and abandoned young boys and girls, overseeing new construction and planning more trips to visit churches and individuals who formed the base of our financial support.

Breakfast is over and I step out into the crisp winter morning air of the mountains. Out of habit—I glance over the foot hills that flow down toward the Rio Grande river and the modern sky-line of El Paso' financial district in the valley beyond. As always I am amazed at the stark contrasts between the two areas. The one shines—almost throne like—as the tall buildings with glass and steel frameworks sparkle in the morning sunlight, while the lower levels of the city of Juarez are covered with a low lying pale of thin dust reflected in the same morning light, rising from the many unpaved streets.

It's another day in the thousands of days spent on this mountain struggling with the problems and needs of the many young lives that had come to be under our care and direction. These were the times and the source of our experiences that God used to bridge the gap between our young years—Marilyn was 24 and I was 28—and the enormous challenges we faced on a daily basis.

**The learning curve:**

Early challenges at a young age can make a big difference in the way one views a given problem. In the case of father/daughter relationships I was only twenty-five years old when I was faced with the responsibility of assuming the role of father and family leader, for dozens of young orphaned girls between the ages of six and thirteen.

When it comes to the mistakes fathers normally make when they are faced with the challenge of rearing a daughter, I have probably made most of them. One of the greatest advantages I have had as a father of daughters is that I have had so many and I started so early. By the grace of God I was given the opportunity to learn from my mistakes and then search for the real answers which work, God's answers. With this in mind, it is my most sincere hope that what you learn by reading this section on *Daddy's Little Girl* will allow you to be successful with your very first and perhaps your only daughter.

When Marilyn and I went to Mexico in June of 1961, I was 24 and she was 20, our first child, Jennifer Lynne, was only thirteen months old. She was just at the age when she was ready to start talking. As it turned out, some of her very first words were Spanish words, and although we were unaware of it at the time, her first language became Spanish.

In the course of developments in our life in Mexico, we were privileged to found a children's home in the border city of Juarez, Chih., Mexico. The children's home is "Hogar de Ninos Emmanuel," located in the foothills of the Juarez Mountains, Colonia Lopez Mateos, about five miles southwest of the center of town. God has richly blessed this ministry and it continues to thrive to this day.

For the next twelve years we worked at building this children's home along with its accompanying school, "Escuela Particular, Vicente Riva Palacio." In all, hundreds of children were reared and cared for in this children's home. In 1974 the on-going leadership of the home was turned over to our Assistant Director, Josue Lopez. Josue and I had worked together in this work for eleven of the twelve years that I was in charge. Josue is still in charge today, and is now married to one of the girls who came to the home, Soledad Gutierrez, who was orphaned of her father, and whose mother was unable to work and take care of her. She was one of the girls in the breakfast scene above.

There were many young girls for whom I was responsible and served as their father. Although I was too young and too inexperienced to be the father of so many young girls, I was God's choice for them and I was committed to be the best father for them that I could be. Their biological fathers—had all either died or had abandoned them—mostly the latter. There were nine girls that were especially close to me and my wife: Soledad (Josue's future wife) and Celia Gutierrez, (sisters), Teresa Carreon, and Lucita Holguin (first cousins), Dina and Ruth Lincon (sisters), Maria de Jesus Molina, Ramona Gonzalez and Esperanza Garcia. I was able to be of more help to these young girls than to the others. These girls were older, eleven to thirteen years of age when they first came to the children's home. This made it necessary for me to take more immediate action in their lives, as opposed to the others. The four oldest of this group moved in to live with us in our new adobe house that we had just finished, in our fourth year, because it was increasingly difficult for us to properly supervise and protect these more mature young ladies in the environs of the larger dormitory style main building.

These four young girls were in no more need of close supervision and family structure (especially the need for a father figure) than the younger girls, but we could only stretch so far. However because of their advanced feminine development they did require more structure and personal coaching for matters of moral values and their future possibilities for marriage—all were between the age of twelve and thirteen. We were a big family, everyday was a new day of discovery and we were constantly challenged to rise to the occasion to give them everything they needed.

Most of the children reared in the twelve years we were directly in charge have been able to establish stable families with long term success. Those with whom we had the most day to day contact were older and more challenging. Yet, five of the nine girls we considered our foster children learned enough to marry successfully and establish stable long term families. These five continue to this day, with strong families and the benefits of a committed love relationship. The other four were not so fortunate; they suffered early divorces and later remarried. However, the second time around has been more successful for them than was the first. Yet, they have suffered a great deal and were not able to realize their God-given dream of successful, committed first love which would last forever. This is always very painful for any woman, and I know that had I been better prepared and known—at the time, all that I know now—it is possible that they would not have made the same mistakes. However, my second biggest challenge with them was their advanced age—12-13 years old—when they first came to the children's home. I learned that starting from birth has enormous advantages.

This early experience came about purely by circumstance. It was not something I had taken time to plan, as one would do with his own courtship, marriage, and subsequent family. It was more like an explosion. One day I had only my little girl Jennifer, and the next I was father for many girls, much older and with more immediate problems. This came to serve both as an advantage and disadvantage to our own daughter, Jennifer.

**The cost to our own family:**

The disadvantage for our first daughter, Jennifer, was that I was so stretched, in my efforts and time commitments with these older "daughters," many times I left Jennifer out of the circle of my activities. Like so many fathers, I had the crazy idea Marilyn, being a woman, would just naturally know what to do for Jennifer. My "adopted" daughters did not have a mother close by whom they could look to, so I felt the need and obligation to take charge. Had I been asked at the time if I thought such involvement on my part with these girls was—normal for a father/daughter relationship—I would have said, "No." For me it was simply a case of first loving them, as daughters, and then trying to make up for all the things they did not know and needed to know. It was creative thinking and action day by day.

Marilyn was very busy during these years, taking care of all of the office and correspondence associated with the financial support of the work, communicating with the hundreds of relationships we had developed along the way. I was left with either taking up the reigns and assuming the responsibility—or watching these girls flounder and fail—with no guidance whatsoever. I chose the former. The irony in this whole experience is illustrated by the fact I still felt that Marilyn, as Jennifer's mother, was the appropriate one of the two of us—to introduce her and any future daughters we might have—into the male world to develop their femininity and understanding of love and marriage. I'm sure that most will agree; this was and is still today our traditional understanding and considered very normal. God had a surprise for me, for in working out His good pleasure in me, He taught me how very wrong I was—how very NOT normal such customs really are!

**Recognizing God's preference for preparing our young daughters:**

One great advantage was that I was able to gain some very valuable experience early in life. I would be able to draw on this experience later, when I began to realize Marilyn, as a woman, was not equipped to handle the aspects of love and romantic development of our daughter Jennifer. It is important that you understand what I mean when I say Marilyn was not equipped to handle this aspect of our daughter's development. I am not—as some might think—saying my wife was in any way neglectful or "unfit" as a mother. On the contrary, she is endowed with tremendous mother instincts. What I have discovered is women—God's created female human beings—are not naturally equipped psychologically, emotionally or spiritually to best fulfill the role of personal guide in matters of love and marriage for daughters. Much to my surprise, and most likely for you as well, I discovered that it is we fathers who are best suited for this role. The strong role for mothers comes in the form of supporting the father in his challenge to meet the early preteen and teen needs of his little girl. Later, after marriage and when grand children come along, we fathers take a decidedly—second role position compared to mothers—the mission of fathers is to get our little girls developed and prepared for that big and important future event!

The fact that you are reading this book indicates that you have some interest or curiosity about this subject and perhaps, even no small concern, for the horrific suffering and subsequent results we see in millions of our young women today. We are faced with times and a culture that demands more compete understanding of these our—most basic and pivotal—family and cultural challenges. The very foundations upon which marriage is built are under open attack by God's enemies in every form imaginable. We will either win this war against the complete God-given development of our daughters—the very future mothers who will rock the cradles of tomorrows leaders—or we will turn it over to others; Planned Parenthood, the left liberal media with their political minions, secular humanistic academia, homosexuals of all types, MTV, Hollywood, our Public schools and of course, the always available "street smarts," of girl friends and boy friends!

I can hear you now—"Yes, I agree we are in the midst of a great moral crisis—the all out war against love and marriage and the family—but is the key to overcoming this enormous problem more in the hands of fathers, would it not be more correct to say it is fundamentally in the hands of mothers or maybe equally divided between both mothers and fathers?"

The short answer is: "NO." The complete answer and proof of what I am saying will take a little longer. Please, hold those more critical thoughts until you have had the opportunity to understand the overall scope and results of what I am saying. Then you may decide; is what you have learned from our discoveries and successful experience a true break through in family wisdom and understanding or—is it just the vain and egotistical imaginations—of a misguided male chauvinist pig? In today's world of hyper critics there isn't much room for anything in between.

**A changing of the guard:**

It was late. We four adults, Josue & Soledad, Zester & Marilyn, surrounded by five Hatfield children, had been sitting together in a major truck stop, just off of the Patriot Free Way, North of El Paso, Texas, for over three hours. We were saying our good-byes, for how long we did not know, but this was the culmination of three years of preparing Josue Lopez to take over the full management and leadership responsibilities of the mission work we had started and worked in together, for so many years. No one wanted to get up and signify the end of our interlude—the memories of the past and the dreams of the future—and offer that last embrace before departing. The inevitable finally came and we loaded our five children into a car we had been loaned to make our return trip back into the American culture we had left thirteen years previous.

I am a missionary by calling, with a mindset that thinks in pioneer terms and perspectives. As such, I was not interested in a long term career in a stateside pastoral ministry, but I felt that we needed breathing space to reintroduce ourselves into the American society and economy. We had left the U.S. with one daughter just thirteen months old, and had returned with a total of five children (our sixth child, Lorena, would come much later) and virtually no experience in our own culture for over twelve years. We were what I would call culturally handicapped. So, when I was presented the opportunity to serve as an interim pastor for a small church until they could find a permanent pastor, I accepted it as God's providence for our needs. It was a good arrangement for them and for us.

Our oldest child at the time was Jennifer, she was approaching her fourteenth birthday and was demonstrably the most up-set and emotionally impacted by our departure from Mexico and—the culture which she had adopted as her own—with all of her childhood close friends being left behind. Struggling with the problem of Jennifer's personal developmental needs; we became embroiled in a diverse set of problems. For thirteen years she had been so closely associated with the Mexican culture and language; she identified more with the Mexican people her own age than she did with the few Anglos she knew. We discovered just how serious this was when we arrived in the small town of Healdsburg, California, a winegrowing rural community near the Napa Valley. As I had agreed to assume the role as the interim pastor for the small Christian church in Healdsburg, this inadvertently placed us into a community-wide rift taking place in the local public schools between the Anglo American children and the local Mexican American children.

**Paying the price for early ignorance's and mistakes:**

We placed all of our school age children in local schools. The Healdsburg area is one of California's most productive wine producing communities, stretching for miles around and many Mexican Americans are employed in this sprawling wine industry.

Jennifer, as a beautiful, blond, blue eyed young girl who spoke Spanish more fluently than even the best of the Mexican American girls in her class, was voted the leader of the Mexican American girls involved in the dispute. As such she was immediately placed in the forefront of the battle. Naturally, she took the side of the Mexican American girls and—defended their cause—which had become her own. Jennifer was so angered at the insensitivity she perceived in the Anglo American girls that she was embarrassed that her parents were also Anglo Americans. For starters, Jennifer was flabbergasted that none of the Anglo American girls could speak Spanish. That along with the personal complaints of the Mexican American girls was enough to convince Jennifer that all Anglo Americans were unworthy of her love and respect—including us!

It would be hard for anyone who has not suffered such a confusing cross cultural situation, to imagine how difficult it was. Jennifer would come home from school and go to her room, turn on the local Spanish-speaking radio station and not come out until supper time. Then she would find it very difficult to talk to us. It was as if she couldn't accept the fact she was the daughter of Anglo American parents. We were a couple of really confused parents.

Finally, it all came to a head when she failed to come home from school one afternoon. Marilyn called all of our friends and asked if she was with one of their girls of if they had seen or heard anything. No one had seen or heard from her. Later that first night, our next door neighbor lady, a Mexican American lady with a daughter a year older than Jennifer, came over and asked if we had seen her daughter. This put us all to thinking that perhaps the two girls had gone somewhere together. When an under aged young daughter does not come home and you can't locate her in any of the most likely places, things really begin to get tense! Given the circumstances of all that had taken place in the preceding days, we made the decision to not call the police and to wait for her to surface. At that point we felt the police would only traumatize the situation even more.

A few days went by and there was no word from anyone about either of the girls. Marilyn and I agreed that if we didn't hear from her within another day we would go to the police. I personally felt very strong that she had gone home with someone she had met from school and that we would find her soon. Naturally, we were in much prayer through this whole time!

The next day, Marilyn was shopping at the local grocery store we frequented and as she was pulling out of the drive—who did she see but Jennifer—walking down the street with a sack of groceries in her arms. Marilyn did not let her know that she had seen her and she pulled over to the curb to keep from passing. Marilyn watched until she had turned the corner—she was on foot—she couldn't be going far. Marilyn eased the car around the corner and watched until she went up the steps to the porch of a small single story bungalow. Marilyn parked the car and went up and knocked on the door. She knew that it was Jennifer she had seen and that this was where she was staying.

A young Mexican American lady came to the door. Marilyn introduced herself and said in perfect Spanish: "I think my daughter Jennifer is staying here with you, is that correct?" The lady was surprised to hear such good Spanish from an Anglo American, but after catching her breath she responded with: "Yes, Jennifer is staying here with me, come in I'm sure you have been worried."

The next thing we did shocked everyone we knew who were aware of Jennifer's disappearance—especially those at the Christian church I was pastoring. We had asked for prayer from many and when we found her everyone expected us to bring her home and pick up the pieces. The truth is, Jennifer had become so rebellious in her attitude toward us and—especially toward me—that I had lost all of my authority with her. This was what was shocking to us, especially to me, her father. I knew that it would take wisdom and a miracle to regain her trust and have a real father/daughter relationship with her. The only thoughts that I could entertain were how to reestablish her as a daughter and to help her make the breakthrough. My final decision was to send her back to Mexico for emotional and spiritual rehabilitation.

I called Josue Lopez, in Juarez, the brother we had only a few months ago embraced in our tearful departure. I told him of our problem and asked him if he would consider taking Jennifer into his home for awhile—until she had time to sort things out. He said he would, and we sent her back to live in the same surroundings in which she had grown up. We had no idea how long it would take for her to adjust to the events that had taken place in her life. We only knew that she was under a lot or pressure and desperately needed time to think it through.

I had great confidence in Josue; he had assisted me in my efforts to structure a proper home for all of our foster teenage daughters who lived with us from the children's home. His wife, Soledad, had come from that group. Josue had also been one of the men who had accompanied me when I attended several conferences for—fathers of faith and grace offered by Howard Watrous—during those crucial years of change for Marilyn and me. Soledad and Marilyn had also attended the conferences designed for the woman of faith and grace. We knew we were sending Jennifer into a great home with every possibility for God to work a miracle. Our surprise was in just how He worked it out.

**Letting go and trusting in God's wisdom and grace:**

This is the conclusion that I had come to and had done before Marilyn discovered where Jennifer was staying. Our plan was as follows: As soon as we found Jennifer we were going to take her directly to the bus station and put her on the next bus to El Paso. We already had her bags packed and in the trunk of the car. So, when Marilyn found her, she called me and told me she would soon be coming by the house and for me to be ready. A few minutes later Marilyn drove up in front of the house with Jennifer in the back seat. I got in the car and told Jennifer she had two options, she could stay and go to Juvenile Hall or she could go back to Mexico and live with Josue and Soledad. In a flash her eyes lit up and she said: "I want to go back to Mexico." Why was I not surprised? We drove to the bus station and within an hour she was on a bus to El Paso.

You cannot imagine the emotions I was feeling at that moment; I was not feeling very good about my success as a father of faith and grace for Jennifer. I had just put my almost fifteen year old daughter on bus for El Paso to live—for I did not know how long—with a Mexican friend and brother in the Lord, that I trusted with my life—and now with my daughter. What would become of her and how, if ever—

would the Lord return our Jennifer back to us—it all seemed so surreal and strange?

The big break came sooner than we could have imagined. At first Jennifer believed that she was really going to like being away from us, but then, after she got back to Mexico, all of the children who were her friends in the children's home wanted to know where her Mom and Dad were. She tried to tell them how terrible it had been in Healdsburg, and how she was so unhappy with her parents, that she couldn't stand to live with us anymore. She tells me they looked at her as if she were a little crazy.

All her friends in the children's home began to tell her their perspective of her parents, and what we had meant to them, and the fact that she was just confused because of the racial prejudices she had witnessed in the Healdsburg public school. Her closest friends told her that they would trade places with her in a minute. This went on for six months. During this time we were able to talk to Jennifer on the telephone several times, and each time we talked, it was obvious she was dealing with her confusion and making good progress. Finally, she asked to come back home, and said she was ready to take her place back in the family. It was truly a miracle for her mother and me.

**Jennifer's new beginning:**

She came back with an entirely different attitude. She was ready and willing to talk with us and to allow me to resume my role as her father and family leader. We began to grow very close to each other, and today she is the most wonderful daughter that a father could ever hope to have. I feel confident the intervention of the children in the orphanage was the determining factor that gave us back our daughter! She was so young and at such an impressionable age, that had we not had this unexpected input into her life from those wonderful children in the orphanage, who had suffered so much and knew how to reach Jennifer, we would probably have lost her for a long time.

Getting back on course with Jennifer was not so easy—as if we had never—had the problem. Yet, she was so changed and so ready to take on a new approach, that as a father/daughter relationship, things improved immensely. She began to develop friends among the Anglo American community, and to our surprise fell in love with a wonderful Anglo American young man, Paul O'Neill. She had always seemed so totally involved with the Latin American community and I was fully prepared to work with her choice of a future young male friend from that community. The fact is, she never really developed any romantic attractions within the Latin American community.

When I first met Paul O'Neill, I felt she had made a good choice. My first question to her was not in reference to Paul, but, instead, was in reference to his parents. I wanted to know what kind of parents he had. I soon discovered, from Jennifer and from my own personal experience of meeting Paul's parents that he was blessed with a strong family leader, in the person of his father, and enjoyed a close family relationship. Paul evinced a great respect and love for his mother and his younger sister, all of which were the positive kinds of evidence that Paul had the basic tools for becoming a real man of faith and grace.

**Learning to pass family leadership to a son-in-law:**

Paul was my second experience in trying to pass family leadership from the father to the husband-to-be. My first experience had been with my "adopted" daughter, Soledad. Soledad fell in love with Josue, who was the Assistant Director of the children's home before he became the Director. There was a seventeen-year difference in their ages, which presented a much different set of circumstances from what one would normally encounter.

Josue Lopez and I had worked together for several years before this mutual attraction took place. Soledad had been living with Marilyn and me for several years, and was going to school and working part time in the office of the children's home. She is a very dynamic lady, a real leader in her own right. With these and her many other qualities of beauty and charm were more than enough to attract Josue, who was single and very much a Christian gentleman.

Josue asked me one evening if he could have the privilege of courting Soledad. I was very confident in Josue's character and honorable intentions. I told him that if Soledad wanted to date him, I would agree, but she was to be treated as my daughter and I would control her activities. He agreed, and it all went so smoothly, I was really not given much opportunity to learn as many things as I later realized I needed to know.

Paul would be the first to say that I was less than completely sure of myself. We had talks about their relationship and about principles, etc., but I was treading a new path, with no advantage of having examples from others whom I could look to for help. The important thing for the three of us—Jenny, Paul and me—was the fact we each knew there was commitment and real love between the two of them and that my efforts were sincerely made to help them develop to the best of their ability.

It was with great pleasure and joy that her mother and I were able to give Jennifer to Paul. On a beautiful day in July, 1982, we celebrated the wedding of Jennifer Lynne and Paul O'Neill. Paul went on to graduate with a degree in construction from the University of California at Chico, California. Jennifer had completed her AA degree at Santa Rosa Jr. College. Paul and Jennifer are now the proud parents of four children: Ryon, Vanessa, Steven, and Shawn.

**Walking the walk:**

Although many men will brag that they run their families, the truth is, few men today can make decisions on family matters which contradict the opinions of their wives. If they do so, they are most likely to suffer such repercussions they will not do it again—or will give up the reigns in disgust and abdicate their role as family leader—from that moment on. A father of faith and grace has not really tested his ability to lead his family until he makes a decision he feels is right, even though it is not in complete harmony with what his wife thinks or would do. These are the really tough decisions to make. Yet, in the case of father/daughter relationships, the need for making decisions which many times are different from what your wife would do, or think, is going to be very normal.

Those fathers of faith and grace who have the privilege to start early with their daughter will generally have less difficulty with their wife's misgivings. Certainly, any wife and mother of faith and grace who reads this book will most likely be supportive of her husband in this and in all aspects of his position of authority as head of her and the family.

My decision to send Jennifer back to Mexico is a perfect example. It was too painful for Marilyn to even consider such a move, much less to have the courage to do so without my support. After all of the input Marilyn could give and all of the circumstances I could review, plus the conviction that God had given me a peace about what I should do, I made the decision—not an easy one to make—but it was mine to make and by God's grace I did it. God honored His word for the leadership of families and answered our prayers through the orphaned children of Mexico—what a miracle!

Had I not been given the opportunity to function in the role of family leader, without the need to feel everything on which I made a final decision must agree with the way my wife sees it, I would have been incapacitated! I would never have been able to develop our daughters into the wonderful women they are today. This willingness, on the part of Marilyn, to allow me to lead, even when she was not sure I was right, but, out of love and respect for me, as her husband and Knight in shining armor, has made my experience as a father extremely rewarding! I am very proud of my wife for many reasons, but most of all for her courage and wisdom, as a woman of faith and grace, who trusts God's revealed Law-Word to let me lead, as God gives me grace and strength to do it.

In God's revealed truth He reminds us many times that we in and of ourselves, with our old hearts of stone, with our natural abilities and with all of our natural intelligence, are not equipped to handle the tasks of life that are before us everyday. He does, however, promise all who believe in Him and who will trust in His revealed truth, His Law-Word, will be given grace sufficient to overcome. This applies equally to both men and women. In marriage, the great challenge is to balance our natural attractions and affections for each other with our need for supernatural guidance to realize our full potential and our foreordained appropriate—though distinct—roles in Him.

These early challenges and over comings served as God's catalyst for more understanding and more personal involvement with the other daughters who were racing into maturity—demanding my attention: Stephanie, Melissa, Robin and last but not least our adopted daughter, Lorena, five daughters in all, how could I possibly be successful with so many?

# Book II
# DADDY'S LITTLE GIRL

## Chapter Two

## Breaking Old Habits Is Hard

**Effective father/daughter relationships:**

Post modern assumptions about father/daughter relationships make it hard for men to develop into genuinely effective fathers for their daughters. This difficulty is only made worse by present day feminist movements which advocate women's independence from men. Consequently, we men have developed some very bad habits with respect to how we perceive and relate with women in general and our daughters in particular.

You may agree or disagree whether women deserve equal opportunity with men in their vocation and compensation, the fact remains there are many differences between the sexes. These differences are not limited to physical appearance or procreation functions. Each of the sexes has just as distinct a role to play after a child is born as they did in procreating the child in the first place. The equality arguments of the radical left feminists will never change the reality of these differences.

So what are we to do men? Are we just to assume there are no bad habits or attitudes on our part, no walls, no differences, and stick our heads in the sand? Or, would it not make more sense to act wisely and try to understand these problems and differences and to discover—if that's possible—what role they play in either helping or hindering us to develop our daughters into fully prepared and successful young ladies?

**Misinformation and bad habits:**

As I have learned more about the role these bad habits and attitudes play in our problems and differences, several unexpected discoveries have been made.

First of all, if you ask women who are having trouble with their husbands what their relationship with their fathers was like, a great many of them will tell you it was good. This is what they feel you expect them to say. But, if you ask them what their fathers told them about men—really the truth—and how they went about preparing them for marriage as well as for relationships in general with men, in the work place, and on a social plane, the answer is almost always that they didn't. In fact, in my experience of having asked this question dozens of times, I have never had a woman—in such a situation—say her father prepared her for any such relationships! So, the women who don't know the secrets to a good lasting and loving relationship with a man, don't get along very well with their fathers—or at the very least—they don't feel they were really prepared for men and a man's world by their fathers.

However, when one asks these same women if they would have liked their father to groom them and prepare them mentally, emotionally and spiritually for their success as wives, lovers of their husbands and mothers, the answer is unanimous: "Most certainly so!"

Many have also added: "I knew he was supposed to—that's what my heart was telling me—but I didn't know how to tell him or how to ask him. He just made me furious that he would not take me into his confidence!"

Are any of you fathers out there experiencing the fury of a daughter? I'm talking about fathers with daughters who are as young as nine or ten, not to mention those who are older. The frustration and "fury" can be evinced very early and only worsens with time. By the time the personal discovery dating age arrives—father is out to lunch—he is now enemy number one.

**Ignorance among women abounds:**

I'm not surprised that so many women have a feeling of emptiness about their relationship with their fathers. It is not that they don't have a sense of love for them. They do! Their problem is that most of them never really know their fathers more in depth than just to be "Daddy's little girl." Ask yourself the question. If young daughters never really get to know their father beyond the superficial minimum of "Daddy's little girl," how are they ever going to learn about men in general? Is it not logical they are left with only alternative sources: mothers, girl friends, sisters and other men through the school of experience?

Certainly they can read about men in many books that taut the pabulum of our Christian cultures common misconceptions—albeit if they don't read this book—I don't know where they will learn the truth about men and their proper role; for which God has uniquely prepared them. Not to mention the grave dangers they face because of this ignorance! The fortunate, are those still at home who have the hope of learning—through the leadership of a father of faith and grace, schooled in God's Law-Word and the applications put forth in this book. Barring that—their best option is to read this book—teach themselves all they can, and trust God to make up the difference. Lacking that, they will learn only some cultural or ethnic bias or superficial knowledge about what men are supposed to admire in a woman: looks, sexuality, and all the latest sex "techniques" from magazines such as Cosmopolitan, Shape, Self, or Playgirl. However—relationally—person to person, with their father—as things stand today—they are going to learn very little. Unfortunately these fathers, even the well intentioned, more often than not, exacerbate the situation by appearing to be relevant but always lacking the zing to pull it off because of their own ignorance of the truth. Such daughters will definitely be limited in their development—especially in their very young formative years—to mother and their little friends at school. Oh yes!—and we mustn't forget those wonderful sex education classes—soon to be introduced even in grades as low as kindergarten! Now get real! Father, please ask yourself this question: "To whom does my daughter have access who knows men, a real live man like me, better than I know myself?"

**Fathers are God's primary element for teaching their daughter the truth:**

Or better still, let me put it like this: Let's say you are building a precision machine. You have master plans and you want to build several of these machines. Do you make each part from the master jig or do you copy each succeeding part from the last part? Every man who knows anything at all about precision building of anything mechanical knows you must always use a master jig and or a computer generated digital master, or the parts will be progressively worse when copied one from the other in succession.

I would like to propose another question: If this is true and you would not trust anything less than a master control for building precision parts, why then would you trust anything other than, the original master control—you her father—for the development of your daughter? Is not your daughter a creation of marvelous precision, as much or more than the most complicated of machines? Furthermore, is she not more valuable than any machine? If the answer to these questions is "Yes," then we have no choice. We must get personally involved with the development of our daughters.

I can hear it now, "I'm personally involved. I personally told my wife to tell my daughter what she needed to know about being careful with boys and not to let her get into trouble." I highly commend any man who reads this book and I know that if you or any man you know has ever said such a thing, you also know that it is a cheap cop-out—I know—because I did it too.

Let's back up a moment. What have we actually been told or what has been indicated to us as men that we should do regarding our daughter's development as young ladies? What did your mother tell you? What did your father tell you? What did you learn in school? Which class did you take in school that would prepare you for being a real father to your daughter? If you are anything like me, you are in trouble. No one told me anything, except that I was to consider myself the head of the family, whatever that was supposed to mean. I know what that means now—I was clueless when I got married.

That's just terrific! Here we are on our wedding day, at the very moment of taking over the role of husband and probably soon to be father, with a 50% chance of having a daughter, and we are supposed to be the "head" of this family, fully responsible for its success, but with little or no instructions on how to do it.

Guess what? If you haven't already figured it out—you were supposed to be watching your father and mother and taking notes on how to do it. For only the rare few, it was probably a good example, but for most it was probably not a good example. So, if those from whom you were supposed to take notes didn't have it figured it out, and were afraid or unwilling to admit it, you are obviously left in the dark! The truth is that when parents know the truth, walk in the truth and enjoy the blessings of the truth, their sons and daughters won't have to learn by just watching, they will be taught! When we are too close-minded or refuse to seek help from somewhere, I would say that our chance of making a real father of faith and grace for our daughter is less than pretty slim—I say it is nil, bankrupt—not going to happen.

**Fathers of faith and grace steeped in ignorance and misinformation:**

These are hard words to hear, especially for the father who has followed the "American Dream," college educated, good career, faithful and generally engaged with his family—I couldn't possibly be talking to such a father—right? Wrong! I am talking to him; being educated, having a good career, being faithful and loyal to your family are good—very good—but if taken alone, they are more often going to deceive such a father into thinking that all is well—including the myth that his daughter is going to do just fine with only the assistance her mother can give her—he will not need to be personally involved. Oh he will worry about it, but when did worry ever solve anything? By the time serious trouble wakes him up—it's too late!

Our number is up fathers! Our present day statistics on broken homes, divorce and child abuse, declare loud and clear that the jury is in and has ruled—and to-date at this time in our Christian culture, we fathers of faith and grace, steeped in our cultural ignorance and misinformation—have been weighed and found wanting!!

**As a small review of the facts**

1. A finding, contained in a teacher opinion poll commissioned by Metropolitan Life Insurance Co., 1007 public school teachers in a survey were questioned twice: in July and August of 1990 before beginning their first school year, and again the next spring after completing their first year.
2. Seventy-five percent initially agreed that "many children come to school with so many problems that it's very difficult for them to be good students." But after a year in class eighty-nine percent held that view.
3. When it comes to marital fidelity in the United States, "Do what I say, not what I do" seems to be the prevailing ethic, according to Peggy Vaughan, author of "The Monogamy Myth." "We give lip service to monogamy, but we actually support and encourage affairs."
4. Dr. Frank Pittman, author of "Private Lies: Infidelity and the Betrayal of Intimacy" says, " Although most Americans are faithful most of the time, nearly fifty percent of married men and thirty percent of married women will be unfaithful sometime during their marriage. "
5. Sociologist Marc Miringoff has tracked 17 social problems for the past 20 years with his Index of Social Health, and after a steady decline its latest reading has sunk to its lowest point. In fact, the index has dropped fifty one percent since numbers were first compiled in 1970.

"It's a warning sign. The fact that so many problems are worsening to so great an extent is a cause for concern. It says something about the soul of the nation," said Miringoff, director of the Fordham University Institute for Innovation in Social Policy at Tarrytown, N. Y.

"It's like the movie 'Jaws.' We can't keep denying there's a shark out there. There are people bloodied on the beach. We can't leave the beach open and let everybody swim. We better take action," Miringoff said.

**The mind of secularism versus the mind of Christ:**

According to Ken Graber author of "Ghosts *in the Bedroom: A Guide for Partners of Incest Survivors,"* about twenty percent of all women have had at least one incestuous experience before the age of 18.

What can be done to correct such a mess? Well, the bad news is we have been born into a difficult time, a time so difficult it challenges our roles as men, it challenges the very roots and fundamentals of God's great commission for fatherhood! The good news is we have within our possession the knowledge and the promise of Christ's—personal presence in us—to overcome this challenge and to re-establish ourselves as true family leaders of faith and grace, fully informed and armed to the teeth!

By walking through each of the circumstances or situations, which are common to our challenge—of being real fathers of faith and grace to our daughters—we can discover what God's wise and uncommon common sense answers are for all our basic needs as husbands and fathers. We have already discovered that God's Law-Word, tells us that we have the mind of Christ. We are not of the same mind that we were before He raised us up from our dead past. We have been given a new heart and a new mind. Now, the challenge we face is learning how to use them. Philippians 2:5, "Let this mind be in you which was also in Christ Jesus." We have the choice to choose to have the mind of Christ. Also in chapter 3:12-15, he reveals a most astounding factor of our life and being: vs. 13, "For it is God in you who works both to will and to do His good pleasure." Let us pray that He should give us more of His mind![119]

119 "I beseech you therefore, brethren, by the mercies of God, that you present your bodies a living sacrifice, holy, acceptable to God, which is your reasonable service. And do not be conformed to this world, but be transformed by the renewing of your mind, that you may prove what is that good and acceptable and perfect will of God." Romans 12:1-2.

# Book II

# DADDY'S LITTLE GIRL

## Chapter Three

## A Time for Victory

### Overcoming Our Fears of Daddy's Little Girl

**Putting our uncommon common sense to work:**

First lets begin by accepting the fact that we have been given a sense that although I will call it common, it is only common for those who believe in and trust in Him! Compared to what the secular world calls "common sense" we fathers of faith and grace, who believe in our Lord and Savior Jesus Christ, are invited by Him to have His "uncommon common sense." Remember, what God calls wisdom and understanding, the secular world calls, foolishness.[120] Remember, Christ's worldview and His uncommon common sense is our new language known only by us.

Using our new uncommon common sense opens a new door for the development of father/daughter relationships. It is not necessary for us to allow the attitudes of fear and low personal self-esteem to dictate how we conduct ourselves with our daughters. Once it is accepted, that the God ordained position of fatherhood is a very necessary element in the proper and successful development of a young lady—then 95% of the problem—is already solved. That is of course—IF ONE ACTS—on such a conclusion and does not procrastinate. Indeed, a new door is opened to us, a door that leads to understanding, God's applied wisdom and to some of life's greatest joys and privileges.

**More than just babies:**

At first it seems impossible. Our daughters come to us in a small, frail bundle and we look at them with a special kind of wonderment. They are more than just babies to men. To us men it's the little boys who are "just babies," they are simply little men, right? All the right parts are there, their little penises, testicles, hands for throwing and catching balls, legs for running, eyes to see with, and ears to hear with, yep, he's all there all right. We can relate to everything we see, because it is just like us. We have a sense of pride and calm when we see and hold our little boy. Some will wonder why I am so explicit in my descriptions of a father's first look at his newborn son compared to his first look at his newborn daughter. It is not my intent to be insensitive or crude—but rather to capture verbally—the emotions and mental reactions experienced by a vast majority of men. The fact is that men are comfortable with their infant sons and all that they represent,

120 "For the message of the cross is foolishness to those who are perishing, but to us who are being saved it is the power of God. For it is written: 'I will destroy the wisdom of the wise, and bring to nothing the understanding of the prudent.' Where is the wise? Where is the scribe? Where is the disputer of this age? Has not God made foolish the wisdom of this world? For since, in the wisdom of God, the world through wisdom did not know God, it pleased God through the foolishness of the message preached to save those who believe. For Jews request a sign, and Greeks seek after wisdom; but we preach Christ crucified, to the Jews a stumbling block and to the Greeks foolishness, but to those who are called, both Jews and Greeks, Christ the power of God and the wisdom of God. Because the foolishness of God is wiser than men, and the weakness of God is stronger than men." I Corinthians 1:18-25.

however, they are—not comfortable with the feminine mystique—and seeing their little newborn baby daughters in the nude is a reminder of this fact.

When we see our little daughter, it's not the same. From the very first moment we lay eyes on her she is different. She is not formed as we are, she has a vagina, her legs don't bespeak of carrying footballs and lifting heavy loads. She may be the same length at birth and weigh the same or even be bigger and weigh more, but she is not the same. When we look into her eyes we see beauty of a different sort, we see her as—feminine—from top to bottom even to the very depths of her soul. We can already imagine her long eyelashes and her teasing look. Her face is but a foreshadow of the beauty she is to become—a beauty which relates to us men in the form of sexual attractiveness—from this moment forward we are on guard. There is not the same calm and pride we feel with a son. Love, yes we sense and feel love! But more predominately we are in awe of her differences. The feminine mystique, the sense that she is woman, makes a little chill run down our spine and we feel a little uneasy. "Can I really handle this little mirror of my wife? Oh God, if ever I needed help I need it now!" Not to worry, my friend! God has indeed equipped us men of faith and grace with all that we need to handle this little bundle of feminine mystique and beauty. Relationally, much better I might add, than most have proven capable with our sweet wives!

**Young daughters are especially drawn to fathers:**

Fathers, we must open our eyes, we've got everything going for us. From the very moment this little bundle of joy begins to examine her new surroundings, she knows her daddy is different from her mother. Sure, her mother has breasts and she nurses her, but I mean deep down she knows you are different. You are someone special. God has blessed her with all that female intuition and it starts to work immediately. She has an insatiable desire to know who you are and why you are different. She has a God-given trust for you and will do anything you tell her. She believes in you and wants your approval. What an awesome responsibility this is.

Dr. S. Appleton, M.D., psychiatrist at Harvard Medical School says, "From the first time he gently cradles his baby daughter to the day he gives her away at the altar, dad is the model for every other man in her life." I would personally add that such is true—even after you give her away at the altar.

So, be wise, break the old habits and bad attitudes, treat her like the miniature little queen she is. Her awe and wonder of you will never cease. You hold all the secrets of your world as a man, as a husband and lover to her mother and as her father. You are much more naturally and spiritually gifted and able to reveal these secrets to her than you think. Once you embark upon such a commitment to her you will be amazed at the power and smoothness with which it can be done. Long after she is successfully married and a mother in her own right, you will still be moved by the thoughts of your relationship with her during her developing years. She literally and frighteningly is "putty in your hands." She will be and become—to a very great extent—what you form her to be.

Don't tell your self that this is over the top and that there is no way you could possibly do this. True, we as carnal men, mere physical biological fathers of faith and grace, cannot do this. But, we have already qualified from Whom and with Whose power, we are promised the gifts of understanding and uncommon common sense of applied wisdom with which to do this, right?

**What is a daughter?**

When properly answered and understood we not only shed a great deal of light onto the scene of father/daughter relationships, but also we open up a new and deeper understanding of husband/wife relationships.

When we look at our newborn daughter we see many things about her which are obviously different. She is definitely not male, right? The physical differences are obvious—but what is she, apart from just being another member of the female sex? Is she different from, say, a son? "Of course!" you say. Ok, I agree, but how is she different? What is a daughter other than just the fact that she lives physically in a female body?

She is first of all a brand new being—a person—not just a body in the vast world of humans. She is completely alone, except for the care and love of her parents. She is a unique being, never before having had any input into her mind as to what to think or know, concerning this vast new world into which she has burst, all of a sudden. She is a new book with all the pages blank. This is kind of scary when you think about it. This is also true of sons, but our focus in *Daddy's Little Girl* is limited to our father/daughter relationships. We will cover the mother/son relationship aspects of this in *Mommy's Little Boy*.

What gets written into those blank pages determines what she becomes in this life. Let's consider for a moment what might need to be written and what areas fathers should consider as important. Here she is, this little bundle of joy and mystery, looking at us with those beautiful eyes which hold such great promise of life and victories to come. We have already made the observation that this new being we are holding is living in a female body. How is her gender associated with what is written into those blank pages? Does it matter what kind of body a person has? Isn't a body a body, and whether it is female or male makes no difference to the person living in either body—right? Well—maybe not.

On the surface it might not seem important whether one has a male body or a female body. But, when you think about it for a moment, and put it into proper perspective, gender makes a big difference. First of all, it is interesting to note our reference to this new being as, "she." Why do we refer to this new person as "she" and not as "he?"

"Of course," you will certainly say, "because of her female body."

Correct, and that is just the point I want to make. This being is referred to by her gender and will be treated for the rest of her existence on this planet in ways entirely conditioned because of the body in which she lives! There is one fact with which most women will agree, regarding the feminist movement for equality. Women are basically crying out for recognition as persons and demonstrating their resentment for being limited to the identity of just a "female" body. They are saying to us men, "We are more than just a female body. Look at us, we are real persons, we are trapped in this female body and we want to be accepted for who we are as persons not just as a female body!" In fact, it is so obvious that some are frustrated to distraction. They would like to escape the female body altogether—lesbians, transvestites—only to mention a couple of Satan's proposed solutions to the unregenerate mind.

**Feminine development and Daddy's little girl:**

Why do you think they are so upset about living in their female bodies? Men seem to accept their own male bodies without question, except for those rare souls who think they would be happier with a female body, another of Satan's solutions to the reprobate unregenerate mind. Why is it so hard for many women to feel complete within their female bodies?

This cry for recognition as a person and not as just a body is evidence of the failure of men to be genuine, effective fathers to their daughters and the failure of those fathers to understand fully the needs and purposes of the female body, in which their daughters live! Remember, the mothers who will rock the cradles of tomorrows leaders—that includes future fathers—are Daddy's little girl today. What is written into their blank pages from birth to the time they launch out on their own determines what kind of women they will be.

So, who has had the most opportunity to write into those blank pages? We already know that fathers have done very little, because we have always been told that mothers are supposed to relate to little girls and daddies are supposed to relate to little boys. The fact is, aside from being "Daddy's little girl," Daddy has done very little to write directly in his daughter's book of life. He has written more by accident and by omission than by direct thoughtful planning. How mothers relate uniquely to sons is the subject of *Mommy's Little Boy*, in Book III.

When we look at the situation from this vantage point, it becomes clearer how many of our current "modern" women are the product of a one-sided input system. In the majority of households, women/mothers are the sole source for what their daughters should know and understand about life and the world at large. They have had the main opportunity to set the stage and to write in the blank pages of a daughter's book of life. Or more correctly stated, we men have abdicated our true role as fathers of faith and grace to our daughters and in fear of them and ourselves we have said—verbally or with our silent abdication—"Here, you take her, I don't understand her—she is woman—you tell her what she needs to know." Hence, their inner sense of value as women is never given an opportunity to connect with the one who has been ordained to develop it. They've never been given the correct place of value nor the tender feminine recognition and yes—the protection of a wise father of faith and grace from the wrong-headedness of only knowing input from other women—equally disadvantaged.

**Fathers leave an indelible impression:**

The women of today's world are who they are because of what has been written in the pages of their heart. The most important pages are those of the first six years, these lead to a good or bad transition into the development years of puberty and beyond. If we fathers of faith and grace do not like the way our daughter has turned out and we want to know whom to blame, we need go no further than the mirror and take a good look. What we do right or wrong either directly or indirectly, through commission or omission will stay with them throughout life. Thus, what we see in the woman of today that we don't like we can know that it has come about because of these truths—in this case for the worse and not the better. For sure, men are not the blame for all of their problems—they have their own sins a plenty—but based on Christ's worldview of our foreordained position as His representatives to be responsible for them—it is safe to say that we carry the lion's share of the burden. The most important thing we can do as men is to realize the fundamental areas of our mistakes with respect to our daughters and we will in the process understand more about our mistakes, with women in general and our sweet wife in particular.

There is little we can do about the mistakes of previous generations of men, but we can determine to no longer live and act ignorantly regarding the women in our lives as they did. This in itself is a great step forward. Without such fundamental commitment to change and to midcourse corrections, our relationships with the opposite sex will only further deteriorate and we will be the losers, with no one to blame but ourselves. If I accept the premise that in God's revealed Law-Word—Christ clearly proclaims a Great Commission for Fatherhood—encompassing the responsibility among other things, for the spiritual, moral, character, romance and marital sexual success for my wife—it goes without saying that I am also the beginning source for all of these same things for my daughter. Albeit there are differences, but the principle and the mandate is the same!

**What does she need, this person living in a female body?**

To begin to understand this, we first need to recognize the role of her body as just an extension of the person inside, it is a tool, a major tool, through which the person living inside can and does relate to the people and the world around them.

The person inside, Daddy's little girl, in this case, is greatly affected by the body she possesses! Looking at it from inside for a moment, we are able to understand how she is hormonally and instinctively regulated and affected by many things foreign to us. She has come equipped to be a mother some day. Her body is uniquely made and suited to conceiving and giving birth to new life. She has inner powers of motherhood which we will never comprehend; they just are, and we have to accept that and work with it. To fight this basic drive of women is only to invite disaster for them and for us.

She is gifted in this body with unique ways which attract the opposite sex. Not just the way she is put together physically, but in deeper ways, spiritual ways. Even as only a child she has but to look at you and she can communicate her power of persuasion and intuition. Without a doubt, she can play catch with us, she can learn to swim, to ride a horse, to ski, to drive a car, fly a plane and do all sorts of things, acting just like a man, but she will always be a woman. She is inextricably united with her body and therefore, as a person who cannot change her female identity, she needs to learn how to communicate through the tool of this body she possesses to be successful in her relationships with the opposite sex. Anything short of this will only cause her pain and confusion. All the PHD degrees, money and political power in the world will never fulfill her as much as her ability to know and relate successfully with her counterparts in this world—men! No—not just sexually. Sexuality is always the first thing that jumps into a man's mind. She must be able to understand and relate well with men in general, with the very concept of man. If she cannot do this, how then can she choose wisely from all of her opportunities for that one special man?

Her feminine drives, as woman and mother to be, will be there for her all of her life. She is a natural domestic in the sense of motherhood and her drive to reproduce herself and to care for and nurture her offspring. Her nesting instincts are legendary, and although the idea of settling down and rearing a family seems very frightening to many men of today—it is the most basic of all—that drives the heart of Daddy's little girl. University of Michigan psychologist David Buss has found that:

> "Because women invest more time and energy in bearing and caring for children, they react more strongly to a threat of emotional infidelity. What women fear most; is the loss of their mates' long-term commitment and support."

Have you noticed the latest reports? There are more women now leaving the work place and returning home to rear families than there are women entering the work place for the first time! Well, so much for the great feminist career revolution. The truth is women cannot escape themselves. I am proud of these women and praise their personal integrity and honesty. It takes a brave person to say, "I need to quit what I thought I wanted to do and go back to what I really want to do." Can we be as honest about our needs, men? I hope so.

For those women of faith and grace who now feel trapped in their new "freedom" to earn extra bucks, seek God's answer for you. Maybe you should stay on the job, or maybe you are wasting valuable feminine time and need to concentrate on the family. There are both kinds: there are women called to be as the woman of Proverbs 31 and there are those who—can do it all—minus the financial part. Prayer and your husbands support will tell you which is right for you. My wife Marilyn has experienced both roles: a stay at home mom for many years and a woman with a professional career outside of the home—interacting with other women and men in the same profession—and bringing home our family income. I consider my wife a perfect example of the woman of Proverbs 31.

For better or for worse, this new person in our lives comes into a male dominated world. As Daddy's little girl progresses from—new-born, preschool, preteens, college age, or older—they have a built-in hunger and urgency to know who is this person, this man they call father. No matter at what age a father finally comes to realize and accept this fact, his daughter will always be ready to listen and respond. By recognizing this necessity early in our experience as a father of faith and grace, we will reap the rewards instead of the regrets.

**What does the father of faith and grace need to fulfill his little girl?**

Unfortunately, many men never come to this understanding, or if they do, they are so overcome with their own bad self-image as a man—or are so afraid of what their daughter would think if she really knew—they keep their daughters locked out. How many daughters have had to go to their mothers and ask, "Mom, tell me about Dad, what kind of man is he, what kind of person? What was he like when you first met him? Such fathers, unless they wake up, will never know the deep resentment their daughters are building up against them.

To hold your daughter off at arm's length, never really revealing yourself as a man and a person to her is one of the cruelest things a father can do to his daughter. Hopefully we all would shudder at even the thought of sexually violating our little girls, yet we can find it all too easy to hurt her by holding her off at arm's length and never opening up to her. How tragic! Don't fall into such cruel escapist traps. Your daughter has a keen inner sense which came with the package, placed there by God, revealing to her that you—her father—is a very important person in her development process. It's part of her feminine intuition. If you don't believe me, just ask her. Ask any woman the following:

> "Do you feel you should have known your father better?", or "Do you feel it would have been helpful for you if your father had told you more about himself and the world of men, in a gentlemanly and honest way?"

Don't ask me—how they know—that we are supposed to assume this role of teacher and guide for them into the male world, they just do. As to why: it is another factor in the mystery of womanhood. God is sovereign and what He has created as woman—specifically because of the fall in Genesis—we have what we have. Consequently, even though we may never know why they know, the fact remains—they do know—and what may surprise you even more is that we fathers know it too. We know that we know, because of the strong protector drives and impulses we have, for our little girl. These strong drives are just the kernel—the beginning and most basic—of what we are really called of God to be for our little girl. This common drive of all men, believers and unbelievers alike is evidence of

God's common grace. However, we men of faith and grace are born of God's special grace—He gives us our gift of faith to believe—and He adopts us into His family.[121] We of all men are especially blessed and equipped by God through Christ to fulfill His commission for fatherhood.

God has given all men a measure of wisdom in leading a family. We know this is true because God always provides for His creation and when He tells man that their natural desire will be to leave their father and their mother and to become one flesh with a new person—a wife—we know that He has prepared the man to do it. When God planned for woman to bear children and to give birth to them He provided a womb and all the necessary equipment to produce such a baby and to allow the mother to fulfill this foreordained purpose. As head of the family and as the designated leader of his wife for spiritual and moral development, a father of faith and grace is also given an inner desire to lead his little girl. Whereas this is true for all men and women under God's—common grace[122]—it is even much more so for all of us who are of His elect! We are those whom He has saved and whom He has promised victory over sin in this life. We have actual victories to not sin and victory in forgiveness when we do sin.[123] Therefore the standards for how to live and how to overcome are unique gifts of God to the elect and not a part of common grace to the unbeliever.[124] Thus we are God's key element in overcoming the enemy of God's institution The Family and we are His ordained authority through which He exercises His good pleasure to use the family for overcoming evil in the world.[125]

**Interacting with Daddy's little girl:**

Fathers of faith and grace must always be asking ourselves, how is our relationship with our daughter? Have we answered that sti11, small voice yet? The one compelling from deep inside of us saying, "Your daughter needs to know who you are, and needs for you to take charge of her development as a woman." Or are we going to be like so many, sitting back and waiting for our wife or some other woman to do it for us? Once we men exercise the courage required to assume our proper role in the development of our daughters, we do very well. When I made my decision to get personally involved I began to take my daughters out and have time alone with them. Sometimes my wife and I would take one at a time to some special event. As my daughters have gotten older and tell me how they felt when they were little, I realize I didn't take them out on father/daughter dates nearly enough.

A father/daughter outing doesn't have to be fancy, although being fancy is something to do once in awhile. More often than not it could be just a trip to the store or the local service station. All father/daughter outings whether fancy and all

121 "Most assuredly, I say to you, he who does not enter the sheepfold by the door, but climbs up some other way, the same is a thief and a robber. But he who enters by the door is the shepherd of the sheep. To him the doorkeeper opens, and the sheep hear his voice; and he calls his own sheep by name and leads them out. And when he brings out his own sheep, he goes before them; and the sheep follow him, for they know his voice. Yet they will by no means follow a stranger, but will flee from him, for they do not know the voice of strangers." John 10:1-5.

122 "That you may be the children of your heavenly Father: for he makes his sun to rise on the evil and on the good, and sends rain on the just and on the unjust." Matt. 5:45

123 "These things have I spoken unto you, that in me you might have peace. In the world you will have tribulation: but be of good cheer; I have overcome the world." John 16:33

124 "O wretched man that I am! Who shall deliver me from the body of this death? I thank God through Jesus Christ our Lord. So then with the mind I myself serve the law of God; but with the flesh the law of sin." Rom. 7:24-25

125 "Jesus answered them, 'Do you now believe? Indeed the hour is coming, yes, has now come, that you will be scattered, each to his own, and will leave Me alone. And yet I am not alone, because the Father is with Me. These things I have spoken to you, that in Me you may have peace. In the world you will have tribulation; but be of good cheer, I have overcome the world.'" John 16:31-33.

dressed up—or just to the local store in jeans—will give you the opportunity to take a few minutes to talk. We all love to talk about ourselves, and our daughters want to know about us, so, we couldn't ask for a better combination. I'm continually amazed at how young our daughters are ready to have serious conversations with Daddy. They always look too young to be interested, but inside of those very young looking bodies is a young lady maturing at lightning speed, ready to soak up everything she can about her world, and especially about her Daddy.

It's a natural feeling for us fathers to embrace our little girl, folding her up in our strong arms and to be all we can be for her. We know for a fact, that we—like her—come equipped with a God-given inner desire to fulfill a certain special role relative to her development. The natural father instinct is to protect our daughter, to want to provide wonderful things for her to make her happy. These are desires and natural instincts we have felt before—for some other woman—our wife!

**Our nagging fears:**

At the same time we are unsettled by certain nagging fears and mixed signals. The similarity of our natural instincts to protect and provide for our little girl, are the same we have for our wife, (listen up, wives and mothers) these also remind us of other natural instincts which are closely related; our sexual responses and attractions for our wife, which we intuitively know are NOT proper for our love relationship with our little girl.

These dual signals, both which are gifts from God but for two distinct purposes, cause many sincere, loving fathers to be afraid of their daughters' sexuality. And instead of feeling more relaxed as their daughters get older, they feel more afraid and uneasy. It starts with the uneasy feeling it can give a man, just to see his little daughter's naked body, as he or mother changes the first diapers. As she grows older and wants to hug daddy and sit on daddy's lap, the feeling persists and becomes more acute. Then, as she reaches puberty, the time for young women to start having menstrual cycles, he really feels uncomfortable when she wants to sit on his lap and hug him.

Men react to these feelings in many different ways. Some remain aloof and distant from their daughters from the very first day. Others go to extremes in the other direction, even so far as to have showers with their young daughters, or take tub baths with them. Where the one responds to his feelings with extreme caution the other throws caution to the wind and thinks sharing baths and being a "free spirit" with his young daughter will promote better understanding between them.

Whereas we fathers must certainly realize our proper role and conduct with our daughters' sexuality, neither fear nor license is the correct response. Neither of the above approaches is appropriate for a father/daughter relationship.

Many men never figure out how to differentiate between these signals. And unfortunately all too many men respond improperly to these signals, never seeming to understand how to bring their proper role or responsibilities into perspective.

As men and fathers, how do we differentiate between these powerful signals and instincts? Which set of feelings and promptings are the Right feelings, and which are the Wrong feelings?

How should we as men and fathers respond to these promptings, and how do we protect our daughters from our male sexuality, at the same time we introduce her into the male mystique and the male world?

These are some of the most important questions we will ever ask ourselves. This is one of the great intersections of our lives as men. We can mess up terribly at this point or we can make a great leap forward into a world of wonder and excitement, a world for which we were uniquely created and from which we will emerge with a sense of fulfillment, more complete than any other adventure that life could provide!

**A father of faith and grace takes charge:**

Taking charge is the first step. We cannot come to grips with the challenges of fatherhood, and the needs of our daughters if we do not put our fears and misgivings aside and take charge. Taking charge means to take responsibility for our roles as fathers and to determine to be personally involved in the development process of our daughters.

At first, it means stepping lightly, not charging like a bull into an unfamiliar arena just to make a good macho effort. Remember, we are dealing with a very young lady here, an amazingly resilient, determined, strong, even stubborn, but at the same time fragile and—tender of heart young lady.

If you want to enter a world of wonder and joy, of dreams and romance, rivaling and in many different ways even surpassing the feelings you had as you dated and courted your wife, then I welcome you to prayerfully continue to finish reading this book. If however, on the other hand you are afraid of what you might learn and of how it might cause you to change—if you are afraid of change—afraid of yourself and your daughter, and you don't have the courage to face these facts and overcome them; then I advise you to stop right here and put the book down.

For those who are both brave and adventurous, I welcome you to enter this new world of living, with respect to your daughters and the world of fathers—especially fathers of faith and grace—a world as you never have imagined it could be. You are to be commended for your bravery and honesty, and your courage of heart. It will not be easy, it often will make you want to give up or to say, "I can't do it," but the truth is you can. Furthermore, you're the kind of man who will never forgive yourself if you don't give it the very best effort possible.

As you continue to read this book, I want you to keep an open mind. Consider the practicality of the things you will hear or be exposed to for the first time. Look at them logically; seek God in prayer that He might allow you to see His great uncommon, common sense. Most of all; reach down deep into your heart—that new heart of flesh—not the old stony one. Tap into the strength of your God-given gift of faith and ability as a man and as a father that I know He has given you. In short—measure up to what you know in your heart God has prepared you to be. You have nothing to lose and everything to gain!

Remember this—fathers and mothers of faith and grace—any male can have sex with a woman and get her pregnant, assuming that he is not sterile. Therefore any such male can also bring a little girl into the world, but only a concerned and brave father of faith and grace—born out of a mother's tender care and instruction of her little boy can he become a real father—fully prepared for some Daddy's little girl—to become a woman!

[illegible]

# Book II

# DADDY'S LITTLE GIRL

## Chapter Four

## Father as Hero and Knight in Shining Armor

**A surprising role:**

FATHER AS HERO and Knight in Shining Armor is a role most men have never considered for themselves. As a Hero—never! As a Knight in Shining Armor, unlikely! Most would think of it only in terms of tales of romance from medieval times, or perhaps think of it as being limited to some romantic notion held by young—teen-age girls with respect to their boy friends. But to be a Hero and a Knight in Shining Armor as a father, Wow!—Where did that come from?

Let's back up a minute and look at that teen-age girl. Your wife was, or maybe still is, a teenage young lady. How do you think she sees you down deep in her heart? Some girls and a lot of women won't talk openly about their fantasies concerning that special man in their heart and life. But when you get them to open up, they all admit to dreaming of falling in love with this image of a man. A man who is to them a Hero, and certainly a Knight in shining armor, no one less in their eyes is worthy of their love and surrender.

Even though we men are rightly accused of acting too macho at times, it is still very difficult for us seriously to consider ourselves as Heroes or Knights in shining armor. I suppose it is our rejection of such a notion for ourselves that causes the woman in our lives to hold her thoughts to herself. She senses that we think it's silly—to her it is anything but silly.

I don't suppose that the expressions, "Hero" and "Knight in shining armor" are truly adequate to express the way a woman in love with a man feels toward her man. It's my opinion that the feminine capacity for love and devotion to a man—at its highest levels—borders on god-like worship. So, for the woman in your life, such expressions are only an attempt to express the way she feels.

Unfortunately for all concerned, we men have a great capacity for proving ourselves to be far less than Heroes or Knights in Shining Armor and much less gods! Some might even think it unfair for a woman to cherish a man in this way. How can we possibly measure up to such expectations? Some might say: "The reality of our inability to measure up to the expectations and fantasies of women should convince them to not have these silly notions. They should think more practically with regard to men, and be more realistic."

God has been merciful to us men. With all of our imperfections, the women in our lives—our wives and our daughters who love us—look beyond our faults and see only what they want to see: a Hero and a Knight in shining armor.

**A daughter's Hero and Knight in shining armor:**

With daughters it is actually worse than you think men. As fathers we are more than Heroes or Knights in shining armor. To a daughter, we are as gods—we can do no wrong. To realize this is the beginning of fatherly wisdom, and the beginning of being a real father of faith and grace for your daughter!

Before we get to feeling too proud of ourselves, let me remind us all, it is possible to destroy this romantic image that the women in our life have for us. It takes a lot of effort, but we men have proven up to the challenge all too frequently. To be loved by a woman is a precious and humbling experience. Indeed, it is amazing how little honest effort in the right way is needed to keep a woman's love. And if such be true, how is it we are so good at losing it? Is it possible we have lost the art of truly loving our wives! And as a result, that the young men of today know more about biological sex than they do about real sex and real love? If you think on this question more than a nanosecond you're in trouble.

What does loving wives have to do with loving daughters? Well, if you don't know the true meaning of love with the full-grown version of woman, how are you going to recognize the needs of the mirror image of your wife—your daughter? The problems we face with expressing our true feelings and attitudes to our wives are the same problems we face when we try to express them to our daughters. So, what is the point; what does all this have to do with father/daughter relationships?

Some things in life are so important; they require learning the basics all over again. For example, I moved to Mexico as a young man with my young wife and our first daughter. Well, when I got to Mexico and began to try to learn Spanish, I came face to face with this very issue. I first had to go back and relearn all the basic English I either had forgotten or had never learned. Without this I could not even deal with the terminology for learning Spanish. If you don't know what a predicate noun is in English, you sure aren't going to know what it is in Spanish—right?

For those who are mechanically inclined, you will relate to this comparison in another way. If you don't know the basic theory of internal combustion or understand the inner workings of a small one-cylinder engine, for sure you won't know how a large complex engine works.

I don't want this to seem harder than it really is. However, based on my own experience in coming to grips with these factors, you can't learn the basics about the love and care that a daughter needs from her father and not deal with the same problems relating to the wife.

**The power of first impressions:**

First, consider this: every wife is some man's daughter. Every wife who had problems understanding her father is probably having trouble understanding her husband. Every wife who lost the vision of her ideal for her father, that is—he managed to shatter her original romantic image of him—as Hero and Knight in shining armor, has a problem. Daughters who lose the romantic vision of their fathers, held as little girls, often grow up to be women who either hate their fathers or who at least have difficulty later in life when they try to relate to their husbands. All the faults and mistakes of their husbands begin to look just like those their father had!

In a not so recent People Magazine publication, Dr. William S. Appleton, M.D., psychiatrist at Harvard Medical School relates some details about one of his patients. He was quoted as saying:

> "The relationship between father and daughter—good or bad—powerfully influences a girl's romantic future."

> "'Not all men are like your father,' her mother assured her. But no matter how hard Anna tried, she couldn't maintain a relationship."

"I'd think, 'Here's a guy who's opposite from my father,' recalls Anna, now 35, but after a while we'd have the same kind of stormy battles. I turned every man I dated into an ogre even if he wasn't.

"I didn't know how to get out of the trap. I was furious with my father. I decided to give up on him—and other men too."

God recorded this reality for us thousands of years ago, but it seems to be more believable if a man of letters says it. I'm not going to get into all that this implies about us, His creation, but it speaks volumes about our lack of faithfulness!

**A future wife:**

To put it bluntly, as fathers we are not just rearing a daughter, we are rearing some man's future wife. This is the central issue to the whole process of father/daughter relationships. Even though your daughter may never marry, your role as her father is first and foremost to bring her to the highest degree of development possible to be a great wife for some other man. To do less is to rob her of the most fundamental of all man/woman relationships. Nothing else you can do for her will mean as much to her as this. Pretty clothes, a new car, education and travel pale by comparison to the importance or her learning to be a great wife, lover and mother to her children.

This is one of the toughest things for modern men to realize: it is fathers not mothers who teach daughters to be great wives. When you married your wife, she came as a complete package with all the—good and the bad—she had acquired from her experience as her father's daughter. Her mother could have taught her all she knew and never come close to what her father could have taught her, if he had understood his role and put his mind to it. And whatever he did or didn't teach her about men comes with the package and you got it. When we say "I do" at the altar of marriage, we are accepting the whole package. You can't send back the parts you don't like. Men—we have to deal with the whole package!

**Her key to happiness:**

Well Mr. Hero, Mr. Knight in shining armor, welcome to the real world of daughters. Every daughter has started off with the vision of her father as a Hero and as her Knight in shining armor. By exercising God's gift of father and His uncommon, common sense, you will not have to disappoint your little girl. You can measure up to what she sees in you. Remember, it is God working in us who both—wills and does—His good pleasure in us![126]

Through the eyes of a daughter you are not just a bread winner, you are the answer to all the mysteries about men. You are her source for all things male, beginning with you. She intuitively looks to you to unfold the secrets to her future relationship with men, and for now—as father—you are the only man in her life.

At this juncture it may seem strange to realize you hold the key to your daughter's future happiness in her relationships with men in general and in particular with you and her future husband. But I know through our discoveries thus far, you have already begun to see yourself differently and you are beginning to see your wife and your daughter in a new and more positive light. You are now seeing—possibilities—where before you could only see—impossibilities! As we

---

126 "Therefore, my beloved, as you have always obeyed, not as in my presence only, but now much more in my absence, work out your own salvation with fear and trembling; for it is God who works in you both to will and to do for His good pleasure." Philippians 2:12-13.

progress further you will come to appreciate more and more about this new you that God has created you to be, as a husband and father of faith and grace.

The joy and privilege it is to be in the role of father for a daughter is hard to express. A daughter gives her father the opportunity to learn as much from her as he hopes to be able to teach her. He is also given the opportunity to learn to communicate the basics of love, sex and family to this mirror image of his wife. This is not only a great blessing and need for the daughter but a blessing in disguise for the father. He will learn—or perhaps relearn—how better to express himself to his wife in the process.

# Book II
# DADDY'S LITTLE GIRL

## Chapter Five
## Knight's Honor

**Fragile—handle with care!**

The honor of a father towards his daughter begins with a deep recognition and respect for her sexuality as a woman. She is a person in her own right, to be respected as such, yes; but she is physically a woman, with all the feminine attributes implied. Her body is female and not male. She has a completely different set of inner drives from a man. She cannot escape these, and we as fathers in the role of teacher, counselor and friend, must arm ourselves with the moral fiber, values and principles required to handle this precious and fragile package we call "Daddy's little girl." From the moment a daughter is born she begins to get impressions about everything around her. At first it is limited to knowing who feeds her and takes care of her dirty diapers. This is not limited to mother.

Little girls are no different from little boys when it comes to wanting to touch everything and to learn about their environment through touch. Yet, at a very early age, you will notice that the femininity of a little girl will predominate. She will not be as rough-and-tumble as a little boy, and her choice of toys will be different. She will be attracted to things of a feminine quality, just as her mother is: soft materials, dolls, a desire to show off with new clothes, and even a desire to want to change clothes several times a day. By age two, and sometimes even before, she will want to paint her nails and put on make-up just like Mommy.

Daddy's little girl can also be a—over the top—"Tom Boy!" Her moments of delicate femininity will only make such characteristics stand out in greater relief and contrast—they in no way make her less feminine.

It's amazing how much formal education one can have and still not see these common sense realities. Jerre Levy, professor of psychology at the University of Chicago, makes her confession in the January, 1992 issue of Time Magazine. "When I was younger, I believed that 100% of sex differences were due to the environment," she says, "My daughter was 15 months old, and I had just dressed her in her teeny little nightie. Some guests arrived, and she came into the room, knowing full well that she looked adorable. She came in with this saucy little walk, cocking her head, blinking her eyes, especially at the men. You never saw such flirtation in your life." After 20 years spent studying the brain, Levy is convinced: "I'm sure there are biologically based differences in our behavior."

These feminine characteristics will differ in strength and intensity from daughter to daughter, but they are unmistakable. They indicate how important it is for us to harmonize our approach to this new little woman in the family and to encourage her in the discovery of who she is.

If our new daughter has older brothers, or even when younger children are born into the family, they all must understand how different their sister is. We treat her more gently and with deliberate tenderness; she is a little lady. There are certain ways we convey our respect for a lady. First, we begin with the tenderness and attitudes shown to her when she is just a baby, and then we expand into areas of privacy and respect for her physical and sexual differences.

**Honor through respecting the difference:**

Personally, I am very much against an all too common practice of parents to rationalize—for time efficiencies—the practice of bathing both sexes at the same time. Early baths and nudity with her brothers is a matter of much more serious concern than modern parents seem to think! Virginity is more a state of mind than just a purity of body. The concept of what is special in the differences of the sexes is dulled and reduced to commonality when such practices are in place. Remember, this tender creature of God is called the weaker sex, not because she is not capable of being muscularly strong, but because she is delicately made up within her reality as a feminine being. As we explore other areas of our little girl and her reactions to structure and her life surroundings we will see more clearly how this is so. It is easy to pressure our little girls into situations that bruise this tender nature. As we fathers write on the blank pages of our little girl's heart we must remember that it is easier to inscribe information and impressions than it is to erase them. When in doubt we should always choose the path that will best prepare her and stay away from the libertine suggestions and encouragements for doing things that are contrary to God's clear and simple principles.

Women are adversely affected by all sexual activity inconsistent with their God-given intuition. It is a master plan, inscribed upon their subconscious mind, and no amount of "sexual liberation" talk or reasoning can remove it. In the case of fathers gone mad—with a rebellious heart against God—they commit the most brutal of sins against their daughters. Incest is the most brutal sexual damage a girl can suffer. Her first reaction to such an experience, so unlike the model God has inscribed upon her subconscious mind, is to bury it deep and to forget it. Then, many years later, often after marriage and children of her own—she remembers it all in a flash! Wow, what a reaction she has. She can no longer function as a lover with her husband as she did before. Their whole life is smashed and must be rebuilt from the bottom up. Unfortunately, in most cases, this rebuilding never seems to be able to put it all back together. The woman's relationship with men is changed forever.

Some react by entering a life of prostitution. This is not something a woman would naturally consider as a career opportunity. However, the many reports on this issue indicate that up 95% come from families in which they were sexually molested as young girls by some family member, most often by their own fathers. Many more struggle bravely on throughout life in a search for peace and answers to their deep inner pain.

**Dishonor at its worst!**

Some years ago I counseled with a young widow and mother of four beautiful children, let's call her Rebecca to protect her identity. She is a graphic illustration of what happens to a little princess—when only the worst aspects of a biological male are functioning in the role of father—and all vestiges of any sense of a real father of faith and grace are dead or nonexistent.

Rebecca and her three sisters, two older and one younger, were all sexually abused by their father, their one brother, their father's brother, and a neighbor friend of their father. Rebecca can remember that her first experience of sexual abuse from her father came between the ages of five and six. Her sisters portray the same abuse, beginning at about the same age.

Her father was one of fourteen children who were orphaned when he was between six and seven. They were all scattered into orphanages and foster homes. She recalls how her father would tell her and her three sisters about the sex he had at an early age with the daughters of his foster mothers. Also, some of the mothers had exposed themselves to him from time to time as he was growing up. He used these early experiences as excuses for his abusive treatment of them. One of the more sobering characteristics of her father is his blindness to his own dreadful deeds. Her father is now old and very sick with a terminal disease, but to this day he still thinks he was a good father. Truly, as C. S. Lewis said: "The thoroughly bad think they are all right!"

Rebecca is a surgical nurse who has won many honors in her profession. To look at her or to talk with her you would never guess the pain and suffering she has been through. She says of herself, "At six years of age I felt uncomfortable and unnatural as a child. I knew something was wrong, but I didn't know what it was. I was always covering up and couldn't be myself. I grew up feeling very inferior to men and very uncomfortable. In a group situation I felt below all people and especially men. When I did have a male friend I assumed sex was expected as part of the friendship. I never thought about marriage until I became pregnant by one of my boy friends." During all their young and youthful years of development she and her sisters were surrounded by men who had never exercised any personal discipline, nor who had developed any sense of true value for women or femininity. The following is only a small glimpse of the many mindless depravities and callous sins they suffered.

> "When I was only about twelve I can remember my father's brother getting myself and two of my girl friends together in a car and telling us to take off all of our clothes and touch each other. He said we were growing up to be beautiful young girls and that it was normal for us to show ourselves to him." Rebecca said.

She relates that throughout all her earlier life the most challenging thing for her to overcome was her use of sex to attempt to fulfill her need, for love and acceptance. She had lots of sex but never felt truly accepted or fulfilled in love.

Rebecca married the father of her children in 1972, and they both accepted Christ as their personal savior in 1976. For the next seven years she grew in her faith along with her husband. When asked how she deals with the old ghosts of her past. Rebecca answers with a firm voice of conviction.

> "By God's grace and by comparing the feelings I have now and the feelings I had in the past. I'm now freed from the pressure to perform in order to be accepted."

Rebecca is truly a different person today. Her old self is no longer evident. Fortunately for her she was gifted by God with faith in Him and through His strength has overcome. Rebecca's most ardent prayer and concern today is for her own daughters to grow up with the proper development as young ladies and enter into adulthood with their minds and hearts prepared for the challenges of love and marriage that lie ahead. This is not going to be easy as Rebecca lost her husband in a helicopter accident in Germany and now she and the children must go on without him.

No small effort was put forth in the fight to reverse the negative impact of all of these destructive influences and tragic occurrences. My wife and I personally met with Rebecca and her children almost daily for over a year. We assisted her in structuring family meeting times, prayer, bible study times, scheduling and discipline issues. Much work and consistency went into this commitment. It was impossible for us to continue at this high level of involvement for a longer period of time. Just how much time is necessary for such a difficult family situation will always depend on the circumstances of each case. In this case much more time was needed for the best results. However, there was great growth and positive benefits for her and the children—just not enough to avoid some of the ultimate results of the damage already suffered.

The full impact of the lack of a father of faith and grace for Rebecca and her four children will not be known for many years. Although she is open for the possibility of a new husband it has not been possible for her, even though her children are now grown. There is evidence of long-term damage to the children and only God's providence and grace will bring the victories desired. The oldest daughter moved in with a man twenty five years her senior when she was only seventeen. They later married, have had some children but are struggling with many problems. Rebecca's oldest, a son, has had to spend some time in jail and is now trying to rehabilitate back into society. The younger daughters are doing better. The negative impacts seem to have been more for the two oldest. It is still too early to know how these lives will ultimately work out. God is still working on them, but their success would have been much greater and more assured through God's—original plan for Rebecca—a father of faith and grace when she was young!

**A virgin's God-given seal for chastity:**

As you can see, the young princess who submits to peer-pressure or other pressures which make her give up on the intuition and the dream inscribed upon her subconscious mind; suffers a lifetime of remorse. The reactions may not be as violent as those suffered when the violations come from intimate family members, but they are painful and do negatively affect her development as a woman and inhibit her relationship with her future husband.

Thus, you can actually say a virgin girl is sealed, with a deep need to fulfill this inscribed intuition of love in the context of true commitment. She has a need first to find the man who will, commit to her for life and prove it by his actions of honor and trust. After he makes his commitment public by entering into a lifetime commitment of marriage—then, and only then—will she be free to let down all of her mental, emotional, spiritual and physical barriers. She can now fully give herself to this man who loves her. This is the fulfillment of the intuition and dream inscribed upon her subconscious mind.

Now, for the first time, she has a basis for building a great sex life with the man of her dreams. A life of sexual intimacy and satisfaction for her and for her husband no other form or quality of relationship can bring! No real father of faith and grace would ever deny such an opportunity to his daughter, or would ever cause some other man's daughter to lose such an opportunity. Yet, every time some macho male (not a man of faith and grace, just a common, everyday, biological male) conquers a young virgin, he is destroying the God-given intuition and dream—every woman—should have the opportunity to realize. The picture should be pretty clear by now. The moral decay and poor self-image of many of today's women comes from not having had a real father of faith and grace, and by the treatment they have received at the hands of—would be—fathers and boy friends.

However, for the man who wants to be a father of faith and grace and measure up to the high calling of God's role for men and have the honor of leaving a positive psychological and spiritual imprint on his daughter, such realities are both a warning and a cry for help. They are a warning that as fathers we cannot take our male sexuality (our sex drive and fascination with the feminine form) for granted. They are a cry for help, pleading with all men to arise to the highest standards of chivalry and Godly fatherhood! Now, in view of the present condition, we must take corrective action to avoid repeating the mistakes and damage caused by generations of other misguided and poorly prepared men. We must not let such individuals set the standard by which we perceive and understand ourselves and women. We must hold our perspective of women, femininity and motherhood above reproach as gentlemen, and not as animals. This is possible, even in a world where many women have lost contact with their inner God-given intuition of their true value as God's women.

**Our power comes from above:**

As fathers we are family leaders, but we are not gods! We, too, must answer to a higher power and receive our strength, faith and motivation from our Heavenly Father, who is God. When we fail to realize our need for faith in, and strength from God, we show our rebellion. We ignore the power of our biological male sexuality to overcome our own limited ability to do what is morally right—we assume too much! Given constant opportunity and exposure, coupled with a lack of proper commitment, appreciation and respect for feminine sexuality, we can be tempted to do things we would otherwise find repugnant and impossible to imagine. As men of faith and grace we are not normally insensitive to God's revealed Law-Word, the real Right and Wrong. On the contrary, all men have normal desires and ambitions to be gentlemen and to be functionally correct in their conduct. These are noble ambitions and I do not deny their existence or wish to denigrate their importance for good self-image. Indeed, it is my intention to help you realize your ambitions and goals of gentlemanly conduct! However, ignoring our propensities for sexual arousal and assuming we are in control without exception, regardless of the circumstances, is not the most intelligent way to accomplish this goal. God's revealed truth says it best: Run—flee—do not stay in the presence of sexual temptation.[127]

**Dealing with our own vulnerability:**

We must first understand and be sensitive to our vulnerability under certain circumstances, in order to have the convictions and courage necessary to protect against those circumstances occurring. Let us pray God's grace and providence that He will not allow us to be tempted enough to encounter the limits of our vulnerability and that He will deliver us from evil.[128] Contrary to the macho attitude of many, accepting the reality of our vulnerabilities is the first step toward protecting against them!

There is not a grown man alive (assuming normal sanity) who does not know exactly what I'm talking about. You know, because the confirmation of what I am saying comes intact with all male bodies. I'm speaking to men, those who have insider information. I am not addressing these comments or observations to the unaware or the uninformed. Furthermore, it is not my intention to impugn your motives as fathers, or as men who will become fathers. I'm simply saying as fathers of faith and grace, we must adopt strict rules for our own sexual moral values and conduct. Otherwise we cannot expect to rear a daughter who will excel in moral standards. Indeed, she just might, but if she does, it will be in spite of us as her father, and not because of us!

---

127 "Flee fornication. Every sin that a man doeth is without the body: but he that commits fornication sins against his own body." I Cor. 6:18. "Flee also youthful lusts: but follow righteousness, faith, charity, peace with them that call on the Lord out of a pure heart." II Tim. 2:22

128 "Therefore do not be like them. For your Father knows the things you have need of before you ask Him. In this manner, therefore, pray:

"Our Father in heaven, Hallowed be Your name. Your kingdom come, Your will be done on earth as it is in heaven. Give us this day our daily bread. And forgive us our debts, as we forgive our debtors. And do not lead us into temptation, but deliver us from the evil one. For Yours is the kingdom and the power and the glory forever. Amen." Matt. 6:8-13.

Confirming a daughter's natural image of her father as Hero and Knight in shining armor is the proper response to our sexual fears and misgivings. Accepting this role with humility and inner pride not only takes the father and daughter into a new path of action and understanding, a path of protection for both the daughter and the father, but also establishes a moral basis for an exciting experience in father/daughter relationships.

Assuming a father is conducting himself as a gentleman and respecting his daughter's sexuality and is actively engaged in the role of a father of faith and grace and family leader, there develops a natural desire on her part to want to be tender and cuddly towards him. She is drawn naturally to his masculinity, strength and leadership and has a tremendous desire to know who he really is. Mother is wonderful in the eyes of a daughter, but does not hold the mysteries of the unknown like father does. As we have said, a daughter intuitively knows her father is different and—to her—very important. She sees him conducting the family meetings and setting standards and hears his comments concerning morals, values and principles.

**Zeroing in on Daddy:**

"Who is this person?" becomes a constant question in her mind. She sees him hugging and kissing Mommy, she hears some of the tender things he says to Mommy like, "I love you." or "You are so sweet." The very vocabulary he uses in his conversation with mother becomes a source of wonder and curiosity. Father uses words and body language with Mommy in a way different from the way he talks and handles her and her brothers. A young daughter is not sure why Daddy does these things, but for sure her curiosity and intuition are on full alert. As she gets older and begins to recognize and understand more fully her own unique sexuality as a female, she is thrilled to see the tenderness and caresses that Daddy gives to Mommy in her presence.

Daddy is her Hero, her Knight in shining armor, but he is also a very special Hero and Knight in shining armor for Mommy. In fact, you would think this would make her jealous. However, she intuitively knows Mommy and Daddy are special for each other, and these actions on the part of father only confirm to her his distinction as a Hero and Knight in shining armor. Intuition is not enough, however; she wants to know more and can be very demanding.

At this age of discovery, some earlier or later than others, it is not uncommon for a daughter to curl up on her Daddy's lap, look at him with deep penetrating eyes and a demonstration of demure sexuality, enough to scare a father to death, and say something in a coy little voice as, "Kiss me daddy, like you do mommy." or "Hug me daddy, like you do mommy."

Wow! Is this scary, or what?

The majority of men who experience this and who will tell you about it will tell you they are so amazed they don't know what to do. All too often there are a lot of mixed feelings and twinges, of fear running through a man's mind at a time like this.

**How not to respond:**

Many men, when this happens, experience such extreme feelings of fear, guilt and discomfort, they no longer want to let their little girls sit on their laps. They begin to push them away and in many little gestures indicate to their daughters that they are not comfortable with their sexuality and their presence.

This is devastating to a daughter. She has no idea why she is being cast off, or why it is no longer proper to sit on Daddy's lap.

"What have I done wrong?" "Is there something the matter with me?" "I'm ugly, and daddy doesn't love me anymore!" "Daddy hates me!" "I'm a bad girl!"

These are the thoughts of a little girl who has been consistently rejected in this way by her Daddy.

I know, and I do understand that those who have done this and who have experienced the fear, misgivings, guilt and discomfort, did not mean to reject their daughter, or indicate any lack of love for her! Don't hate yourself. Self hate will not help you or your daughter, who still needs you and who still wants to know who you are. You are a victim of a society which knows a lot more about making automobiles and going to the moon than it knows about developing genuinely effective fathers! However, ignorance and a corrupt "Christian" society will not carry water with our Lord! He will never accept an attitude of victim-hood—He has already gifted us as over-comers!

Unfortunately for all too many fathers, even—sincere, responsible, caring fathers—regardless of their education and position in life, they find these negative responses to a young daughters developing sexuality necessary. Let's face it, the response of most men in these situations is to feel uncomfortable and threatened by a young daughters developing sexuality. What is the proper response? What does a father do to respond properly and at the same time not be insensitive to his little daughter's needs and feelings? This is a very tender and precious moment for daddy and his little girl. A lot of points can be made or lost at a time like this!

**Responding properly:**

There are many ways you could phrase your response, but the objective is to let your daughter know there is a difference between the way you kiss and hold Mommy, and the way you kiss and hold her, and why.

First of all don't act surprised at her show of femininity and curiosity. Accept it as a normal developing response. Accept with pride her love and care for you and her desire for your tenderness. Rejection or any semblance of it is not what you want to do.

Laugh with her, be playful, and give her a big hug and a Daddy kiss. Then simply say, "Honey, Daddy is Mommy's husband and I kiss Mommy the way husbands kiss and I kiss you the way Daddies kiss."

Keep it simple and to the point. Some will respond with other questions and requests for more information. Use the opportunity to explain further the special relationship between you and her mother. These conversations will please her very much. She is very interested and curious to know how you fit into the picture. She will come to you again and again and indicate her desire for you to tell her more. Mostly, she wants to be reassured of your love.

The fact of your relationship with Mommy being different from your relationship with her is no big surprise. However, you are her Hero and Knight in shining armor, and at first she is not sure she wants to share you with anyone, not even Mommy. Fortunately this is only a momentary fear. Through your wise actions and tender words she quickly realizes Mommy is very special for you and it becomes a privilege to share you.

By God's grace—you are and will always remain in her sight a Hero, a Knight in shining armor!

# Book II

# DADDY'S LITTLE GIRL

## Chapter Six

## Daddy's Little Princess and Her Virtue

**Virtue and the Princess:**

The virtue of every daughter begins at the level of Princess. Mother is the "Queen of the Universe," Daddy is "King," Sons are "Princes" and daughters are all "Princesses."

You can't use the word princess without thinking of someone young, special, tender and innocent. This is the true picture of every newborn daughter. She is a new beginning. She is a new book whose chapters have not yet been written. She is like new snow on a mountain side before the first track has been made. She is brand new; she is a virgin in both mind and body.

Virginity signifies much more than is commonly accepted. Prevailing attitudes in today's world have reduced the state of virginity to a limited perspective, relative to sexual activity. If a young girl has not had intercourse, then she is considered to be a virgin. Although this is one correct use of the word "virgin," it is a very limited perspective relative to all that it signifies for a newborn baby girl!

The tragedy of so many young, pregnant girls and unwed mothers in our society is evidence of how ungodly fatherhood is being practiced in far too many American homes. For many, these tragedies among our young female population indicate the state of "princess" did not last very long.

Virginity is a state of mind and being much more so than it is the absence of sexual activity. The essence of virginity, in mind and body for our young princess begins from the moment of birth. Abstinence from sexual activity and the protection of sexual virtue come after the state of virginity has been well-established in a young girl's mind and being—not before.

In addition to the proper attitudes and actions of a real father of faith and grace towards his daughter he makes it a point to emphasize the reality of his daughter's newness and special place in life, while she is still a young girl. He will tell her plainly and to the point how like a new book she is, full of blank pages and future chapters yet to be written. He will emphasize the importance of by whom and how these pages are written upon.

When a newborn baby girl is blessed with such a father, one who will take on the responsibilities of family leadership, as we have outlined, she grows up with a special kind of love for Daddy. She trusts him, respects him, looks up to him, obeys his instructions, and knows he is a true Hero and Knight in shining armor. Her natural, God-given intuition of who he is has not been shattered. In short, she loves him so much he is her first choice to be the man of her dreams and to be her future husband. The latter is much more than just a childish dream. A stark example is found in the women who come from abusive fathers and who are attracted to abusive men—think about it—our imprint on our daughter is so strong than even when we are vile reprobates this becomes an attraction for her! Our hope and prayer to God must be for the positive imprint that we can leave!

**A daughter's most important author:**

A new thought perhaps, challenging for sure, but we must accept it—the person who writes the most in the first chapters of the book of life of each little new princess—is her father! These first chapters in her book of life establish forever who she thinks she is and how she should conduct herself in her quest for life's goals. Without the role of a real father of faith and grace who will accept the challenge to inscribe the Right things in these first chapters, the little princess begins to languish and becomes disoriented and lost.

At 57, Gloria Steinem, the famous feminist movement leader, co-founder and editor of "Ms. Magazine," revealed for the first time some of the details of how and why she became so enraged at men and suffered her loss of self. She reveals in her new book, "Revolution from Within: A Book of Self-Esteem" that when she began keeping company with billionaire real estate developer, Mort Zuckerman, in the late '80s, what she really fell for was his car. Not just any car, you understand, but a warm, chauffeur-driven cocoon of transit Zuckerman had dispatched to meet her as she returned to La Guardia Airport late one night from one of her many fund-raising trips, so exhausted that the auto's "sheltering presence loomed out of all proportion." She says she sank into the soft leather interior of the car that night at La Guardia, and felt as insecure as a junk bond, without energy, without hope and without enough self-esteem to resist this inappropriate but eager suitor. "This relationship," she writes, "became a final clue that I was really lost."

She traces her loss of self to the day her 300-lb. father, an itinerant salesman, abandoned her when she was 10 years old in a rat-infested, dilapidated farm house fronting on a major highway in Toledo. She was left to care for her mentally ill mother. Through her strong determination she managed to escape to Smith College but never escaped the trap of being the caretaker. Once she became involved in the feminist movement there was no campus, community group or benefit so small that she wouldn't hop a plane and raise money for it. She seemed to take "personal responsibility for every oppressed woman in America." Steinem says.

In reality—although she doesn't know this even to this day—her father had abandoned her—emotionally, spiritually, morally and as her guide and champion for feminine success—long before he physically left her in that rat-infested farm house. He had abandoned her by not being a real father of faith and grace—and by default—he wrote all the Wrong things in the first chapters of her book of life—she is still not over it!

**Bad or missing authorship from father brings destructive results:**

Young girls and women like Gloria are truly lost without a father of faith and grace and until they find themselves—which is very hard if not impossible to do—they will continue to be lost. They are lost to the hopes and dreams that God intended for them to have: namely, a love that will be true and faithful to them all their lives, a true home, an environment in which to bear and rear a family and to express their natural inner drives to be ladies and mothers. Instead, all they get are frustrated lives with men who lead them into premature, premarital sex, male partners who don't understand the meaning of love, much less how to live it, and for many, babies not much younger than they are.

This is more than just a personal tragedy, this is a national tragedy. Millions of young girls are not just lost to themselves; they are lost to their families, their communities, their states, and to their nation. Furthermore, they are producing many more millions of offspring, who will be just as lost as they are! Short of a massive effort to have their offspring adopted into families with real fathers of faith and grace, who would take on the task of being responsible for them, there is little or no hope for their proper rearing. As this is very unlikely to happen, words cannot express the depth of this tragedy; only time and many years of suffering will show us how tragic it really is.

In 1988, according to The Children's Defense Fund, about one million teenage girls got pregnant and almost two-thirds of all births to teens were to unmarried girls, compared to less than one-third in 1970. The numbers are staggering and only continued to get worse until the nineties. We now have stats that show a slight annual decrease in the numbers of unwed mothers, but these "improvements" in stats seem to be coming from an increase in teenage marriages not from a decrease in America's overall moral decay.

How is it possible to have a society which produces young girls who can get pregnant at ten and twelve years of age? How is it possible for us to have allowed our family structure in this great country of ours—America—the land of the free and the home of the brave, to be so destroyed? How is it possible that of all new born babies in our great land, over 25%, based on 1991 reports are born to unwed mothers? When broken down into different ethnic groups, the figure goes as high as 70% of all births, in some groups. How is this possible?

Let me tell you. There is only one way that it is possible. It is possible only in a land where men have abdicated their most important and most sacred role, that of fathers of faith and grace. It can happen only in a land and a society where men refuse—for whatever reasons—to accept their God-given role as fathers of truth and grace. Only fathers of faith and grace can successfully embrace God's Great Commission for Fatherhood and accept the responsibility of being moral role models, teachers, counselors, disciplinarians and leaders for their families. Men—we either stand in the gap or we surrender to the enemy—running is no option!

**Gone with the wind:**

This is what has happened to America, the land of the free and the home of the brave. Where are the free, and where are the brave? All too many of our men are not very brave—where bravery counts the most—in the family! Consequently, not very many of our men are free, for to be free is to have the power to do what is right and to be in control of your family and its destiny. Unfortunately, the majority of men in America have accepted license and cowardliness in place of God's power to give us courage and freedom!

In addition to the creation of millions of lost girls, the abdication by men to be no more than just biological fathers has also produced a whole generation of women who have no idea who they really are, or how to go about finding real happiness and success. Thus, in spite of the reality of every woman beginning as a Princess, and a virgin, the daughter of some man, somewhere, a great many have turned to such hollow substitutes as "Feminist, " "Equal Rights," and "Pro-Choice" movements as substitutes. Yet, regardless of the "pros" and "cons" of these movements, they will never take the place of a real father of faith and grace.

The anger and disappointment over lost virtue, lost "virginity" of mind, soul and body, of millions of women, is expressed in these movements. In reality they are using these movements to express their displeasure over never having had real fathers of faith and grace, and as a hopeful medium to find meaning and purpose in who they really are. These bruised women, of which at least half claim to be Christian, are ignorant of the facts and of God's revealed truth that speaks volumes concerning the cause of their problem—but all they seem to be able to do is to lash out. They bash Christianity, blame society, hold the government responsible and offer as solutions ideas that could—only be born—in hell!

In fact you may rest assured that this book, *Daddy's Little Girl and Mommy's Little Boy,* and everything we are discussing relative to fathers and mothers of faith and grace and the present state of our affairs as a "Christian" nation—especially our claim of ungodly fathers and mothers—will be reduced to a claim that all we are doing is, bashing men and women! Remember, you only "bash" something when you simply offer endless criticism without any viable solutions. Unfortunately the very people[129] who are—most responsible for our corrupt "Christian" society—will also cast blame and dispersion our way for bashing the Church and ministry leaders! So be it—we're in good company.

Insofar as there are injustices towards women and their needs in this life—that too—is a demonstration of the lack of male leadership in our society. Consider: true male leadership starts at home, not in business or political office. Either one of the sexes is competent to officiate in the latter roles, but only men can be fathers of faith and grace. Only men have the God-given role to establish their daughters' virtue and personal self-image. Real fathers of faith and grace are concerned about justice, rights and equality for their women, whereas men who just use them as sex objects are—tools of Satan—and couldn't care less.

**Abortion—an evil of the male heart!**

Unfortunately, of the three movements mentioned above, the most despicable and unworthy of a real mother is the concept that abortion is merely a physical matter over a sexual inconvenience. If you don't want it, or you don't think you can rear it properly, kill it! This is the response of pro-abortionists to the lack of fatherhood in the American family! In addition, women who have had abortions and have suffered the consequences of post abortion syndrome joined together into several different support groups: Women Exploited by Abortion, Victims of Choice, and American Victims of Abortion. Their research proves that 75%-80% of all abortions are done because of pressure from a male figure somewhere in the relationship: fathers, husbands, lovers, and even bosses. Her abortion is a solution to "their problem!" The only freedom of "choice" is revealed to be more that of the man and NOT the woman!

With fathers of faith and grace, virtue is established and cherished, good self-image is attained, personal discovery and a sense of belonging are achieved. The unwanted pregnancy never occurs, and if one does occur, for whatever reasons, abortion would be out of the question except perhaps in very rare cases to save the young mother's life.

You don't have to believe me. Just ask any woman who has been reared by a real father of faith and grace; she will tell you the same thing. Ask any young girl who is now experiencing the reality of such a father; she too will tell you the same thing. These women have virtue, they have a good self-image, they know who they are, and they know what it takes to experience and attain the love and family goals that they want for themselves and their children.

Now, if you don't know any such women or girls, or you think they are in short supply that is another matter. This is because we have so few males who are willing to accept their roles as real fathers of faith and grace. Being born—male—only identifies one's biological sex. A man of faith and grace is a product of the Holy Spirit; it is definitely not a product of elitist social engineering! In stark

[129] "Then the scribes and Pharisees who were from Jerusalem came to Jesus, saying, 'Why do your disciples transgress the tradition of the elders? For they do not wash their hands when they eat bread.' He answered and said to them, 'Why do you also transgress the commandment of God because of your tradition? For God commanded, saying, 'Honor your father and your mother;' and, 'He who curses father or mother, let him be put to death.' But you say, 'Whoever says to his father or mother, 'Whatever profit you might have received from me is a gift to God'—then he need not honor his father or mother.' Thus you have made the commandment of God of no effect by your tradition. Hypocrites! Well did Isaiah prophesy about you, saying: These people draw near to Me with their mouth, and honor Me with their lips, but their heart is far from Me. And in vain they worship Me, teaching as doctrines the commandments of men."' Matt. 15:1-9.

contrast—it is all such biological males who seek—the role and responsibility to be a real father of faith and grace, who make the first step toward becoming one!

**Even hearts of stone aspire to honor a daughter's virtue:**

How to protect the virtue of his daughter is the secret desire of every father. It is truly amazing! Rare would be the case where a father—any father—would self consciously think of his little girl in degrading terms. No matter how immoral a man he is, or how reduced in his own self-image he might be, or how evil in the eyes of society he might be, he will always—at least tell—you that he wants his little baby girl to grow up protected and to be a lady of virtue. How rare in deed that you should hear him say such gross things as:

> "I hope my little girl turns out to be a good whore." or "I sure hope my little girl turns out to be a good stripper and man teaser." or "I sure hope my little girl gets pregnant as soon as she can."

Nonsense! These are things that only happen to—other men's—little girls. No sane man consciously desires or thinks that such degrading experiences will ever happen to—his—little girl. Remember, even an appeal of insanity for such crimes will not stand in the Lord's court of justice. Such attitudes and statements of desire are not normal; they are contrary to God's revealed Law-Word. It is the natural desire for a father, any father—even the unregenerate—to want to protect his daughter's virtue and to envision personal protection and success for his little girl. This being true, as I'm sure all will agree, then why are there so many girls living unprotected, bruised, damaged, abused, lost and aimless lives?

The dismal record of our nation's young women indicates there is a big difference between just wanting a daughter to be virtuous, protected, have a good self-image and actually seeing her attain these goals. As we said before, a young princess's virginity is more than just physical.

**Virginity Is:**

1. Mental

2. Psychological

3. Spiritual

4. Sexual

**God's key element for a daughter's virtue:**

Developing these four areas properly is the beginning of her personal self-discovery and self-image as God intended her to have—not as the world would teach her. And no one plays a more important role in helping her develop properly in these areas than does her father! This unique and very important role of father is most definitely needed by all "Daddy's little girls" but it will only be provided and best assured by a father of faith and grace. Such faith in action by these fathers is their best assurance that their little girl's virtue and chastity will be successfully protected.

But be assured of this: nothing good is going to happen if all we fathers do is intellectualize these facts. This book is not written to give you information for discussion—our purpose is to motivate you to action! This is a how—TO DO—book not a how—to know—book!

Although many might say they know, even if true, so far in recent history few—very few—have taken action. This is not a new phenomenon in the spiritual struggle of men. James had to deal with this same problem of knowing—but not doing—in his ministry in the first century. Fathers of faith and grace do not have the luxury of not making a decision—this is war—and a call to action is our only possible response! The spirit and principle of what the Apostle James says in James 1:22-25 is this:

Knowing is not enough—we must apply! Understanding is not enough—we must do! Knowing and understanding in action is what distinguishes the life of a man of faith and grace from those who only have illusions and who only talk. The father of faith and grace knows he receives his power to perform from above, thus, he demonstrates genuine faith through action—for faith is not an adjective it is a—verb, it is action—or it is nothing.

Let me emphasis again, this is not machismo, the fathers of faith and grace know they are not the source of their power to overcome. The action they demonstrate through their gift of faith is based on God's revealed Law-Word, which promises them the power to overcome through Christ in them. John 15:15-21 and I Cor. 15:56-58.[130]

James is often mistakenly characterized as someone who actually taught salvation by law. Contrary to such unenlightened conclusions is the overwhelming context of all that James says. What James is clearly saying to the redeemed is that this gift of faith from above is spiritual in origin but manifests itself in visible action.

**First; her mental development:**

In your position as family leader, moral role model, counselor and teacher, you have the first opportunity of feeding her mind the correct data, she needs to know, concerning how to think of and accept her self. This is more than just class-room type instructions, such as you will have in family meetings. In addition to these meetings, she needs action. Action beginning with the father's attitude towards her mother! She needs her father's words of kindness and appreciation. Our establishment of the family moral structure, our discipline and respect for her personal sexuality, all play an important role in her mental development.

**Second; her psychological development:**

Her psychological development is in parallel with her mental development. She will develop sound, dependable emotions in general and in particular where men are concerned, based on the quality of your efforts and actions. A young girl is very tender in many ways, but she is especially tender, psychologically. Her natural propensity for high ideals, high standards of virtue and moral character make her especially susceptible to life's rude awakenings, and moral disappointments. One of your objectives as a father is to introduce her to these realities gently and with understanding. This protects her natural tendency for idealism; at the same time it prepares her for dealing with the lesser reality at large.

---

[130] "If you love Me, keep My commandments. And I will pray the Father, and He will give you another Helper, that He may abide with you forever—the Spirit of truth, whom the world cannot receive, because it neither sees Him nor knows Him; but you know Him, for He dwells with you and will be in you. I will not leave you orphans; I will come to you. A little while longer and the world will see Me no more, but you will see Me. Because I live, you will live also. At that day you will know that I am in My Father, and you in Me, and I in you. He who has My commandments and keeps them, it is he who loves Me. And he who loves Me will be loved by My Father, and I will love him and manifest Myself to him." John 15:15-21.

"The sting of death is sin, and the strength of sin is the law. But thanks be to God, who gives us the victory through our Lord Jesus Christ. Therefore, my beloved brethren, be steadfast, immovable, always abounding in the work of the Lord, knowing that your labor is not in vain in the Lord." I Cor. 15:56-58.

**Third; her spiritual development:**

Her spiritual development can be appreciated only when one understands the magnitude and importance of what has already been said. Her natural propensity for high ideals, high standards of virtue and moral character brings with it a special need for help. A young woman has an inner sense of her own delicate nature and her need for protection, mentally, psychologically and physically which young men do not share. It is as though her own need for protection and proper moral structure, added to her natural drive for motherhood, give her this added dimension of spiritual sensitivity and need.

**Fourth; our young Princess has all of these:**

Our young Princess has all of these characteristics, mental, psychological and spiritual, embodied within her unique total sexual make-up. She is female, she is woman, she is a virgin. All of these characteristics are part and parcel of her virtue and her virginity. She is a virgin in all of these areas. She is a virgin mentally—no one has yet written any data on her blank mental pages of life concerning her sexuality and future attitude toward herself and men. She is a virgin psychologically—she will develop her emotional maturity and reactions to femininity and role as a woman and future wife as she receives input into her blank mental pages. She is a virgin spiritually—she has not yet sensed her God-given role as a woman and as a unique soul and spirit. Her physical virginity is in reality only a fourth element in the total picture of her state of virtue and virginity. To deal honestly and successfully with the virtue and virginity of our Princesses, we fathers must accept the perspective of the whole picture, and not just think of their virginity in the singular concept of physical intercourse with the opposite sex.

**Good beginnings make for future successes:**

When she surrenders her physical virginity in marriage, her sexual development and success after marriage will be in direct proportion, good or bad, depending on the quality and success of how and with whom she surrenders her virginity in those unique feminine areas that are—NOT—physical. Ideally and in keeping with the goals of this book and our ministry, this surrender should be to her father. In order for her to understand how and with whom to share her physical virginity, she must first have had understanding and experience in sharing the virginity of her mental, psychological and spiritual make-up. As you now know, our culture has mistakenly assumed that this would be an experience she would share with her mother. Now we know that it is her father who is uniquely gifted to lead her in these areas. It is her father who actually writes these first important chapters in her book of life. He does so, even if he has abandoned her or is deceased while she is yet a baby. A father's mark is left on her either by his action or his inaction.

A young daughter intuitively desires to share the first three aspects of her virginity, her innocence of mental, psychological, and spiritual make-up with her father. It is natural for her to open her mind, her emotions and her spiritual make-up to him first.

- Mentally, she will submit her mind to his teaching.

- Emotionally, she will condition her emotional responses to life based on what she learns from him, in word and by example.

- Spiritually, she will respond quickly to his spiritual leadership. In essence the sum total of all her expressions of moral character and sexual conduct as a woman will be what she has learned or not learned from her father.

**Being drawn to Christ by our Heavenly Father:**

A young girl, when exposed to the possibility of a personal relationship with God through prayer and an awakened awareness of His presence, will respond much more quickly than will a young boy of similar age. Young boys are not spiritually insensitive. Boys simply attain strong sensitivity to their spiritual needs at a later age.

As an adolescent young boy, did you respond positively to your inner sense of your own spiritual needs, or did you listen to the voice of temptation and accept the notion of God as dead and make up your own rules, that is, draw your own Map of life's Right and Wrong?

I am writing this book especially for men who have already recognized and acted on God's gift of faith in them. However, if you are reading this and you have not yet done so—then I urge you to begin by taking these first steps toward discovering your gift of faith. Many men resist the move of the Spirit. If you are one of those, and you have not yet dealt with your own spiritual needs honestly, openly, and with a sincere heart, you need to deal with this important area. I suggest you begin by, first of all, secluding yourself and offering a short and simple prayer. Something like:

> "Heavenly Father, I need to know you. Forgive me for having been wrong about you and your part in my life and the life of my family. Help me to understand and to know your reality and your personal involvement with men."

This is not a prayer of confession of faith in Christ, but rather an appeal to God the Father to consider your sinful state—to draw you to Christ your Savior through His gift of faith. God's revealed Law-Word is clear, unless you be drawn to Christ by the Father you cannot believe. Some will tell you that all you have to do is "raise your hand," don't believe it! Seek the Father. He and only He is faithful to know your heart and to give you the gift of life eternal through faith! Unfortunately, our churches are filled with individuals who raised their hands but whom the Father has never drawn.[131] Much needs to be said and done about this but for now—seek the Father. He is faithful.

**Actions must follow the words of a sincere man or woman:**

Follow this up by including regular church attendance in your family's activities. Visit several churches and be sensitive to getting the answer to your prayer. You will get answers. You will get insight as to where you should go to church and what you should do. Only consider churches offering at least three spiritual growth basics:

1. One that consistently teaches salvation by faith only in Jesus Christ and that as a gift and act of God: Read: John 1:12-14; Eph. 2:8-10; and II Cor. 2:14-16

---

[131] "Beware of false prophets, who come to you in sheep's clothing, but inwardly they are ravenous wolves. You will know them by their fruits. Do men gather grapes from thornbushes or figs from thistles? Even so, every good tree bears good fruit, but a bad tree bears bad fruit. A good tree cannot bear bad fruit, nor can a bad tree bear good fruit. Every tree that does not bear good fruit is cut down and thrown into the fire. Therefore by their fruits you will know them." Matt. 7:15-20.

2. One that teaches personal responsibility for one's actions and for repentance and submission to the sovereign will of God for one's life. Read: Acts 20:22-24; Gal. 2:17-21; and Mk. 5:36, 10:30

3. One that teaches strong support for parents as the primary family leaders, and for fathers as the heads of the family leadership. Read: I Pet. 3:7; Col. 3:18-21; I Tim. 3:4-5; and Eph. 6:1-4

You cannot be a father of faith and grace without God so—just do it—and expect Him to guide you. I have focused on this reality from several different perspectives. At the risk of over emphasizing; I continue to remind us all of our dependence upon our Heavenly Father for the source of our faith, grace, wisdom, understanding—the motivation and strength to express our love for our little girl in actions—that reflect His uncommon common sense.

As I have said before: A father of faith and grace is an oxymoron if there is no personal reality of experience in walking in this way. None can be a spiritual leader in his own family if he doesn't know anything about God, or doesn't have any experience of trusting in Him to be a part of his own daily life. Our descriptive term—father of faith and grace—is not a physical badge of identification. This is not something you show off—like the radical left atheist liberals—who wear ribbons, pins and bumper stickers every time they do a "GOOD WORK!" This is a term that describes not the physical man—but the inner man—a man who trusts in the revealed truth of fatherhood in God's word. A man who takes his marching orders from the—Father of fathers—from the source of all truth. There is nothing wrong with ribbons, pins or bumper stickers in and of themselves, but we need to examine our motives when we use them.

**Our enemy is not external but internal:**

Ideally speaking, the Right aspects of these developmental processes should be the same her mother learned from her own father, and which she continues to experience now, in a deeper and much more intimate way with her husband, the father of this young princess. Our present post modern culture has afforded us only a scant few examples of the trans-generational possibility. To salvage what little moral fiber we have left in our Christian culture and to renew the battle, we must enlist the self conscious commitment to action from millions of Christian fathers. Nothing less will do. God need not bring our rightly deserved discipline through external means—our enemy is within. All Christian fathers who refuse to accept their own personal responsibility in this war against the spiritual and moral decay of our culture are the enemy within. Our Heavenly Father is not looking to the unbelievers for elements with which to change our spiritual decay and moral morass! He only disciplines sons. If we look to the secular social engineers of our post modern culture—we are looking to the children of Satan to do the work God has called us to do. May God have mercy on us—forgive us our sins—corporately and individually and lift us up from the dust of our unbelief to the heights and glories of what is possible in Christian family development.

The need of a woman for this emotional, moral and stabilizing leadership never ends. The only difference between the relationship of the father with the mother of this young Princess, and herself is that the young Princess does not share her physical sexual intimacies and physical virginity with her father. This is reserved for the young man who will take her father's place and provide the ongoing role of emotional, moral and stabilizing leadership. In addition to family leadership, it is clearly God's intention that this future male relationship will provide a new, deeper and much more intimate love for our Princess, which will include fulfilling all her sexual desires and needs.

**A young Princess of faith and grace knows:**

When our Princess decides with whom to share her physical virginity it encompasses a great truth concerning her feminine sexuality, one not entirely lost to the moral and social structure of our times, but certainly badly damaged. As men and fathers we must be open minded and determined to understand this truth and refocus our perspective.

Physical virginity is not something for a young girl to surrender just to experience her first act of sexual intercourse. Sexual intercourse is an expression of surrender and love far beyond sex. In fact, good sex, which leaves you feeling satisfied physically, emotionally, and spiritually, is possible only by doing at least two things:

**First:**

One must decide and commit to a life-long love for the person with whom they are going to have sex.

**Second:**

They must have the experience of being reared by a real father and mother of faith and grace. As we have said, such a father will have already written in the first pages of her book of life. Through both word and deed he will have reinforced the basis for her moral fiber, values, principles and good self-image. She knows who she is and with her father's help, she even knows why it is wrong to give her sexual virginity to a man who has not decided to love and be committed to her for life.

Our young princess knows this for two basic reasons: The first is from her own God-given inner source of intuition. Giving her virginity to a man without his life-long decision of love and commitment to her is wrong and in her heart she knows it. Plain and simple, it is wrong. She might not know exactly how to explain why it is wrong, but her sensitivity—read gift of faith—to God's revealed Law-Word assures her that it is. Left to herself, without—Satan's tools—the distracting influence and claims of "free love" and "sexual liberality" of our present morally bankrupt society, she would never experiment with the idea of such behavior being Right.

**The unregenerate mind rationalizes that no harm is done:**

The prevailing situation leaves a great deal to be desired! Virginity—in America's "Christian," morally bankrupt society—is considered to be more of a liability than a virtue or blessing, to share with one special person—one love. It is regarded by far too many, as something to give up as soon as possible so you can get on with your "normal" sex life of seeking more and better orgasms. For the uninformed I suggest that you look around in your congregation and take note of how many couples are living together before marriage. This blatant form of sexual experimentation is open rebellion against God, it is sexual sin, as well as the many other forms—that can be easily picked up on, if you're looking—are only the tip of the iceberg.

> "This is the way of an adulterous woman: She eats and wipes her mouth, and says, "I have done no wickedness."" Proverbs 30:20.

Let's face it, the experiment has been made, the findings are in. In reality, the results are not better and better orgasms or "better" sex of any kind. What happens is a monstrous atmosphere of sexual, emotional and spiritual poverty and frustration!

Without the presence of a resolute father to provide the family leadership, as we have described, there is no reason to assume anything other than chaos will result from such unrealistic attitudes about virginity. The young girl who gives her physical virginity to a man, young or old, whose only interest in her is his own limited, short-sighted single-dimension perspective of sexual intercourse and orgasm is not one who has had the advantage of being reared by a real father of faith and grace! This girl, young or old, is simply yielding to pressures other than those which will bring her satisfaction. If you know in advance you are not going to get the kind of results and satisfaction you want, you don't do it. It's not necessary to experiment with sex to know if you are going to get the results and satisfaction you want. To know the difference simply requires understanding what real sex is!

**Leadership is more than warnings:**

Mothers can and do warn their daughters about sex. They tell them the kind you get in the back seat of a car with the local hot football jock, or with any other man, for a one-night fling, is not the kind that satisfies mentally, emotionally or physically. Mothers know, all too often, from their own mistakes. However, daughters resent this information from mothers. The daughters intuitively know and are expectant that such information and instruction will come from their father.

Allow me to digress for a moment. Are you one of those men who think they are good fathers, but who won't assume the direct responsibility for their daughters' moral development, but instead will insist their wives assume the role and tell their little girls about boys and sex?

After all, isn't the mother supposed to do it? Well, yes, if we allow ourselves to be controlled by the stereotypes of the past and spiritual wimp girly men stumbling all around us. However, if we're resolute in our pursuit of fulfilling our—Great Commission in the experience of fatherhood—definitely not! It is this myopic view of the stilted role of "father" that creates the castrated male "Christian" within our midst. I do not believe that men who have been given the gift of faith to believe in Jesus Christ as their savior are men who will knowingly acquiesce to the cacophony of Christ's enemies!

When we fathers don't accept our proper role as fathers, then when it doesn't work and things go from bad to worse, our first line of defense is to blame our wife for not teaching our daughter how we wanted her to be. I'm the first to admit that I did just that! When things began to go wrong with my oldest daughter at about the age of 12, I blamed Marilyn and took up the reigns thinking I was doing sacrificial duty because she had failed. I later came to understand how wrong I was. Then I asked her to forgive me and I also thanked my Lord for animating me to take action.

**Leadership is more than angry outbursts:**

It is all too easy in these tense moments to even disavow our own parent and father relationship with the "Princess" we used to lovingly call: "Daddy's little girl. Now up-set and angry with the results of our non-activity and non-commitment—we verbally strike out at our sweet wife with—"Your daughter this and your daughter that." At this depth of ignorance and misinformation we unrealistically assume that by doing thus we drive our point home more successfully to the little wife letting her know we—really mean business—and that we want better results! Accusations begin to fly, like:

> "Why do you let her go out with a boy like that?" "Didn't I tell you I didn't want her to see the bum?" "How many times do I have to tell you not to let her date any of those boys?"

However, as we have discovered, such instructions from the mother only invoke resentment from the daughter. Daughters will not accept moral values about sex from their mothers. All such instructions and introduction into the realities of the male world that hold any promise of being successful will come from their fathers; they intuitively know it and won't accept anything less. If this very sensitive instruction does not come from the father, it only frustrates them and makes them bitter towards men in general and bitter towards their biological fathers in particular.

These futile efforts—by mothers—to attempt to do for their daughters what their own mothers could not do for them, is one of society's real life tragedies. The concern is natural, the effort, without a father of faith and grace, is tragically inadequate!

**The empty fruit of warnings and angry outbursts:**

Get the picture: Consider the situation of a woman who has never had the advantage of a real father of faith and grace. She deeply resents her mother's efforts to control and instruct her in the ways of men. She could easily see the lack of success on the part of her own mother, concerning her biological father. She wants no advice from her. She intuitively knows it should come from her father. But, by now she has lost all hope that he will ever be what she thought in her heart he should have been—in the absence of such responsibility on his part—she figures she must be mistaken, so she turns to a morally bankrupt secular liberal society to teach her. At this point some will exclaim:

> "Wait a minute; she should go to her local Christian community leaders!"

Oh, I see, you mean like the leaders who are helping all of those others—their wives, daughters and single moms—in their congregations, right? If you haven't noticed—it is for lack of such qualified leaders, that so many assume must be out there—that our Christian culture is in the corrupt state that we are!! Granted, if a congregation has proven qualified leaders—in romance, sex, love and marriage—by all means these should be considered.

However, this is normally an exercise in futility and usually reveals the pathetic state of our current post modern Christian culture! It's like turning the lambs out to the wolves! All of the many Christian leaders I have personally interviewed on the matter—agree with the evidence supporting my claims concerning our problem—but they all have refused to take action for lack of preparedness to be involved in such an enormous personal undertaking. The good news is that a few leaders—very few but enough to give hope—are beginning to take action. This is extremely encouraging and a factor, on which I am hopeful, will prove to be the forerunner, of a great revival in families of faith and grace in our Christian culture, now and in our time!

Enter the transgenerational tragedy: This same woman, now a mother, now full of all the natural concerns of a mother for her daughter, resorts to the same empty, pathetic and powerless drivel her own mother used on her!

> "Don't let boys put their hands on you honey!" "Please don't get your nose and eyebrows pierced, and don't you have any better clothes to wear than that?" "Oh, Honey, are you sure that is a good boy you are seeing, he looks so rough?" "Sweetheart, you know your daddy doesn't want you going out with boys at your age, of course you can't date that boy!" "Etc., .etc. etc......."

You fill in the blanks, you can be the judge; you have all heard them.

**We must rise above our guilt feelings:**

Fathers and mothers who already have girls of a personal discovery dating age and who identify with the above—could easily feel guilty and frustrated when they read this book. As we have already discovered, in Chapter Two, *Recapturing Virtue*, once we come to grips with our sins and loss of virtue God is faithful to lead us into the paths that lead to recapturing our virtue.[132] None of us like the feelings we get when we are faced with the things we do that are wrong. This is especially so when a lot of those are things—we did to others or had done to us—when we didn't know or perceive them to be as wrong as they really were. At such times it is natural to feel remorse and guilt. Although feelings of guilt and remorse—in and of themselves—have never made anything right, they can be a blessing. They are a blessing in as much as they can and should prompt us to action—to REPENT of the old bad habits—and to be committed to actions based on truth.

Guilt and remorse are like worry; they grow only in an atmosphere of introspection without constructive or corrective action. Once we decide to take action and put our minds and efforts to work to solve the problem, we become excited about the possibilities of the new solution. Once we make a commitment and step out on faith—God in faithfulness to His promises for enablement—begins to direct our efforts into His prepared steps[133] of victory for our lives.

**Personal Discovery Dating:**

How a father and mother of faith and grace establish dating is a very important discovery in this book. It applies to both sons and daughters and I have chosen to place it in: Book III, Chapter Three, *The First Discovery Date*. If you can't stand to wait until you reach that chapter, turn to it now and read it next.

---

[132] "O LORD, I know the way of man is not in himself; it is not in man who walks to direct his own steps. O LORD, correct me, but with justice; not in Your anger, lest You bring me to nothing." Jeremiah 10:23-24.

[133] "When a man's ways please the LORD, he makes even his enemies to be at peace with him. Better is a little with righteousness, than vast revenues without justice. A man's heart plans his way, but the LORD directs his steps." Proverbs 16:7-9.

"The steps of a good man are ordered by the LORD, and He delights in his way. Though he fall, he shall not be utterly cast down; for the LORD upholds him with His hand. I have been young, and now I am old, yet I have not seen the righteous forsaken, nor his descendants begging bread. He is ever merciful, and lends; and his descendants are blessed." Psalms 37:23-26.

"Your testimonies are wonderful; therefore my soul keeps them. The entrance of Your words gives light; it gives understanding to the simple. I opened my mouth and panted, for I longed for Your commandments. Look upon me and be merciful to me, as Your custom is toward those who love Your name. Direct my steps by Your word, and let no iniquity have dominion over me. Redeem me from the oppression of man, that I may keep Your precepts. Make Your face shine upon Your servant, and teach me Your statutes. Rivers of water run down from my eyes, because men do not keep Your law. Righteous are You, O LORD, and upright are Your judgments." Psalms 119:129-137.

# Book II

# DADDY'S LITTLE GIRL

## Chapter Seven

## A Daughter's Dream Come True

**Bonding is a decision of Fatherhood:**

Father/daughter bonding is the foundation for love and trust, through which all the dreams of a daughter can come true. This bonding begins the moment the father decides to be a real father of faith and grace and to accept his God-given role of family leader, moral role model, counselor, teacher, and disciplinarian. These actions by a father pave the way for a very important future time when his daughter becomes old enough to notice seriously the existence of young boys outside of the family. This age comes sooner than fathers are ready for it—much sooner—but it does come.

In addition to the fundamental bonding process which has been going on between father and daughter from birth, there is a moment—a very special moment—in the life of every young daughter when she needs for her Hero, her Knight in shining armor, to be committed to her in a new way. Up until this moment you have been laying down the foundation of your daughter's moral fiber, values and principles. You have strengthened your relationship and trust. Your daughter trusts you, looks up to you, and now at this very crucial moment, when she begins to notice members of the opposite sex, outside the family, she needs you as never before. She never thought she would notice anyone but you. But she senses a certain interest in these other members of the opposite sex, and she needs your approval and support to be able to know how, when, where and with whom to relate. Our little girl is hoping for a champion of romance and marriage to be her coach and mentor.

**Hero and Knight in Shining Armor is more than a mere fantasy:**

This is the point where most of us men of faith and grace fail miserably! Our concern for our daughter's welfare is so mixed up, with our own male ego and pride. We carry so much guilt over past and—for a large percentage—even present sexual misconduct that we freak out. Most men cannot bear the thought of some strange boy, man, of whatever age, kissing and holding his little girl. The idea of her being sexually intimate with the opposite sex is unthinkable! So, rather than take the responsibility for the development of his daughter, the average Christian man of today succumbs to his fears and doubts. He proceeds to push the whole matter off onto his wife, and then, as we have noted, complains because it doesn't seem to work that way.

Today's young American Christian daughter of faith and grace goes through her early formative years longing really to know who this Hero, and Knight in shining armor is. She gives him every opportunity and is completely willing to be developed by him into a trusting and obedient team player, only to find herself locked out from him when she needs him the most.

As we have already discovered, one of our main objectives as fathers for our daughters is to prepare them, in every way possible, to be not only ready for introduction into the male world, but to be the best women men could ever have, as wives and lovers within God's Institution of The Family.

She will always be a person who lives in a woman's body. As we have seen, she may become President of the United States, but she will always want to express her femininity and to be successful in her relationships with men. In spite of any other career motivations a young daughter of faith and grace can have—the one most likely to bring her long term satisfaction and joy in this life is—being a great Christian wife, lover, and mother. Everything else falls into place, with little or no problem, if she has been prepared for her role as a woman, first and foremost.

**Mothers of faith and grace are Queens not Heroes and Knights:**

Again, I repeat, a young girl will not accept this instruction from her mother. Those mothers who insist on being the main instructor for their daughters' entrance into the male world only show how little they really know about it, and they reveal the failure of their own fathers to accept their responsibility to prepare them. The appropriate and only really effective role for the mother is to support her husband's efforts and encourage him not to lose heart or confidence in his ability to do the job.

**Heroes and Knights develop into great coaches:**

As a father of faith and grace, you will have developed an attitude of support for your daughter in all her stages of development. When she walked for the first time, you were there to cheer her on. Although she had fallen many times before, this time she actually took her first step. I know you cheered her on and felt proud of her accomplishment. In fact, if she walks sooner than most babies, you will brag about it at work and everywhere you can.

How about other signs of her development? Do you encourage her in her performance of small tasks? Do you reward her when she is obedient and respectful? Do you help her with her school work and encourage her in her studies? When she takes part in some school activity, are you proud to see her accomplishments?

In the case of fathers of faith and grace, the answer to the above questions is always "yes." The challenge comes when our task is to prepare her for those areas of development which scare us the most—her romantic relationship—with some other man.

However, instead of fear, we should experience great joy. This process, although fraught with many opportunities for mistakes by all, is the most exciting time the two of you will ever share together. This is what being a father of faith and grace for a daughter is about. This is the Super Bowl of father/daughter relationships. All the other victories have been achieved just to get to this point. Don't freeze up now; you are just getting to the best part! Some would suggest that the realization of your daughter's gift of faith should be the greatest experience. Yes, for God her heavenly father, because that is His special relationship with her—this is your special relationship with her—His gift to you so that you can rejoice as He does!

Coach and cheerleader might seem a strange title for a father, but this is exactly the role your daughter needs you to fill at this crucial juncture in her young life. It will definitely make the difference between mediocrity and success, and in many respects it will actually save her life!

**Her Knight and coach prepare her for her future Prince:**

When you stop and think about it, you have really functioned as a type of coach and cheerleader all along. Maybe you never thought about it in those terms—but never-the-less—this has been a role you have played. Only now it is more serious and more delicate. Now, you are playing for the biggest stakes of her life. There is no doubt about it; you are entering into a real Super Bowl event.

Being a good coach and cheerleader includes being prejudiced about your team players. When they make a touchdown—you cheer—but you also cheer even if they are having trouble, or are behind in the score. Your role as cheerleader is just that, to be a dedicated supporter no matter what happens. On the other hand, you are also the head coach.

Being a good coach requires being honest with the players. You have to be willing to tell it as it is, and to offer that kind of strong leadership. You must inspire trust and confidence, even when the going gets tough. The real father of faith and grace is supportive of his daughter's dreams from a very early age. This enables the relationship to grow into a real life-long trust. It encourages the daughter to believe that her Daddy is indeed interested in her development and personal welfare. Getting interested in her welfare only at the time she is showing an interest in boys you don't like, is not going to convince her you really care.

Young daughters at the age of six or seven will say they want to be this or that when they grow up. Fathers, don't let the opportunity pass unnoticed. It does not matter how much money you make or how little. A daughter has no idea, at that age, how money may or may not play a part in her dreams. So don't fall into the trap of thinking that—what she says she wants to do or be—is more than you can afford to give her. On the contrary you must be supportive, no matter what she says her dreams are. It is amazing how over the years her dreams will change. Also, your financial status can change, up or down. It doesn't matter. What matters in this relationship is for her to know beyond the shadow of a doubt that she has your support!

**Personal experience:**

My daughters experienced many different kinds of dreams and desires for their future, all the way from veterinary medicine to professional ballet. My reaction, in spite of my money concerns, was always one of great support and interest.

For example: If a daughter wants to be a dancer, let her make a deal with you. Tell her if she wants to be a dancer, you will provide her with dancing lessons, but only after she has shown you her interest by practicing every day for a period of time. Give her time to practice dancing in the garage, back yard, on the sidewalk, in the living room, wherever—just practice. Then praise her progress; encourage her to keep trying. Find a way to get the lessons; there is always a way when you want to do it. If she is really cut out to be a professional dancer, you will not be sorry for having encouraged her. If she is not, don't worry about it; she will know before you do and will come and tell you that she has changed her mind. That's OK too. Move on to the next dream and keep supporting her efforts. Remember, these are her dreams not yours.

My daughter, Melissa, told me, at a very young age, that she wanted to be a professional dancer. I have never been very interested in ballet or the stage. But my little girl had seen something that she liked and was interested in being a dancer. I made her a deal. If she would practice for a few weeks by herself, and show Daddy how serious she was about putting in the effort, I would get her dancing lessons. She said she would. She did. She danced her heart out every evening after school in our garage. She would put her tape player on the garage floor, work out her routines, and really do a surprisingly good job with no instruction at all. Then I got her some lessons. She would work on her routines and even include her sisters in the production. Then she would put on a show for the family. We would all come together in the family room and she would bring on her show. It always filled me with great pride to watch her live her dream, even if it never got any farther than our garage and our family room.

**It's about investing in your daughter and your relationship:**

One evening, after several months, she came to me and asked if I would be terribly disappointed if she stopped her lessons. She said she liked to dance but she didn't think she wanted to be a professional dancer. I told her that was OK and that she didn't have to take the lessons if she didn't want to.

What about the money I had invested in her dancing lessons? Good point, the money wasn't invested in the dancing lessons; it was invested in Melissa and in our relationship, and is still bringing dividends, even to this day.

My daughters always changed their minds as they grew older. Their perspectives changed and so did their interests. But, my own goals did not change. My investment in their dreams and goals, with the interest of a true coach, was consistent and helped to develop deep roots in the overall bonding process.

By the time your daughter is eight to ten years old—about the time you are going to introduce the greatest plan in the world to her—she will be accustomed to your support and trust in her. The transition, from being her coach and cheerleader in all the other aspects of her life and dreams to—her need for understanding boys and the male world—will be very natural. In fact, she will have been expecting it. Remember, she intuitively knows it is your role and place to introduce her to your male world. Scary isn't it?

**There is no set time:**

The age at which a young girl will first begin to show signs of interest in boys outside the family structure will vary from one daughter to another, even within the same family. Consequently, it is highly advisable to establish yourself as her coach and cheerleader in matters of the opposite sex as early as possible. I recommend anytime between eight and twelve years of age to be appropriate. However, be sensitive to your daughter's development, most will be ready between nine and ten, but nothing is cast in stone.

Commitment to share the male world with his daughter is a father's finest hour! This is a daughter's dream come true! This is the moment that her inner senses were telling her would come true some day. This is the moment, above all others—which proves to her that you are indeed her Hero—her Knight in shining armor!

You have been supportive of her as she moved from one dream to another. Now you will anticipate the dream of her life, a dream that lies latent in the heart of every young girl—always ready at any moment to spring forth—the dream of romance and love that lasts for ever and ever!

**A most important proposal; second only to the one you gave your wife:**

Sit down with your daughter somewhere quiet and private. Tell her as straight-forwardly as you can about your desire to propose a plan and a life-time commitment to her. For this to work you must be committed all the way. This is not a "pick and choose" list of possibilities; you must be committed to tell her that you are committing to be her personal champion, coach and cheerleader for her success in love and marriage. She does not need your half-hearted attempts at this. Such an approach would only hurt her and leave her frustrated. Tell her in your own words, the following points of this plan:

1. You want to be the champion of her cause and her desire to know all about men and boys and you will answer all of her questions.

2. You are committed to sharing with her all that you now know or will learn about men. You will tell her the good and the bad.

3. Tell her how important her virginity is to her for her overall development as a woman and for the most successful and satisfying sexual relation with her future husband. (This portion will vary depending on how well you have prepared her.) This is a good time to share with her the three deeper and more complex aspects of her virginity. Book II, Chapter Six, *Daddy's Little Princess and Her Virtue*

4. You are the guardian and protector of her virginity, and as she learns more about men and boys, she will understand why it is so important

5. You are committed to her in her development as a woman; you are committed to prepare her and to support her in her desire of someday finding the man of her romantic dreams.

6. Your counsel and guidance in these matters will prepare her for the most exciting, romantic and sexual satisfaction that any woman can have.

7. You believe in her and in return you only ask one thing from her. You want her complete trust. You want her to demonstrate this by telling you, about all the boys that she finds interesting.

8. She can ask you any questions she wants to and you will do your best to give her the answers.

9. Ask her if she likes this plan, and will she promise to trust you and to be transparent with you! (You might have to explain the concept of "transparency" to her with different words.) Transparency can be taught at a very early age.

**Personal experience:**

My experience with this proposal has always been one of amazement and excitement. The amazement was mostly on my part—as to how willing and ready my daughters were—for me to make such a proposal. Exciting for both of us, especially for the daughter of the moment! (When you have several daughters, you are blessed with the opportunity to do this many times.)

Believe me, they do get excited. There is a glow and a brightness in their eyes that is unforgettable. They begin to express a new appreciation in the way they view father, the depth of trust and transparency go so much farther than you can imagine it blows your mind. For the first time father this whole experience will revolutionize his understanding and appreciation for his daughter. His love for her grows in a way far beyond what most fathers ever dream possible. It is love based on shared trust and commitment of the most sacred kind.

I have explained this to men who have been doing their very best to be real fathers of faith and grace to their daughters, excluding their role as champion and coach in matters relating to their romantic and sexual dreams. Being real men of faith and grace and fathers of truth, they have responded with a desire to take up this cause, even as late as with daughters twenty years of age who have not yet found the man of their dreams. To their pleasant surprise, their daughters accepted their proposal whole-heartedly—with tears of joy! This is cause for hope.

**Personal discovery dating (Book III, Chapter Three for details):**

The personal discovery dating agreement: This is the one area where most men find it very hard to get results. However, in contrast to the disaster that is taking place in most American homes today, where there is little or no personal discovery dating but plenty of sexual discovery dating, real fathers of faith and grace are given the opportunity to have tremendous success establishing the right methods and the right age for their daughters' first date, through personal discovery dating!

The great reward for all—in a true father's efforts is summed up—in her trust in him. This trust, the one thing you have asked for in return for your role as champion and true coach, is the backbone of what makes everything else work so beautifully.

Determining the correct personal discovery dating age involves simply stating to your young daughter that with good training and preparation as a team, she should be ready to have her first real date sometime after she is sixteen.

**Personal experience:**

I found it very successful to tell all my daughters how the world would not be ready for them until they were at least sixteen. I told them they were so wonderful and special that it would be unfair to the world to reveal them too soon, how it would take time, working together, to get her ready for her debut. It's the truth; it does take time, sometimes even more than this. I meant every word, and it was worth it, especially for each one of them!

Once you have committed to her completely, to be her champion and coach for her romantic and sexual relationship with her future Hero and Knight in shining armor, she will follow your leadership. The age you set will not be upsetting to your daughter. This whole process is so important and exciting to your daughter; she will ignore the pressures of others, outside your family unit and will be drawn to you and to your counsel. She trusts you and she wants to learn these things from you, more than from anyone else in the whole world.

# Book II

# DADDY'S LITTLE GIRL

## Chapter Eight

## The First Kiss

**Nonverbal messages:**

Physical expressions of tenderness and love are very important. Like appearances and dress styles, they convey nonverbal messages and therefore can be, and often are, misunderstood. For this reason, it is very important to establish a good understanding, for your daughter, as to—which—messages are sent with different kinds of physical expressions.

Physical expressions, such as kissing, hand holding, and different kinds of physical contact short of intercourse, must all be clearly understood, before they can be respected, appreciated and properly used. Such expressions have become common-place for many, thus, they have—lost any true meaning—of communication. If your young princess is going to go out on dates whose main activity is the exchange of kisses, hugging, and caressing, she will be embarking on a wide road crowded with travelers suffering—spiritual and emotional—long-term damage.

Definitely, such activity brings a certain amount of superficial pleasure to the participants, (albeit in different degrees, male vs. female), it is inappropriate for two people to try to get to know each other in this manner. We can't overemphasize the need of those in personal discovery dating experiences to refrain from this temptation and to stick to the business of getting to know each other's character and values. If not, one might find that the "prince or princess charming" that they thought they were kissing—was in reality—a wart-hog in disguise!

As previously stressed, kisses affect a man in a very dramatic way, and your daughter must not overlook this. There is much more involved in a kiss than she may have ever considered. The man who is doing the kissing is highly sensitized by her physical form and presence and even more so by her touch. When he kisses her and holds her close, she must realize he will feel the pressure of her breasts on his chest and, depending on their position; her hips could be pressed against his groin area. All of these actions generate a tremendous sexual arousal within the male body. This is not appropriate or wise activity for two people trying to get to know each other's character and values—unless of course—it is their lack of the same!

**Reason for disqualification:**

If such activity continues, she will find her escort trying to get more and more body contact. On occasion he will stand with his legs spread apart and have her stand between them. Although a girl might not realize the importance of such a position for her male friend, it gives him a great sense of sexual arousal because of the close contact with her hips and vaginal area. All these tactics are pursued by the male simply for the purpose of sexual arousal and sexual satisfaction. If they are married, these are normal responses and appropriate methods of sharing tender intimacies. This is not the code of conduct for a personal discovery dating experience; it is very dangerous and does nothing to promote the basic objective of good personal discovery. Many will say that any proper young man should know better than to engage in such conduct. I agree, but knowing better and doing better, is not the same thing. Here we want to prepare for whatever possibility might occur and then decide based on the outcome of the overall conduct. Any young man who would do so and who would not immediately correct his actions would be disqualified.

It is a sad commentary on the progressively deteriorating moral conditions within the Christian community that there is no way to know which young men are going to conduct themselves the way one might expect. I have first hand knowledge of young men from outstanding Christian leadership families that have conducted themselves very badly. This is also not unknown among their daughters; we all can remember the phrase—preacher's kid—or preacher's daughter. In the matter of good character and morals no one can be taken for granted.

Under the best of circumstances, it takes good understanding and even better determination, not to allow one's self to be drawn into these kinds of compromising situations. Your young princess will be the big loser in any situation such as this that gets out of hand. Consequently, the best form of protection is not to allow an escort to have such physical freedom in the first place. The first rule for successful abstinence from sexual intercourse is not to play the kissing and petting game that leads up to intercourse.

Undoubtedly, your princess will be told by practically everyone at her school that kissing and petting are normal, healthy activities and that "everyone" is doing it. I always tell my daughters: just because—everybody else—is in a hurry to jump off of a building and kill themselves, is not a good reason to imitate them.

**Amazing transparency:**

The first kiss your daughter receives from her date is very important. You have prepared her with good understanding, she has communicated this to her date, and when the first kiss does occur, it will most likely be in the context of a sincere expression of personal care and tenderness. However, one or a thousand kisses are not necessarily an expression of true love! Remember, true love is a decision, not a physical expression of sexual arousal or intercourse. There are many kisses exchanged between men and women looking for sexual arousal and intercourse, which have nothing to do with love—lust for sure—but not love!

One very special experience for me was the first kiss received by my daughter Stephanie. She became interested in a young man at church who exemplified many of the qualities we considered important. We discussed each date before she left the house and what things she should be concerned about learning. On about the third date she came home with a special glow and excitement which indicated something very special had taken place. I was waiting up for her, as I had done on the previous occasions, and she could hardly contain herself, she was so excited.

She sat down beside me on the sofa, and with tears in her eyes, related to me how she had let him kiss her and how wonderful she thought he was. I can't even write about this without tears coming to my eyes again, as they did on that occasion. She hugged me and we held hands for awhile as she told me all the things she was learning about him, and how he just might be her true Knight in shining armor.

Not every daughter will come back from her date and be so transparent with you, and you should not feel left out when such an experience doesn't occur, but when such things do transpire between a daughter and a father, you experience one of the many blessings reserved especially for true fatherhood the product of faith and grace. You are able to perceive—if only for a brief moment—God's purposes in calling men to be real fathers of faith and grace!

**Good conduct brings good results:**

Stephanie continued to date this very good candidate for some time. She was always very frank with me, and kept me up-to- date on all of their activities, and discussions. We kept them close to home most of the time, but they did have occasional dates out alone. I was very approving of this young man, and would have been happy to see this relationship become the discovery of Stephanie's true Knight in shining armor. But, alas, it was not so serious for the young man in question. Later, when he went to college in Portland, Oregon, he found the lady of his dreams. He wrote to Stephanie and told her what he had discovered. It hurt her a lot, more than she was prepared to admit at the time.

Limitations on physical expressions are very wise for a number of reasons. One of the most important reasons becomes clear when you realize the person you have been personal discovery dating is not the Knight in shining armor for which you are searching, but you are still morally and emotionally intact. This experience that Stephanie and I shared with her first boy friend is a good example. We discussed her commitment to good morals and behavior in keeping with her principles, not allowing their relationship to become physical. If she had allowed the relationship to become physical, this young man would have left her bruised and damaged for life. Oh, she would have gone on to meet her present Knight in shining armor, the wonderful man whom she did marry, but she would have had to carry the scars of her first love forever.

Without this firm commitment to values and principles before the personal discovery dating begins, a young lady has no guidelines or boundaries. She is left to the mercy of the moment. Such a situation is asking the impossible. No one can create moral fiber, with values and principles at the moment he or she is faced with the need for their use and understanding. To attempt to do so is like going into battle before deciding what kind of weapons you need. This very lack of preparedness is what causes many promising young ladies to fall prey everyday to smooth- talking sexual con artists!

Without clear understanding of her guidelines and moral boundaries, a young lady is often tempted to believe that if she will just show this wonderful guy how much she loves him by giving him sex, he will love her in return. Sorry, ladies, it doesn't work that way. Haven't you heard the expression: "Why buy the cow when you can milk her through the fence?"

**Wisdom is experienced in the father/daughter romance team:**

The beauty of good personal discovery dating practices and devotion to sound moral behavior is the protection it offers. You can move on to someone else without a load of life-long emotional baggage. In contrast—for our present post modern Christian culture many of our young couples are not so well disciplined—and after about two or three hot romantic affairs, the average woman is so emotionally destroyed she loses the ability to function as a normal woman. She loses her original God-given dream of true love and commitment. For all practical purposes regarding marriage and developing a good family she is almost, if not completely, dead! Her ability to ever trust again and commit to any person, thing, or cause, even, God himself, is greatly impaired.

Sharing with her father all the important details of her personal discovery dating experiences gives the daughter added strength to her resolve. She not only knows her father supports her 150%, she also knows that he is there to counsel her and to help her make sense out of her emotional fog. Unfortunately, when father/daughter relationships are either strained or non-existent, as they are in the majority of American homes, then there is little or no desire to trust or to share anything with her father. When it comes to learning about men and marriage, most

Daddies' little girls in American are on their own!

This process of sharing information with her father is the catalyst in which the daughter becomes wise in her use of all the information her father has taught her during the years she was preparing for her debut into the male world. Everything up until this moment of personal discovery dating and sharing has been just theory. Now, in the actual process of personal discovery dating and sharing, the two of them become a formidable team. This is the transparency she promised her father when he first committed to champion and coach her development in love and marriage. Together they will accomplish their original goal, the discovery of her Knight in shining armor, and the promise of life-long love and happiness.

# Book II

# DADDY'S LITTLE GIRL

## Chapter Nine

## The Knight Appears

**Discovering the Knight:**

The moment of truth is when the daughter makes her discovery of a real man of faith and grace, one to whom she can surrender her love and devotion, and who will return the same commitment to her. Mutual commitment is the key to knowing she has the correct one. If she is the only one of the two who wants to be committed to the other—to make that very powerful decision to love—then it is not a match! It must be a mutual decision—of love and marriage commitment—in order for there to be real love—a product of faith and grace—in the relationship. Let us be reminded: the secularist concept of "love" is better described as—lust—seeking for a physical experience of release in sex. Men and women of faith and grace know that as purely physical beings without God's—gift of love—they would have no hope of true love for each other. Our hope is not in our fallen flesh. Our hope is based in our Savior's promises of support and victory that are clearly the exclusive—unmerited favor—of those to whom the Father has drawn to Christ and to whom He has given the gift of faith.

> (..."For if by the one man's offense death reigned through the one, much more those who receive abundance of grace and of the gift of righteousness will reign in life through the One, Jesus Christ.) Therefore, as through one man's offense judgment came to all men, resulting in condemnation, even so through one Man's righteous act the free gift came to all men, resulting in justification of life. For as by one man's disobedience many were made sinners, so also by one Man's obedience many will be made righteous." Romans 5:17-19.

> "For by grace you have been saved through faith, and that not of yourselves; it is the gift of God, not of works, lest anyone should boast. For we are His workmanship; created in Christ Jesus for good works, which God prepared beforehand that we should walk in them." Ephesians 2:8-10.

**Doing due diligence is a normal activity:**

For example, no one enters into a contract to buy a home with just one side of the two parties in agreement. If you give someone money for the house of your dreams, but he refuses to give you clear title, there has been—a fraudulent sale—leaving you with only the courts for recourse. Your money is now in jeopardy, your dreams are smashed and now you're left with only the courts to untangle the mess. Why does this sound so much like secular love and marriage followed by divorce? Likewise, when a young princess thinks she has found a real man of faith and grace, a man with whom she wants to make a decision to love, and this man does not want to make the same decision with her, there is no basis for continuing the relationship. As the country western ballad says: "He ain't nothin but a walk away

Joe!"

No one reading this book would even think of buying a home or making an important business deal without the counsel of some professional, who is knowledgeable in the matter, to help them cover all the details. In the heat of a hot real-estate or a business deal—we seem to sense our need for a level head, someone with experience—to make sure we ask all the right questions and understand the details. We all consider this normal.

This being true, how is it possible then—for adult males, all of us who call ourselves fathers of faith and grace—to let our daughters go about the process of making the most important decision of their lives with little or no meaningful counsel, structure or help? Are daughters not as important as material things? Who will stand up for the daughters of America? Who will help them set the stage so they can know with whom and with what they are dealing? Let us not cop-out on our daughters with the idea that—her mother, her pastor, her youth leader, her school coach, or someone else—will assume our personal responsibility under God.

**Behind the scene but in control:**

Setting the stage for our daughter to have a successful relationship is the foundation through which any prospective male candidate really gets to know the father, the man behind the scene. The process of preparing the playing ground for this important experience of personal discovery dating and determining who is the real Knight in shining armor and who is not, is something only for a father to implement.

If a young girl has lost her biological father through death or divorce, then some other father should have been brought into the picture as soon as possible after such loss, to further her development. This is not easy, but is never-the-less possible when a mother understands how important it is for her daughter to have such a relationship and such development. In reality, such a girl is an orphan. The original meaning of "orphan" is a child who has lost their father.

I have personally served as a counselor and assistant coach for several young girls, some with extremely good success. It is a tremendous challenge, even with one's own biological daughters, and much more so with those who are not. However, it was worth the effort.

Once a daughter brings home the news that she has found her Knight in shining armor, or she thinks she has, it is time for father to set the stage. Most fathers of today would probably imagine that their daughter has already dated this young man. On the contrary, if the daughter is following her training instructions properly, she will not date anyone she has not first presented to her father as a possible candidate for marriage. The process of elimination should have already taken place. Your daughter should undergo her first date having already determined the young man in question is potentially qualified, otherwise, why date him?

You don't drive a car off the dealer's lot to try it out if you don't even like the make or model he is showing you. So, why would your daughter make a date with some—dude who just happens to ask her—without her even knowing anything about him? The daughter of faith and grace who has been properly prepared—is one who will not give in to the pressures of her unwise peers—she won't accept unqualified dates to no where!

**Personal experience:**

My daughter, Melissa, brought me this startling news at a very early age—so early in fact—that I was tempted to believe she was joking. However, it only took a second look into her eyes to know how serious she was. As I said earlier, I tried to look calm and collected.

After making my own investigation into the young man she had revealed as her candidate, I was encouraged to follow up with the next step. I called him on the phone and asked him to come to my office to talk with me. It could easily have been at our home, where I have talked with others. But in this case it was a matter of timing, so I asked him to come to the office. He accepted and arrived at the appointed time.

When Jay came into the office, I could tell he was a little nervous. I wanted him to feel relaxed so we talked awhile about his schooling and some of his interests. He is a naturally gifted mechanic and loves to talk about cars and engines. Finally, we got around to the purpose of his visit.

Jay and Melissa had met each other at church and had talked to each other quite extensively at the different youth meetings and church functions. Jay had dated several girls of personal discovery dating age in the congregation, and had not found his Queen for Life. All of these girls were attractive young ladies and some were quite beautiful. Yet, because of the discussions in which he and Melissa had engaged, he knew there was something special about her. Likewise, Melissa had come to a conclusion about Jay; he was her Knight in shining armor!

I wanted Jay to know, as her father, I had several unique responsibilities. I told him about my responsibility and commitment to Melissa to protect her virginity and her virtue from the time she was a just a baby, and that any young man who would date her would have to agree to join with me in protecting her virtue and virginity. I revealed to him the pact which I had made with Melissa when she was ten years old and how important our relationship was. When he heard me tell about my role as her champion and coach for successful romance and a life-long committed love relationship, his eyes got wide with keen interest.

We spoke at length about moral fiber, values and principles of life. He expressed his own conviction to remain a virgin until marriage, and held strong convictions about everything we had discussed.

I told him about my efforts to focus all of my instructions and guidance for Melissa's benefit in order to prepare her for the most fantastic of all love experiences possible. I told him that if he was interested in such a girl as Melissa, and could wait until she was sixteen before asking her out on a date, he had my permission.

Jay answered immediately in the affirmative. He said he was very interested in a girl like Melissa, and that he could wait until she was sixteen to ask her out on their fist date.

I congratulated him on his level-headedness and his commitment to good moral values and principles. I also made very clear my desires to develop a relationship with him, man to man, and encouraged him to come to me for any information or advice concerning himself and Melissa. He seemed genuinely pleased about the whole meeting and the arrangements upon which we had agreed.

**Discovery dating is a father/daughter team effort that includes the escort!**

Developing a relationship with the prospective candidate is very important. This gives the father an opportunity to establish good communication and mutual respect between himself and the young man. Be sensitive to the interests of your daughter's new discovery. Take the time to talk to him just as you have taken the time to talk with your daughter. Both of you made failing grades in your "mind reading" classes, so don't expect to be able to read his mind and don't ask him to read yours.

Many of the more important and proper aspects of father/daughter relationships are beyond the scope of today's young male suitors. It would be hard if not impossible for you tell him everything you know about this concept. If he had been raised by a father who did these things with his sisters he would understand more than most. However, even in the case of my own son, he will probably learn more from his own personal experiences with his own daughters than he learned from watching me.

If I could have written this book before I met Jay or the other young men who came into the life of our family, I would have had them read it and discuss their reactions with me. I did not have the advantage of such a book—but you do—so put it to good use. There is more immediate impact and teaching material in a book like this than you would be able to convey personally in as short a time span. Yet, a book cannot take the place—of the strong personal relationship—that must be built with a serious prospect for your daughter's love.

Committing to honor your daughter's virtue and virginity is a must for any young man who wishes to date her. You exemplify a courageous heart simply by taking a young man aside and talking straight to the point with him. Your actions will strengthen the positive aspects of his moral character. There are millions of young men who have high moral standards when they are young. The desire of their heart is to love and cherish a virtuous woman. The changes in their standards begin when they are discouraged in their dreams and hopes by the loose morals they see in movies, TV soaps, TV sit-coms, magazines, novels, and in the everyday life they witness at school. Also, sad but true, the things they witness among the older youth at church!

**Knowing the truth gives your daughter confidence:**

With so called "safe" sex being the topic of the day, and premarital sex the assumed norm for every young person, it can become very threatening to let your peers know of your positive stand on virtue and virginity. This is true whether you are male or female. Much of today's young adult sex is the result of bad information and deliberate misinformation by rank liberals who aren't satisfied with their own personal, moral, emotional, and relationship failures—they demand company—misery loves company!

My daughter Melissa says:

> "The daughter should have formed her own personal relationship with Christ. I was never embarrassed to stand up for good morals when it was brought up. I had confidence in myself and none of my high-school friends put me down. They respected my confidence. It was because of my relationship with Christ that I felt this way. I think high-school kids cling to someone who does things right and are proud of it. It is when you are unsure that the peer pressure is hard!"

**I've asked this question before, but it's worth asking again:**

> "If so called "free love" and "safe sex," or any other expression you want to use to describe premarital, promiscuous sex, is so good and so healthy, why does it promote such disasters as sexually transmitted diseases, and why does it destroy emotions and relationships? Will all those who advocate such practices please stand up and demonstrate their wonderful successes? Please show us your outstanding families full of faithfulness, love, devotion, commitment, and truly satisfied sex partners. Give the world a parade, show off your model, obedient children, and all those you have reared and who are successfully and happily married, with life-time committed partners!"

The silence is deafening! Perhaps Hollywood, which is so dedicated and creative in its efforts to portray its many seemingly endless and passionate "love" scenes and relationships, could make a documentary to show the successful committed families of its secular, atheist, activist actors.

People, who cannot do this and thus open up their personal lives and the lives of their children to public scrutiny, should shut up about the glories of premarital and promiscuous sex habits. The reality of their—low moral standards, emotional and relationship bankruptcy—does not give them license to spread their deadly venomous ideas and moral practices, with high-handed assumptions of normalcy! They are not normal! They are very disturbed, morally and emotionally sick people. Listening to the tirades of so many so-called enlightened people about "safe" sex, makes as much sense as—listening to some mentally deranged person trying to sell the world on putting sand in the engines of new cars—and then lessening the deadly effects by using a special oil to protect the insides from being destroyed! It would be funny if it were not so serious and so deadly for all our young people! Does not this scenario give us ample reason as to why our young girls and boys must not be allowed to watch such programs as MTV?

No matter how badly you have performed in your own moral habits before reading this book, take charge of your moral standards and do not allow yourself to be controlled by those who would only encourage you to be as miserable and sickly as they are! Sexual immorality is a self-inflicted blindness. It is not controlled by your glands or by the opinions of others. You, the real person who lives in your body, have the last word. It is up to you—you set the standards—and you reap the rewards, good or bad![134]

We must be courageous, change our perspectives and our personal habits, and stand firm in our resolve to speak straight to the point when interviewing prospective suitors for our daughter. Make them agree to join with us in protecting her virtue and virginity. If we feel they are vacillating in their comments and commitments, we must dismiss them as unfit to date our daughter.

**Taking on a partner:**

Outlining the objectives of good personal discovery dating practices is a must, when speaking with any prospective suitor for your daughter. The whole process of interviewing prospective suitors is to facilitate the first stages in the transfer of your role of protector and family leader to this new—prospective—Knight in shining armor. When a young princess is properly prepared for the experience of searching for a true life-time love and Knight in shining armor, it can often be the first candidate. So, you don't have the luxury of sitting around waiting for some long list of candidates to appear and then deciding which one you like. You must treat each candidate—as if he were the special one—the Knight in shining armor who is going to take your place and much more.

This is an ongoing relationship-building process. You can not expect to do this in one five or ten minute quick, "get to know you," interview. This young candidate must be brought up-to-date to meet your standards, the same standards which you and your daughter have been working on for years; you will need to commit time and energy to working with this candidate. If you fail to take on this part of the process—you will leave your daughter open and unprotected—to the enormous pressures an unstructured relationship will bring. It is possible for her to be destroyed before you gain a second chance. Don't make the mistake of assuming

134 "Flee fornication. Every sin that a man doeth is without the body: but he that commits fornication sins against his own body." I Cor. 6:18. "Flee also youthful lusts: but follow righteousness, faith, charity, peace with them that call on the Lord out of a pure heart." II Tim. 2:22

you can take your sweet time about these matters; they won't wait!

Taking on a partner in these matters probably seems strange at first. But think about it—if you don't develop this young suitor into a loyal partner and friend, you will have assumed that he is not going to help protect your daughter—and that in fact—he would encourage her to disobey you and to do the very things from which you want to protect her.

**Sowing the seeds of one's own destruction:**

This is exactly the kind of situation all fathers fear. Trust me; it will be a self-fulfilling prophecy for all fathers who do not take seriously everything I am sharing with you in this book! Your daughter wants very much to honor you as her father of faith and grace and to follow your instructions to the letter. She will be greatly aided and supported in this natural and basic desire because of your courage in speaking with her candidate, boldly and straight to the point, on each issue. Your daughter's behavior and personal safety—while out on dates, learning more and more about her candidate—is dependent upon the quality of all your efforts. In most cases, such training and preparation of your daughter, and the close relationship developed by this, will give you enormous control over the situation. She will even surprise you with her ability to stand firm on the lessons and directives you have taught, as to how she should respond to her candidate.

Many were the times my daughters have come back from talking with their suitors and have said to me. "Boy, Daddy, he sure didn't like to hear what you told me to tell him. He thinks you don't trust him. "

My answer was always the same:

> "I trust him—but not his body. He is a young male who can be very sexually tempted from the pressures of his male sexuality. When he has finally made it to the altar of marriage with you, he will be very pleased and happy about everything I told you to do."

He will not only be happy because of their virtue and virginity, but also because he will have confidence in their ability to maintain themselves in a state of continued faithfulness and loyalty to him.

Males who are successful in winning a daughter's loyalty and obedience away from a father only create their own hell. Later, after they think they have won, and they steal the daughter away from the father in an adversarial contest, the daughter will prove to be just as unfaithful and disloyal in her treatment of him as he taught her to be towards her father. Take care, young men, don't destroy the very heart of the most precious thing you will ever have, the trust and loyalty of a loving wife!

**Wisdom brings forth great joy:**

So, the new Knight in shining armor has been identified. You are moving ahead in your relationship with him, and he is developing into a responsible partner, in the objectives which you and your daughter have set out to accomplish. These objectives are now his objectives, and you will experience the moment when he will come to you and ask you the big question: "May I have your daughter's hand in marriage?"

This is a great moment; it opens the door to a whole new aspect of your daughter's development, the engagement period.

# Book II

# DADDY'S LITTLE GIRL

## Chapter Ten

## The Engagement

**Transition manager, a new role for Daddy and the romance team:**

Understanding the value of the engagement period is vital to the success of your daughter's transition from searching for her Knight in shining armor to becoming his wife. The engagement period affords the father/daughter team time and opportunity to make the family leadership change, from father to husband and from daughter to wife.

The transition from being Daddy's team partner to fiancée is a time that can provide a wonderful experience of self-discovery for the bride and the husband to be. Up until now they have dated. They have talked about themselves, their goals, dreams, values, principles, love, sex, family, and how many children they want. What they have not experienced is how to function as a team. When understood properly, the engagement period provides a time of team practice.

Each needs to know how the other presents themselves when he or she is taking a leadership role. The daughter needs to know how her new Knight in shining armor approaches the matter of leadership and his methods of communicating his desires and instructions, for various social, personal and future family concerns and the prospective husband needs to know how his prospective wife also handles leadership.

Every prospective husband should experience the role of family leader, taking the reigns in matters of decisions that are vital to their future family goals and structure. By doing so he can see how his new Queen reacts to his leadership, and what adjustments he might consider necessary in presenting his desires and concerns.

**The engagement experience can be dangerous:**

Unfortunately, in the experience of most engaged couples of today, the engagement ring and the whole concept of being engaged are merely a continuation of their premarital sex patterns, with tradition and a formal marriage ceremony being the main reasons for the engagement announcement. Even in those less frequent occasions when there has been no premarital sex up to the point of the engagement, a majority will make the mistake of assuming the engagement gives them sexual privileges. This attitude is usually stronger in the man than in the woman, but, wanting to please her Knight in shining armor, the woman will usually give in if she is pressured enough to do so.

This is another good example of how males are capable of thinking more with their hormones than with their brains. Consequently, the whole concept of why a wedding is so important to women is lost on the minds of most men. The woman's natural drive is to submit sexually to a man who is strong in his commitment to her, and one who is willing to wait until he can make such a commitment formally, for all the world to see. The marriage ceremony is the best opportunity to do that.

When women, especially virgins, are pressured into sex before the marriage vows are taken, it gives them a feeling of uneasiness and shallowness about the whole relationship. Giving in to male pressure for premarital sex during the engagement period will carry deep emotional bruises into the marriage and will have negative effects on the ultimate success of their sexual relationship. A woman comes naturally equipped with a keen sensitivity to the Real Moral Law within her. She is particularly sensitive to the act of surrendering her body in sexual intercourse. What might seem like an atmosphere of complete trust and commitment to a young man, i.e. his sincere intentions to follow through with the wedding, is quite another matter for the woman. The woman is very sensitive to the fact that sex before the wedding, no matter the verbal commitment from the man, is still sex before the actual public and official commitment is made. The Right of the public wedding vows and the ceremony of joy and emotional support supersede any logic presented by a man in an effort to erase the Wrong of having the sex first and the vows later. Consequently, the woman suffers a sense of true loss. This guilt and sense of loss will cause feelings of resentment toward her husband that she might not even recognize as having anything to do with the premarital sex.

Ask yourself the obvious questions: Are such demands for sex now, ahead of the official public ceremony, really necessary? Is the demand for sexual intercourse so great you have to risk destroying a lifetime of sexual bliss for a few weeks or months of stolen privileges? A wise man will not risk anything that will cause his future bride to be less than one hundred percent emotionally satisfied and happy with his commitment and the responsibility demonstrated by waiting.

**Secular post modern subjective moralism:**

In today's world—morals by convention, if it's popular—do it. This same approach to morals is unfortunately all too common among young men who consider themselves to be men of faith and grace. For such males it is common to act unwisely, and to insist on their assumed rights to sexual privileges, once they have promised marriage. For some macho dudes, this is nothing more than their way of getting sex; they go from one broken promise of marriage to another. They get what they want—one-dimensional sex and the woman gets jilted—as soon as the game is over.

The popular excuse for many males who are insistent on sex before marriage is based on their macho comparison of cars with women, as he says: "Who wants to buy a new car without driving it first?"

So, with such great wisdom, he embarks on his quest for a "new car," believing he has the right to a few test drives before he makes a life-time commitment. How stupid!

The virtuous woman, who can perform as well sexually before the wedding vows, given all the psychological, emotional, and mental pressure this brings to her, has not been born yet. Therefore, if this macho dude thinks he is likely to get a good sampling of what is really possible in a marriage based on real values of commitment which understands these sensitivities of women, he is badly mistaken. On the other hand, should he find a woman who could be so abandoned in her mind and emotions, so as never to have a problem with premarital sex, he probably is in a personal discovery dating situation with a woman who—after a few good healthy problems come along—will find some other man's arms more inviting. So either way, the big macho/wimp is the loser!

**Engagement allows for proper transition into a lifetime of commitment:**

Understanding the engagement period and using it to the advantage of the engaged couple, will greatly increase their understanding of each other, and contribute greatly to the total success of their marriage. In some ways it's like pre-season practice in sports. It is not official game time, but what is learned, in the life-like experiences of building their personal relationship is very important to the success of their marriage after the official "I do's" have been said.

The engagement period is the time frame where the theory of the young couple's commitment to each other for life begins to find form and substance. This is the time during which they will touch the nerve endings of those many deeper feelings and attitudes they missed during the personal discovery dating period. The newly engaged couples begin to test their ability to work out problems and to overcome the frustrations they will feel when they are misunderstood, or are taken for granted by the other.

Our society today is willing to enter into a marriage in ways they do not consider proper, even for playing a game of football or basketball. More and more couples who walk down the aisle today are not willing to commit until "death do us part." It is said by many that such a vow is not realistic. They say divorce proves that marriages don't last forever, and therefore, it is unnecessary to make vows of commitment until death.

What are they actually saying, with such reasoning? Are they saying that when things get a little too tough, divorce and dissolution of the wedding vows are acceptable? Are they saying that they know it can't last forever, so why make such a statement of commitment?

Put their attitude into the context of a coach and his football or basketball team. They are planning the up-coming season and laying out their strategy for victory. The coach tells the players there is a tough road ahead, one fraught with many problems and difficulties. The school he is coaching has never won the championship, and he doesn't want anyone to get his hopes up too high this year. Just go out there on the playing field and have a good time. If you win, OK. If you lose, OK. It doesn't really matter.

To some I suppose that would sound like a great speech, but to the world of competitive sports it sounds sick and uncommitted. No coach or team with such an attitude of preconditioning for defeat has won, or ever will win a championship. Likewise, no marriage starting off with divorce as a viable solution to future problems will survive for life!

**Divorce is abnormal:**

Every marriage will have problems, some of which will be serious. Divorce is NOT—a normal option for solving the problems of marriage—no matter how serious. To the extent that divorce is accepted by couples as *normal,* it weakens their commitment to overcome the serious problems that—should be expected—in any marriage. You can overcome any problem in a marriage—if there is a commitment from the beginning of the marriage—which will not accept divorce as a viable option.

Although it can be compared to sports in its need for a winning attitude, marriage is certainly not a game. In marriage you are competing only with yourselves. Everyone can win. However, as in any function of life, if there is no commitment to succeed then there is a preconditioned attitude of defeat. You cannot have it both ways. Either you are committed to each other for life to win the battles. or you are resigned to defeat.

Marriage is the most challenging endeavor one can enter into; yet it is also the most resilient and the most rewarding of all human undertakings. The late billionaire, Forbes; said of his own life that he would give up all his money for just one good marriage. He never had a good marriage. He was married several times, but never was able to handle successfully the challenges of marriage.

Such men as Forbes and many other rich men and women have proven over and over again that money cannot buy happiness, and it certainly cannot buy a good marriage. This is great news! If money were the main ingredient in a successful marriage, then only the rich could be assured of success. However, in the context of—Christ's Great Commission for Fatherhood and Motherhood—all men and women of faith and grace can have a successful marriage, all the poor, all the rich, and everyone in between. All they need is the knowledge of what is required and the courage and commitment to pull it off! A woman of faith and grace—beautiful in virtue and loving commitment would rather live in a tent with a real man of faith and grace—than in a castle with a rich male who thinks he is real macho and God's gift to women. See the Walt Disney movie (or read the story) "Beauty and the Beast."

If you or your spouse have already suffered the consequences of a divorce—you are not without hope—you are only challenged to start all over and do it right! Your challenges will exceed those who have done it right the first time—which is the price for making mistakes, right? There is no alternative—repeating the old mistakes will only guarantee failure—so change is mandatory NOT optional!

**Personal experience:**

By now the reader has learned many of our personal experiences and there are more to come—but our experience with NOT divorcing—is most important at this time. Engagement leads to only one of three things:

1. Broken engagement
2. Marriage for life
3. Divorce

During our first fifteen years of marriage—a time span that most American "Christian marriages" will never see—by God's continued faithfulness to answer our prayers for wisdom and victory, we were enabled to overcome at least a dozen excellent opportunities to choose divorce as a solution. With each new crisis there was always the temptation to look for a way out—or a way around—anything but straight up and over the mountain.

I hope that it doesn't come as a surprise to you that God doesn't provide—ways out—nor does He provide—ways around—because He specializes in providing strength, and providential wisdom to go straight up and over the mountains of life.

> "Strengthen the weak hands, and make firm the feeble knees. Say to those who are fearful-hearted, 'Be strong, do not fear! Behold, your God will come with vengeance, with the recompense of God; He will come and save you.' Then the eyes of the blind shall be opened, and the ears of the deaf shall be unstopped. Then the lame shall leap like a deer, and the tongue of the dumb sing. For waters shall burst forth in the wilderness, and streams in the desert. The parched ground shall become a pool, and the thirsty land springs of water; in the habitation of jackals, where each lay, there shall be grass with reeds and rushes. A highway shall be there, and a road and it shall be called the Highway of Holiness. The unclean shall not pass over it, but it shall be for others. Whoever walks the road, although a fool; shall not go astray. No lion shall be there, nor shall any ravenous beast go up on it; it shall not be found there. But the redeemed shall walk there..." Isaiah 35:3-9.

> "But those who wait on the LORD shall renew their strength; they shall mount up with wings like eagles, they shall run and not be weary, they shall walk and not faint." Isaiah 40:31.

Time to pray, to think, to consider the errors of one's decisions allows for the Spirit to minister to us and to provide insight into His uncommon common sense. After deep reflection coupled with a constant faith that God works only that which is—good for us, no matter the pain—will always bring more positive results than we can imagine!

> "Likewise the Spirit also helps in our weaknesses. For we do not know what we should pray for as we ought, but the Spirit Himself makes intercession for us with groanings which cannot be uttered. Now He who searches the hearts knows what the mind of the Spirit is, because He makes intercession for the saints according to the will of God.
>
> "And we know that all things work together for good to those who love God, to those who are the called according to His purpose. For whom He foreknew, He also predestined to be conformed to the image of His Son, that He might be the firstborn among many brethren. Moreover whom He predestined, these He also called; whom He called, these He also justified; and whom He justified, these He also glorified.
>
> "What then shall we say to these things? If God is for us, who can be against us? He who did not spare His own Son, but delivered Him up for us all, how shall He not with Him also freely give us all things? Who shall bring a charge against God's elect? It is God who justifies. Who is he who condemns? It is Christ who died, and furthermore is also risen, who is even at the right hand of God, who also makes intercession for us. Who shall separate us from the love of Christ? Shall tribulation, or distress, or persecution, or famine, or nakedness, or peril, or sword?" Romans 8:26-35.

**Accepting a proposal for marriage:**

Permission granted to marry is a very special moment between the prospective son-in-law and the father of the daughter. It can happen many different ways. When Jay, Melissa's Knight in shining armor was ready to make the big step, he was in Blacksburg, Virginia, in his junior year at Virginia Technological University. He called on the phone one day in October, 1986, and asked if he could present Melissa an engagement ring during the upcoming Christmas holidays.

I had actually been expecting his request, but I had not been given any indications when it would happen. She would graduate from high-school in May of 1987 and Jay would graduate from college May 21, 1988. I knew that Jay wanted to get married after college, but neither had said just how soon. It turned out to be the very next week after Jay's graduation.

I gave Jay my permission and also expressed my desire to discuss some details concerning certain changes this would make in our relationship. He agreed, and I said that when he came up the next week-end to visit Melissa, we would get together and talk about them.

Delegation of authority from the father to the husband-to-be is the first step the father takes in transferring his role as family leader to the new Knight in shining armor.

When Jay came up from Blacksburg the next week end, I'm sure he couldn't imagine the nature of the details I wanted to discuss with him. We went for a long walk, as I recall, and I told him that after he had presented the ring to Melissa, as soon as possible I wanted the whole family to get together and share in this very special moment. I told him of my desire to take the first step passing my role as family leader for Melissa to him. Thus, establishing the basis for the new roles"; we would have during the engagement period.

During the engagement period, I instructed Jay to make all the final decisions regarding any of their activities or plans. He would then come to me to see if I had any concerns about their proposals or decisions. As the father, I would have veto power over any plan or proposal, but I would always be available for alternatives. The idea of my role as father including the right to say "No" had already been well established in the personal discovery dating relationships of my daughters. The daughters and their prospective Knights must always allow the father the right to say, "No." "No" is a good answer, and should never be taken as insensitive or uncaring. It simply means—I don't like that option—give me another. The more options they presented the better chances they had of getting a "Yes."

**New changes in responsibilities and roles:**

As a family affair, the engagement period changes certain aspects of responsibilities and leadership roles. I had always been the one to whom Melissa would come when she had a question, problem or need. I was always the one to whom she would have to explain what she felt or what she liked or did not like, about the family structure and how it affected her. She had always looked to me to set the family structure and to counsel her on what to do and not to do. The whole family would be affected by Melissa's new status.

Also, our son, David, had often played a very important role in Melissa's life. In times of my absence, I would delegate certain family leadership roles to him. In this capacity, he would often counsel Melissa and his other sisters and took on the responsibility of supervising their activities while I was away. Melissa would no longer be able to come to me or go to her brother for such counsel, but would focus on Jay for the solution of all of her needs.

So, in order to make it clear, we brought everyone together to share in a precious moment of transferring family leadership, through delegating new authority to Jay.

**Jay receives new authority and responsibilities:**

Delegation of authority is best accomplished with witnesses and, when appropriate, it should be strengthened by prayer. Building strong families without believing and trusting in God to give you added strength and wisdom is like trying to design and build an airplane while denying the existence of the laws of aerodynamics!

Jay had presented to Melissa their engagement ring while they were visiting his parents in Pennsylvania. Later, we all met in Lake Tahoe, California for Christmas.

One morning after Christmas, Jay and Melissa met with my wife, Marilyn, all of our other unmarried daughters, my son, David, and me.

I explained in the presence of all that from that moment on, Jay would be taking over the role of family leader for himself and Melissa. I told them of the details that Jay and I had discussed earlier, and that Melissa would no longer come to me for permission to do anything. She would, in effect, be required to discuss all her desires, plans and needs with Jay. After she and Jay worked out the details, Jay, not Melissa, would come to me or call me and get my approval or veto.

After explaining the new role that Jay would play in Melissa's life and the way it would affect the whole family, we gathered around and held hands and asked God in prayer to bless Jay and Melissa in their new roles and in their efforts to establish a new family of love and life-time commitment to each other.

We all took turns praying and felt great strength in our family love and commitment to each other. It was one of the most moving family experiences I have ever had.

**A new chain of command:**

The wisdom of such a plan becomes apparent once it gets underway. The new family leadership begins to take form. No longer could Melissa deal with me, as father, in the same way as before, often times wrapping me around her little finger. She would have to learn how to communicate with Jay, and he would have to learn how to be an effective leader for Melissa.

Strengthening the new relationship of the engaged couple now becomes the main function of the father. Father is always there to respond when called upon, but not in the same way as before. The objective now is for the engaged couple to deal with their problems as a team, focusing on each other in the solution of those problems. The last thing a daughter needs at this stage is for father to tell her what her new Knight in shining armor should do or not do. Such was the case before, during all of those years of training and instruction, but now is the moment of reality. Now is the time to execute our—lessons learned—to build a new relationship.

In Melissa's experience, as in the experience of my other daughters, she would come to me and say something like:

"Daddy, Jay thinks this, or that, or wants to do this or that, and he said this or that. What should I do?"

My answer has always been the same.

"Melissa, talk it over with Jay. I know that when you put your mind to it, you can come to understand what he is trying to say or do. You might have to ask more questions in order better to understand what he is trying to communicate. The important thing is to put your energies into discussing your need for more understanding with Jay and not with me. "

**The new chain of command always requires some adjustments:**

I could often see and feel the frustration they were experiencing in their new roles. This gave me opportunity to share ideas and experiences with Jay when we would get together for personal talks. Once the couple have made a true love decision and have committed their love to each other for life, and I have delegated the role of family leader to the new Knight in shining armor, I never impose my views on what I believe to be Right or Wrong!

I may veto their plans and ideas for activities and require an alternative to their first proposal. This is for their own good, as I see and understand it, while they are still engaged. However, they would not have to agree; they would just be expected to obey what I said at the time. Later, in the setting of their own home, they could do it their way.

In actual practice I can't think of anything that I ever had to veto. When a daughter and her new Knight are properly prepared for real love and marriage, by the time the engagement becomes a reality, it is amazing how compatible and committed to excellence they can be. By always being open and seeking moments to communicate with Jay and others of my sons-in-law, during the engagement period and after the marriage, I have been able to share many things with them. They have all shown remarkable ability to use what ever they learned to good advantage for their family. I always leave the decision with them to use or not to use the things that I might share with them. They are the new family leaders and responsible for their own families. As their father-in-law, I'm a source of information, experience and support, not a substitute for assuming their responsibilities.

# Book III
# Mommy's Little Boy

## Introduction

The Words of King Lemuel's Mother

"The words of King Lemuel, the utterance which his mother taught him:

What, my son?
And what: son of my womb?
And what: son of my vows?
Do not give your strength to women,
Nor your ways to that which destroys kings." Proverbs 31:1-3.

King Lemuel's mother is a biblical role-model for a real mother of faith and grace. Through her words we discover Christ's world view of women as leaders in the home for cultural and economic prowess, but also we hear her telling her son about the character and moral quality of a virtuous wife:

**The Virtuous Wife:**

"Who can find a virtuous wife? For her worth is far above rubies. The heart of her husband safely trusts her; so he will have no lack of gain. She does him good and not evil all the days of her life. She seeks wool and flax, and willingly works with her hands. She is like the merchant ships; she brings her food from afar. She also rises while it is yet night, and provides food for her household and a portion for her maidservants. She considers a field and buys it; from her profits she plants a vineyard. She girds herself with strength, and strengthens her arms. She perceives that her merchandise is good, and her lamp does not go out by night. She stretches out her hands to the distaff, and her hand holds the spindle. She extends her hand to the poor, yes; she reaches out her hands to the needy. She is not afraid of snow for her household, for all her household is clothed with scarlet. She makes tapestry for herself; her clothing is fine linen and purple. Her husband is known in the gates, when he sits among the elders of the land. She makes linen garments and sells them, and supplies sashes for the merchants. Strength and honor are her clothing; she shall rejoice in time to come. She opens her mouth with wisdom, and on her tongue is the law of kindness. She watches over the ways of her household, and does not eat the bread of idleness. Her children rise up and call her blessed; her husband also, and he praises her:

'Many daughters have done well, but you excel them all.'

"Charm is deceitful and beauty is passing, but a woman who fears the LORD, she shall be praised. Give her of the fruit of her hands, and let her own works praise her in the gates." Proverbs 31:10-31.

**To be—Virtuous—is to describe an action:**

Virtuousness in a wife—by definition—means that one would expect to see the physical and obvious fruit of such virtue. Our present day post modern Church uses virtue and the whole concept of virtuousness so loosely that it is almost impossible to know what they are talking about. King Lemuel's mother makes it very clear that she is—not simply tagging a name on something—she is describing a woman whose actions bespeak and live the meaning of the word—virtue—she is therefore—VIRTUOUS! The fact that she poses her words in the form of a question indicates that it was something not every young man had, but it was and is certainly something that God wants every young man of faith and grace to have! It is Christ's worldview of the NORMAL Christian wife!!

**What does our post modern Church call normal?**

Josh McDowell, an outstanding spokesperson for evangelical youth for several decades said years ago that evangelical youth are only ten percent less likely to engage in premarital sex than nonevangelicals.

The Southern Baptist Convention has a program called: *True Love Waits* and it is one of the most famous evangelical efforts that attempts to reduce premarital sexual activity. So far, 2.4 million young people have signed a pledge to wait until marriage to engage in sexual intercourse. However, the Columbia University and Yale University reported in their findings of March, 2004 that after seven years of study involving twelve thousand teenagers who took the pledge; they found that—eighty eight percent—of those who made pledges reported having sexual intercourse before marriage and just twelve percent kept their promise. The rates for having sexually transmitted diseases "were almost identical for the teenagers who took the pledges compared to those who did not."[135]

On a more positive note: there are some character based abstinence programs that produce have documented higher success rates. These programs allow for a longer exposure time for each student than that which is applied in the True *Love Waits program.* Those students that have taken virginity pledges under the strong character based training show on average, an eighteen month delay in initiation of sexual activity and in many cases until marriage. [136]

Though small, these successes serve to emphasize the dramatic impact for success that a family with parents of faith and grace—living the principles of God's revealed Law-Word set forth and illustrated in this book—can expect to have! Results for the general Christian culture is much less, as Barna reports in a 2001 poll that cohabitation—living with a member of the opposite sex without marriage—is only a little better among born-again "Christians" than the general public.

**We report on Barna's 2001 poll with the following comments:**

1. Thirty three percent of all adults have lived with a member of the opposite sex without being married. Among these "Christians" the rate is twenty five percent for born-again individuals.[137]

---

135 Lawrence K. Altman, "Study Finds That Teenage Virginity Pledges Are Rarely Kept," New York Times, March 10, 2004, A20.

136 For more information call Greg Williams, Lexington, KY (O) 859.278.8109, (C) 859.229.6504, (F) 859.277.7999,

137 "The Barna Group, The Barna Update, "Born Again Adults Less Likely to Co-Habit, Just As Likely to Divorce," http://www.barna.org/FlexPage.aspx?Page=BarnaUpdate&BarnaUpdateID=95.

John C. Green, a Christian political scientist and director of the Ray C. Bliss Institute of Applied Politics at the University of Akron. Green has discovered that:

2. Twenty six percent of traditional evangelicals—do not think premarital sex is wrong—and forty six percent of nontraditional evangelicals—read liberal—see nothing morally wrong with it.[138]
3. Thirteen percent of traditional evangelicals say it is okay for married persons to have sex with someone other than one's own spouse.
4. Nineteen percent of nontraditional evangelicals say adultery is morally acceptable.[139]

Green says that although evangelicals fare better than mainline Protestant and Catholic "Christians" on these issues, the number of evangelicals that outright reject biblical sexual moral standards is astonishing.

**Adopting the lies of the unbelievers as truth is killing us:**

Our current post modern Christian culture has predominantly accepted as—truth—what the revealed Law-Word of God declares to be lies. Actually, God is much more emphatic, He says that to adopt such lies as truth—is to commit spiritual adultery—to be idolaters! The secular atheist humanist academia has been spoon feeding the believers lies about family, sex and sin for centuries. This is not a new phenomena—this is old hat—remember Satan and the Garden of Eden? What were the lies that Satan told Eve? The lies that she believed then, are the basics of the same lies that our present day Christian culture has adopted as true. They are—the same old girl—she just has a different dress on!

For centuries Christians have been moving away from the basic truths of God's revealed Law-Word and little by little we have been adopting the ways and beliefs of the atheists and saying to ourselves that—we have learned—something new.[140] Now we see our homes divided with the larger majority of Christian fathers and mothers acting as though they didn't know the difference between Right or Wrong—or even if such a thing exists—as Right and Wrong. Everything is relevant, everything is gray—no black or white—that is something that sounds like racism for today's post modern men and women. Yet, in a world not too distant from this one when you said that: "Right and Wrong are as clearly different as black and white." everyone understood that you meant the contrast was plain to see. Even black people knew the term and used it the same way. Stark contrasts between Right and Wrong are just that—STARK—and you can't get starker than BLACK and WHITE!!

---

138 Ibid., p26

139 Ibid.

140 Alan Wolfe, director of the Boisi Center for Religion and American Public Life, has just published a study of American religious life. Evangelicals figure prominently. Today's evangelicalism, Wolfe says, exhibits "so strong a desire to copy the culture of hotel chains and popular music that it loses what religious distinctiveness it once had." The Transformation of American Religion (Free Press, 2003), p. 257.

Wolfe says, "The truth is there is increasingly little difference between an essentially secular activity like the popular entertainment industry and the bring-'em-in-at-any-cost efforts of evangelical megachurches." Michael Horton, "Beyond Culture Wars," Modern Reformation (May-June 1993), p. 212.

**My mother of faith and grace:**

It was a sunny summer afternoon in the Ozark Mountains just thirty miles East of Springfield, Missouri on my parents' new dairy farm. It was black berry picking time and we: my sister Joanna, my father, mother and me were all out picking black berries. My mother came over where I was working—I was eleven years old—and this was my first summer to live on a farm, so I was very excited about the new experience to pick black berries. My mother worked by my side silently for some time and then in a soft voice she said to me: "Son, have you ever thought about your relationship with God and His Son Jesus Christ?"

This was the first time anyone had ever spoken to me personally about my relationship with God or anything at all about Jesus Christ. I remember thinking how odd it was that she was asking me this—but on the other hand—I felt honored that she cared. I answered her with a simple: "Yes" and kept right on picking black berries. She then said: "That's good, I want to encourage you to do that and I would like to read the Bible with you."

Our family had not been big on church attendance or Bible reading before my dad had purchased the farm. My father never read the Bible in my presence but he did always say grace at the table. So, for my mother to say these things to me and to offer to read the Bible with me was really something! This was the beginning of what I remember most about her instructions to me over the years to come. When I got old enough to go out to ball games, school activities and to date girls she would always tell me to come into her bedroom and kiss her good-night when I got home—no matter how late that might be. Later she told me that she did that for two reasons: one she wanted me to know that I was special to her, and two that it would give her an opportunity to check and see if I had been drinking or smoking. Mothers do need to check.

**Grandmothers are very important also:**

My grandmother Hatfield was a woman of strong faith. She read the Bible from cover to cover as many times as life would allow. She prayed for many years that my father would finally give his heart to the Lord—he finally did the same year that my parents bought the dairy farm in the Ozarks. During my years in the Navy, while I was stationed at North Island in San Diego, her little house in Fontana, California became my weekend refuge from the constant chatter and attention given by most of my fellow service mates about their illicit sex, bars and whore houses in Tijuana, Mexico, just fifteen miles south of the city. I did not have a car in those days and so I hitch hiked up and back every weekend I had liberty. From her little house I would hitch hike to near-by Riverside where I had found a church with a very active youth group. The hundred and twenty miles back and forth from San Diego seemed like nothing to me.

**Paul speaks of the importance of Timothy's grandmother and mother:**

> "To Timothy, a beloved son: Grace, mercy, and peace from God the Father and Christ Jesus our Lord. I thank God, whom I serve with a pure conscience, as my forefathers did, as without ceasing I remember you in my prayers night and day, greatly desiring to see you, being mindful of your tears, that I may be filled with joy, when I call to remembrance the genuine faith that is in you, which dwelt first in your grandmother Lois and your mother Eunice, and I am persuaded is in you also." II Timothy 1:2-5.

It is important to notice two distinct aspects of these words to Timothy.

**First:** They convey an attitude of thanksgiving for past generational passage of spiritual example and blessing for Paul—Timothy's forefathers.

**Second:** They convey the message of successful transgenerational passage of spiritual and moral values from Timothy's grandmother to her mother and then to him—two generations of women blessed Timothy.

God promises us transgenerational blessings if we believe in Him and follow His commandments.

> "Therefore know that the LORD your God, He is God, the faithful God who keeps covenant and mercy for a thousand generations with those who love Him and keep His commandments; and He repays those who hate Him to their face, to destroy them." Deuteronomy 7:9-10

**Mothers of faith and grace are champions too:**

Mommy's little boy is in great need of a champion for his development as a man of faith and grace. Nothing reaches a boys heart—soon to be a man—like the voice of his mother and if possible a grandmother to confirm her words. You, mother of faith and grace, are the hope for the moral and spiritual future of your sons. No one on earth has the words of life that can penetrate as deeply into a son's heart as does his mother.

As we have discovered in Book I and Book II, the father of faith and grace is God's foreordained head and spiritual leader of His institution—The Family—as such, father is certainly in charge and in the forefront of teaching by example and personal instruction. Yet, father can do all of this and much more for his son: wrestle with him, take him hunting and fishing, throw him fast balls and cheer him on in soccer or football—but only you mother—have the most penetrating words to open the door to his spiritual heart!

As we discovered in much more detail in Book I, the mutual support from both fathers and mothers of faith and grace are key elements in God's foreordained plan for successful marriages as stewards of His gift of the children that He has given to us, to love, teach and rear. The intricate detail of God's design of interdependence between a man and woman for planned success of love and marriage serves to illustrate why Christ's worldview on divorce is that it was never sanctioned from the beginning and is only allowed because of the hardness and sinfulness exemplified in our rebellious natures.[141]

So, we see that whereas both a father and mother of faith and grace are God's primary elements to serve as champions of sex, love and romance for their children of the opposite sex—they can only do so successfully—with the whole hearted support of the other! Like the support columns and cross sections of a large and intricate bridge—if one fails—the whole structure fails.

---

141 "The Pharisees also came to Him, testing Him, and saying to Him, 'Is it lawful for a man to divorce his wife for just any reason?'

"And He answered and said to them, "Have you not read that He who made[a] them at the beginning "made them male and female,' and said, 'For this reason a man shall leave his father and mother and be joined to his wife, and the two shall become one flesh? So then, they are no longer two but one flesh. Therefore what God has joined together, let not man separate.'

"They said to Him, 'Why then did Moses command to give a certificate of divorce, and to put her away?'

"He said to them, 'Moses, because of the hardness of your hearts, permitted you to divorce your wives, but from the beginning it was not so. And I say to you, whoever divorces his wife, except for sexual immorality, and marries another, commits adultery; and whoever marries her who is divorced commits adultery." Mathew 19:3-9.

**Mother as a champion of love and marriage for her son:**

As a mother of faith and grace part of your commitment to your son as coach and champion of his development in love and marriage is to share with him the female world and to magnify his understanding of his role in developing that world. All of the things that a husband of faith and grace must teach his daughter are also the same things that must be taught to Mommy's little boy. The virtue of a son is the key element for God to use in protecting the virtue of a young sister and also the young daughter of some other family. It is painfully obvious but apparently—not very embarrassing to many—that our America Christian culture understands how to spell the word virtuous but—little or nothing—about how to live it. God's revealed Law-Word—in language that only those with the gift of faith can understand—reveals to us that MOTHER is God's primary source for teaching and molding moral character and virtue in the heart of a son.

Book III, *Mommy's Little Boy;* will lead us into discoveries of the great importance that God's revealed Law-Word has to tell us about mothers of faith and grace and their sons. We will discover—the worldview of Christ as revealed by Him the Word of Life—and how mothers have been used by God to work His special work in their sons and how that impacts the woman of faith and grace in today's Christian family.

# Book III
# MOMMY'S LITTLE BOY

## Chapter One

## Haloed Queens

"My son; hear the instruction of your father, and do not forsake the law of your mother; for they will be a graceful ornament on your head, and chains about your neck." Proverbs 1:8-9.

**Women who can do no wrong:**

If you want to start a fight anywhere in the world just tell a man—any man—that his mother is a whore, or some other despicable thing and you will have your fight. It will not matter that you should possibly be telling the truth. Truth in this instance is focused solely on the honor and emotional ties that men carry in their hearts for their mothers—no sin, known or unknown—is sufficient to dispel this bond between a son and his mother. Every man sees his mother as much more than just a woman. She is always a queen to her son—even when she has been rejected as nothing by her husband—the man that he must call father.

**Mother and Wisdom are characterized as nearly synonymous:**

In the book of Proverbs we discover that Wisdom, here characterized as a mother—a mother's law, calls her son to a meeting. In this meeting she—Mother/Wisdom—gives her son certain instructions that she says will be so important for him that if he does not heed her words and obey what she tells him—he will lose all that he holds dear in this life. Wisdom also speaks out to men in general with these same instructions, not to her son only—but to the broader audience of all men. In Proverbs, chapter 3, we hear the mother speak:

> "My son, do not forget my law, but let your heart keep my commands; for length of days and long life and peace they will add to you. Let not mercy and truth forsake you; bind them around your neck, write them on the tablet of your heart, and so find favor and high esteem in the sight of God and man. Trust in the LORD with all your heart, and lean not on your own understanding; in all your ways acknowledge Him, and He shall direct your paths. Do not be wise in your own eyes; fear the LORD and depart from evil. It will be health to your flesh, and strength to your bones. Honor the LORD with your possessions and with the firstfruits of all your increase; so your barns will be filled with plenty, and your vats will overflow with new wine. My son, do not despise the chastening of the LORD, nor detest His correction; for whom the LORD loves He corrects, just as a father the son in whom he delights. Happy is the man who finds wisdom, and the man who gains understanding; for her proceeds are better than the profits of silver, and her gain than fine gold. She is more precious than rubies, and all the things you may desire cannot compare with her. Length of days is in her right hand, in her left hand riches and honor. Her ways are ways of pleasantness, and all her paths are peace. She is a tree of life to those who take hold of her, and happy are all who retain her. The LORD by wisdom founded the earth; by understanding He

established the heavens; by His knowledge the depths were broken up, and clouds drop down the dew. My son, let them not depart from your eyes—keep sound wisdom and discretion; so they will be life to your soul and grace to your neck. Then you will walk safely in your way, and your foot will not stumble. When you lie down, you will not be afraid; yes, you will lie down and your sleep will be sweet. Do not be afraid of sudden terror, nor of trouble from the wicked when it comes; for the LORD will be your confidence,..." Proverbs 3:1-26.

**Christ is synonymous with Wisdom:**

Christ is declared in the gospel of John to be the incarnate Word the—very Word, Christ incarnate—that God the Father used to create the universe, our world, mankind and all of His creation.[142] I find it striking that here in Proverbs it is also clear that this same Word, our Lord and Savior Jesus Christ is also the Wisdom with which God states here that He used to create the world. There can be no coincidence that this Wisdom is characterized as feminine and also as the Word incarnate in John. This doesn't mean that I fully understand it, but it does cause me to have tremendous respect for this mystery of Christ and Wisdom being one—after all—I am said to be one with my Marilyn because she is my wife. I don't fully understand that either, but that doesn't ameliorate or negate the truth of the fact!

**All mothers know they are special to their sons:**

Both the unbelieving mother and the mother of faith and grace know that they are special in the eyes of their sons. A mother is close to her daughter but she is bonded in a way with her son—like she is to no other—including her husband. Mothers are deeply hurt when their sons fail to live up to the dreams that they have had in their hearts for them. A father is displeased and his pride is wounded, but a mother truly grieves for her son when he fails. His failures tear at the deep bonds that she feels for him and they become her failures and her pain. Unlike politicians who use the phrase—"I feel your pain—mothers actually do, especially mothers of faith and grace!

"The proverbs of Solomon: a wise son makes a glad father, but a foolish son is the grief of his mother." Proverbs 10:1

"A wise son makes a father glad, but a foolish man despises his mother." Proverbs 15:20.

"Listen to your father who begot you, and do not despise your mother when she is old." Proverbs 23:22

God began His relationship with Women as a help meet for His created being, Man. Unlike Man—who came directly from the dust—Woman came from Adams rib, removed from his side by God. True—the origin does not change—both man and woman are from the dust and to dust we shall return until the resurrection. However, because of this method—chosen by God to make woman from a piece of Adam—there is a unique bond between man and woman! Adam noticed the importance immediately and made special mention of it:

[142] "In the beginning was the Word, and the Word was with God, and the Word was God. He was in the beginning with God. All things were made through Him, and without Him nothing was made that was made. In Him was life, and the life was the light of men. And the light shines in the darkness, and the darkness did not comprehend[a] it." John 1:1-5.

"And the LORD God said, "It is not good that man should be alone; I will make him a helper comparable to him. ... So Adam gave names to all cattle, to the birds of the air, and to every beast of the field. But for Adam there was not found a helper comparable to him.

"And the LORD God caused a deep sleep to fall on Adam, and he slept; and He took one of his ribs, and closed up the flesh in its place. Then the rib which the LORD God had taken from man He made into a woman, and He brought her to the man.

"And Adam said: 'This is now bone of my bones and flesh of my flesh; she shall be called Woman, because she was taken out of Man;' therefore, a man shall leave his father and mother and be joined to his wife, and they shall become one flesh. And they were both naked, the man and his wife, and were not ashamed." Genesis 2:18-25.

The mystery of oneness within the bonds of matrimony began with the miracle of God when He took the rib from Adam's side and used that as his beginning point to create Woman. Adam immediately picks up on the reality of her creation—as being also a part of himself—and says that because of this she will be called Woman. Man and Woman were never more one than at this time until Christ died and rose from the dead and made it possible for Man and Woman to be one—both physically and spiritually—in the same sense that Christ and the Church are one.

"So husbands ought to love their own wives as their own bodies; he who loves his wife loves himself. For no one ever hated his own flesh, but nourishes and cherishes it, just as the Lord does the church: For we are members of His body, of His flesh and of His bones. 'For this reason a man shall leave his father and mother and be joined to his wife, and the two shall become one flesh.' This is a great mystery, but I speak concerning Christ and the church. Nevertheless let each one of you in particular so love his own wife as himself, and let the wife see that she respects her husband."" Ephesians 5:28-33.

Spiritually speaking we are all one in Christ[143] but functionally speaking for the purpose of God's chain of command for His institution; The Family, there are differences in positions and separations of powers. The position of the man—the husband/father is the head—the wife/mother is his second in command, his chief assistant.[144] Power flows from God through Christ to the man and from the man through delegation to the wife. Thus, the commission of the wife/mother is so great that she can be the greatest blessing or the greatest source of destruction!

**God's Commission for Mothers of faith and grace:**

As with the men among God's elect, there is a special commission for the daughters of God and their roles in the affairs of His Kingdom.

143 "For you are all sons of God through faith in Christ Jesus. For as many of you as were baptized into Christ have put on Christ. There is neither Jew nor Greek, there is neither slave nor free, there is neither male nor female; for you are all one in Christ Jesus. And if you are Christ's, then you are Abraham's seed, and heirs according to the promise." Galatians 3:26-29.

144 "For a man indeed ought not to cover his head, since he is the image and glory of God; but woman is the glory of man. For man is not from woman, but woman from man. Nor was man created for the woman, but woman for the man. For this reason the woman ought to have a symbol of authority on her head, because of the angels. Nevertheless, neither is man independent of woman, nor woman independent of man, in the Lord. For as woman came from man, even so man also comes through woman; but all things are from God." I Corinthians 11:7-12.

"Wives, likewise, be submissive to your own husbands, that even if some do not obey the word, they, without a word, may be won by the conduct of their wives, when they observe your chaste conduct accompanied by fear. Do not let your adornment be merely outward—arranging the hair, wearing gold, or putting on fine apparel—rather let it be the hidden person of the heart, with the incorruptible beauty of a gentle and quiet spirit, which is very precious in the sight of God. For in this manner, in former times, the holy women who trusted in God also adorned themselves, being submissive to their own husbands, as Sarah obeyed Abraham, calling him lord, whose daughters you are if you do good and are not afraid with any terror. Husbands, likewise, dwell with them with understanding, giving honor to the wife, as to the weaker vessel, and as being heirs together of the grace of life, that your prayers may not be hindered." I Peter 3:1-7.

**Great commissions bring great responsibilities:**

A virtuous wife is praised highly and her value is compared to that of the highest order. There are seven examples of woman's special and highly valued relationship with man. Four of the seven are juxtaposed against—the potential volatility of woman—therefore in the fourth one you will notice that a—good wife—is said to obtain favor from God for her husband:

"For a man indeed ought not to cover his head, since he is the image and glory of God; but woman is the glory of man." I Corinthians 11:7.

"An excellent wife is the crown of her husband, but she who causes shame is like rottenness in his bones." Proverbs 12:4.

"The wise woman builds her house, but the foolish pulls it down with her hands." Proverbs 14:1.

"He who finds a wife finds a good thing, and obtains favor from the LORD." Proverbs 18:22.

"A foolish son is the ruin of his father, and the contentions of a wife are a continual dripping." Proverbs 19:13.

"Houses and riches are an inheritance from fathers, but a prudent wife is from the LORD." Proverbs 19:14.

"Better to dwell in the wilderness, than with a contentious and angry woman." Proverbs 21:19.

**A virtuous woman is covered:**

The concept of a covering for Woman has long been a contentious point of doctrine for many different Christian groups. I have chosen to bring it up here to alleviate the fear and apprehension that comes when certain groups such as the Catholics, the United Pentecostals, the Apostolics, and the Amish, along with some other less known groups, attempt to force upon women the custom of wearing a headscarf at all times. Their intention is to fulfill in a literal way the—symbol of authority on her head—mentioned in I Corinthians 11:10. "For this reason the woman ought to have a symbol of authority on her head, because of the angels."

Although Paul suggests that she should have a "symbol of authority on her head" he does not say that such symbol is limited to just a scarf. Quite the contrary! Paul is highly recognized among biblical scholars for denying the superior value of physical symbols over the reality of a spiritual value expressed in a person's heart and exemplified in their day to day life. The wearing of scarves by Hebrew women of the First Century was common to show respect before God and men—likewise and of greater Hebrew importance was the common practice of circumcision for men to show their submission and respect to God. Nevertheless, Paul makes it very clear that symbols will never take the place of the reality in the person's heart! A scarf can be a symbol of submission for a wicked rebellious woman the same as it can be for a respectful submissive woman of faith and grace.

In Mexico I saw many women who were dressed most extremely provocatively—those actually preparing for a night of prostitution—going up the steps of some local cathedral seeking God's favor or pardon—I'm not sure which—all wearing a beautiful scarf with long lacy borders over their heads. Likewise, I know for a fact—because of my work with hundreds of their husbands—that the women of those groups who insist on the wearing of scarves are no more submitted to, or respectful of their husbands than those who don't. The point is not the scarf or the circumcision but the attitude of the heart and the life-style of the believer!

> "For circumcision is indeed profitable if you keep the law; but if you are a breaker of the law, your circumcision has become uncircumcision. Therefore, if an uncircumcised man keeps the righteous requirements of the law, will not his uncircumcision be counted as circumcision? And will not the physically uncircumcised, if he fulfills the law, judge you who, even with your written code and circumcision, are a transgressor of the law? For he is not a Jew who is one outwardly, nor is circumcision that which is outward in the flesh; but he is a Jew who is one inwardly; and circumcision is that of the heart, in the Spirit, not in the letter; whose praise is not from men but from God." Romans 2:25-29.

**The true covering of a virtuous woman:**

It has been said many ways and from many different points of reference since we first started our journey of discoveries in this book—though we did not use the term covered—the husband/father is God's true covering for Woman. If this does not make sense to our readers at this point in our dialog—then I am guilty of having done a very inferior job of directing you into God's uncommon common sense—and I apologize.

1. The husband of faith and grace is God's true delegated covering for his wife—whom the Lord has given him.[145]

2. The father of faith and grace is God's true delegated covering for his daughter—whom the Lord has given him.[146]

---

145 "Wives, submit to your own husbands, as to the Lord. For the husband is head of the wife, as also Christ is head of the church; and He is the Savior of the body." Ephesians 5:22-23.

146 "So she said to him, 'My father, if you have given your word to the LORD, do to me according to what has gone out of your mouth, because the LORD has avenged you of your enemies, the people of Ammon.' 37Then she said to her father, 'Let this thing be done for me: let me alone for two months, that I may go and wander on the mountains and bewail my virginity, my friends and I.' So he said, 'Go.' And he sent her away for two months; and she went with her friends, and bewailed her virginity on the mountains. 39And it was so at the end of two months that she returned to her father, and he carried out his vow with her which he had vowed. She knew no man." Judges 11:36-39.

This text is an excellent example of a daughters submissive attitude and loyalty to her fathers rule over her—it is not however an example of a wise father—for he acted very rashly and he too was sorry for his actions. ZH

3. When neither husband nor father is available, then God's institution the Church is God's delegated authority to serve as the provisional head for the woman who has lost all her other options for covering.[147]

**An excellent wife is the crown of her husband:**

I wish I could testify that simply by walking down the aisle and saying: "I do," we married couples could realize the ultimate levels of God's calling and the perfection of His grace in our development. The truth is not so idealistic—promised and possible—but not so easy. I always envisioned Marilyn as my Queen of the Universe—certainly my universe—but my own ignorance and pride of self, served as major blocks for me to allow God to unlock all that He had stored up for me, in this person I call my wife. As I was able to submit more to God's revealed Law-Word and apply the uncommon common sense of Christ's worldview to all aspects of my life and relationship with Marilyn—God began to unlock her secrets of value and blessings!

**Mission impossible:**

If you choose to accept it—dear wife and mother of faith and grace—your mission, indeed your commission in life—is to understand God's revealed Law-Word and His great commission for you as your husband's help meet and second in command and to raise your son to know what that means for his understanding of both himself and of the woman that one day he will ask to be his wife. Unlike the TV series—Mission Impossible—this mission really is impossible for you alone.

Know this for certain, God has not left you weak and unable. Our trust is always in His perfect sovereign will and the steps that He has foreordained that we might walk in them. Understanding who we are in Him and in His Christ is 95% of the battle—for now our attention can be refocused from our weaknesses—to His infinite strength, wisdom and faithfulness. Remember dear wife and mother of faith and grace, it is God who works in you both to will and to do His good pleasure. You are His gift as a Queen to your husband and certainly as the image of the Queen that one day your son will want to marry!!

> "Therefore, my beloved, as you have always obeyed, not as in my presence only, but now much more in my absence, work out your own salvation with fear and trembling; for it is God who works in you both to will and to do for His good pleasure." Philippians 2:12-13.

[147] "Do not rebuke an older man, but exhort him as a father, younger men as brothers, older women as mothers, younger women as sisters, with all purity. Honor widows who are really widows. But if any widow has children or grandchildren, let them first learn to show piety at home and to repay their parents; for this is good and acceptable before God." I Timothy 1:1-4.

# Book III

# Mommy's Little Boy

## Chapter Two

## Introducing the Male World

### Introduction

"Blessed is the man who walks not in the counsel of the ungodly, nor stands in the path of sinners, nor sits in the seat of the scornful; but his delight is in the law of the LORD, and in His law he meditates day and night. He shall be like a tree planted by the rivers of water that brings forth its fruit in its season, whose leaf also shall not wither; and whatever he does shall prosper. The ungodly are not so, but are like the chaff which the wind drives away. Therefore the ungodly shall not stand in the judgment, nor sinners in the congregation of the righteous. For the LORD knows the way of the righteous, but the way of the ungodly shall perish." Psalms 1:1-6.

**From cradle to the altar—he is all boy:**

As fathers and mothers of faith and grace part of your commitment to your daughter and son as their coaches and champions of their development in love and marriage is to share with them the male world. The father for his daughter—who will one day marry a man and the mother for her son who will someday be a husband for some other man's daughter—and head of his own family. This chapter presents some, but not all, of three areas of the male world that are important for Daddy's little girl to learn to prepare her for what is and what could be. Also, this chapter presents the same information for the mother's use in preparing her son to know himself as both from the dust—and yet saved by grace—as God's tool in Christ to be the spiritual leader of his future family.

Ultimately each father and mother has to decide how much and in what detail these matters should be presented to their respective charges. The objective is not—to frighten or scare them—but to give them a good concept of the challenges they face. Each with their own unique needs and challenges for development will become well prepared for success in love and marriage to the degree that they—providentially receive and assimilate—this information. Father and mother team work is very important in the cross application of this information, as this endeavor is so important for the development of wisdom and understanding in the son and for his future role as a father of faith and grace for his daughter.

**By the grace of God we must prevail:**

As we discovered in Book II, without the spiritual and moral character development of sons, the women they ultimately marry will be greatly disadvantaged. Successful transgenerational spiritual and moral character depends upon our success as parents, by the grace of God—to mold our sons and daughters into the high calling of Christ, that they become His mature man and woman of faith and grace!

"And He Himself gave some to be apostles, some prophets, some evangelists, and some pastors and teachers, for the equipping of the saints for the work of ministry, for the edifying of the body of Christ, till we all come to the unity of the faith and of the knowledge of the Son of God, to a perfect man, to the measure of the stature of the fullness of Christ; that we should no longer be children, tossed to and fro and carried about with every wind of doctrine, by the trickery of men, in the cunning craftiness of deceitful plotting, but, speaking the truth in love, may grow up in all things into Him who is the head—Christ—from whom the whole body, joined and knit together by what every joint supplies, according to the effective working by which every part does its share, causes growth of the body for the edifying of itself in love." Ephesians 4:11-16.

**The three sections of this chapter:**

Part I, "The Status Quo," is a composite of present conditions, attitudes, historical influences and personal experience which illustrates the wide margin of inappropriate and incorrect responses of many men to their own male sexuality.

Part II, "Normal Male Sexuality," is a frank and candid glimpse of male sexuality, its early biological development before emotional or mental maturity and the pressures that our modern society puts on this development.

Part III, "A Real man of faith and grace," offers a positive affirmation of Right responses to male sexuality which a man should exemplify and gives a breakdown of what a young princess should look for in a real man of faith and grace.

# Book III

# Mommy's Little Boy

## Chapter Two-Part I

## Introducing The Male World

## The Status Quo

"Therefore lay aside all filthiness and overflow of wickedness, and receive with meekness the implanted word, which is able to save your souls. But be doers of the word, and not hearers only, deceiving yourselves. For if anyone is a hearer of the word and not a doer, he is like a man observing his natural face in a mirror; for he observes himself, goes away, and immediately forgets what kind of man he was. But he who looks into the perfect law of liberty and continues in it, and is not a forgetful hearer but a doer of the work, this one will be blessed in what he does." James 1:21-25.

**Mommy's little boy must develop into a doer and not a hearer only:**

The present status of American males, as a group leaves a lot to be desired. However, bad as it is—it is not all bad—it is not without hope. We all have dreams of what we consider to be ideal and of what we think we want. Our inner sense of God's revealed Law-Word—our source of a real Right and Wrong—inspires us to want what is Right, but then our fears, lack of commitment and failure to make mid-course changes keeps us heading in the Wrong direction. As a result, many men are suffering great pain and personal destruction.

Many business leaders in high places, politicians in all levels and branches of local, state, and federal government, teachers and school officials in the highest ranks of our educational system, military leaders in all branches of our armed forces, and even the ministers of our churches, both small and great, are guilty of a morality that says, "Do as I say, but not as I do!" Honesty, integrity, and moral role modeling have in more than a few instances become mere platitudes of meaningless rhetoric—something far too many of our present leaders in all ranks and categories seem to have raised—to a new level of sophistication and deceit. Slick media, newspapers, magazines, radio and especially television; produce an endless stream of names and faces of men and women who are supposed to be perfect or near perfect models of honesty, high integrity and moral example. Only in rare instances is there much truth to what we are reading, hearing or seeing. Such conduct adds new meaning to an old saying that was common with our forefathers, "Don't believe anything you hear and only half of what you see!"

**Ministry Leaders and Sexual Promiscuity:**

In the Introduction to Book I, page 1, I quoted Jennifer Roback Morse: "Far from being a losing strategy, we can only win if we bring the divorce issue out of the closet."

Yes, we must bring the issue of divorce out of the closet. I only wish that divorce were the—only thing—we had locked up in our closets! To our great disgrace as a culture and especially as Christian people, our closets are overflowing with hidden sins that we—as a Christian culture—have not been willing to discuss, much less to admit and certainly from which we have yet to repent and seek God's healing. By saying this I run the risk of your disdain—"Here we go again, just another diatribe against the church." I know—I'm sorry it looks that way, but nothing could be farther from the truth! Before you pass judgment, let me share with you the results of a little known poll, taken by a well known and highly respected Christian leader and minister, Chuck Swindoll—of Dallas Theological Seminary. The time was July, 1994—the place was Colorado State University at Boulder Colorado—I was there. I participated and I am a personal witness of this poll.

We Americans are very familiar with polls—all kinds of polls—from what we like to eat, to whom we are most likely to vote for. Before experiencing this poll that I am about to describe, I had never heard of a poll to measure the moral health of our nations ministry leaders. This was a public—on the spot—poll, not your typical phone survey or mass mailing. I don't think that Pastor Swindoll was thinking in terms of a poll. We were all gathered together in a small indoor stadium of approximately 5,000 seating capacity. We numbered between 3,500—4,000 men, ministry leaders all. There were pastors, assistant pastors, youth pastors, elders, deacons, Sunday school teaches, evangelists and missionaries, representing every ethnic and social strata from all of the lower 48 states. Polls taken from a broad geographic section with ethnic and social diversity and in numbers exceeding 1,200 participants are considered to have an error factor of no more than three percent. This poll was truly a representation of a major cross section of American Christian leadership.

**Personal witness:**

We were in the last night of a three day leadership training conference sponsored by *Promise Keepers* of Colorado Springs, Colorado. Chuck Swindoll was the featured speaker for our last gathering before departure the following morning. Excitement and a sense of expectation filled the air. We had heard many speakers during the previous three days and had participated in many study groups to share problems unique to men and their roles as leaders in church, family and business. This last meeting would be the pinnacle of our experience. Chuck Swindoll's message would be the hot iron to—cauterize—our open wounds and to bring a measure of final healing to this group of men.

Pastor Swindoll held forth in his delivery for almost an hour. He began by giving an over-view of the general problems of men in ministry; work-a-holism, family and spousal isolation, self importance, insensitivity to spousal needs for tenderness and romance and last but not least—ministry leadership tendencies for blindness to our own sexual misdeeds. Pastor Swindoll was very transparent and graciously shared his own experiences with many of these problems, especially his past failings with regard to his having isolated his loving wife from his ministry life and his failings to appropriately cultivate her personal needs for tenderness and romance. He shared his failings and his victories through the grace of God and praised Him for giving him back his wife and his ministry, during this difficult time. We all were on the edge of our seats, hanging onto each word, expecting a testimony of victory and overcoming of evil—we were not disappointed!

Then came our moment of truth; Pastor Swindoll changed from his personal experience and challenges and began to focus—on our personal—potential for problems and challenges. He reviewed the need for all men in leadership to accept ownership for their actions and to be committed to face their problems and to seek God in honest repentance and commitment to positive change. Only through personal ownership of our problems and frank admission of our errors—could we gain God's blessing—of healing and over-coming.

Pastor Swindoll was very clear on his subsequent request for a personal declaration of guilt and an honest request for God to forgive and to heal. Not just twice did he clarify to whom he was speaking and from whom he was asking a decision for repentance—but many times—he clearly stated that he was addressing this challenge only to those who were now—present tense—involved in and guilty of sexual misdeeds for which they knew they were wrong and for which they desperately needed to repent and ask God for forgiveness. He was very clear on just what he felt constituted such sexual misdeeds: adultery, fornication, pornography, incest and homosexuality. He introduced his challenge with a qualifying statement, which I will paraphrase:

**Pastor Swindoll:**

> "Men and brothers I have spoken to many men concerning the problems we are about to discuss. I am aware that although this is a group of ministry leaders from all over the country, there are those among us who suffer from these very problems. In a group of this size it would be impossible for there not to be such men who are even right now involved in sexual misconduct with secretaries, mistresses, pornography, adultery, fornication, incest and homosexuality. At the close of my comments I am going to ask all of you who are now involved in anyway in any of these sexual sins, to be honest and to seek God's forgiveness. I want you to stand where you are and I am going to lead you in a prayer of repentance and forgiveness. God is faithful and He will hear your prayers and lead you to victory."

After repeating this explanation and challenge many times from several different perspectives it would be impossible—or so it would seem—that any of us present did not understand what was being said and what the challenge was. It was crystal clear to me and personally very impacting and of great interest.

It was a great impact personally because I too had had a problem with sexual misconduct from 1974-1985 during which time I deluded myself into believing it was alright for me to occasionally frequent "gentlemen's" bars—the oxymoron—for topless bars. The lunacy of my ways was brought home to me through a small men's prayer group I helped to form and attended, beginning in the summer of 1985. This was my first experience of real—man to man—openness and spiritual delivery. After coming to my spiritual senses—pure intellectualism will not work—I told my wife. From that moment on, I have been blessed by a deep understanding of God's wisdom on limiting my visual focus of the feminine form and—all things sexual—to my wife, Marilyn. Amazingly, this happened during a time when I was working very close with my daughters as their champion for successful romance and marriage—how willfully blind I was!

It was also of great interest to me because I too had been involved, in the years since my own delivery, in counseling men in their struggles with sexual sins. I was very interested to get a pulse on the level of such activity within the broader scope of ministry leaders from all across America. I'm not exactly sure what I expected the response to be—but be assured of this—I did not expect what actually happened! After doing all that is humanly possible—to make clear and unambiguous—his challenge and his request for personal action, pastor Swindoll came to a point where he said:

**Pastor Swindoll:**

> "Alright men, those of you who want to respond to this call for repentance and forgiveness on any of these matters, stand up now."

I knew that there were certainly too many men gathered to allow for any possibility that there were none present who did not have problems with some—if not all—of these areas of sexual sin. What I was not prepared for was the impact I felt, from the public response to this very personal polling of sexual sins and misdeeds. The response impacted me then and continues to bring serious reflection to me as I see our Christian culture suffering increased attacks from without while dying from within.

**The response shows evidence of our decaying Christian culture:**

The response was so over-whelming that it was hard to see—who was not—standing up! As I already had experienced my own delivery many years prior to this gathering and not because of any—superior personal holiness—I did not stand in response to this challenge. The view from a seating position was advantageous for determining who else was still seated. In this oval shaped, bleacher style arena, it was easy to look both ways, up and down the aisles. I spent the whole time, listening and at the same time looking to see what percentage was standing and what percentage was still seated. My most conservative calculation is that at least 90 percent of the men present were standing and only 10 percent were still seated.

Albeit this was not announced or characterized by *Promise Keepers* to be a poll—but non-the-less—a poll it is. In the interest of not over-stating the case and given the possibility that in spite of pastor Swindoll's clear explanation of to whom he was addressing this challenge; let us say that only 75 percent were actually having personal sin problems of a sexual nature. Aside from the fact that these men were courageous in their admission of guilt and in their commitment to repent and to seek God's forgiveness—the big message here for America—is that our Christian culture is decaying and dying from within—as a church nationally—we are without moral leadership.

**God will magnify the Kingdom through the elect not the unbeliever:**

Thank God for every pastor and ministry leader who is living the victorious life over sexual sin, and thank you pastor, ministry leader, whom ever you are! May God continue to give us the victory—for it is not by flesh and blood that we overcome[148]—it is an unmerited gift from our Heavenly Father.

Even so, the fact that our ministry leaders are having personal problems with sexual promiscuity gives us a clear understanding that they are mere men and not gods. Also it is sobering for all men, for if those who are proclaimed leaders of spiritual and moral values are having problems what can we expect from those who are more ambivalent about their commitment? The answer is in our faith: the faith we either have or do not have. We, as carnal men, regardless of whether we are in ministry or not—although in possession of the gift of faith and grace—are no more powerful than those men who reject our Lord and Savior, if we self-consciously disregard His commands and deny His gift of wisdom and power to overcome. Remember that old saying: "You can lead a horse to water, but you can't make him drink." God can and does give us the answers and the power we need to be

---

[148] "He was in the world, and the world was made through Him, and the world did not know Him. He came to His own, and His own did not receive Him. But as many as received Him, to them He gave the right to become children of God, to those who believe in His name: who were born, not of blood, nor of the will of the flesh, nor of the will of man, but of God" John 1:10-13.

successful in all that He has commanded us to do—but only if we accept His Lordship and His guidance. Remember, He does not indwell the unbelievers nor does He promise them power to overcome. Their failures should be—no surprise—to us who believe. But what should be of—great surprise and concern—is our rebellion against our Heavenly Father evidenced in our lack of exercising His gift of faith and the power to overcome. We men of faith and grace do not have the luxury of pointing are fingers at the atheist in our midst and thinking that by comparing ourselves with them we afford ourselves some measure of success. Christ is our King and we live and move and have our being in Him—not in and by the standards of the unbelievers!![149]

**Honesty, integrity and Mommy's little boy:**

In our present political environment the legislature meets and decides the laws for which the government is responsible, and the executive branch executes the new law by signing it into existence and authorizing the actions or expenditure of the funds necessary to make it happen. The majority of our politicians do not exercise personal or professional accountability. That is, they can say they are going to do certain things, take responsibility for certain tasks, perform their duties with honesty and integrity , but in reality they often work hardest of all to feather their own nests. In short, they are not honest, have little or no integrity and they don't keep their word. Those who keep their word are so rare that when one appears it takes some getting used to—President George W. Bush for example.

This kind of character deficit and lack of moral fiber is no less than a mirror image of the smooth-talking womanizer seducing an unsuspecting young girl. In the case of the politicians—society as a whole—is seduced.

In the absence of fatherhood for such a large segment of our society, we hear the hue and cry of the liberals for more intervention by government in the lives of children and in our schools. Many liberals, who for decades have preached against family authority, and equally against fathers as heads of families, are seeing the destruction of millions of families, their own included. Now they scream for help and for answers, but not once do they admit their mistake, of rebelling against authority and against fathers in the role of family leader. How can they? Like Gloria Steinem, the famous feminist, they really don't know exactly how or why they were hurt.

In addition to our attempts to pass the responsibilities of fatherhood onto government, public schools and churches, we also find it convenient to blame our women for our lack of leadership. It's so easy to blame anything or anybody but ourselves! Apparently, we men are so afraid of taking the reigns of responsibility for our own sexuality, wives and family, that we are desperate to find someone or something to take over in our place. We seem to want all the laurels and all the sex, but none of the responsibility. For Mommy's little boy to develop into a man of honesty and integrity—indeed a well equipped man of faith and grace—something has to change!

[149] "God, who made the world and everything in it, since He is Lord of heaven and earth, does not dwell in temples made with hands. Nor is He worshiped with men's hands, as though He needed anything, since He gives to all life, breath, and all things. And He has made from one blood every nation of men to dwell on all the face of the earth, and has determined their preappointed times and the boundaries of their dwellings, so that they should seek the Lord, in the hope that they might grope for Him and find Him, though He is not far from each one of us; for in Him we live and move and have our being, as also some of your own poets have said, 'For we are also His offspring.' Therefore, since we are the offspring of God, we ought not to think that the Divine Nature is like gold or silver or stone, something shaped by art and man's devising. Truly, these times of ignorance God overlooked, but now commands all men everywhere to repent, because He has appointed a day on which He will judge the world in righteousness by the Man whom He has ordained. He has given assurance of this to all by raising Him from the dead." Acts 17:24-31.

**Historic influences:**

The temptation to put money, sex: and other things; ahead of the high calling of fatherhood has been around since Adam and Eve. However, it has never had the lopsided proportions which it has today. This lopsided sense of male priorities has been on a constant increase, ever since the industrial revolution and the migration from the farm to the city. On the farm it was easy to stay close to the day to day needs of each family member. The success of the family depended on the success of all of its members.

The city does not offer the same close-knit interdependent structure for family awareness offered on the farm. Also, the nemesis of every man is more available in the city than in the country—the eye gate—the ability to be aroused almost instantly, simply by seeing a pretty girl walk by. No need to know her or to think seriously about her, just the fact that she is there is enough. Our modern cities provide a lot of material for the eye gate. Add to this our present cultural propensity for cultivating and accepting pornography and all manner of female dress styles that stimulate and titillate the male eye-gate, and you have a formula for disaster. In a recent CBS news report, 1-21-1992, Gentlemen Magazine revealed that over ten million men each year are now spending more than three billion dollars on topless and nude bars. It is now in the tens of billions.

When men accept the possibility of some women being only sex objects, toys to be played with and then cast aside, while asserting others are "different" and suitable for respect and marriage, they open the door to unlimited sexual titillation and promiscuity. With such "distinctions" there ceases to be any moral basis for limiting one's sexual stimulation and satisfaction to only one lifetime partner. It also debases womanhood.

The whole world of pornography, topless bars, prostitution and extramarital affairs, stems from this fundamental mistake of assuming there are two levels of respect for women. One level allows men the freedom to look for the "sexually liberated" women, whom they use as sex objects and for limited, short-term relationships. This kind of woman does not require or challenge a man to be faithful or accept the high calling of fatherhood. She can be used as a toy, flirted with, trifled with, pawed over, oiled, and then cast off, like a throw-away ball-point pen. The other level constrains a man to ferret out the virtuous women, preferably virgins; he idealizes them, he respects them, he admires them, and his dream is to marry one of them. This is the kind of woman every man wants for the mother of his children. This kind of woman expects her man to be faithful and to accept the high calling of fatherhood, even if she doesn't really know the details of what it is.

**The inconsistency of the double standard:**

With this mistaken concept of women, men are free to exercise the infamous double standard. After all, if some women are no more than sex objects and sex trinkets, it is only natural to want to play with them. A wife is always looked at by these men as one of the respectable women. This is true even if she came from the worst of experiences and sexual habits. He takes the awkward position that—if he wants her and she will marry him—that makes her respectable. Thus, the expression, "He married her and made a decent woman out of her" That is why, if she plays around on him, he feels betrayed in his efforts to reform her and must now divorce her. After all, she has proven to him that she is unworthy of him; she is really one of the—other kind.

This rationalization also gives him the feeling he is free to flirt around and explore the female population. He feels free to test the women he meets, to try and see which women are sexually "liberated" and easy to play with and which are not. In the minds of such sexually disoriented men, this kind of woman is fair game, and his actions regarding her should not cause anyone to criticize him. Look at the dichotomy this creates. However, this same kind of man tends to want and expect his own wife to be sexually satisfying to him, but not to be raunchy or overt. These are characteristics he attributes to the women he considers mere sex objects and playthings. In fact, this myopic view causes many of today's men to be inhibited in their sexual expression and their sexual needs with their wives. If their wives are too aggressive or are too willing to engage in any sexual position or exchange, they're all too often considered whorish and suspected of belonging to the other sort of women.

How ridiculous to assume that there are two kinds of women! This is like saying there are two kinds of gold. With one kind you make nude, erotic feminine artifacts to be viewed as toys and with the other you make a Madonna to adore in a shrine. Gold is gold and the only difference is the shape the craftsman has given it. Likewise, the only differences in women are those which men have created. If the male population did not seek loose, shallow, and trivial sexual experimentation, then even if a woman wanted to be available for such practices, she would not find any willing customers. When there is no demand, there is no supply!

We now have young pre-teen girls and teen aged girls hitting on male class mates and older men. I ask you—who is rearing these promiscuous young ladies of our times? It is no defense to say that these all come from the "wrong" side of the tracks. There is virtually no measurable distinction within the different ethnic, social or economic strata that would suggest a single source from within our culture. This cultural reversal further justifies the double standard in the minds of many men.

**The double standard destroys real femininity for the carnal mind:**

Obviously, the "two kinds of women" theory is nothing but a convenient rationalization of sexually irresponsible and morally disoriented men.[150] A general disrespect for women has been invented by the male mind. Once the habit of using women as sex objects and sex toys is well established in the lifestyle of a man, it becomes more difficult for him to respect any woman.

Some men express this general disrespect for women through verbal mistreatment and sexual harassment in the work place and other normal gathering places. In the more extreme cases, this pattern of disrespect spirals down to much lower levels and becomes resentment and hate. At this level anything from rape to murder, or both, is possible. Such men reduce women to a sub-human level; they become nothing more than objects without rights or feelings.

**Mommy's little boy and the influences of the military and war:**

With the industrial revolution and the migration of the majority of America's men to the cities, we men as a group have been extremely damaged by our military experience. This experience seems to be at its worst when we are assigned to overseas duty, whether in time of war or peace. Men have tremendous challenges keeping a clear head and a proper perspective with regards to their sexual arousal and sex drive, even when they are surrounded by good influences and good role models. But, when you take them away from these standards and put them in countries thousands of miles from home, their sense of personal responsibility and

[150] "Now the Spirit expressly says that in latter times some will depart from the faith, giving heed to deceiving spirits and doctrines of demons, ²speaking lies in hypocrisy, having their own conscience seared with a hot iron,..." I Timothy 4:1-2.

self-discipline can plummet to near zero.

The very psychology of war and its destructive environment of death, wounded and dying, make men change. It gives them a sense of urgency to experience all that life is supposed to be—in just days, even hours—if need be. Caution about proper sexual behavior goes berserk. What was a tremendous challenge even in a good environment becomes even more difficult in a state of war. This whole experience of war, military service in other countries thousands of miles from home and its devastating effects on American men, can be traced from World War I. When "Johnny came marching home" from Europe after World War I, the American male perspective of fatherhood began to die. This war, and the many that have followed, served to fuel the fires of sexual promiscuity and sexual disorientation of the American male from the family on a national scale. These wars of global or near global proportions have also produced large numbers of families for whom headship was placed in the mother because of the father's absence or death. Those returning soldiers, and the millions since that time, have brought back home a badly bruised conscience, full of sexual guilt and disorientation from the reality of what sex is all about. So much so, that as a group, men have lost the high ground of sexual morality and have been unable to regain the sense and attitude of a good sexual role model. Certainly good chaplains in all branches of the service are a much needed element of spiritual and moral encouragement. More importantly, the greatest need of all—for our American Christian culture—is for all of her sons to have true mothers of faith and grace!

**Personal experiences:**

My own personal experiences with military service might not be a specific example of every military unit. However, it is my opinion that it is representative of the average service man's exposure to sexual promiscuity and moral sexual decay. The following is an account of only a very small portion of the kinds of peer pressure and sexual opportunity which often confronts the average service man today. I think this information is important for those who have never served in the military, to give them some idea of the impact our military service has had and continues to have on the moral development of our young men. Women especially need some grasp of what kind of world a large segment of the male population is exposed to. With more and more women going into the military there are sure to be additional concerns.

From December 1, 1954, through December 10, 1958, I served in the U.S. Navy. I enlisted in Kansas City, Missouri and was sent to basic training in Great Lakes, Illinois. From there I was sent to Norman, Oklahoma for additional basic training for service in the Naval Air Force. From there, I was sent to Memphis, Tennessee, where I spent eight months, in the Naval Electronic Technicians training center. I was then given my first duty assignment, as an electronic technician, on Hutchinson Naval Air Station, Hutchinson, Kansas. I was stationed there for the second year of my first two years in the Navy. The closest I came to water was the Olympic-sized swimming pool we had on base.

After a year at Hutchinson, I was given orders to the sea plane squadron VP-42, located on North Island, in San Diego harbor, San Diego, California. I was to report for duty in early January, 1957.

Just a month prior, in December, 1956, I had asked Marilyn to marry me. She accepted and we were formally engaged. I had just turned twenty on the 11th of December; Marilyn would be sixteen on the 17th of February, 1957. We were very young, very much in love, and California seemed a world away from our close family ties in Overland Park, Kansas.

**A new duty station brings new problems:**

Being stationed in the U.S. at training centers for the first two years of my military service, I was exposed to only a small amount of male promiscuity. There was the normal amount of tough talk, women being a topic of sexual fantasy, but no real exposure to rampant promiscuous behavior.

I had been raised by Christian parents. My last four years before entering the Navy had been spent as a young man growing up on a Missouri dairy farm three miles south of Grovesprings, in the middle of the Ozark Mountains. I was a virgin and committed to stay that way until I was married. My overall perspective of the male world was one of respect and admiration. I had not yet been exposed to the prevailing sexual moral decay. I would soon get a glimpse of what was then growing out of control in many sectors of our society, especially in our military organizations, and from there into the American family.

From the first weekend I was stationed on North Island Naval Air Station, I was rudely awakened to the reality of the sexual moral decay among American service men.

Tijuana, Mexico, is just about fifteen miles south of San Diego, CA. All the guys in my barracks were either talking about their plans for getting Mexican girls in Tijuana for the weekend or about those they had taken out or slept with the weekend before. Right away I was asked if was going to go along and what I intended to do on my first weekend off the base. I felt strangely alone, confused and even a little scared. I knew I did not want to be exposed to the kinds of temptation these young men were telling me could easily be had in Tijuana. In fact, I immediately determined not to go to Tijuana while I was stationed on North Island.

In order to keep my head straight and to occupy my free time, I spent a lot of time in the gym, working out and thinking about Marilyn and writing her at least one letter a day. I was so lonely I could hardly stand it, but I knew it would not last for ever, so I just kept my cool and concentrated on my job.

**Standing up for principles:**

This was easier said than done. Guys in military service can be very cruel. I was respected because of my job capabilities and my physical condition. But not a week went by that I did not get asked at least once why I didn't go to Tijuana with the boys; get me a girl and "get laid," as men like to say? I used lame excuses at first, but nothing less than the truth would satisfy these guys. So, finally, I told them I was a virgin and that I was engaged to a young girl back home for whom I intended to stay a virgin until I was married.

Wow! I don't have to tell you what kind of response I got from that one! They couldn't believe I was for real. For a long time my closest buddies thought I was joking. Some even wondered if maybe I was homosexual. They just couldn't understand how anyone could be so far from home, with no one to say no to you, and still pass up the opportunity to go to a place like Tijuana and play with the girls.

At this point the only men I was exposed to in close quarters or a social way were the unmarried enlisted men. I had not yet been exposed to the personal habits of the married enlisted men or the commissioned officers, single or married. Our squadron was equipped with what was considered for those times to be the state-of-the art electronically equipped airplane for sea/air rescue and submarine detection, the twin engine Martin Marlin P5M-2 seaplane. We had a crew of twelve. The P5M-2 was powered by two 3350 compound radial engines. These were the state-of-the-art radial engines of the day, equipped with four-bladed propellers. We called it the flying goose because of its large white fiber glass nose and gull wing design. The *P5M-2* had four pilots. Two functioned as navigators while the other two flew the plane. We had three electronic technicians who served as the radio, electronic surveillance and radar operators, two mechanics, one ordinance man, one electrician, and one hydraulic technician. Thus, our total crew assignment was four officers and eight enlisted men. I was the 1st radio operator on the plane in which I flew, and as a result I was in charge of the other two electronic technicians.

Working and living together in such close quarters broke down the normal distance usually maintained and required by the navy between officers and the enlisted personnel. As a result, I became a very close friend of one of the pilots of our plane, Lt. David Benjamin Pitts. We all called him Ben.

**Other men of faith and grace make strong allies:**

Our crews had the normal routine of practicing our patrol duties and submarine detection skills for several months before deploying to overseas active patrol duty. During this period, while going through our training for overseas duty, Ben told me of his last experience overseas. He said it was terrible, that the peer pressure and temptation to live a life of constant promiscuity and womanizing was intense. He said he was not looking forward to our upcoming departure. He was determined not to be overcome by the group peer pressure and was very committed to his wife and family. I told him of my own commitment to Marilyn and of my desire to remain a virgin until marriage. We agreed, then and there, to stay close to each other and to be strength to each other.

We began to spend more time together. He invited me to visit him and his family a few times before we flew out to the Philippine Islands. We read the Bible together, prayed, and in general prepared ourselves with strong mental and spiritual fortitude for the challenge ahead.

The day of our departure from North Island, I got my first inkling of what to expect on this overseas assignment. Our day of departure dawned clear and beautiful. The entire squadron of twelve planes was all keyed up, packed, and prepared for take off. Our planes were especially equipped for long over water flights, and everyone except our support staff would be making the trip in our own squadron planes. Everyone else was flown over by Military Air Transport, or MAT, as we called them.

Prior to take off, the families of all the officers and married enlisted personnel were allowed to tour the base. Our plane commander, who was our acting 1st pilot and the officer in charge of the crew, brought his family aboard our plane. He was married to a very attractive young woman, had three children as I remember, two sons and a daughter. They squealed and jumped around from one place to another, and I remember being concerned for their safety and the safety of the equipment, so I watched them pretty closely.

Soon the moment arrived for departure and all family members were ordered to stand clear of the planes. There were the usual kisses and tears experienced at such partings. The wives seemed especially grieved to see their men leaving for the long eight month stay overseas. Launching a sea plane of our magnitude, 109 feet in length and weighing 80,000 lb. required a team effort. Each plane was towed into launch position at the head of a long sloping cement ramp leading down into the water. A winch was attached to lines that were connected to both the bow and the stern of the seaplane. The winch pulled the plane into the water; once in the water we would release our wheels. Our wheels were only temporary. They were fastened with long pin mechanisms and attached to large tanks. The ground crews would haul them back ashore after we released them.

**Shipping out brings new and deeper challenges:**

Our plane number was five (5), so we were fifth in line for take off. Our plane commander and 1st pilot was at the controls; Ben was 2nd pilot at this time and was in the co-pilot's seat. (Ben would later become commander of his own squadron.) We took off down the San Diego harbor sea-lane, engines at full throttle, propellers kicking up a wild spray and water jetting out from under the plane, as we moved up on "the step," the transition from boat to airplane. Once on the step, our speed increased to take-off capability and we became airborne just as we came up on our squadron's recent home base. As we came abreast of our old parking area, the families of all the pilots and married service personnel were lined up along the shore waving us good-bye. We made a beautiful sight as we flew by, dipping our wings in a farewell salute.

We had just reached cruise altitude and had settled in for the first leg of our trip, a one-night stop-over in San Francisco, California. Our plane commander came on the ICS (internal communication system) and announced to his fellow officers, and anyone listening, how glad he was to be getting away. All flight crew members were required to wear a head-set at all times. So, in effect he was telling everyone, which did not seem to bother him. On the contrary, it was obvious that he was quite proud to be telling it. He said he had called a girl he knew in Hawaii, which would be our immediate destination after departure from San Francisco. He said she would be waiting for him when we arrived in Honolulu the next day. He said he could hardly wait to see her again. She had the biggest breasts he had ever played with, and he was looking forward to a repeat experience!

A couple of the officers commented that he was really lucky to have such a girl friend. I thought to myself, "What about his wife? I just saw her moments ago standing on the parking ramp, crying, kissing, and hugging this big lug, as if there were no tomorrow. What about her?" The tears were not yet dry on the woman's face and her "Hero and Knight in shining armor" was making plans and fantasizing about some other woman's breasts! The contrast in scenes and moral inconsistency made me sick at my stomach. However, it was the cold, calculating, insensitive way many of the men commented about it and enjoyed the fantasy along with our 1st pilot that really put me on alert! From a moral perspective, this trip was not going to be a walk in the park.

For eight long months I was bathed in a sea of sexual promiscuity. The lack of moral fiber I had witnessed in my 1st pilot was not an aberration, it was the norm! Our squadron consisted of 375 enlisted men and commissioned officers. I got to know all of them on sight, and many by name. Almost half of the squadron was flight personnel. We had twelve planes with twelve men in each crew for a grand total of 144 flight personnel. I trained and flew with all of these men. Even the support crews, ground mechanics, electronic maintenance and parts people, were all a part of our very close-knit group. It was impossible not to know what was happening.

I could account for only a dozen men, including officers, who did not either live off base with a mistress or jump from one sex partner to another. Based on a report from our electronics division chief, our squadron's health records showed that during our eight months in the Philippines—over 85% of the squadron contacted some form of venereal disease—ranging from gonorrhea to syphilis.

The officers lived in two-story structures with small apartments, and the enlisted men lived in a row of Quonset huts, metal arched structures about 20 feet by 60 feet. Each hut was comprised of twenty men, married and single thrown together. The number one priority of everyone, with only hard-to-find exceptions, was women, women, women, and more women. What they were doing with their present women, what they did with their previous women, and what they wanted to do with their next, was all you could hear.

Fortunately for me, there were two other guys in my hut who had vowed to stay away from the women, and we spent many evenings reading or playing cards together to pass the time. In those days there was no TV to be enjoyed in a place like the Philippine Islands.

By 7:00 P.M. on almost any evening, the row of Quonset huts where we lived was quiet, with hardly anyone around. Unless they were on duty, most were off the base pursuing their latest girl friends. They never called them whores unless they were mad at them, but certainly that is all they were.

It was hard for those who kept going out almost every night to see someone stay in the barracks. The pressure was constant and always to the point. "When are you going to get a woman?" "Why do you always stay on base?" "Come with me, I'll show you what a *"real man* is." It was hard to keep one's cool under those situations—only by the grace of God.

Actually, it was only a matter of a very short time until I began to feel extremely sorry, for those men. Not in a self-righteous way. I did not feel "better" than they, but from my perspective I could see their pain. They really demonstrated a tremendous amount of pain and confusion. One of the married men in my hut who had been particularly unkind in his remarks to me—He was always insisting that I should get a girl—came down with a severe case of syphilis and had to tell his wife. He suffered both physically and emotionally as a result of wrong responses to his sexual arousal and sexual drive. I wanted to reach out to this man and help him, but he was much older and was not willing to listen.

**The fellowship of the saints is a gift from God:**

As for Ben and me, we found a great deal of peace and enjoyment in some of the family groups that were stationed on the base and also some of the people in other government capacities based in Manila. We met most of these people by attending local church services and being invited by them to visit their homes. One family with the CIA agricultural advisory group, (before the time of AID, Agency for International Development), was especially wonderful to us, Mr. & Mrs. Frate and Ludwina Bull. The Bulls were on their last assignment before retirement and lived in Manila. Ben and I spent more time with them than with anyone else. In fact, they practically adopted us. I felt so close to them, that when Marilyn and I were married on June 20th, 1959, we traveled to their home in Milledgeville, Georgia, and spent a week with them as part of our honeymoon.

**The return to America and our native shores:**

The return trip from the Philippines left an indelible impression on my mind, something that in many ways has served to strengthen my resolve in matters of sexual behavior and moral standards.

When we were preparing to return to the states, we got word that the relieving squadron had to leave their planes on North Island for a major overhaul. They would have to fly over to the Philippines by MAT, (Military Air Transport) and take over our planes. In the meantime we would also be going back home via MAT, and not flying our own planes. We weren't too happy about it, but that's military life: you follow orders and learn to like it.

This provided a unique experience, one I could never have foreseen or imagined. After long over-water flights in four engine propeller driven aircraft, we finally arrived back on North Island. Our planes landed on a bright sunny day with mild temperatures and spring-like weather. We taxied up to the unloading area, out in the middle of a large aircraft parking zone. There was no terminal as such. We could see a large band assembled and could hear the rousing music as we opened the aircraft doors. All the family members who could get there were there. The wives and girlfriends of most of the men were there, waving and crying with joy.

The whole scene should have been one of great joy for me too, but instead I experienced more sadness than joy.

I just happened to be sitting in a seat in the plane that made it impossible for me to be one of the first to deplane. As it turned out, I was one of the last to get off. The scene I witnessed was in such sharp contrast, in its moral context, to the promiscuous behavior I had witnessed in the Philippines, that it struck me like a hard blow to the stomach. All you could see were wives and girlfriends hugging and kissing their Heroes, laughing and smiling such smiles of joy, as only such a reunion could bring. Romantic on the surface! But, tragic in the knowledge that, only days before this reunion, almost every man out there had crawled out of some other woman's bed. In addition, these same men were bringing back bruised consciences and bruised and infected bodies. "For what"—I asked myself? "For a few months of sexual diversion and titillation would they destroy the lives and relationships of the most important people in their lives?" The obvious answer was all too sad.

**Sharing God's revealed Law-Word provides new understanding:**

Many times during my military experience I had the opportunity to counsel several different men. Some were personal friends, others just men who knew about my stand and would look me up. They all were having problems with the guilt and the remorse which they felt over their sexual habits. I would do my best to give them a different perspective. I encouraged them to focus on the real goals of their heart, a good woman and a true love.

As I got to know the older married enlisted men better, I would question them about their goals in life and their families. They all expressed fear that their wives were possibly playing around on them while they were overseas. Each and every one, without exception, believed that what his wife did not know would not hurt her. They could see no inconsistency in their own sexual behavior and their desires for their wives to be faithful. However, when I asked them what they would do if they discovered their wives were being unfaithful, all of them said they would divorce them. Are we talking double standard here?

The single men always provided a curious sense of logic. I would talk to them about their goals for a wife and a family, and without exception they were all going to marry a virgin and rear a family of strong moral fiber, with high standards for values and principles. When I would ask them if they expected to find the girl of their dreams in the bars and on the street, they would just laugh and say:

"Of course not, Hatfield, do you think I'm crazy or something?"

They never could explain just how they were going to find such a woman—and assuming they ever did—just how they were going to establish themselves as moral role models in their future families.

I'll leave it to you. What do you think happened to most of these young men and their dreams? One thing for sure—for anything good to happen—a change would be needed, a drastic change! Remember, if you don't change directions you will end up where you are headed.

Some of you may feel this is very unlike your own experience, never-the-less, for me it was a positive life-molding experience in many ways. I must and do thank God for His grace and strength which helped me overcome the challenges. I am no stronger in natural ability to overcome such temptations than any other man, so I know I had more than just a little help. During my early experiences in reading God's Law-Word as a teenager, I came to the conviction that as a mere mortal man in the flesh, I was capable of all of the sins recorded in the Bible. This proved to be a great strength to me as I grew up and encountered such exposures to moral decadence and temptations as I describe. Knowing that we are capable of the worst is important for the man of faith and grace. Our focus turns from our own weakness to His great strength. This is what Paul was talking about when he said: "When I am weak then am I strong." That is strong—not in himself—but strong because of Christ in him.

> "And He said to me, 'My grace is sufficient for you, for My strength is made perfect in weakness.' Therefore most gladly I will rather boast in my infirmities, that the power of Christ may rest upon me. Therefore I take pleasure in infirmities, in reproaches, in needs, in persecutions, in distresses, for Christ's sake. For when I am weak, then I am strong." II Cor. 12:9-10.

> "But I rejoiced in the Lord greatly that now at last your care for me has flourished again; though you surely did care, but you lacked opportunity. Not that I speak in regard to need, for I have learned in whatever state I am, to be content: I know how to be abased, and I know how to abound. Everywhere and in all things I have learned both to be full and to be hungry, both to abound and to suffer need. I can do all things through Christ who strengthens me." Philippians 4:10-13.

Given the events of military history such as the Vietnam War, where drugs became an additional factor with which our young men have had to grapple. Plus the reality of so many Amerasians, the children engendered by all our service personnel in Asia. Now our most recent military challenges are perhaps going to be our longest and most difficult for many years to come—the war against world-wide Islamic terrorism. Things are obviously worse from the standpoint that the stress and temptations, long deployments, lonely men and women—separated for too many months at a time, is not good.

**Serious questions we must consider for both sons and daughters:**

1. Who is in control of your family as a wife/mother of faith and grace?

2. Do you take part in supporting your husband in this control?

3. Who is the moral role model, teacher, counselor, disciplinarian and leader of your family?

4. As a wife/mother of faith and grace do you receive delegated authority from your husband to support his role?

5. Have you accepted the challenge of being the champion and coach for your son's emotional and sexual development, for his possible future relationship with a wife? If not, would you like to?

Statistics from all quarters: divorce, unwed mothers, dead beat dads, sexually transmitted diseases, poor educational performance, street gang violence and child abuse indicate a rapid decaying of today's families. Such evidence of family decay is further confirmed by a general lack on the part of many who refuse to address the real source of the problem. This large and growing segment of our population seem to have only one answer for everything—the government. Contrary to this current trend, we men and women of faith and grace are the key elements of God to introduce light into the world where in it concerns family leadership.

**Now think seriously with me for a moment about government's involvement!**

1. Is our government to blame for our country's drug problem?
2. Is our government to blame for the unwed mothers in our country?
3. Is our government to blame for the alcohol abuse in our country?
4. Is our government to blame for the fact that many of our children don't want to study?
5. Is our government to blame for the teen-age gang violence running wild in our schools and on our city streets?
6. Is our government to blame for a society of unfulfilled women?
7. Is our government to blame for the deviant sexual life styles of all the men and women who seem to think it is their only hope of fulfillment?
8. Is our government to blame for the venereal diseases and the AIDS epidemic in our country?
9. Is our government to blame for the racial tension we see growing in our country?

**Easy escape goats:**

The government is such an easy target for the frustrations of our problems. Every time society demonstrates it is in need of change we quickly assign the role of responsibility to the government. Let's be intellectually honest. Is it possible for men who are elected into public office to solve moral problems as a group which they can't or won't solve individually in their own personal lives? Government is not the cause of our moral decay, nor can it be blamed. As we have mentioned before, moral decay is not a group function, it has happened in the wake of Wrong navigational decisions made by—each man and each woman—who has decided against the need for a real Map of Right and Wrong. Without God's Law-Word as our guide we are left with only laws and situational morals of convention—such as are espoused by those in the radical left liberal elitist camp.

No, there is no evidence with which rightfully to accuse our government directly. On the contrary, the evidence points in the other direction. Through incorrect responses to their male sexuality, all biological males who refuse to be real men of faith and grace and who repudiate fatherhood are to blame for the poor quality of our politicians and subsequently the declining quality of our government. Consequently, when government is made up of a majority of such men, and they rule by democratic process, then it is only natural for the decisions they make and the laws they pass to reflect their personal lack of commitment to good morals and principles? Conversely, when the majority of men in government are committed to high standards of a Real Morality, accepting the reality of a real Right, independent of what people think, then government reflects those higher values. Consider Proverbs 29:1-3:

"He that is often disciplined becomes more stubborn, will suddenly be destroyed, and that without remedy. When the righteous are in authority, the people rejoice: but when the wicked are in power, the people mourn. Whoso loves wisdom pleases his father: but he that keeps company with harlots wastes his substance."

**Many political leaders are morally adrift in a sea of promiscuity:**

As an example of how Wrong morals in government leaders can adversely effect all who are governed by such people, Atlanta psychiatrist, Dr. Frank Pittman, says, "People who commit infidelities and try to keep them secret from their marriage partners are setting up a dangerously split secret life. "

Political history has shown, Pittman says, that presidents who were secret philanderers easily deceived the people who elected them to office.

Presidents John Kennedy and Lyndon Johnson, whose biographies are rife with affairs, "got us into a secret war," Pittman says, referring to the Vietnam War. "Such people don't really believe they're accountable. They believe image is the important thing. They don't feel they have to be honest with people."

Remember what C. S. Lewis said, "A moderately bad man knows he is not very good: a thoroughly bad man thinks he is all right.—Good people know about good and evil: bad people do not know about either."

As for Bill Clinton, who can deny that the continuing outbreak of oral sex among our young adolescents and teenagers does not stem from the personal sins of this past president?[151] He not only admitted it but also established it as a—non-sex act—because it is not intercourse. This misinformation is so accepted as truth by today's young people that when they are polled with regards to their sexual habits, many who have participated—only in oral sex—will say that they are also virgins. Well—virgins in the strict biological sense—but given what we know and have discussed about the complete scope of virginity, we also know that—deep, very deep—and lasting damage has taken place in these young girls and boys. These girls now are first in line for out-of-wedlock pregnancies and many future problems in their efforts to establish a successful marriage. The boys will use this as just another justification that some women are just sex toys and will increasingly dissociate them from the "faithful" wife.

**Government can assist but it is not the main catalyst:**

Governments, local, state, or federal, churches and school systems can and should be supportive of the family, but they can in no way take the place of the family. A family is a unit—a whole—it has parts and it has different members, but it functions as a whole living organism. It has a life, a pulse beat, a sense of being and a good sense of Right and Wrong or a lack of such a sense. It is moving forward or backward; it is never static. The Gift of Gods' uncommon common sense truths about fatherhood and family cannot be looked upon as mere factual knowledge. True, the bare facts can be taught in a class room, just as we are putting forth in this book, but to be successful and to develop a sense of their reality, they must be lived and experienced within the family unit. Otherwise, they are no more than an accumulation of dead facts, like so many dead cells in a

---

[151] "But ever since the whole Bill Clinton/Monica Lewinsky thing, oral sex has been on everyone's lips (excuse the pun). The Clinton scandal raised a bunch of issues: Is oral sex considered "sex"? If you have oral sex, but "don't go all the way" (have vaginal intercourse), are you still a virgin? And is oral sex safe — or can it pass infection?

"According to some recent studies, most teenagers define "sex" as vaginal intercourse — they don't consider oral sex to be "sex." This isn't surprising, since that's how our culture has traditionally defined sex (which, incidentally, leaves out gays and lesbians altogether). So, there are a lot of self-proclaimed virgins out there who haven't "gone all the way," but will do "everything else but," including oral sex." Posted on Teenwire.com April 19, 2001.

cadaver. You can say they are there, but without animation you cannot say they are alive. Such details of facts are revealed in God's Law-Word but they are only animated by the Spirit and through the gift of faith and grace in the elect.

**Government reflects the leadership of a nation's fathers:**

Consequently, governments can only demand that fathers be accountable in the role of fatherhood in things material. Whereas, forcing fathers to pay child support or alimony is an attempt to deal correctly with only one symptom of the lack of fatherhood; it does not address the cause. Moral fiber, values and principles cannot be instilled in the hearts of men by government legislation or decree. Men have to desire them and seek them individually at the hand of our creator God who has promised them to us if we will just seek. Matt. 7:7-11

Do you now begin to see why it is a nearly impossible task to teach such a sense of family to children with only one parent? Teaching single-parent children these truths in a class room and then sending them home to a single parent, especially when the parent is a single mother, is like teaching music theory and never practicing the art of singing or never playing a musical instrument. You may learn a lot of facts about music, but you will never make beautiful music! No matter how hard we try—we can't replace father—with schools and text books, mothers, church congregations, or government! Father is unique—he is father! However, you mothers of faith and grace, as you work in harmony with your husbands, are Gods' primary element in the faith and character development of your sons!

In spite of these very negative situations of historic impact—incorrect responses to male sexuality, double standards, single parent families and homosexuality—the majority of today's women are hoping and praying that men as a whole will come to their senses and stop running from the high calling of fatherhood. This is good and it offers real hope for those men of faith and grace who understand what it means. The irony is that it is women who suffer the most direct damage from this character fault in our men and yet it is women—mothers of faith and grace—whom God has uniquely gifted to overcome this great sin. Women of faith and grace, this is your Great Commission! Support your husbands' leadership. Let your sons see your role as the wife, lover and mother of faith and grace. Teach your son to respect your husbands' role as family leader and to respect and care for all women as he knows you are teaching him to respect and care for you! If God be for us, who can be against us?

> "What then shall we say to these things? If God is for us, who can be against us? He who did not spare His own Son, but delivered Him up for us all, how shall He not with Him also freely give us all things? Who shall bring a charge against God's elect? It is God who justifies. Who is he who condemns? It is Christ who died, and furthermore is also risen, who is even at the right hand of God, who also makes intercession for us. Who shall separate us from the love of Christ? Shall tribulation, or distress, or persecution, or famine, or nakedness, or peril, or sword? As it is written:
>
> 'For Your sake we are killed all day long; We are accounted as sheep for the slaughter.'
>
> "Yet in all these things we are more than conquerors through Him who loved us. For I am persuaded that neither death nor life, nor angels nor principalities nor powers, nor things present nor things to come, nor height nor depth, nor any other created thing, shall be able to separate us from the love of God which is in Christ Jesus our Lord." Romans 8:31-39.

The experiencing of these truths is positive and productive when expressed through the minds and hearts of men and women of faith and grace. Thus, they are committed to the best for themselves and their families. When such truths are born and are given life through faith and practiced—in the daily reality of living—such a family will walk in God's revealed Law-Word and experience His victories, one day at a time. They are life to the family, as the spirit is life to the soul. Only God can separate life from the soul, and no Government, church, or school can separate the living dynamics of these truths from the family. The three institutions established on earth by God are these: The family, (which includes all aspects of education and finance,) Civil government, and the Church of Christ universal. There is separation of powers and authority in and for all three; but know this—there is no separation—of God and His revealed Law-Word from any. We individually and corporately, for good or bad, are disciplined and blessed according to His sovereign will expressed in all of these institutions!

# Book III

# MOMMY'S LITTLE BOY

## Chapter Two Part II

## Introducing the Male World

## Normal Male Sexuality

**What is normal?**

Secular atheist humanists pride themselves on defining the terms of our culture. They never miss an opportunity to tell the American public that there is no such thing as—normal—and that to attempt to define anything as normal is to be intellectually dishonest. It is often said that he who defines the terms wins the argument. The truth is that—*normal*—is dependent upon the worldview of the person or persons who are defining the term. The worldview of the unbelievers—the left wing liberal radicals of America—is a world where all is transitory and conventional without absolutes. With this as their worldview they then assume an attitude of the all knowing elitist and declare that there is no Right or Wrong—no real morality—and certainly nothing that can be described as normal. For the secular atheist to accept—*normal*—as possible is to accept that there is also a—real abnormal—or in other words, a real Right and Wrong and that is something they cannot accept.

For the man and woman of faith and grace, normal is what ever Christ says that it is supposed to be, supposed to happen—or that does happen and He accepts as normal. The worldview of Christ must become the source of our presuppositions of life, God's creation, time, history, the future and our place in His Kingdom, for now and for eternity. Thus, when we use the term—normal—we are referring to a state that is accepted by Christ to be normal, His world view of the matter.

**Mommy's little boy comes with normal sexual construction and design:**

Normal male sexuality is almost lost in the confusion of our "so-called" present day "sexual liberation!" In spite of all we have said about the improper responses of many men to their sexual arousal and sex drive, there is such a thing as—normal—male sexuality for the man of faith and grace.

Young boys, even as little babies, exhibit certain unique sexual aspects that are quite obvious. If your daughter has little brothers she will understand this from experience; if not, you will have to bring her up-to-date. These genetically—built in—overt sexual responses of the male are not duplicated in young females, such responses from the female need to be cultivated.

Little baby boys experience an erection of the penis even while they are still in the womb. On the lighter side, I suppose one could say they are getting ready. However, on the more serious side, it illustrates the directness with which a man is confronted by his male sexuality. When mothers or little girls, in the case of older sisters, change his diapers, it is not uncommon for them to notice his erection. Sometimes this can result in getting sprayed with urine, as he will often urinate while he is having an erection and will spray it straight up. He has no option to address the issue passively. His organs and his hormones are designed to react to certain stimuli whether he likes it or not. In fact, it is his response to these normal sexual reactions which will determine his attitude toward himself and toward women—for better or for worse.

**Self stimulation—normal or abnormal—as a design feature:**

The more direct term to use in this case would be—masturbation—but it has unfortunately become a very pejorative term. In order to avoid such unnecessary baggage we will limit our discovery process for more clarity and understanding to the term of self stimulation.

Little boys are quick to realize that when the penis is in a state of erection, it feels good to rub it against something soft, the sheets, the pillow or what ever happens to be there at the time. There is no way for a young boy, at one or two years of age, to understand the moral aspects—the Right or Wrong—of this experience or of his sexuality. Given the almost hysterical anti-self stimulation attitude of many religious leaders and not just a few church members as well, one would think the Bible was full of texts and commandments against self stimulation. Contrary to these—highly held opinions—there are many texts that warn men against adultery and fornication, but there is only one text that I know of—which is most often quoted—as a reason for such hysteria.

> "And Judah said to Onan, 'Go in to your brother's wife and marry her, and raise up an heir to your brother.' But Onan knew that the heir would not be his; and it came to pass, when he went in to his brother's wife, that he emitted on the ground, lest he should give an heir to his brother. And the thing which he did displeased the LORD; therefore He killed him also." Genesis 38:8-10.

This is the account of Judah one of the twelve patriarchs and his sin of not fulfilling the law of Israel to carry on the name of his brother through taking his brothers widow as his wife and thus through his seed—read sperm—giving her children in his name. This was done only for the widows of brothers who had been barren and had no children by their husband while he was yet alive. This is the sum total of the context of this account. Only those who come to these verses and bring with them a—wrong headed presupposition—of sin and sexual perversion can find any relevance with the subject of self stimulation. Let's examine the text.

Verse 8 tells how Judah ordered his son to take his brothers widow as a wife and raise up children to this brother. Then we see in verse 9 where Judah's son, Onan takes her as a wife, has sex with her but—spills it on the ground—read sperm for "it." It is obvious that Onan didn't seem to mind the extra sexual privileges but for sure he did not like the idea of rearing a child by his brother's widow. This would have meant that he would have to share some of the inheritance with this off-spring and he wanted no part of it.

The sin here and the reason, as stated in verse 10, that God was so displeased and thus killed Onan comes—solely from the disobedience of Onan to inseminate—Tamar. Onan knew that if he ejaculated his semen on the ground that the possibilities of impregnating Tamar would be slim. It is no where indicated directly or indirectly in any biblical text that thus avoiding a pregnancy is—of itself—a sin. It was a sin in this case because the only reason for Onan to have the privilege of having sex with Tamar was in return for having children by her and thus fulfilling the law of passing the inheritance on to the family of his dead brother.

There is another text—I Thess. 4:4—that is sometimes quoted but which actually is not referring in anyway to self stimulation but rather to adultery and fornication which was rampant among the Greeks and Romans of the day.

"For this is the will of God, your sanctification: that you should abstain from *sexual immorality*; that each of you *should know how to possess his own vessel in sanctification and honor, not in passion of lust,* like the Gentiles who do not know God; that no one should take advantage of and defraud his brother in this matter, because the Lord is the avenger of all such, as we also forewarned you and testified." I Thessalonians 4:3-6.

We will consider this powerful set of verses—especially the words where incorrect inference is placed—by those who appeal to them for support of their narrow thinking against any self stimulation for sexual relief. You will notice that I have italicized the most pertinent words as—*sexual immorality*—which may also be translated as—fornication—and this is really the overall context of the entire passage. The call is for men of faith and grace to honor their sexuality in—*sanctification and honor, not in passions of lust*—which is an appeal to the men of faith and grace to not lust after women in general as the Greeks and Romans were famous for doing. He is reminded that God avenges the husband and father of the daughters that are thus abused by such lustful and destructive activities.

**Moralists are forced to superimpose their own fears and opinions:**

As we can easily see: there is nothing here to indicate the subject of self stimulation. Those who oppose self stimulation simply take everything out of context and make their ruling based on their wrong-headed moralist presupposition. They wrongly conclude that if God was displeased to the point of killing Onan for spilling his sperm on the ground that this surely proves that God will be just as displeased if a male self stimulates himself to ejaculation and spills his sperm onto the ground. Only if your presuppositions of—the Right and Wrong of the matter has been defined by some other source—than God's revealed Law-Word. Men and women of faith and grace must be led by the wisdom and truth as expressed in God's Law-Word—through this source alone we must form our presuppositions—and reject completely the alternative sources provided by secularists and moralists who imagine wrongs that do not exist! This bad habit often leads even men and women of faith and grace to fall into the trap of ignorantly rejecting the Wrongs that are clearly defined by God, calling them lies, but the "wrongs" of their own construct—they embrace as truth.

All those who have been influenced by this kind of thinking need to run their own test. Take every word you can think of that might relate to this subject and check out every reference you can find in Strong's Exhaustive Concordance. Also, use a Bible with a cross reference feature and see where the topic of "issue," "sperm," "ground," and any other word group you want to and see where they lead. I have included here all of the cross references for these texts; but you might find others:

1. Sperm or issue on the ground: Genesis 38:8-10[152]

2. Issue of sperm in bed alone: Leviticus 15:16-17[153]

[152] "Then Judah took a wife for Er his firstborn, and her name was Tamar. But Er, Judah's firstborn, was wicked in the sight of the LORD, and the LORD killed him. And Judah said to Onan, 'Go in to your brother's wife and marry her, and raise up an heir to your brother.' But Onan knew that the heir would not be his; and it came to pass, when he went in to his brother's wife, that he emitted on the ground, lest he should give an heir to his brother. And the thing which he did displeased the LORD; therefore He killed him also." Genesis 38:6-10.

[153] "If any man has an emission of semen, then he shall wash all his body in water, and be unclean until evening. And any garment and any leather on which there is semen, it shall be washed with water, and be unclean until evening. " Leviticus 15:16-17.

3. Issue of sperm in bed with a woman: Leviticus 15:18[154]
4. Issue of sperm in bed alone: Deuteronomy 23:10[155]

See the full text in the footnotes below.

**Lust and self stimulation as a necessary result:**
Both the Old Testament and the New Testament are consistent in that—lust—which precedes sinful acts is a mental process, which leads a man or a woman into a course of action that is against the laws and revealed principles of God. However, each and every time that the issue of—lust—is discussed with regard to which action it leads to, the details of the context are also listed in the following texts in each instance. It is clear that the subject—of lust—as a prerequisite for self stimulation is never addressed, nor is sex in marriage, nor the desire that a husband has for sexual pleasure with his wife, nor that of the wife for her husband, none of these are in the category of the LUST that leads to sin. Given the realities of what is both stated and not stated in God's revealed Law-Word, we must conclude that—lust—is not a prerequisite for self stimulation. Thus, to include issues of life, such as self stimulation, as proof of a failure to overcome lust where lust has never been declared—as the root of the problem—is to do as the Jews did which was to invent many doctrines of men and to impose them upon others. We are not above doing this, and we must not do it!

**Self stimulation and lust as a possible result:**
Many things and many actions can lead to the lust that produces both the sins of our minds and the sins of our actions. Lust is not limited to actions, but clearly is first a factor of our carnal minds. As we have clearly stated and indicated many times, there is a clear difference between our carnal minds, which we still have after the gift of faith, and the mind of Christ, which we have access to through faith. In spite of this great privilege we do sin and self stimulation can certainly lead to lusting after that which is not ours. Any individual who allows an act of self stimulation to include or lead to lusting for a sex partner—real or imagined—not already theirs through the institution of marriage, is committing sexual sin. This lust can and often does find complete expression at great spiritual and moral cost.

**Self stimulation within marriage:**
It is well documented by reputable sources that most women are not orgasmic. It is also very well documented that a large majority of those who are not orgasmic would be orgasmic if they would learn to self stimulate during the act of intercourse. Especially it is very important for all wives of faith and grace that their husbands learn how to stimulate their wives in all of her erogenous zones. Tenderness and much patience are needed to deal appropriately with the needs of all wives and especially those who are not so naturally blessed.

**God's revealed Law-Word gives us the correct worldview:**
As we have said, mature males can and often do experience what is referred

[154] "Also, when a woman lies with a man, and there is an emission of semen, they shall bathe in water, and be unclean until evening." Leviticus 15:18.

[155] "If there is any man among you who becomes unclean by some occurrence in the night, then he shall go outside the camp; he shall not come inside the camp. But it shall be, when evening comes, that he shall wash with water; and when the sun sets, he may come into the camp." Deuteronomy 23:10-11.

to as a "wet dream," or—more literally—the ejaculation of sperm, during sleep. Such an experience usually occurs during a period of time in the mature male's life when he is not experiencing any sexual contact with the opposite sex. In such cases the male usually dreams of an imaginary sexual experience during which he has intercourse. The details of his dreams may or may not be remembered. However, fantasizing about a known individual of the opposite sex could bring about such a "wet dream" experience. Should the fantasy be with or about some female other than the man's—wife—it could lead to problems. See: Leviticus 15:16-18, Leviticus 22:4 and Deut. 23:10: The full text is in the footnotes below.[156]

In Leviticus 15:16-18, Moses makes a clear distinction between what we would call a—wet dream or self stimulation—and the act of intercourse. Verses 16 & 17 deal with the wet dream or self stimulation, we are not told which method actually caused the issue of sperm. It should be noted that the issue of sperm is distinguished from the infectious issue of a sore or disease—such as leprosy—and thus only a bath and washing of clothes is required to regain cleanliness.

In verse 18 Moses deals with the sperm that is spilt onto the bed clothes and the two individuals—a man and a woman—who have just finished intercourse. It would be illogical and bad hermeneutics to believe anything else. If verses 16 & 17 include the act of intercourse then the specific stipulations of verse 18 are unnecessary. Moses did not see it that way and thus we have two accounts of the sperm issue from the man—one without a woman—the man being by himself and—one with a woman.

**Different opinions should not create adversity!**

There are far too many divisions among Christian groups in our post modern society. Certainly there is room for different opinions about texts that are unclear—especially those which do not seem to have any other scriptural clarification—that lead to a full understanding to the intended message. Honest differences about difficult to understand texts—although normal—does NOT justify the rancor and bullheaded divisive spirit that continues to thrive in our midst. I contend that the crucible of our doctrinal divisions is centered entirely in our fractured worldview.

To the extent that we adopt Christ's worldview—wherein that is clearly discernable in His Law-Word—as the only viable Christian worldview, we will be united and speak with one voice. Conversely, to the extent that we insist on providing interpretations of His Law-Word, where none is either required nor advised—due to the absence of any way to confirm such interpretations as forming the basis for a so called "Christian worldview"—then we will not be united.

We are duly warned against such attitudes and divisions—so far all to no avail—as is so clearly evident in the cacophony of doctrines and miscommunication

---

[156] "If any man has an emission of semen, then he shall wash all his body in water, and be unclean until evening. And any garment and any leather on which there is semen, it shall be washed with water, and be unclean until evening. Also, when a woman lies with a man, and there is an emission of semen, they shall bathe in water, and be unclean until evening." Leviticus 15:16-18.

"Whatever man of the descendants of Aaron, who is a leper or has a discharge, shall not eat the holy offerings until he is clean. And whoever touches anything made unclean by a corpse, or a man who has had an emission of semen, or whoever touches any creeping thing by which he would be made unclean, or any person by whom he would become unclean, whatever his uncleanness may be—the person who has touched any such thing shall be unclean until evening, and shall not eat the holy offerings unless he washes his body with water." Leviticus 22:4-6.

"When the army goes out against your enemies, then keep yourself from every wicked thing. If there is any man among you who becomes unclean by some occurrence in the night, then he shall go outside the camp; he shall not come inside the camp. But it shall be, when evening comes, that he shall wash with water; and when the sun sets, he may come into the camp." Duet. 23:9-11.

to the secular world of what constitutes a Christian or a Christian worldview. It is impossible to communicate effectively on such enormously important matters when we refuse to agree on what constitutes a Biblical standard for measurement. As I have made very clear—my contention is that the only Biblical standard for measurement—is Christ's worldview and none other!! Our energies will be better spent in the search for more clarity and understanding of Christ's worldview.

**Divergent approaches:**

There are other sources and other perspectives on this culturally delicate subject. Although not as clear cut as the one we have considered here, in our discovery of the most clearly referenced view in God's revealed Law-Word; Douglas Wilson has a very acceptable approach to the matter.[157] In 1999 Pastor Wilson wrote *"Fidelity—What it Means To be a One Woman Man."* In the chapter on, *Masturbation*, page 109-113 is one of the closest alternative perspectives. Our most notable difference would be in the way we might understand the meaning and application of lust, and the damage that over indulgence of the practice of self stimulation might pose for a man. Wilson warns against overindulgence and I agree, as there is nothing that God has given us—save the gift of faith and love—that cannot be abused or overindulged. Consider eating, drinking too much water, staying up too late, doing too much work, being too engrossed in ministry, taking too many vacations, sleeping too much, to mention only a few. There can be no serious argument against the advice to exercise—all of God's gifts with moderation—self stimulation or sex within marriage not exempted.

**Moral and character inconsistencies belie our wicked hearts!**

Our present moral morass and ambivalence with regard to what we say we believe—versus how we structure our "Christian" life styles—reveal our deeply ingrained hypocrisies! To site only a few: we say we believe in one husband and one wife but we construct life styles that allow for serial—multiple husbands and wives—through no fault divorce. We say we believe in the sanctity of life but we accept abortion within our midst to the same degree that the unbelievers accept it. We say we believe in sexual integrity, even to the point of—denying personal freedom to work out one's own salvation through personal government of one's sexual drive—specifically through wet dreams and self stimulation. However, we at the same time construct life styles that allow pornography, X-rated movies and magazines in many "Christian" homes! We also refuse to deal with our flagrant sexual misconduct in adultery, fornication and even in some cases the acceptance of practicing homosexuals as members in good standing.

Personal and corporate repentance is the only viable response to these gross inconsistencies in who we say we are and what we say we believe. Repentance calls for change and the—change that must be effected is a change in the standards we adopt—for our Christian worldview!

**Mommy's little boy makes a normal discovery:**

Yet, for our very young little boy—as early as between one and two—it is a very natural thing for him to discover how to reach an orgasm by rubbing his penis against something soft. (No ejaculation of sperm occurs until after the testicles have reached maturity, around 10 - 14 years of age.) At varying ages, the young boy will soon realize he can also use his hand. As he becomes older, he learns that the

---

157 Douglas Wilson is pastor of Christ's Church, Moscow, Idaho and editor of Credenda/Agenda magazine. He is author of: *"Recovering the Lost Tools of Learning," "Reforming Marriage," "Federal Husband," "My Life for Yours," "Future Men,"* "Fidelity, What it Means To be a One Woman Man." Contact: www.canonpress.org

ideal place to rub his penis is inside the vagina of a woman. For young boys being raised by real fathers and mothers of faith and grace, this knowledge is gained intellectually from them and not through premarital sex.

There is absolutely nothing abnormal about his discovery of the functions of his penis. Given his experiences with erections in the womb and orgasm at such an early age, it should alert young girls and perhaps even mature women to a very important aspect of norma1 male sexuality. It should become a matter of common sense for all females, that there is no—Off –button on the male sexual drive. It is turned—On—in the womb, and it stays—on—until death or some outside force, physical or psychological, turns it off. If this were not so, then the mere presence of a fully clothed modest woman would not be the powerful attraction that it is.

**Mothers of faith and grace have their own discoveries:**

God's physical design of Eve, the first woman, was the same as is the design of every woman God has created—believers and unbelievers alike—all must embrace the scope and limits of that design. For Woman the reality of God's design feature in her clitoris is that it serves no functional purpose what so ever—apart from sexual stimulation and pleasure—much to the chagrin of the uninformed and misguided moralist. As straight forward and simple as this design feature is, one would think that men and women of faith and grace would have no problem implementing the use of this tool in the purpose for which it was designed—to give the wife of faith and grace sexual stimulation and satisfaction. A mother of faith and grace will, with God's help, find the words she needs at the correct time to begin to inform her little boy about the correct understanding of this design.

At first glance it would appear that much of this discussion should have occurred in Book I on *"Love and Marriage."* However, once a discussion on the more intimate areas of our sexual design is begun it needs to be balanced, between both the male and female aspects, so as to not create confusion. Therefore I have chosen to give a more complete investigation of these sensitive areas here as this offers the best opportunity to address the issue for both sexes. Everything we discover about one needs to ultimately be known by the other. We must admit, however, that there is considerable ignorance among many of the adults within our Christian culture. Consequently, it is wiser to not assume a level of understanding for the reader that might in fact not be present.

**Misinformation and ignorance prevail:**

Today's so called "liberated woman" when examined from the perspective of her track record in—love, sex and marriage—is found to be anything but liberated. On the contrary the overwhelming evidence is that she is now a prisoner of secular moral relativism with its post modern subjective convention as its only source for Right and Wrong. As a result, she is more a sex object today than ever before when she was considered "unliberated." This would not be so tragic if it was isolated to the unbelieving atheist woman—alas such is not the case—for the truth is that the woman of faith and grace more often than not, has adopted the same worldview as the unbelieving "liberated" woman. The hope for the woman of faith and grace is the possibility that she will rethink her source, for what she considers to be a Christian worldview on love, sex and marriage.

**God's design for the woman of faith and grace is for her pleasure:**

1. "Shall I who cause delivery shut up the womb?" says your God. "Rejoice with Jerusalem, and be glad with her, all you who love her; rejoice for joy with her, all you who mourn for her; that you may feed and be satisfied with

the consolation of her bosom, that you may drink deeply and be delighted with the abundance of her glory." Isaiah 66:9-11.

2. "Your head crowns you like Mount Carmel, and the hair of your head is like purple; a king is held captive by your tresses. How fair and how pleasant you are, O love, with your delights! This stature of yours is like a palm tree, and your breasts like its clusters. I said, 'I will go up to the palm tree, I will take hold of its branches.' Let now your breasts be like clusters of the vine, the fragrance of your breath like apples, and the roof of your mouth like the best wine. The wine goes down smoothly for my beloved, moving gently the lips of sleepers." Song of Solomon 7:5-9.

3. "Let your fountain be blessed, and rejoice with the wife of your youth. As a loving deer and a graceful doe, let her breasts satisfy you at all times; and always be enraptured with her love." Proverbs 5:18-19.

4. "Let the husband render to his wife the affection due her, and likewise also the wife to her husband. The wife does not have authority over her own body, but the husband does. And likewise the husband does not have authority over his own body, but the wife does." I Corinthians 7:3-4.

**A review of God's revealed Law-Word on the woman's pleasure:**

In number one above; we are given Isaiah's words of revelation concerning God's desire to bless the elect through their possession of Jerusalem, and later in other more detailed descriptions of the city of Jerusalem we also discover that it is also a spiritual possession and also is illustrated as the future bride of Christ or another vision of the Church. The points of our immediate concern are in the language that is used. "that you may feed and be satisfied with the consolation of her bosom, that you may drink deeply and be delighted with the abundance of her glory."

We discover very quickly that God has chosen to liken the city in all of its illustrations as being feminine and possessing delights with which men can relate as being of extreme pleasure and satisfaction. God is not prudish—only misinformed moralists are prudish—for He uses the language that he knows will cut to the chase and strike the deepest emotional response from His audience. These words of feminine delicacies are the same as God uses in the words of number two above.

If we leave it there and know nothing further of God's design for woman, then these words would seem to be solely for the benefit of the man—his pleasure and satisfaction—with femininity and have nothing to do with any such personal pleasure and satisfaction for the woman.

However, the whole point of reading all of God's word—cover to cover-at least once a year is to provide the man and woman of faith and grace the understanding and wisdom of God as it relates to the whole matter of His revelations for us and not just small bits and pieces.

In number three and four above we see the focus of God's revelation more clearly and directly located in the simple joys of sex aside from any use as a means for procreation. For example:

When God's word refers to the procreation and its blessings to man he refers to it as the fruit of his loins—conversely to procreation—when He is referring to simple sexual pleasure He refers to the—man's fountain or penis—as the focus of discussion. This is very obvious in number three.

The reality that under-lays this statement: "Let your fountain be blessed and rejoice with the wife of your youth," is the fact that, when wisdom and understanding are applied to sexual pleasure the selfish habit of all too many men in their—slam-bam-thank you-mama sex performance—is not satisfying to either the man or woman! To accomplish the stated goal of the verses in number three the man must also fulfill the stated objective of the verses in number four!

Number four brings us to the more complete understanding of God's design for the sexual pleasure of the woman. "Let the husband render to his wife the affection due her." In the process of rendering to his wife such affection as is due her, the husband of faith and grace will find it impossible to ignore any of her erogenous zones of sexual pleasure—especially the clitoris—being the most sensitive and central to allowing a woman to experience an orgasm.

**Gentle and mutual exploration:**

In a world of perfect understanding none of this explanation would be necessary. The sexual world of our Christian woman of faith and grace is anything but perfect. The sad truth is that most women—unbelievers and believers alike—are not orgasmic and find only limited satisfaction in sex. In Mexico it is so bad that Christian feminine counselors estimate that as many as 30% of Mexican women married to Mexican men in ministry will not even let their husbands see them naked, much less to be involved in assisting them in being orgasmic. It is also noteworthy that promiscuity is the most prevalent problem within the Mexican ministry to date. For sure, the American ministry is deeply wounded by the same problem but not in the same severity, as in the Mexican ministry. The ignorance among the Mexican woman of faith and grace—although not the sole cause—is certainly a very strong element and contributor to the cause!

Ignorance is not part of God's plan—ignorance is the fruit—of our own self-righteousness. Discovering God's worldview for the sexual pleasure and delight of both men and women of faith and grace is the only way to overcome these misinformed, wrong headed ideas of self-righteousness. Doing so will be the first step to making the more important discoveries of how each husband and wife of faith and grace can enjoy the gentle and mutual exploration of what is sexually pleasurable to each and to then pursue those discoveries for the benefit of each other. Only thus will you be able to receive the greatest blessings from God's foreordained plans for your most intimate and complete sexual pleasure and satisfaction.

**Mommy's little boy must not be reared in ignorance:**

Our present day husbands of faith and grace are—ignorant about the femininity and sexual needs of their wives—due mainly to the prevalence of misguided understanding and self-righteous moralism on the part of our wives of faith and grace. Both men and women of faith and grace have suffered tremendously from this same source of wrong headedness, but none more severely than the woman. This cycle of ignorance must stop if we are ever going to produce the kind of successful love and marriage unions that is central to God's foreordained purposes for His institution The Family!

**Mommy's little boy must deal with the powerful force of feminine attraction:**

It is also very important for fathers to recognize and bring to the attention of their little girls certain basic aspects of normal male sexuality. Young girls are not unaware of the special attraction they are for the opposite sex. Even at the early age of eight or nine, a girl already knows when the boys, in her young world, are looking at the girls with more than just curiosity. By understanding what factors are involved in the essence of her power to attract the opposite sex, she will better understand her own sexuality and also acquire a hea1thy respect for her role in the art of femininity.

As I have mentioned. I worked very closely with *Promise Keepers* during the nineties and one of the things we discovered about men was very revealing about male sexuality. If a female walked in the back door of a room full of over a thousand men—all of whom had there attention focused forward to the speaker—within less than two seconds every man in the place knew a woman was present and the whole atmosphere of openness and transparency would disappear. Immediately in its place would descend a cloud of—macho superficiality—and the former state of attention would not be regained until the female had left the room. Now mind you—this is a fully clothed—respectful and loving Christian woman—an assistant to the leadership group. Assistant or not, they were not allowed to attend the all male sessions, but on occasion, a message or some other exception of the rule would allow one to come into the room for a few seconds. In only takes a few seconds for one female to change the focus of a whole room full of men.

**Wisdom brings peace and order—not confusion:**

Although the reality of preadolescent boys to experience orgasm is probably a factor of male sexuality most women either don't know, or choose to disregard as unimportant; a closer look at the situation should make it clear that it is very important!

In boys who are quite young and preadolescent, self stimulation is a common and not at all abnormal reaction to the erect penis. Yet, some men testify that this was never true for them. However, these same men also testify that their first awareness of ejaculation came in their sleep as they were dreaming about having sex with a fantasy woman. These sexual releases continue throughout the normal male sexual experience. However, because of a great deal of ignorance, and sometimes religious prejudice, young boys are scolded and punished when they are discovered rubbing their penis or some other form of self stimulation. Some mothers will even tell their sons not to touch—"that's nasty" they might say. This unrealistic response to their normal sexual drives and development can cause a great deal of psychological damage. Young men who are treated this way grow up pressured by two great forces.

These young men grow up with the natural desire to stimulate themselves into orgasm, a phenomenon which begins at a very early age. Then, they are told by well-meaning parents—whom they have been taught to believe and want to respect—that they should not do it. Unfortunately, the young boys will continue to have erections and will continue to self stimulate, but now with guilt feelings and confusion.

**There is no escaping the exposure of femininity on display:**

In the real world a young boy will continually be exposed to our present-day parade of female exhibitionism. He will not have to frequent the local X-rated movie theater or sneak out and have some older boy buy or lend him a Playboy or Hustler magazine, to be confronted with more than he needs for sexual stimulation. All he has to do is get up in the morning and walk around, turn on the TV, read a paper, look at a magazine, or even simply go to school and feast his eyes on all the young feminine forms on display. As far as the "girlie" magazines, pornography books and Internet porn are concerned—in all too many homes—the father has already provided a good supply. This happens in homes where the father is a Christian who is struggling with his own problems of misdirected sexuality.

**Men of faith and grace must speak out!**

Many parents are guilty of fear and ignorance, and let misguided religiosity take control. However, the father knows better; he has lived the experience. Thus, many men are so afraid and unsure of their own sexuality, they won't speak out. What common sense is trying to say, is the very opposite of what many people fear. Self stimulation is not abnormal behavior; it is natural and represents a God-given way for men to control themselves. Without this alternative for se1f-control and relief from sexual arousal, the only remaining possibility is the pursuit of the opposite sex. This is in fact one of the excuses offered by many men who seek sexual gratification through prostitutes. They reason that prostitutes are more honorable than self stimulation—not according to God's revealed Law-Word.[158] Or, as in the case of those unfortunate young boys who have grown up without the advantage of a real father of faith and grace and who become afraid of the opposite sex, they are tempted to experiment with members of their own sex, thus adding to our present growth in homosexuality.

Because of the controversy in our society today over homosexuality I think it is important to elaborate on a particular aspect of human sexuality, applicable to both sexes. Living beings of flesh and blood pose some unique problems. What is in fact a natural phenomenon within the context of our human sexuality can be cultured and nourished to do evil and wrong things, through exposure to and involvement in improper concepts and practices. My big question for all men of faith and grace is this: "Where are the fathers when all of this is going on?" The normal sexuality of God's males should not be a closet item. Respected with the highest degree of sensitivity—yes—but never denied or ignored.

Janice Juraska, a biopsychologist at the University of Illinois at Urbana-Champaign, has an interesting thing to say about differences between the sexes, she says, "Hormones do affect things. It's crazy to deny that, but there's no telling which way sex differences might go if we completely changed the environment. There is nothing about human brains that is so stuck that a different way of doing things couldn't change it enormously. "

**Two examples:**

Death, which is a normal phenomenon of our human nature, is not evil or wrong. (If necessary refer back to Book I to review our establishment of Right and Wrong.) However, death caused by murder is not a normal phenomenon of our human nature, and it is evil and Wrong. It is a sin against God the creator of life.

Sexual intercourse, which is a normal phenomenon of our human nature, is correct, enjoyable and healthful in the context of marriage. Sexual promiscuity and sexual perversion are not natural phenomena of the—redeemed man of faith and grace although still living in a human body—they are evil and wrong.

In both instances we see where it is our abuse of the normal aspects of our nature which were never created for such use that are evil and Wrong.

---

158 "All things are lawful for me, but all things are not helpful. All things are lawful for me, but I will not be brought under the power of any. Foods for the stomach and the stomach for foods, but God will destroy both it and them. Now the body is not for sexual immorality but for the Lord, and the Lord for the body. And God both raised up the Lord and will also raise us up by His power. Do you not know that your bodies are members of Christ? Shall I then take the members of Christ and make them members of a harlot? Certainly not! Or do you not know that he who is joined to a harlot is one body with her? For "the two," He says, "shall become one flesh." But he who is joined to the Lord is one spirit with Him. Flee sexual immorality. Every sin that a man does is outside the body, but he who commits sexual immorality sins against his own body. Or do you not know that your body is the temple of the Holy Spirit who is in you, whom you have from God, and you are not your own? For you were bought at a price; therefore glorify God in your body[c] and in your spirit, which are God's." I Corinthians 6:12-20.

**Unbelievers abuse the normal and make it an abomination:**

Likewise, in the context of comparison, self stimulation in young boys and men is an instinctive phenomenon of our human nature, a method of sexual release when necessary. However self stimulation as practiced among homosexuals, men with men and their anal and oral sexual intimacies, are not instinctive or normal phenomenon of our human nature. They are evil and wrong. Paul makes this clear in the letter to the Romans congregation:

> "For the wrath of God is revealed from heaven against all ungodliness and unrighteousness of men, who suppress the truth in unrighteousness, because what may be known of God is manifest in them, for God has shown it to them. For since the creation of the world His invisible attributes are clearly seen, being understood by the things that are made, even His eternal power and Godhead, so that they are without excuse, because, although they knew God, they did not glorify Him as God, nor were thankful, but became futile in their thoughts, and their foolish hearts were darkened. Professing to be wise, they became fools, and changed the glory of the incorruptible God into an image made like corruptible man—and birds and four-footed animals and creeping things.
>
> "Therefore God also gave them up to uncleanness, in the lusts of their hearts, to dishonor their bodies among themselves, who exchanged the truth of God for the lie, and worshiped and served the creature rather than the Creator, who is blessed forever. Amen.
>
> "For this reason God gave them up to vile passions. For even their women exchanged the natural use for what is against nature. Likewise also the men, leaving the natural use of the woman, burned in their lust for one another, men with men committing what is shameful, and receiving in themselves the penalty of their error which was due.
>
> "And even as they did not like to retain God in their knowledge, God gave them over to a debased mind, to do those things which are not fitting; being filled with all unrighteousness, sexual immorality, wickedness, covetousness, maliciousness; full of envy, murder, strife, deceit, evil-mindedness; they are whisperers, backbiters, haters of God, violent, proud, boasters, inventors of evil things, disobedient to parents, undiscerning, untrustworthy, unloving, unforgiving, unmerciful; who, knowing the righteous judgment of God, that those who practice such things are deserving of death, not only do the same but also approve of those who practice them." Romans 1:18-32.

The message here is clear and focused entirely upon the unrighteousness of the homosexual community. It is true that all of us are guilty of some of the attitudes listed here—that is not the issue! The issue is this—homosexuals know they are rebelling against God—not because I or you say so, but because God says so. Consider closely verses 18-19: here we are told what part of the issue Paul's message is focused on:

> "...all who hold the truth in unrighteousness; because what may be known about God is manifested to them; for God has shown it to them."

Paul continues by revealing to us how that such people have no excuse and later in verses 22-24 we see how they respond:

"Professing themselves to be wise, they became fools, and changed the glory of the uncorruptible God into an image made like to corruptible man, and to birds, and four-footed beasts, and creeping things. Wherefore God also gave them up to uncleanness through the lusts of their own hearts, to dishonor their own bodies between themselves: who changed the truth of God into a lie, and worshipped and served the creature more than the Creator, who is blessed for ever. Amen."

Men and women of faith and grace need to hear loud and clear what God means when He says: "Wherefore God also gave them up to uncleanness through the lusts of their own hearts, to dishonor their own bodies between themselves:" Through these words we have the opportunity to understand Christ's worldview regarding homosexuals and the source of their rebellion. Thus, we are forever given the clear truth of—who these people are—and what the nature of their sin is, as we read further:

"For this cause God gave them up unto vile affections: for even their women did change the natural use into that which is against nature: and likewise also the men, leaving the natural use of the woman, burned in their lust one toward another; men with men working that which is unseemly and receiving in themselves that recompense of their error which was due."

It is important to notice here that this whole set of verses is directed at men—male individuals—as it is clear Paul is stating that their sins of "holding the truth in unrighteousness" is justification for what God is saying that He has done to them and that this has also affected their—women! See verse 26

**Confirmation of the Great Commission for husbands:**

Some—perhaps even many—who are reading this book started off with a lot of doubt about the premise of the book as stated in the introduction. Given the upside-down state of our Christian cultures ignorance and our progressively deeper romance with secular thought and education—it is only natural—that many would have early misgivings. However, this and many other texts that we have already reviewed and the many more yet to come, will forever confirm the truth of our early claims. We men are responsible for the spiritual, moral, educational, romantic and sexual developmental success of our wives. Now is a good time to reread Ephesians 5:23-33.

This is terrible news to the unbeliever and very—sobering news—to even the husbands and fathers of faith and grace. It so terrifies the weak in faith, that I have had men actually yell out from the audience that this is a lie and that they were not going to stand for it—they get up—and storm out of the auditorium. Such a demonstration of rejection doesn't mean that these men are unbelievers, but we cannot deny that they are scared.

One more example and we're through with this comparative analysis. Mental fantasies are a natural and commonplace part of our human nature. The unfortunate individuals who have had accidents in isolated areas of the world, imprisoned by enemy forces during wartime or imprisoned by civil authorities, have all testified that their sanity and ability to survive the ordeal was in large part due to their ability to escape into a world of mental fantasies. Likewise, in our everyday life, mental fantasies are very healthful and relaxing. Fantasies of love and devotion with those we love and cherish are normal and healthy. However, fantasies of the woman next door or of some other person who you know, or see via printed or broadcast media, can lead to lust and many sexual abuses. These are not a normal part of our humanity. Such fantasies are evil and wrong.

**Sex is much more than an orgasm:**

If sex is more than just biological titillation and orgasm, then males who pursue the opposite sex solely for the purpose of satisfying their fantasies or release from sexual arousal, do so for the wrong reasons. This type of motivation will result in only superficial sexual satisfaction and will develop a completely distorted perspective of the concept of love. When thus motivated, such men do not find either true love or good sex. This distortion becomes a perversion when carried to the level of homosexual activity.

One of the greatest sexual challenges to the male population is the reality of this constant—on—condition. I mentioned earlier about the eye gate being the nemesis of all men. Obviously, this would not be true for those born blind or who become blind. But, barring such handicaps, all men must live every day with the reality that the female form and presence, and even the memory of her form and presence, are enough to create instant sexual arousal, with a fully erect penis and a very high motivation to pursue a course of action which will satisfy the desire to stimulate the erection until an orgasm is reached. The more naturally viral the man is—the more intense the reaction. Christ recognized that not all men had the same level of libido. He cut to the chase when he said that—some had so little that total control was within their possibilities—but that others needed to pursue the goal of finding a wife.

> "They said to Him, 'Why then did Moses command to give a certificate of divorce, and to put her away?' He said to them, 'Moses, because of the hardness of your hearts, permitted you to divorce your wives, but from the beginning it was not so. And I say to you, whoever divorces his wife, except for sexual immorality, and marries another, commits adultery; and whoever marries her who is divorced commits adultery.' His disciples said to Him, 'If such is the case of the man with his wife, it is better not to marry.' But He said to them, 'All cannot accept this saying, but only those to whom it has been given: For there are eunuchs who were born thus from their mother's womb, and there are eunuchs who were made eunuchs by men, and there are eunuchs who have made themselves eunuchs for the kingdom of heaven's sake. He who is able to accept it, let him accept it.'" Matthew 19:7-12.

Obviously, such a sensitive condition in men can create a temptation for improper fantasies, especially under the age of 50, but many men much older report extreme sensitivity and easy sexual arousal to the feminine form. Single men are those who suffer the most. Married men have the opportunity to go home and seek solace and relief in the arms of their wives.

We males of the post modern era, living as we naturally do with a constant—on—condition in our sex drive, are confronted—almost attacked—as the female form is literally thrown at us day in and day out. Every waking moment, if we are not concentrating on something else, we are potentially exposed to the female form in varying degrees of nudity. The daily newspaper is full of semi- clad female forms. The department store catalogs we receive in the mail have some pages dedicated to the female form, in such a way as to suggest light porn.

All kinds of advertisements use the female form in varying degrees of nudity to attract attention. Whose attention are they trying to attract, women's, or men's? Driving to work or to school, you can see billboard signs with semi-clad women. In addition to all of the media exploitation of the female form, we have women of all ages vying for first place in the art of seduction. The male eye gate is constantly being flooded with the very forms and images most likely to stimulate his sexual arousal.

**Communicating with feminine sexuality:**

Putting this into perspective, with the world of female sexual arousal, will give a more distinct outlook for the benefit of all women and for mommy's little boy to understand the difference in God's design for women.

Female sexuality is much less affected by the eye gate. At the same time that the ladies appreciate and enjoy the good looks of the masculine form, they are not particularly aroused sexually by viewing it. However, tender words of love, devotion and expressions of appreciation for their beauty can have an arousing effect. Couple this kind of conversation with kisses and touching the right erogenous zones on their bodies and you can get complete sexual arousal.

Now let us imagine—it could not really happen—but it will do for an illustration. Let us imagine that it is both possible and a common practice for advertisers to appeal to the sexual arousal of the female world, as they do the male world. Imagine that it would be possible to have TV, radio, and all manner of printed matter which could actually talk and physically caress at the same time. Imagine, ladies—if you can—what it would be like to be experiencing constantly the effects of sexual arousal. The sound of just the right endearing words, the actual touch to your erogenous zones by caressing hands, and kisses from out of the blue to make you feel loved and cared for. How would this affect your day to day relationship with men?

Some might even wish such sexual titillation were possible. Believe me, if Madison Avenue advertising executives had the technology to use such sexual marketing inducement methods, groomed especially for women, they would do it. Well, after years of it, I think you would be just as bent out of shape as the average male!

Far from any intention to be insensitive to women, it is hoped that this illustration will help women who read this book to understand what the male world lives with everyday. Ladies—there is a place for modesty and I pray that its practice will soon return to our Christian culture.

**How will mommy's little boy see his wife?**

The lessons we learned in Proverbs where the teacher taught his son how important it is to focus on the wife of our youth. This has been and continues to be a great blessing to me! As I mentioned before: I see my wife through the eyes of love—eyes which God has given me—much as He has given me a new heart. I have learned to use the wisdom of focusing on my wife as a means to counter the negative effects of all the female stimulation that is provided by our post modern society. Every married man has a wife in whom he can see with eyes of love, as no one else can see. Our counsel is to increase our perspective of her beauty—both physical and inner beauty—to a point that when we are out and about or something suddenly appears on TV, our previous focus on our wife gives us peace. The forms and the exhibitionism is the same, but the sharp tug and negative sexual response is greatly reduced. It probably cannot ever be totally eliminated—that will have to wait—until after the resurrection. We men of faith and grace do not have the luxury of ogling all that is passed before us. We do so at our peril and with great danger of moral corruption. We can't keep our eyes from being exposed to the gratuitous display of the female form, but we can keep from seeking it out.

**Will mommy's little boy focus on his wife or the wife of someone else?**

When I speak about focusing on our wives, I am not referring to passive focusing. I am saying that by taking the time necessary, I self consciously look for and program where possible—tender moments—of caressing and cuddling with my wife. It is very important for a husband of faith and grace to pay more attention to Paul's writings to the Corinthians. It is clear that the sexes belong to each other, neither has priority over their own bodies. The husband's body belongs to the wife and the wife' body belongs to the husband. Since the husband is the one most affected by the exhibitionism of our culture, focusing takes on a more acute role. Many cultures have had different levels of exhibitionism and overt feminine exposure to the general male populace. The first century was one of the worst. Much like our own, the feminine form was on display in the public arena—even worse—it was for sale in any of the pagan temples. Romans considered this an act of piety. Promiscuity and homosexuality was rampant. Paul must not be considered a man out of touch with times like ours. If he could know and compare our time with his times, he might even think we have less of a problem than he and the men of his day had to deal with.

> "Do you not know that the unrighteous will not inherit the kingdom of God? Do not be deceived. Neither fornicators, nor idolaters, nor adulterers, nor homosexuals, nor sodomites, nor thieves, nor covetous, nor drunkards, nor revilers, nor extortioners will inherit the kingdom of God. **And such were some of you.** But you were washed, but you were sanctified, but you were justified in the name of the Lord Jesus and by the Spirit of our God.
>
> "All things are lawful for me, but all things are not helpful. All things are lawful for me, but I will not be brought under the power of any. Foods for the stomach and the stomach for foods, but God will destroy both it and them. Now the body is not for sexual immorality but for the Lord, and the Lord for the body. And God both raised up the Lord and will also raise us up by His power.
>
> "Do you not know that your bodies are members of Christ? Shall I then take the members of Christ and make them members of a harlot? Certainly not! Or do you not know that he who is joined to a harlot is one body with her? For 'the two,' He says, "shall become one flesh. But he who is joined to the Lord is one spirit with Him.
>
> "Flee sexual immorality. Every sin that a man does is outside the body, but he who commits sexual immorality sins against his own body. Or do you not know that your body is the temple of the Holy Spirit who is in you, whom you have from God, and you are not your own? For you were bought at a price; therefore glorify God in your body and in your spirit, which are God's." I Cor. 6:9-20: Emphasis mine.

Some groups make special efforts to create a more modest environment for their men. They have certain dress codes that were once common place but that are so distinct from what is considered modern as to seem ridiculous. The counter part to the male nemesis of the eye gate is the female nemesis to want to show off. I'm sure that very few women would think that they dress—just to be attacked! Yet, it is without doubt that they do dress to be noticed. Even the ladies of these groups who have strict dress codes find ways to be noticed. However, more than just modest apparel—modest attitude—is what is needed. When a woman adopts a modest attitude she will dress in a fashion that will not embarrass her father, her husband, her neighbor or her God. More importantly, with that modest dress she will exhibit a modest attitude. You can dress a woman in a Muslim burqua and all she has to do to get—noticed—is to walk and act in an overtly immodest way. This is another of the many examples we can make about how it is—God only—who can change hearts. More literally, he gives us a new heart. Just changing the clothes is not the answer. Without heart change there is no answer, there is only self-righteousness and religiosity.

**As a father what will mommy's little boy teach his little girl?**

Fathers; daddy's little girl needs to know how the young men in her world are being affected, how they respond many times to the female form and presence and how this is sometimes correct and sometimes incorrect. She needs to know what to look for in a young man who has his sexual arousal mechanisms under control, and who has been reared by a father and mother of faith and grace, who have given him a perspective of respect and honor for women. If she knows what is happening inside the mind and body of the men, both young and not so young, to whom she is exposed, she is more likely to be able to protect herself from those who could cause her irreparable damage. As with any potentially dangerous element, our little girls must be taught the proper respect and caution for the dangers presented. Our sons must be taught how to teach and coach their future daughters.

Being born a male, in our present world of sexual commercialization of female exhibitionism, presents many challenges that former generations of males did not have to overcome. The Madison Avenue practice, of encouraging standards of dress for women that constantly puts them in the spotlight for male sexual arousal—has definite economic advantages for the promoters—but also causes tremendous pressures for males. At some point, women must assume the responsibility for the effects of their dressing habits on the male world. One of the natural biological drives of women is to want to show off their feminine form. This is the nemesis of women. Whereas the women enjoy showing off and even being exhibitionists, we men enjoy looking. These two biological factors are not always in harmony for productive and positive results. Consequently, women must assume the responsibility for their actions. They are constantly looking for new ways to be alluring and to stimulate the male sexual arousal mechanism. Then, when they are successful, and some man goes beyond just being satisfied with the effects he gets through the eye gate and wants to touch her and make advances towards her, she cries foul play—sexual harassment.

The combination of misguided women, pushing the limits and going over the top with their "sexy" dress habits and men who are hard wired to be aroused by such actions creates a perfect atmosphere for sexual harassment, date rape and a host of serious problems for all! Both non-Christians and Christians of both sexes are involved in these sinful acts. Of the two groups—only Christians—have the gift of a new heart and the gift of faith and are thus able to bring change into our country. Change from our moral morass and the spiritual warfare we are suffering against the family can only come through us who are adopted into our Fathers family, His Kingdom. We are all here—we are just asleep in our unbelief—our Father is calling us—as never before—to shake off our stupor and accept our God-given role as men and women of faith and grace. Once awakened and animated by His Spirit we will arise to build a Christian culture in which men do not abuse the females of that culture.

**The wise man of faith and grace knows his bounds of conduct:**

Men of faith and grace do not overstep the bounds of decent conduct to force their sexual interests on a person of the opposite sex! Should such actions occur; he is grossly out of order and will—we pray and hope—be made to answer for his actions. Our challenge is not an easy one, but in spite of that fact, there is no excuse for a man to think he has—rights or privileges—with a woman just because she dresses alluringly or provocatively, or even if she is acting in such ways as to make him think she is interested. In a perfect world men of faith and grace would be of such moral fiber and character that—even a nude woman—would be considered someone who just needs to get dressed. This not a perfect world and men of faith and grace must flee the presence of nude women—except that of their own wife—and not look back!

Nevertheless, women must assume the moral responsibility for their femininity and the way they present themselves in public. Dressing alluringly or provocatively and strutting around the office and other public places as if they wanted every man in the place to make a pass at them, is not in their best interest. In the light of our present moral decay among men and the lack of discretion on the part of many women, I would not be surprised if companies begin very soon to require certain dress codes for the ladies. Even if such actions are never done or allowed by our over litigious society, we the men of faith and grace can and must set the moral standard in contrast to all those men who have rejected God and refuse His gift of faith and grace.

Indeed, overcoming the temptations associated with our constant—on—condition and our natural sexual arousal's and general sex drive is a full time job, not impossible—by the grace of God—but certainly not something one can just assume will take care of itself. On the contrary , leaving it to itself is exactly what has spawned such disastrous results in the sex habits of the average American male, and in fact, in males throughout the world.

**God's worldview of love, romance and sex is fulfilled only in marriage:**

From the positive perspective, it is very normal for a man to want to express himself sexually to the woman he loves. However, great sex is not sex which only produces an orgasm. Sex that only produces an orgasm is one-dimensional sex. I mentioned earlier that we would share more on this: Such sex brings about biological orgasm and ejaculation, but it is void and empty of the deeper joys and significance of sex. In contrast, great sex is three-dimensional—it satisfies three ways—it satisfies mentally/emotionally, spiritually and physically. When a young boy is reared by a father and a mother of faith and grace, who have this kind of sexual relationship, he too will seek the same quality in his relationship with his future wife.

Every young man who dates the opposite sex is tempted to explore and to follow his sexual arousal instincts. This does not mean that he has no control over his responses to these arousals; it just means it is natural to be tempted to pursue the response. He does have the ability to control his responses and this is very important for your daughter to know. She must also know when she is creating an environment that could lead to things neither of them really wants. Her firm statement of "No" to advances from a young man is not an insult to him, nor is it unattractive. A real man of faith and grace is much more attracted to a girl who has principles and will stick by them than he is to some wishy-washy female who offers herself as a plaything for every pair of male eyes, hands and lips that comes along.

Earlier generations of American families handled this male exploratory temptation by insisting that the personal discovery dating couple never be left alone. Couples were expected to accept a chaperone and to restrict their visits to the house of the young ladies parents. These and many other means to maintain a higher standard of relationship building between the sexes are most often deemed by the young to be—old fashioned—funny how that sex is never old fashioned. Only the methods to control and supervise are ever considered old fashioned.

In post modern America; Christians and the family are under a brutal attack on the issue of love and marriage as never in our history! Liberal secularists of all stripes and political persuasion are attacking our children through abortion, the media, the school room, the press, the theatre, the arts and are now pressing for same sex marriage. Is it any wonder that this has concerned parents looking for alternatives to the post modern American dating scene and all the opportunities for temptations and wrong headedness that it produces? As a consequence, some families are looking for new ideas as alternatives to the current dating game.

**What is love?**

Love and sex are so commonly presented to our young people of today as—one and the same thing—few actually know the difference. This distortion of the facts is so great and causes so much confusion, the majority of young men and women assume there is no love, unless there is sexual activity in their relationship.

It is essential for every young son/daughter to know when he/she is being loved and when he/she is giving love. Without this knowledge he/she will never be able to distinguish between sex and love. Fortunately, this is very easy to understand. Yet, it amazes me how something so easy to understand is so seldom demonstrated.

Love is a decision, not a feeling. One does not—feel—in love. One feels emotions and sexual arousal. Love is not a feeling it is a decision of commitment to a person. A young man is in love with a girl when, and only when, he is committed to her for life. Anything short of such a commitment is either nothing more than infatuation, or just an excuse to get into her pants.

A woman, who is dating can know she is definitely not loved when all the men in her life want are to have sex with her. Such a woman is indeed a sex object, pure and simple.

Petting, kissing and fondling the female body without a life-time commitment of love and marriage to the person living in that body, are not expressions of love! These acts are mere mechanics of further male stimulation through female contact, solely for the purpose of reaching sexual orgasm. It is of little consequence for the woman involved to enjoy such attention and also want to reach orgasm. It is also of no consequence for this woman to have openly invited such activity. Enjoying sexual arousal and the physical release of orgasm—in and of themselves—have nothing to do with true love. Such sexual activity that truly satisfies and fulfills the participants is that which is born out of a committed marriage relationship. I said—born out of—not prior to!

Our daughters need to know that when a young boy gets all hot and bothered on a date and engages in a lot of kissing and petting, he is fully aware of his actions and knows he is using her as a sex object and a means for self gratification. Sexual intercourse on such a date is not necessary for this to be true. Many young boys will simply go home from the date and within thirty minutes or less stimulate themselves to orgasm, fantasizing the moments of their embraces.

Sexual activity between the sexes without a lifetime commitment is just that, sex, nothing more, it's not great sex—it's not even good sex—just biological sex. To engage in such activity only distorts the perspective of what great sex IS, and what love IS. If you want your son to have a life-time commitment of true love, to give and receive great sex, then by all means teach him the truth!

# Book III

# MOMMY'S LITTLE BOY

## Chapter Two Part III

## Introducing the Male World

## A Real Man Of Faith And Grace

**Secular humanism's worldview of a "real" man:**

What is a real man? A question every man must answer for himself. There are certainly many versions floating around, but do you have a good understanding of what constitutes a real man? The question will seem out of place to some—but remember today's "Christian man" more often than not—takes his worldview about men from secularists, not from God's revealed Law-Word. So, from where did you get your concept of a real man? Did it come from "Playboy Magazine", Hollywood movies, the locker room or God's revealed Law-Word?

Today's stereotypes of what constitutes a real man are continually promoted, massaged and refined by these and other sources of male machismo. Unfortunately, these sources adopt a narrow view of masculinity, limiting their focus to the basest of our biological elements, brawn and sex. Such a limited focus not only debilitates the emergence of real men of faith and grace but—even fails miserably in its portrayal of true—masculinity, personal character development and sexual boundaries!

As a result, we men of faith and grace must come to understand as early as possible that being born male, with a penis and testicles, only makes us biologically male, not real men of faith and grace. It gives us the right to aspire to be real men of faith and grace, and through God's gift of faith, we can become such. Our bodies come amply equipped with male hormones and male sex organs with which to demonstrate our biological reality. Consequently, being biologically male is something we men—do not have to expend any thought or energy—to accomplish. However, being a real man of faith and grace encompasses a lot more than being a biological male. In order to excel in the art of being a real man of faith and grace we must accept the presence of a Real Morality within which are encompassed two basic aspects of true manhood.

**Mothers of faith and grace are God's key elements for their little boys:**

The tender approach of a mother of faith and grace for her son—from the moment of birth to the time he says, "I do," at the altar—sets the foundation for his attitude and development as one of God's real gentlemen toward women in general and—especially in particular toward—the women he perceives to be God's gift to him as a wife. Our sense of Real Morality begins with this unique relationship with our mothers—either for good or for evil—we will take our cues from our mother, long before we learn anything about morals from any other source. With the help of a mother of faith and grace a little boy will grow to accept and understand his masculinity and embrace God's worldview for Real Morality—the Real Right and Wrong—for the guidelines of his life.

**First:** there comes the aspect of responsibility. Such a man has, as his first priority to be responsible for his biological characteristics. He accepts the responsibility for his penis and his testicles, and the male sex hormones driving his sexual arousal. With this attitude, he knows he has the capacity for misusing his sexuality and that he also has the capacity to use it properly. Therefore, he is very careful to structure his life so as to make the most positive and productive use of his male sexuality!

**Secondly:** there is the aspect of accountability. Being accountable for our actions is the difference between simply saying we are responsible and actually following through with the appropriate actions to make it so. Being accountable as men and as fathers does not have the highly visible profile of a politician in public office, but the principle of being accountable is no less important or demanding. We can pay lip-service to the fact that we are responsible for certain things: our sexuality, personal development, financial commitments, our family and our role as good citizens; however, keeping our word and making it so, is another matter entirely. Accountable men of faith and grace can be trusted to honor their commitments and follow up on their responsibilities—they keep their word.

**God's common grace blesses all men:**

Positive male characteristics help to balance the account. Males and the male world are not without redeeming qualities. Through God's common grace, manhood and masculinity are physical expressions of beings that are capable of great courage, strength of character, vision and ambition. With these qualities men have conquered oceans, mountains, forests, jungles, and space. These qualities are the driving force behind our great cities. Men are fathers by nature. They want to bring new things into existence; they thrive on discovery and protecting their discoveries. The art of fatherhood begins in the family, but can and does encompass more than just the family unit.

In the heart of every man is the desire to be responsible for his life and the lives of his loved one's. Men have a great capacity for being noble and for choosing to suffer great hardships for the benefit of their loved one's and their country. Every man is born with a natural potential for leadership. Some are just better at it than others.

Men come equipped by God to be strong moral leaders in their own lives and in their families, and to inspire and to lead others who have given up on their higher callings. It is the ability of a man to inspire others to positive action that provides his finest moments.

**We men were all once some mothers little boy:**

These are the qualities our daughters want to see us demonstrate and thus to know how to identify them in other men. It is a man who has these qualities and who will accept the responsibility to use them for good that you want to attract your daughter. Mothers of faith and grace want to instill these same qualities in their little boys.

The level of respect and admiration we have, as real men of faith and grace, for women will be determined by the success of how well we handle these two steps! They teach us to hold women, womanhood and all things feminine in the highest regard. Our own personal responsibility and sexual accountability do not allow us to put women in different categories of respect. As real men of faith and grace we will not view some women as mere sex objects and others as more than just sex objects. The attitude of such men toward women in general is not selective, it is without question one of respect, love and compassion, including those women who have not lived up to this image!

This attitude of respect and compassion for women is important for the real man of faith and grace to focus completely and exclusively on his wife.

**Men and women of faith and grace learn the value of a limited focus:**

Focusing on one woman—one's wife—is the key to overcoming the distractions of a world filled with provocatively dressed female forms and a social fabric that says, "Anything goes." Focusing is a type of mental blinders. One simply blocks out the easy approach to accepting the status quo of responding to the many avenues of available temptation! Deciding to be totally satisfied with the female form and femininity of one's own wife—refusing to allow oneself the "luxury" of frequenting places or sources where the female form is going to be the main attraction—we are better able to fantasize and savor the beauty of our own wife, without the need for outside stimulation. I find the more I concentrate on my wife Marilyn and on her beauty and femininity, the more attractive she becomes to me physically, and as a person. This is a two way experience; we are both mutually blessed with more satisfaction from our relationship.

In a world—where so much feminine form is available—it is impossible to eliminate all outside stimuli, however, it can be greatly reduced, and the more we eliminate the more we will experience increased joy and satisfaction in our marriages.

When we men and women of faith and grace resolve to focus on one woman and one man, the quality of everything we do with our one spouse becomes greatly improved. Our conversation, our curiosity, our appreciation, our feelings of romance and affection all increase. Contrary to the fears of many—such focusing does not produce boredom or burnout—with your partner. On the contrary, there is a constant discovery of new things and new realities of persona that were hidden before, or blurred by the many other distractions that clutter the mind when focusing has been over-looked. The idealistic sexual and emotional satisfaction—alluded to in the world of promiscuity but never realized—becomes a reality within the honesty and romance of focusing on the one woman and the one man to whom we have pledged ourselves for life before God.

## Personal Moral Values and Principles That Exemplify The Day to Day Life of A Real man of Faith and Grace

1. By the grace of God he will remain a virgin until marriage and will be faithful to his wife for the rest of his life. He will focus his attentions and energies before marriage on preparing himself to be a husband and father of the highest quality.

2. He will desire and seek a life-time partner and lover in a marital relationship. He will choose such a woman from among those women he knows to be virtuous, preferably a virgin, but a virtuous widow is not out of the question. His respect and compassion, not passion, for all women, allow him to exercise self-discipline and self-respect in his pursuit of the right woman for him. Once he finds the right woman for him, he will make his decision to love her, and will obligate himself to allow nothing to change that decision!

3. All of his sexual desires and passions will be focused on this one woman whom he has chosen to be his wife and lover for life! Mutual communication of these desires and needs will be a high priority.

"Let the husband render to his wife the affection due her, and likewise also the wife to her husband. *The wife does not have authority over her own body, but the husband does. And likewise the husband does not have authority over his own body, but the wife does.* Do not deprive one another except with consent for a time, that you may give yourselves to fasting and prayer; and come together again so that Satan does not tempt you because of your lack of self-control. But I say this as a concession, not as a commandment. For I wish that all men were even as I myself. But each one has his own gift from God, one in this manner and another in that." I Cor. 7:1-7: Emphasis mine.

"Husbands, likewise, dwell with them with understanding, giving honor to the wife, as to the weaker vessel, and as being heirs together of the grace of life, that your prayers may not be hindered." I Peter 3:7.

4. He avoids the slippery slope of the double standard and considers all women to be worthy of his respect and compassion. He has compassion for women who have elected to participate in the pursuit of male titillation, the topless dancers, prostitutes, porno stars and the sexually promiscuous. He understands that they are the legacy of men who would not accept the high calling of a father of faith and grace, or even the common grace fatherhood of an unbeliever. He is painfully aware of the many dangers such women present. Pursuit of such women only leads to the death of his self-respect and of his dedication to his own husbanding/fatherhood and in effect, the death of his own personal life as a husband/father of faith and grace.

5. He is not out to "conquer" everything wearing a skirt or a tight pair of pants. His self-control and self-respect are not—just tempered—by his knowledge of the evil they represent, but by the sustaining power of Christ through grace to enable him to do so. Such a man of faith and grace knows that he cannot hope to focus his complete sexual needs and desires on just one woman if, his lifestyle were to demonstrate, that in fact his—true attitude toward women—is one that considers them as mere sex objects and sex trinkets.

6. He is not confused concerning erotic sexual arousal. Sexual arousal, by itself, is purely a biological function, whereas love is a decision, which, when once made never has to be changed. He knows one does not "fall" in love, one decides to love. Thus, he decides anew, everyday, to love this woman which he has chosen to be his wife. Likewise one cannot "fall" out of love; it requires a selfish, faithless decision to stop loving.

7. He accepts the responsibility of providing the commitment and leadership necessary to establish a successful family structure and the high calling of fatherhood based on God's gift of faith and grace. He accepts the challenge of creating a love relationship with his chosen mate, one which includes her fulfillment in all areas. He puts a top priority on her continued spiritual, emotional development, her need and desire for motherhood, her educational and vocational development. He is not threatened by his wife's

potential or realized education or vocation. He understands both of them will experience their greatest romantic and sexual satisfaction as a result of this complete understanding and commitment.

8. He protects the bonds of their relationship and intimacy from all intrusions, especially from his or her immediate family members who might be tempted to criticize them or their relationship.

9. He does not abuse his wife or his children, verbally or physically.

10. He wants to pursue the best possible approach to realizing his full potential and destiny in life. He accepts his own creation with humility and seeks a personal relationship with God.

11. He will not reject the inner stirrings within his heart and soul to reach out and ask God for help and guidance in this, the most complex of all challenges, the challenge of fatherhood! He walks in faith, knowing that alone—without God—he cannot hope to fulfill the blueprint for husbands, as stated in Eph. 5:23-33.[159] He refuses to be controlled and manipulated by disoriented male counterparts, who use intellectual pride, secularist mentality, selfish ego, machismo, and so-called "male virility" as a substitute for God's revealed Law-Word. He does not delegate his spiritual development to others, such as Rabbis, Priests, Pastors or Sunday school teachers. He has the courage to read the Bible for himself. He is a man of prayer, both alone, deep and personal and also with his wife—daily seeking—God's grace, wisdom and mercy in their lives. He makes his own decisions regarding what God is saying to him and about his role in this life. He is open-minded and therefore accessible to counsel from his wife, pastors and others—but more importantly—his greatest source of wisdom is from his continual reading of God's Law-Word. Thus armed for life's battles, he makes his own final decisions!

12. He is committed to seeking His answers for the proper worldview from Christ and to—search His Law-Word in the pursuit of all the answers to the demands of day to day living routines, vocational excellence, child rearing challenges, spousal romance and sexual satisfaction with and for the benefit of his wife—encouraging and including her in all his pursuits through wise counsel and prayer.

**Rethinking who we are and where we are going:**

Men and women of many different back grounds, experiences, biblical understanding and spiritual maturity will be reading this book. If you are a man or woman of faith and grace, I know that God is exercising His good pleasure in you

---

159 "For the husband is head of the wife, as also Christ is head of the church; and He is the Savior of the body. Therefore, just as the church is subject to Christ, so let the wives be to their own husbands in everything.

"Husbands, love your wives, just as Christ also loved the church and gave Himself for her, that He might sanctify and cleanse her with the washing of water by the word, that He might present her to Himself a glorious church, not having spot or wrinkle or any such thing, but that she should be holy and without blemish. So husbands ought to love their own wives as their own bodies; he who loves his wife loves himself. For no one ever hated his own flesh, but nourishes and cherishes it, just as the Lord does the church. For we are members of His body, of His flesh and of His bones: 'For this reason a man shall leave his father and mother and be joined to his wife, and the two shall become one flesh.' This is a great mystery, but I speak concerning Christ and the church. Nevertheless let each one of you in particular so love his own wife as himself, and let the wife see that she respects her husband." Ephesians 5:23-33

and you are progressing in your development along these lines. I thank God for you and pray that you grow to excel in all of these standards in your life. May God continue to guide and give you—overcoming grace to succeed—in the paths which He has chosen for you.

If for what ever reason you have doubts as to whether or not you are a person of faith and grace—then above all do not despair—"...for it is God who works in you both to will and to do for His good pleasure." Philippians 2:13." He will use all manner of means to fulfill His will in you, perhaps even this book! Above all—do not—feel threatened and put-down by the prospect of His high standards. Whatever the case might be—put all personal pride aside—face the reality of your situation and embrace these standards to the best of your ability. If any who read this should be one of those who have already failed miserably, and are under heavy feelings of guilt, read again the sections on *Recapturing Virtue*, Book I Chapter Two. You have nothing to lose by taking charge and acting on the need to change, and you have everything to gain!

In fact, we could all do with a review of the material in the area of recapturing virtue. Not one of us is living up to his highest potentials to be a Real man or woman of faith and grace. Consider this: it is the level of our trust in Him and in His promises to enable us and to deliver us that determines His positive actions of overcoming and—conversely to that—it is our lack of these elements that brings about His greater discipline in our lives. Therefore, if you are feeling His discipline—know that you are blessed and loved—for He only disciplines those that are His. Likewise in the face of these realities how can we possibly feel threatened by the need for change? In this biological state of life—CHANGE—is the name of the game. In our voyage of life, change and mid-course corrections are not only necessary but are the very heart of our ability to stay on course, or to come back to course, if we have lost our bearings. Be assured of this—course changes become a fact of life—an almost daily occurrence. We suffer our greatest troubles when we act Macho as a man or Liberated as a woman and exercise our male and female pride and ego which does not admit we are wrong. No real Captain and his First Mate sets a course and then refuses to change their course when the map says they must, or the voyage will end in disaster!

**Yesterday has gone with the wind—TODAY—is our day of salvation:**

We cannot afford to whitewash the truth because of our own faults or past mistakes. If we are candid about our mistakes and sincere about our commitment to be a moral role model for our family, we will find our daughters and sons to be very understanding. However, don't assume I am referring to dumping all the family skeletons. As we have discovered in earlier chapters, we must keep propriety and relevance in perspective when we are confessing faults.

One of the great weaknesses we have as men and women is the desire to appear perfect to our spouses and children, while exercising moral habits—in both mind and deed—that are contrary to such an image. Men and women of faith and grace—we cannot have it both ways—either we are committed to being moral role models for our families and reaping the tremendous positive rewards that such a commitment will bring for all, or we are not. We cannot have the rewards of lasting respect, honor, satisfying love and sex with our spouses, and the joy of rearing wonderful, sensitive children, prepared for the art of love and marriage—and at the same time—reserve a secret area or our minds and life for promiscuity. It is tantalizingly tempting—the secular world of sexual liberality around us is telling us that—"Oh it's all right."—but you know in your hearts that it just won't wash. God has given us a new heart and that heart says this is a doctrine right out of Hell!

Spare yourselves the embarrassment and your children the hypocrisy of whitewashing this world and our part in it. They deserve and need to have a clear picture of the present status of the male world and how that relates to God's worldview on love, sex and romance for both our little girl and our little boy! There is little doubt that in our present times—they know plenty! The benefit to you is—that when you start with them while they are yet young—you can bring them along slowly and by the time they are getting input from the street, school and friends, etc. they will have already been prepared by you. What you don't know until you have experienced it is how much they will grow in their respect for you for having taught them in advance. This will all increase their appreciation, love and respect for your unique roles as their—champions of love, romance and marriage—as only fathers and mothers of faith and grace can do!!

**Small and consistent corrections make for smooth sailing:**

Remember, short, informal meetings on a regular basis, with small and consistent inputs are the best way to share your introduction of the male world to your son and daughter. Expanding the details as you see they are maturing and are thus able to assimilate them.

A young daughter or son does not expect to receive all that you know in one sitting. It would not accomplish the depth or understanding which you want and would probably confuse them. So, determine to share your introductions of such matters in small doses. You should always include both the negative and the positive in each session. Giving only the negative or only the positive does not offer your daughter or son the best opportunity to understand the art of perceiving a balance. Creating balance in your children's perspective is very important.

Keep a good sense of just what you have shared with your daughter or son in past sessions. If need be, keep a record of what you have covered so that you can systematically cover all the important material and review the areas which seem to be the most difficult for him or her to understand. Using this book as a guide and a source for lesson planning is a good idea. The Appendices are especially designed to give you easy access to all of the different topics and numerations of steps and points to teach. Each teaching aid may be photo copied and will allow you total control of how much and how soon you expose your children to the material.

After some time has passed, giving this kind of instruction, you will notice an interesting development. Your son and daughter will start to counsel other children at school. They will invite home those with insensitive fathers and mothers or especially those without fathers or mothers in the family, so they can meet you. It won't be long until you will find yourself counseling other young children. Sometimes you will see your efforts with these other children reap rewards in successful behavior, other times it will have little or no effect. Not every father and mother of faith and grace will feel led to offer counsel to such girls and boys—but some will sense that God is giving them an opportunity—to serve where no answers or Godly wisdom have been available. In these moments we must all make it a matter of serious prayer to determine if any counsel should be given.

Remember, these young girls and boys who would seek or admit to a need for help most often do not have a father or mother of faith and grace in the home. The non-existence of a constant real father or mother of faith and grace present in the home makes such—sporadic and hit-or-miss—counseling difficult to implement. In stark contrast to this tragedy: it is your close day-to-day relationship with your daughter and son in the whole family atmosphere of family structure—implementing God's Family Chain of Command, His Family Charter, and your Confession and Vows of commitment to His Great Commission for husbands and wives—which you—by and through the grace of God—have structured, that make your relationship of love and marriage so special, so powerful and so successful!

[illegible]

# Book III

# Mommy's Little Boy

## Chapter Three

## The First Personal Discovery Date

**Seeking God's special person:**

Finally the time will arrive when our daughter or son will seek to have social contact with others of the opposite sex for the purpose of determining if this individual who has attracted their attention is perhaps that—one and only—special person that God has chosen for them. There are two options for—how we are most likely to react—at this moment in time and history for the daughter or son in question and for our family in general:

- **Option one:**
  Panic and fear is all too often the reaction to the unknown consequences that could come from this action.

- **Option two:**
  Excited anticipation for participating with God: in the process of this most important undertaking for the launching of a new element, of faith and grace for God to use, in His institution The Family.

Nothing is completely perfect in our lives of faith and grace—but God's revealed Law-Word is clear that our obedience to Him and to the application of Christ's worldview on this issue or any other matter in our day to day lives—is the course of our MOST PROBABLE success! Such a reality in our lives will result in our reactions being more like *Option two*. The lack of such a reality in our lives will invoke a reaction more like *Option one*—there is NO neutrality in the matter—we either SUCCEED in Christ with the application His worldviews or we FAIL as we attempt success by applying the worldviews of secular atheists!

**Defining the term:**

The process of venturing outside of the spiritual and moral security of a home of faith and grace, to pursue the natural desire to seek a mate is most often referred to as dating or—*to date*—and is the most important discovery process our children will ever undertake, second only to their personal walk in Christ. To say that it is very important for parents of faith and grace and their sons and daughters is—at best—a gross understatement. Therefore, if the term "to date" is not clearly understood, in its proper context, then it follows that the experience of—this personal discovery process—"to date:" will be full of misunderstandings and create an environment for disastrous trouble. We will describe our concept of this first step—outside of the security of your home—in the process of love and marriage as a—*Personal Discovery*—experience. Thus, we will seek to understand and apply the discoveries we have made to this concept of a Personal Discovery Date.

A personal discovery date means—daughter—is picked up at the house by her escort for the occasion and brought back to the house by the same escort. Whereas in the case of mommy's little boy—now a full grown young man—is the candidate of faith and grace that is escorting some other young lady from a different family home of faith and grace. This includes everything from a short trip to the grocery store to a formal dinner and an evening on the town. For our daughter this escort is a true friend, not in the sense that so many young girls refer to them, as "boyfriends," meaning everything from a "hot" romance, to a "live in" sex partner. For our son who is now the escort— understands his role as an escort of good character and integrity—is to be a co-supporter to the father of the home of faith and grace, for protecting the virtue of his daughter!

Personal discovery dating, as opposed to sharing an event such as a party or ball game with a group of friends, is much more serious stuff. Your daughter will never learn the difference between correct—personal discovery dating and frivolous entertainment—from today's post modern high pressure, church youth group, school yard society. You are her only hope to learn the difference! The post modern concept of anything goes has created a concept of male and female dating that is repugnant to all men and women of faith and grace. Secular "dating" begins with a worldview that there is no God[160], that sex is an adult form of recreation and that the only serious thing to consider is that there be no negative downside to this hedonism. Therefore we cannot be surprised that every effort is made by this powerful group of "believers" and unbelievers to discredit any—worldview of absolutes—such as God's revealed Law-Word!

**No safe haven is guaranteed in the church youth group:**

Those who have no experience in the matter will take issue with us over the inclusion—of church youth groups in the same context as the school yard for high pressure post modernisms—moralistic subjective convention towards dating, sex among teens, sex before marriage and sex outside of marriage. The truth is that one of the most dangerous moral environments within the greater majority of today's Christian churches in our post modern society, that is—all denominations, evangelical, non-evangelical, conservative, liberal, Pentecostal or charismatic—are youth group outings and trips away from the supervision of their parents. As a rule, Christian youth groups can be a positive influence and moral haven for social contact with the opposite sex—so long as—the activities are properly supervised and they remain in the immediate area of the church facility. Records show that when this same group takes to the highways for events—even the most "spiritual" events—or they go to parks and recreational areas away from the church facility or a supervised event in the home of a father and mother of faith and grace—sex and sex games are going to happen to some of these young people.

**Environment for disaster:**

Secular dating has become "the" source of entertainment for today's average young person. If you are not "dating," then you are not having "fun." When most young people today talk about partying, they are referring to drinking, drugs, and sex. So, your "date" for the evening is your party partner. I wonder if all of the unwed teen-age mothers in America are having fun yet.

The peer pressure behind the secular style dating as a status symbol in junior high and among teen-agers leaves no time for an intelligent approach. The concern is more for the popularity of the candidate than the quality. The true

160 "The fool has said in his heart, 'There is no God.'" (Psalm 14:1).

objective of something as in-depth as personal discovery dating is never even discussed, much less given serious consideration.

The most tragic aspect of this whole scene is the apparent ignorance and impotence of the parents and adult community in general. We hear a lot about how important it is to teach young people all about "safe" sex, how to—just say no—to drugs, and how to have other goals besides being a member of some gang.

The idea that giving out condoms at school or making them available at no charge in places like Planned Parenthood, will produce "safe" sex, is assuming that getting sexually transmittable diseases and getting pregnant are—the only unsafe—things about premarital or promiscuous sex. The truth is, that getting a disease and getting pregnant, are only two of the many elements which are unsafe about such sex habits. The most damaging element of truth—of which we hear almost nothing from secularists—namely—the destruction of the God-given intuition and dream of every woman for true committed life-long love, family and happiness in the arms of her chosen Hero and Knight in shining armor and the destroyed dreams of a young man to be such a Knight in Shining Armor and establish himself as head and priest of his future family! Giving out condoms to young teen-agers is like giving a fire extinguisher to a small child and telling him he can go play with fire. Or—on a more personal note—If I know a very pretty young girl who is infected with the AIDS virus, would the protection of a condom make me feel free to have sex with her? In truth Proverbs says: "Those who hate Me love death!"

The only safety from sexually transmitted diseases is abstinence. The only sex capable of bringing us complete joy and satisfaction is the three-dimensional sex we have with a mutually committed lifetime partner in the bonds of marriage! In the latter case, if both partners are uninfected by sexually transmittable diseases, then it is impossible for them to infect each other.

**Satan's worldview of the value of life:**

Then, of course, we have those very enlightened groups of adults who tell our young people that if you cannot keep from getting pregnant, don't worry about it—just get an abortion—and kill the thing.[161] After all, according to these learned souls, it isn't human anyway, not until after it has been in the womb three months, and has no rights as a person until after it is born. Some even go so far as to say that it doesn't matter if it is even a full-term baby, if the mother and or as is most often the case—some man—in her relationships somewhere doesn't want her to have that kid!

Clearly 70%-80% of all abortions are done because of a man or men who are seldom seen but who in fact are the real reason the mother is having the abortion. They range from the husband who is committing adultery, the boy friend who doesn't want the hassle of a baby in his life, the father or grandfather who cannot stand to have it known that the daughter or grand-daughter has had a baby out-of-wedlock and even a boss or supervisor can indirectly be a strong force to push a mother into choosing abortion as a solution to an untimely career interruption.

Imagine if you can: this young girl, who is already morally, emotionally and spiritually damaged, is now being told to add murder to her conscience! That's

---

[161] "Two tidal waves of death: the tsunami late in December and 32 years of massive abortion since the Roe vs. Wade decision on Jan. 22, 1973.

"Television images and Internet blogs have brought home to Americans the reality of one disaster. Ultrasound images have shown many young women and their boyfriends the reality of lives that can be saved. We have fewer excuses than we once had for not loving our neighbors as ourselves, no matter how far away or how small they are." From the www.worldmagblog.com "Two tidal waves: tsunami and abortion" Marvin Olasky
January 13, 2005

terrific advice. It makes one wonder how the adults who advocate such things were reared. Most certainly not by men and women of faith and grace who were committed to the high calling of God's Great Commission for fathers and mothers!

**Timing is everything:**

Establishing the right age for our son and daughter to start personal discovery dating is something we should have established and agreed upon back when we first made our commitment to them—to share all we know about the male and female world, to be their champions and coach in love and marriage.

There seems to be a constant war going on in today's families over how soon a daughter should start personal discovery dating. If you have read this book in time to set up a proper—father/daughter, mother/son—relationship, you are not going to have any trouble establishing the right age or living with the commitment. On the other hand, if you are just now reading this book, and you have a son or daughter who is already screaming at you that they should be allowed to date and do what all the other boys and girls are doing, you have a more difficult challenge.

Take heart, your son and daughter are really open to every principle and concept that you encounter in this book. They are hoping against hope for you to have the courage and the strength of character to take up the reigns of their life and to start giving them the structure they so desperately need!

If this is your situation, and you are getting a late start, it will seem like an insurmountable mountain when you begin. However, no mountain is insurmountable, and every son and daughter comes naturally equipped to be structured in these matters by their father and mother. So, you have everything going for you. All you need to do is get your game plan together and go to work.

We have previously discovered that sixteen is—most likely the earliest and most proper age—to begin personal discovery dating for our young princess. However, our young prince would be well advised to postpone any—out the house—discovery dating until seventeen or eighteen. My wife, Marilyn, was only fourteen when her father first allowed me to date her. I'm sure his decision was affected by the fact we had known each other for so long, and that he felt as if he knew me and trusted me. However, even though my wife was very mature for her age and very close to her father, there was still a lot of preparation lacking. Two more years would have given her a much better opportunity to be prepared, and would have made our courtship and our subsequent marriage less risky.

As a consequence of this premature secular styled dating experience, we were challenged with the need to make up for the lack in our maturity and her general state of unpreparedness. By the grace of God we were able to keep our commitment intact long enough to overcome this handicap. The majority of such cases are not so fortunate, as there can be a great deal of damage done to the immature young girl who is allowed to date at such an early age.

**Continuing a friendship:**

This first discovery date is really a continuation, on a more responsible level, of a friendship that has already shown some promise with these candidates. Both parents as champions for their son or daughter should already be very well acquainted with this young man or young lady candidate.

The occasion of the first discovery date is one of special significance for all concerned. This is like the first official performance for which your son or daughter has been training. They want it to be special and they want to demonstrate to you how well they have learned all you have taught them. Their first response, after this date, will be to tell you everything that happened.

Setting the limits for your son and daughter's personal discovery dating practices is the next step in your objectives as a good champions and coaches. Every good coach knows that you don't set high standards and goals you expect to reach in a week or two. In order to insure your son or daughter's success in love and marriage, you must begin teaching them from the very beginning that real personal discovery dating is not like in the movies, or like what some of their friends might be telling them .

To introduce new ideas and different perspectives—than what their friends or acquaintances might have—will not overcome either son or daughter. The reality of your caring and having sincerely committed yourself to their development has already set them apart, in a positive way, from almost everyone they know. They are proud of their relationship with you, not threatened.

The most important thing to establish in your son and daughter's mind about personal discovery dating, is how different and much more rewarding it is than the incorrect and dangerous secular dating practices—sexual experimentation opportunities—of the majority of boy/girl relationships. What you are leading them into is not only a superior experience but an assurance of blessing from their Lord that He will reward them—now in this life—with results that will fulfill their deepest heartfelt desires for love, sex and marriage!

**Dressing for the occasion:**

Clothing styles and dressing habits play a big role in how a young girl is perceived by the male population. Because the male sex drive and sexual arousal mechanisms are in a state of constant "on," it is important to establish dress codes for your daughters.

This does not mean you must go to the extreme. However, it does mean that you have the responsibility to take the initiative, to establish a standard of dress, which highlights your daughter's natural physical qualities, giving her an attractive appearance without accentuating her sensuality.

The average American woman of today, a creature of Western civilization has either chosen to ignore the effects her feminine form has on men, or just doesn't care. The present practice of low neck lines, high skirts, split skirts, and a general tendency to dress as alluringly as possible, indicates a great deal of insensitivity. Often this is accompanied by an attitude which implies, "look at me, but not too long, notice me, but don't stare, know that I'm beautiful, but don't get fresh! And—sometimes it means exactly what it implies—I'm here if you want me.

Your daughter should adopt a dress style which is in harmony with the moral standards she has embraced—because of your home of faith and grace and her understanding of those values being the implementation of Christ's worldview—for her protection and her future happiness. To go out on a date with a young man dressed in such a way that he will have a hard time keeping his eyes off her neck line and on the road, is a sure way to send the wrong message.

Mommy's little boy must develop into a young man that will know how to choose a candidate that shows moderation and wisdom in how to dress and how to represent herself in his presence.

**Discovery dating is—NOT—a contact sport!**

The current practice of expected physical interaction, hand holding, kissing, hugging, and, in the minds of a majority of today's young people, even sex, totally ignores common sense. Personal discovery dating is not a contact sport, nor a playground, for sexual exploration! In order not to become a victim of bruised and damaged emotions, thus greatly reducing their possibilities for marital happiness and success, your son and daughter will need high standards and a strong character. Personal discovery dating at its best is an opportunity to get to know someone personally, as opposed to knowing him or her physically. In fact, a father and mother of faith and grace need to develop a new way to communicate with their son or daughter about this experience. This is all part of the goals of their championing of love and marriage. The secular liberal left has stolen many of our God-given terms and turned them into words that now have no meaning for us: sex, gay, right, wrong, liberal, morals, truth, love and marriage. These and many more terms have been stolen from what we would consider their normal and historic meanings to be. It is powerful because—he who defines the terms—wins the argument. Thus, as a result of this theft we find ourselves searching for words and phrases to say what we should be able to say with these words, but now they represent and say something else to a growing majority of people.

As the experience of personal discovery dating is intended to get to know someone, intellectually, spiritually, politically and morally—in stark contrast to today's secular dating habits—that are counter-productive to getting to know someone on any of these levels—save one—sex. If you are spending all your time with someone, kissing, hugging and petting, all you learn is the capacity of your mutual sexual arousal and even this will only be a blind alley—as God has saved the best sexual arousal and satisfaction—for His elect in marriage. You will never learn anything about the person, nor vice versa. In order to learn something about the person, there has to be an intelligent interchange of thoughts and ideas. A person must be willing to reveal his or her mind, which is the only link there is between the real person and the body. Knowing his or her body does not reveal who is living in that body. In order to really know someone, you must communicate with that person's mind and discover who—the real person is—what are their goals, how well he or she relates with other people, how that person feels about family, what values and principles they have, and what attitudes he or she has about marriage, sex and love. With such an approach your son or daughter can get a very good idea, of the quality of their prospective candidate and their attributes. Success in this matter depends greatly on the quality of our roles as champions and coaches for romance, love and marriage. Together, with God's enabling grace and the wisdom of His uncommon common sense applied as consistently as possible, our sons and daughters will—want to discover these very deeply important aspects—of life under our leadership. Without this leadership and knowledge they are both—flying blind without a map—and have little or no hope of making an intelligent decision concerning either.

**If the plane is not going when and where you want to go, why get on it?**

Many young men and women think they can discern a good candidate just by meeting them and being in their presence. They rely on their intuition or machismo to tell them if he or she is really a "good" choice. What a disaster! For example: the one area of a woman's life that has proven very elusive to her—otherwise remarkable intuition—is the area of choosing a "good" man! Just look around. If a woman's intuition about the quality of a man were very good, we would not have up to sixty percent divorce rates for first marriages, and even higher for second marriages. Some mommy's little boy—all grown up now—is that dummy on the other end of the marriage debacle, when he has not had the advantage of a father of faith and grace and especially a mother of faith and grace! Our sons desperately need a mother of faith and grace to be their champion and coach for romance, love, sex and marriage!!

The objective of good personal discovery dating for our son or daughter is to discover a real man or woman of faith and grace, a man or woman of good moral character, one who can be attracted to these same qualities of our son or daughter. Without such an objective, all we have is—the secular dating game—an endless stream of male and female candidates looking for an opportunity to engage in sexual experimentation with the opposite sex—or worse yet—the same sex! This is something you hope your son or daughter will have learned as a result of all you have said and demonstrated to them. By this time, you will have spent years communicating to them about girls and boys, and about your own search for his or her father or mother, when you were seeking your mate and love for life. You have learned a lot from your own mistakes in personal discovery dating—or the sad estate of secular dating—and in witnessing the mistakes of others. With your commitment to them as their champions of love and marriage, your son or daughter should be well positioned to receive the greatest blessings possible in this life.

**Walking the walk with God's uncommon common sense:**

The process of discovering a real man of faith and grace among the many male possibilities is a great adventure! The father/daughter—romance and true love—discovery team goes to work. Father, with mother's support, teaches the daughter what to ask her prospects and how to respond to their answers or advances, should that be the case.

Likewise the process of discovering a real woman of faith and grace among the many female possibilities is a great adventure for the mother/son team! The mother/son—romance and true love—discovery team goes to work. Mother, with father's support, teaches the son what to ask his prospects and how to respond to their answers or advances, should that be the case.

The following is a list of questions which will help prepare your son or daughter to understand what kind of young lady or young man they are meeting or considering for a personal discovery date. Any potential prospect for their life-time commitment of love and devotion in marriage should be able to respond properly to the following questions. These questions are stated as from our Princess—Our Prince however must also qualify for his prospect with or without any questions! From the perspective of his parents of faith and grace his character and moral lifestyle founded and lived in Christ must be a given at this point!

**Qualifying Questions and Answers for Candidates**

**1. What do you think of your father?**

**Wrong Answer:**
Any response that shows a young man does not respect his father and is openly hostile to his father, is a wrong answer. Such a response is demonstrating that he has not been successfully prepared for leadership by his father. This is a very poor candidate.

**Correct Answer:**
A young man should respond with a strong response of respect and admiration for his father. He should be proud of the things his father has taught him and be able give details. Score one point

**2. What do you think of your mother?**

**Wrong Answer:**
A young man who does not respect and speak highly of his mother will not be able to maintain a high level of respect and honor for any woman. Not a good candidate.

**Correct Answer:**
The response to this question should be one of obvious tenderness and great respect for his mother. It should be natural for him to talk about her qualities and about her love and marriage with his father. Score one point.

**3. What major are you planning to study in college?**

**Wrong Answer:**
Any response not expressing a strong commitment to further education is evidence that this young man lives in a dream world, and is not a good candidate.

**Correct Answer:**
Any young man who has serious plans for his life and his future wife and family will have definite educational objectives. College is preferred, but is not the only form of higher education. Score one point.

**4. What is love?**

**Wrong Answer:**
Any indication showing the young man in question equates sex with love, is a wrong answer. Any serious candidate should be able to articulate the difference between love and sex, and should know that it is a decision based on a commitment and not an emotion. A wrong answer here indicates the young man has parents who don't know either, or they would have told him.

**Correct Answer:**
The ideal response is one showing good understanding of and strong attachment to the principle of love as a decision, based on commitment. Score one point.

**5. What is your opinion about virginity?**

**Wrong Answer:**
Look for an expression of surprise on his face, like: "You've got to be kidding me." The eyes will tell you what he really thinks. If a young man thinks a girl is a virgin, he is likely to say that he is for virginity. The next question should be: Are you a virgin? This will get the truth out in the open, even if he lies. Your daughter will be able to pick up on a lie most of the time. There are mitigating circumstances which sometimes may allow for past mistakes, but there should be no doubt about the level of understanding or commitment to virtue and protection of the state of virginity until marriage.

**Correct answer:**
The best response to this question is a strong and sincere commitment to virginity, both for the man as well as the young Princess. Score one point.

**6. What plans do you have for being a father?**

**Wrong Answer:**
Any response not showing a strong desire to be and family leader is an automatic wrong answer! There is absolutely no room for error in this response. Any doubt on the part of a male regarding his future role as a father and family leader, spells disaster for unsuspecting woman unfortunate enough to end up with him.

**Correct Answer:**
A young man who has been reared by a father, who taught him the joys of fatherhood and the basics of moral role modeling and principles, will answer this with strong feelings of commitment to the role of father and family leader. Score one point.

**7. What kind of discipline structure do your parents have?**

**Wrong Answer:**
Any response showing anger and deep frustration with the discipline structure or lack there of in a family setting, is a sign that there is not much understanding or experience with good discipline. Also, a person with such reactions to discipline will usually show signs of his own lack of personal discipline. This is not a good candidate.

**Correct Answer:**
Expressions of appreciation for the discipline that he has received and a willingness to talk about the need for discipline in our lives, are a good sign that a young man will develop into a responsible disciplinarian. The honesty and sincerity of this response should also be measured by the individual's demonstration of his own self- discipline. Score one point.

**8. Does your father show his affection for your mother?**

**Wrong Answer:**
If the response to question number one is negative, then the honesty of any response to this question is in serious doubt. However, assuming the response to question number one is positive, you could still get a wrong answer to this question. Any response indicating embarrassment or surprise usually indicates that a father does not show affection for his wife in the presence of the children. This could also indicate the presence of some physical abuse. A tendency for physical abuse is one of the easiest character faults to hide. Even when there is open affection there can sometimes be severe abuse behind the scenes. It will take some time and persistence to really know the truth. This could be an undesirable candidate.

**Correct Answer:**
There should be a genuine joy and appreciation for the affection that a son sees his father show for his mother. No marriage is without its disagreements, but the overwhelming impression that a son receives about his father's love and tenderness for his mother should come through loud and clear. Score one point.

**9. Has your father or mother ever been divorced?**

**Wrong Answer:**
An affirmative response to this question is undoubtedly all too common in our present state of family decay. However, divorce, in and of itself, is not the deciding factor in such cases. There is a need for further questioning and understanding of the circumstances really to have a feel for how much it should count against a young man. More than one divorce on the part of the father or mother, or recent divorce, or evidence of extreme bitterness over a divorce, are all signs that permanent damage has probably taken place. Once children witness their parents' use of divorce as a solution to their relationship problems, the same option remains

open as a possibility for them in solving their own future relationship problems. Not a good candidate.

**Correct Answer:**
The best answer is not only a negative response, but one that indicates a strong commitment to solving mutual problems, with divorce as an unacceptable alternative. The truth is—ALL—marital problems can be solved without divorce when both parties are pledged to reject divorce as an alternative, no matter what! Divorce never solves the problem; it only moves the problem forward to another place and time, for solution. On the contrary the damage caused by the divorce itself far outweighs the alternative costs or sacrifices, which could be implemented to deal directly with the problem and achieve a victory. Score one point.

**Debriefing, a most important experience:**

Needless to say, there are no perfect lists of questions and answers for such complex discoveries. However, imperfect as this list might be, it is never-the-less very important to—know in advance—what qualities must be present in a candidate to whom you are going to pledge your love. Once a commitment to love is made by our son or daughter and agreed upon by the other party also to pledge their love to them, there can be no turning back. From this point on, the only response to problems is to solve them within the relationship. Life will always present its exceptions to this rule, but it should be so rare—in the life of God's elect—as to be almost non-existent.

After the date—the father/daughter team or mother/son team—goes into debriefing—not formal perhaps—but certainly, in principle, it is a debriefing. This is very important for both teams. The son or daughter cannot expect to learn much from the date if they are not completely transparent with their coaches. The father cannot expect to be able to advise the daughter, nor the mother the son, if they do not have access to the facts and events of the date.

As stated in Book II, Chapter Eight, being transparent with Dad is the proper response of the daughter to her father's pledge to be her champion and coach in love and marriage. When properly prepared for this adventure, there is never any doubt in the mind of our son or daughter about being—completely open—and telling their father or mother everything about their dates. However, we must remember that each one—the daughter for father and the son for mother—will be most open to their natural confidant. Certainly there are feminine things a daughter will find easier telling her mother because her mother is a woman, but in the special relationship of the daughter with her—champion of love and marriage—father is the natural preference, the same can be said for the son and his mother.

**Reliving precious moments:**

A father and mother's first experience with this adventure will prove to be almost as exciting as their first date with each other, if not more so! The results of several years of work will be realized in an exchange of confidence and trust that only those men and women, who have the courage to be real fathers and mothers of faith and grace, will ever know. When you realize what is really taking place and you feel like crying, don't be ashamed. These are the tears of joy given to every real father and mother of faith and grace—as a special blessing—in place of the tears of rage and despair suffered by all those who are ignorant of the truth.

Personal discovery dating activities within the scope of this great adventure take on a different form from the—kissing, petting let's have sex norm—of today's post modern secular, "values reoriented" pre-teen or teen-age date. The structure of the personal discovery dating adventure for the son or daughter of the father and mother teams of faith and grace; is to give this—personal discovery dating couple—an opportunity to get to know the essence of each other's character, principles and goals for life.

As part of your teaching sessions with your son or daughter, you will discuss the different types of activities which you feel will best provide for this kind of structure. This will be somewhat different for each—father/daughter, mother/son—coaching team. Some will be able to afford things that others will not. The important thing is to select those activities and places that give them the opportunity to be with other young people near their age, and who are also committed to good morals and serious relationships. Seek out other committed parents of faith and grace—get to know them better—then decide if they are rearing the kind of son or daughter that you want your children to socialize with. If such parents have never read this book, encourage them to do so. If necessary buy them a copy. They will be greatly handicapped if they have not had any such training!

Unfortunately, in today's public school system, it is not wise to assume that a school activity provides the kind of structure in which you want your daughter and her escort to participate. However, participating in the context of a well-disciplined group, such activities can be quite successful.

The personal discovery dating practice should begin with the agreement from both your son or daughter and their candidate that they will keep their projects and pursuits limited to things they can do with an approved group of friends and acquaintances. In most instances, a youth group at your local church or some other church in your neighborhood will provide the best opportunity. There are other kinds of acceptable group activity, but it has been my experience that a local church with a good youth leader, one who exemplifies the kind of moral character you want your son or daughter and their candidate to emulate, is the best kind. Check it out and know who you are dealing with.

Also, when a youth group has a good solid leader, you will get third-party support for your role as father and mother family leaders. In fact, the only kind of youth group I will permit one of my sons or daughters to become a part of, must have such leadership! It is very important to have principled third-party influence, to allow your daughter the opportunity to get confirmation of what she is learning at home. This is not to say such parties have to agree in every detail with your standards or your approach in working with your daughter. It is the overall respect and appreciation for parents, especially the father, for which you want third-party support. The details of your relationship with your son or daughter are between the two of you, and you will find the relationship strengthened, when you have such support.

**Everything is not what it seems:**

However, be forewarned: not all pastors, priests or rabbis have a good grasp of fatherhood. Some of them are among the worst offenders of God's Great Commission for parents of faith and grace in the pursuit of a successful family! [162] There is a tendency among religious counselors to think they have a pre-eminent position over the parents in spiritual guidance for the child and, hence—to usurp—many things which must remain—in the realm of parents.

---

162 The worst example I have ever read of was posted just this last January on the Unitarian Universalist Church website. How anyone can say all of this about themselves and still say they are Christian only illustrates the extreme apostasy present in our country in some circles. ZH

"I come to this conversation as a big fan of marriage, both same-sex and straight, and with a background as a Catholic seminarian, a Unitarian Universalist for twenty-seven years, a university professor, and a practicing marriage and family therapist." William J. Doherty

> "We must also be careful as many pastors and churches have 'sold out' to the contraceptive message of 'free sex' as they claim they have to live with 'reality'. As I tell them the only reality you are living with is that of the flesh outside the Truth of Christ and you and those you counsel will reap destruction. The True Reality is the Truth of Christ, no matter what this temporary world may look like, at this present moment (all brought on by the Church 'selling out' on the Truth!" Greg Williams, State Director of Heritage Services of Kentucky.

It is your responsibility to check out such leaders before you recommend your family or your daughter to participate. Also, we fathers and mothers all must understand that we cannot delegate our son or daughter's spiritual, moral and maturity in love and marriage growth to a pastor or youth leader! We are God's delegated authority to be the major players in this process! We must be the point persons in all such development. This we will do as their champions of love and marriage and by practicing our faith day by day as we grow together with them! They are much more likely to do as we do, than to do only what we tell them to do.

**Positive third party influence:**

As an example of how much we fathers benefit from morally principled third party influence—with Christ's worldview for love and marriage—consider my situation with my high spirited daughter, Melissa. As she approached the age of twelve she was not too sure Dad was as all important for her development as I and her older sisters were telling her. She was open and obedient but not totally convinced. The gravity of her lukewarm response was cause for many moments of reflection and prayer for wisdom and direction.

Her big breakthrough came in the fall of 1983, she was 13. Early that year we had received an invitation to attend a family retreat conducted by Dr. Orv Owens, founder and director of "The Gold Card Family Retreat", a unique family structured conference held once a year in up-state New York on the shores of Lake George. My wife, Marilyn had reminded me several times of her perspective of positive influence for our daughters and the value she felt such a conference could have on all our family. Although I agreed with her in principle, I was deeply involved with business and felt the timing was bad. As time drew closer to make our reservations, Marilyn again brought up her perspective of the opportunity and the overall good it could be for our family. I could not argue against the value it could be for our family, I just could not see how we could financially afford to do it. Finally, I made the decision that we should go, not because I felt like the timing was right or that we could afford the money. I decided that Marilyn's intuition on the family and the benefit this retreat would have for us all had to take precedence over my business and financial concerns.

We took the three youngest, Stephanie, Melissa and Robin. Jennifer was married, David was away at college and Lorena was not yet a part of our family. The conference lasted five days. Adults and children were divided into separate groups. The children were further divided into age groups, thus allowing their instructors to better communicate with them on their level. Aside from meals and afternoon playtimes I didn't get to see or talk much with the children. The whole experience seemed to whiz by much too fast.

On our second day of travel as we were heading back home to California, Melissa leaned over the front seat and whispered in my ear that she had become convinced I was the most important person in her life at the moment. She said, "Daddy you can ask me to do anything you want to and I will do it. You have my complete trust and my word of honor that I will do as you say." It was like a bolt of lightning out of a clear, blue sky! I was overwhelmed with gratitude for her experience—and God's providence in using Marilyn to help me see the value of going—to the family retreat and for the positive influence of Melissa's instructors. I was speechless for several moments and could not hold back the tears.

Her instructors had confirmed many of the things I was teaching her at home about how important our relationship was to her present and future success and happiness. For her, that is what it took. I have experienced this kind of blessing many times over the years. Each of our children has at one time or another been assisted in their moral and character development by positive, family supportive third party influence.

Sometimes these third party influences come from the most unexpected places. Remember the children in the children's home in Mexico and how they were such a vital part in the process for Jennifer, our oldest daughter, revising her perspective of family and her part in it? Think what would have happened if she had been counseled by some of the kinds of children we have in today's schools—ours was an exceptional experience, a real miracle.

You might want to know: Melissa never broke her promise.

**Counting our blessings:**

The rewards of our trip were so stupendous I never did regret the money we spent. We ultimately attended a total of six of these conferences. Marilyn and I have a great deal of gratitude for these experiences and for those who made it possible. These experiences along with many other sources of encouraging people, as with third party confirmation of fatherhood and family values have greatly aided in the development and success of our family. You must seek out opportunities to get this kind of support. Don't assume that you are an island unto yourself and that you can go it alone. Such opportunities will be the best investment of time and resources you can do for yourself and your family. My only sadness at having mentioned this at this time—in the history of our post modern Christian culture—is that there are so few, almost none that I know of that will teach a husband and wife a truly biblically balanced worldview of Christ and His Great Commission for husbands and wives of faith and grace. By His grace we are committed to focus the rest of our lives along with—all who will join us—to be His messengers of this Great Commission for husbands and wives and for the glory of the Kingdom! Those who are like minded and who also feel motivated by God to be a part of this ministry, please see the Contact Information on page 327.

**Sons and daughters mature into marriage at different paces:**

Ladies first: her Knight in shining armor; the one who is someday to take your place as her new leader—in romance, love and family life—will appear at different times for different daughters. Some daughters need more time to mature and to learn the basics of accepting responsibilities. Such girls will not feel comfortable in launching into a life-time relationship until they have had more time to develop themselves. For some this will include going all the way through college or beyond. The desire of others will be apparent; they will want to start this life-long relationship much earlier. When—this new Knight appears—is not as important as—HOW—you handle this occurrence, and how well you have prepared your daughter to handle it.

Likewise, Mommy's little boy becomes a man and now it is your son who is that special Knight in shining armor for that special daughter of faith and grace from a Christian family like yours, a family of faith and grace, praying for God to work in their lives and to bring them His choice for their daughter. Your son will be the answer to that daughter's prayers and dreams!

The moment of their "discovery" might happen for them when they are away at college, or right in your own local church or neighborhood. When it happens, they need your support for them in this process. The—how you do it—is all in the faith, conviction and creativity you will put into it.

**Personal experience with one of our daughters:**

In order to give you an example of how soon a daughter can be ready to start a life-long commitment, I will share the moment, when I first learned from Melissa, our third oldest of five daughters, that she had discovered her Knight in shining armor.

We were living in Alexandria, Virginia, at the time. We had been attending a local church, primarily because of the quality of its youth leaders. Melissa, who at the time was only fifteen and a half years old, came up to me after church one day and said: "Daddy, I have found my Knight in shining armor."

Of all my daughters, Melissa had always demonstrated more maturity for her age. I used to tease her and tell her she was my fifteen-year-old, going on thirty. Never-the-less, a father is never quite ready for such a statement, especially from a daughter who has not even had an official date. I did my best to appear calm and collected.

I responded with the obvious question. "Honey, who is this young man, and how can you be so sure?"

"Daddy, he is the drummer boy in the church band. You taught me how to know when I found the right man, and I know he is the one! "

You must remember that by now this young girl had acquired several years of instruction and preparation for this, but never in my wildest dreams did I think she would make her discovery so rapidly. This is an example of how important it is to teach your daughter to recognize the qualities which represent the character, good moral fiber, and principles unique to a real man of faith and grace.

I did not find out until later, she had actually been introduced to Jay for the first time at a church party when she was only fourteen and knew then she was very attracted to him. We were living in California at the time and she never knew if she would ever see him again. It didn't seem important at the time to tell me about it. As providence would have it, we later moved to that community and began attending services at that church.

Love at first sight, you say? If you believe it is possible for God to bring your perfect mate to you, then that could have been her love at first sight. Believe me; I was quick to find out more concerning this young man and I was extremely pleased with what I discovered. He was highly regarded by all of the youth leaders and was known among his friends to be a very serious-minded young man. He was attending Virginia Tech, studying to be a mechanical engineer and was presently in his sophomore year.

"Like father, like son," is a good thing to remember. Without a doubt, a young man is going to reflect a lot of his father's qualities or lack thereof.

Understanding this, I proceeded to ask about his father also. I approached the men I knew who also had known him for some time. The reports I got were very good, and I was encouraged to continue to the very important step of "setting the stage."

How does a young man or woman know when they have discovered the woman or man of their dreams, their lifetime partner, Princess and Knight in shining armor? If she is a young girl or woman who has had the advantage of a true father of faith and grace, one who has taken the time and effort to teach her all the things I am sharing with you in this book, she will know! She is not alone—she is walking in God's wisdom—which she has learned from you and her own spiritual walk with you in this search. She will be as absolutely correct as this journey can be, you can depend on it. The same is true for the young man of a mother of faith and grace who applies Christ's worldview of love and marriage for her son.

When God has the victory over a majority of Christian men and women in America the pollsters will be blown away by the difference between—love and marriage for the families of men and women of faith and grace—and those who are uncommitted half hearted "believers" and those who do not believe!

> "These things says the Amen, the Faithful and True Witness, the Beginning of the creation of God: 'I know your works, that you are neither cold nor hot. I could wish you were cold or hot. So then, because you are lukewarm, and neither cold nor hot, I will vomit you out of My mouth. Because you say, 'I am rich, have become wealthy, and have need of nothing'—and do not know that you are wretched, miserable, poor, blind, and naked—I counsel you to buy from Me gold refined in the fire, that you may be rich; and white garments, that you may be clothed, that the shame of your nakedness may not be revealed; and anoint your eyes with eye salve, that you may see. As many as I love, I rebuke and chasten. Therefore be zealous and repent." Revelations 3:14-19.

Most important of all, once our son or daughter has made a decision, we must give them our undivided support. You have had years to give them all the input, in the form of advice and training possible, all in keeping with the best of your abilities as you have learned from God's revealed Law-Word. Once this is accomplished a father and mother of faith and grace must trust their son or daughter to use all they have given them and through God's grace and enablement to make the right choice.

Sometimes there is only a tentative response to a certain discovery, such as, "Maybe this is the right one." When this occurs, then it is yet to be determined if, indeed, this is his Princess or her true Knight in shining armor. However, as you and your son or daughter move through the different phases of following up on positive responses, they will soon know which one is for real.

# Book III
# MOMMY'S LITTLE BOY

## Chapter Four

## Sons and Posterity

"My son, keep my words, And treasure my commands within you. Keep my commands and live, and my law as the apple of your eye. Bind them on your fingers; write them on the tablet of your heart. Say to wisdom, 'You are my sister,' and call understanding your nearest kin, that they may keep you from the immoral woman, from the seductress who flatters with her words." Proverbs 7:1-5

**A son is born:**

It was a little past midnight on March 24, 1964, and the nurse was wheeling Marilyn into the delivery room at the Centro Medico, Juarez, Chihuahua, Mexico. In those days we did not have the advantage of sonograms to let us know the sex of our unborn child. It would be a few more minutes before I would be told that our second child was a boy—David Michael Hatfield—our only child to be born a citizen of Mexico.

They soon had Marilyn all setup in her own room and we were both giddy with the realization that we were now the proud parents of a new baby boy. We often spoke to each other of our desires to have a big family—at one point we had dreamed of having twelve—but more importantly we wanted at least two sons. My father and mother had only had one son; me. Marilyn's parents also had only had one son; Curtis—now a missionary in China. We had mentioned in many of our prayers that we would love to have at least two sons—by the size of our family—it is obvious that we were serious, but God had other plans for us—lots of daughters!

As there were no sonograms—our choice of having this baby born in a Mexican hospital—was solely a matter of providence. I remember thinking it would be so great if my son could have more freedom to work in some ministry capacity in Mexico, as the legal limitations are very strict for foreigners in almost everything in Mexico and especially in ministry. There might never be a call on our son's life for ministry in Mexico but he has been a great positive impact on one family—that of his lovely wife Elia—from Chilpancingo, Guerrero, Mexico.

David and Elia have only one child, David Zester, named after his father and grandfather. However, for many years they were the foster parents to Sarah a much younger sister of Elia's, who is now back with her birth mother and her new step-father. Elia's mother, Sabina and her new husband Bill are both Christians and have started a new life together after having been single for many years.

**Foster and adopted sons:**

You might remember that I mentioned in Book II, Chapter One that I had also other sons, from our work as missionaries in Mexico. I mentioned only one in particular, Jose Compean and his wife Clara.

Jose, in some ways, is very much like what you will discover when you meet our adopted daughter, Lorena, which I will present to you in the *Epilog, Chapter Two, The Rest of The Story*. *Jose* was one of five brothers who came to live in the

Hogar de Ninos Emmanuel. He was only seven when he came, the next to the youngest. It was always in my heart to develop the same kind of deep relationship with each boy in the home that I possibly could. We are blessed that many of the boys grew up to be good providers for their families, not all, but many professed a strong faith in Christ. However, Jose was the—only one—who actually responded as a true son of faith and grace. There were many times during Jose's development that the possibility looked bleak. At first he was very responsive, and then later as a teenager he used his considerable intellect to explore and embrace a communist form of reasoning. We had many heated discussions about this and when it seemed like there was never going to be any compatibility on the subject the Lord blessed Jose with the gift of faith and his whole life took an entirely different direction.

Jose and Clara; after many years of struggle—coming from early circumstances that looked impossible, to what God has blessed them with today—have accomplished things that are truly remarkable. They are blessed with four children, a successful business and the largest native missionary work in all of northern Mexico. Clara is a great example of a Proverbs 31 wife for Jose, as she now manages most of the arts and crafts business that they use as their main personal financial support. Their ministry work is strongly supported by both native Mexican and American sources.

This last July, 2004, as a foster father and foster grandfather, I was honored to assist in the wedding of their oldest daughter, Perlita and her Knight In Shining Armor, Mark Livengood, to serve as their translator for the service. There were about three hundred in attendance with almost half being from the USA and speaking only English. So I was challenged to translate from Spanish to English and English to Spanish, as there were participants from both ethnic language groups. This is another proof that transgenerational success in love and marriage is possible for those who are blessed with God's gift of faith.

**A call to missions:**

In 1993 I wrote the book *"Knights In Shining Armor"* which was my first literary work on the subject of father/daughter relationships. Only a limited number of this work was ever printed as it was intended primarily for my own sons, and son-in-laws. A copy of the Spanish translation was given to Jose, who at the time was a young father of two daughters and one son, Perla being the oldest. Jose has testified to other men that the principles discussed and discovered in this work were fundamental to the successful relationship he and Perla were able to experience. He was a successful father of faith and grace to bring her and God's chosen Knight for her, to their point of mutual commitment of love and marriage!

Mark is a graduate of Moody Bible Institute. Mark met Perla while on mission trips from his home church, in Ohio as a sophomore and as a junior in High School. On a subsequent trip two years before finishing his schooling at Moody, Mark asked Perla if she would wait for him. She said that she would wait for him. True to his word, Mark came back to Mexico in 2003 and he worked with her father Jose, founder of Juventud Con Vision of Mexico, for almost a year while he and Perla grew in their love and appreciation of each other. They were committed to serve the cause of Christ in Mexico even from before the day of their wedding.

Jose and Clara are very blessed and grateful to Christ for His manifold evidences of grace and wisdom—in their efforts as parents of faith and grace—for Perla and their other three children. Perla is the first to make the complete transition from their family of faith and grace to one of her own with her new husband Mark. This is always a time of great hope—but never more so—than when it becomes a reality, for those who have applied the principles and discoveries that you have made or reinforced while reading in this book.

**Sons and the next generation:**

The life of every man and woman of faith and grace is lived out as part of God's sovereign will—that awesome mosaic, master plan—of which we only get small glimpses once in a great while. The dreams that they have for a son take on different proportions than those they usually have for a daughter. A son brings a very special possibility to a family, especially as regards the family name. Both father and mother have made sacrifices and huge investments in their family and the name goes with the family—a son is their hope[163] for the continuation of their name and life as a man of faith and grace for the next generation—hopefully to be used mightily by God for great things in the Kingdom.

**A mothers' love for her son:**

A son establishes a new family; becomes the head and spiritual leader for his wife and children. This creates a more pronounced separation for a mother than the new family of a daughter. Fathers are rarely competition for the new father and head of a daughter's family. But it is quite common for a new wife—to assume that there is pressure to crowd her position as the new Queen of the Universe forever—because of the strength of the close relationship her husband had with his mother! Thus: we have the age old stories of the; "wicked mother-in-law."

Marilyn has always been there for all of the children in all of their needs and joys—yet her heart and her prayers for our son David can only be characterized as—very special! Her love as a mother is most especially demonstrated in the surrender of her special place—as his first one and only queen, while he grew to be a man—to Elia his new Queen of the Universe forever. Mothers of faith and grace must accept God's new role for their little boy! They must cut the apron strings that so often cause pain and heartache in new families—because mother won't let go!

**The ties that bind:**

Mothers and fathers of faith and grace will always feel a special connection to their children. Yet, these children are only gifts from God our Heavenly Father. We are His foreordained stewards and guardians of these precious souls that He lends to us as children for a time. They are our joy for the present and our hope as our progeny for future generations—but always first and foremost—they are His! All our prayers for them and the many grandchildren they bring into our lives are for their good and for their overcoming, of all the challenges and problems that life might bring. We pray fervently for God to bless them with the gift of faith that He will become the strength and source for all of their success through Christ their Savior.

**A mother's prayers and perspective transcend time and space:**

My mother always prayed for me and was so careful to let me be the leader of my family. She would always tell me what she thought I needed her to say for my—personal benefit—but she always had only praise for Marilyn, my new Queen of the Universe forever. My mother told me many times before she died at the age of 100 that no matter how old I lived to be—I would always be her little boy!

---

163 "The father of the righteous will greatly rejoice, and he who begets a wise child will delight in him. Let your father and your mother be glad, and let her who bore you rejoice. My son, give me your heart,..." Proverbs 23:24-26.

[illegible]

# Epilogue

# Chapter One

# The Wedding

**Timing is everything:**

Setting the date for the wedding is more than just a decision about the best time for the families to get together, the time of year, or how much money to spend. The date for the wedding can certainly take all of these things into consideration. However, it is—not the overriding principle—determining when an engaged couple should get married.

We have discussed the many important factors about virtue: virginity, morals, principles, sexuality and sexual expressions, which greatly affect a father's young princess who is preparing for marriage. These factors and how they are protected or abused form the foundation of your daughter's femininity. These aspects of her thinking and experience are the very moral fiber and building blocks of her character. You must now be convinced. Your daughter is a very complex and precious being—one who deserves the best opportunity possible to establish her God-given dream—of love and marriage that lasts forever!

By this time, you will have spent years helping her—build this strong and wonderful character and nurturing her God-given intuition—for virtue and true love. To risk damaging such important and precious moral fiber and building blocks, which are so central to her future well being and happiness, is unthinkable!

All of these factors put together form the emotional, psychological, and spiritual make-up of your daughter. Consequently, protecting the integrity of your daughter's delicate and complex nature is the primary factor for setting the wedding date.

As proof of my commitment to protect my daughters, I let them know that all of the wedding plans and ideal times to get married—were secondary—to their successful intimate relationship with their husband. Therefore my instructions to my daughters were simple and to the point. If at any time during the engagement she finds herself in a romantic situation in which she does not feel she can restrain herself much longer before engaging in intimate sexual activity with her Knight in shining armor, then she is simply to say so, and a wedding date will be set immediately. The wedding can take place within a week or less, if necessary. None of our daughters had need for a wedding within such a short time, but wedding dates were definitely accelerated in more than one case.

**The daughter's Champion of love and romance seeks only her success!**

This kind of support and commitment from the father gives the daughter more self-confidence every step of the way. Even if things move too fast and too hot, she knows you are there to provide her with the structure and back-up she needs to be successful. The very knowledge that you support her all the way increases her resolve to live up to the standards of her intuition for virtue and life-long love and marriage. This kind of father/daughter understanding is a fail-safe mechanism offering the kind of security and peace of mind every daughter needs.

My daughter Stephanie, who is three years older than Melissa, attended Eastern College in Saint David. Pennsylvania. Her mother and I went with her to inspect the campus, which is built on a beautiful old estate property fifteen miles west of Philadelphia. Stephanie took us up on a wooded hillside overlooking the campus directly in front of what had originally been the estate owner's family mansion. Stone stairways wound down from the mansion on two sides of the hill and met about half way down in a large stone-fenced landing. From the landing the steps continued down the hill to a beautiful small lake with a picturesque water wheel, turned by the water discharging from the lake.

It was in the fall of 1986, bright autumn colors and wooded hillsides with a mixed variety of evergreen and deciduous trees dominated the landscape. We all went down the steps leading from the mansion to the first landing. When we got there, Stephanie put her arms around me and said:

"Daddy, when I get married I want you to have the wedding right here, and I want to walk down these steps to meet my Knight in shining armor."

I said it was indeed a beautiful spot for a wedding and that I would do all I could to ensure it happened right here, just as she wanted it.

During the fall and winter of that year, Stephanie met her Knight in shining armor, Keith Avellino. After they were engaged, they thought they would continue their education at the college in Saint David, Pennsylvania. Things did not work out that way. They needed to be closer to me and to the support and structure which I was able to afford them during their engagement period. Also, the time span from the beginning of the engagement to the original wedding date was over two years. Many parents and young couples make disastrous mistakes when they try to force themselves into preconceived molds—set by a materialistic hedonist society which places a higher value on education and career planning—than it does on moral fiber, strong character, and successful marriages.

**Changes are sometimes necessary:**

It was a career and educational sacrifice for Stephanie and Keith to change colleges and move their education closer to where I could help them with their romantic structure and development. It is not necessary in every case to do something like this, but in their case it was. The change in educational location and the time table for their continued education were of small consequence, compared to the life-long value of their proper personal discovery dating and engagement experience.

At the time they mentioned their wedding date, I said to them that it was nice to have such long-range plans, but if they began to feel pressured and strained in their efforts to maintain their objectives for sexual virtue, they should consider a much earlier date.

During this period the romance between Melissa and Jay was moving ahead, and by the end of 1986, Jay had presented to Melissa an engagement ring, and a wedding date had been set for May of 1988. About a year later, still unaccustomed to the idea that I would be giving Melissa away to Jay in May of 1988, Stephanie and Keith told me they had reconsidered their wedding plans and felt it would be better to get married in June of 1988.

Just try and imagine, if you can, what it is like to prepare for two weddings only one month apart, and to experience the emotions of giving away two precious daughters who had discovered their Knights in shining armor. My feelings and the whole combination of emotions are very hard to put into words.

**Father moves aside and makes way for the new Knight in Shining Armor:**

These two weddings represented the culmination of many years of father/daughter instructions, love, relationship building and team effort. Thousands of hours of talking and sharing had gone into these two wonderful daughters, much more than I had done for my older daughters. I had learned a lot from my earlier mistakes, and these two girls were the results of my greatest efforts. After these daughters we still had one daughter at home, Robin Elizabeth, twenty years old and in college, and a future adopted daughter that we did not even know at this time. So, we were not finished yet. The challenge goes on, and so does the joy and the rewards of living the victories.

Breaking such a strong tie between father and daughter is not easy. In the traditional wedding, in which the father acknowledges that he and his wife are giving the bride away, it seems easy. In reality, for fathers who really care for their daughters, and especially for those who have invested much effort and time in preparing their daughters for marriage, it is anything but easy.

By the time the wedding ceremony is underway, most brides are caught up in the wedding itself. They are immersed in such a world of beauty, romance, aspirations and nerves, I don't imagine they have much time or emotional energy left to consider what their fathers are feeling.

However, this breaking of the tie is as close to the daughter's death that you will ever feel, short of the real thing. The emotions to hang on to her longer are strong. The reality of her new role now and forever, as the Queen of some other Knight in shining armor, some other man, is overpowering. The new relationship will be much more intimate and sexually oriented than the father/daughter love and marriage team you will have experienced together. This is the moment you both have worked and prayed would come about—now it is here—you are about to walk her down the aisle to give her away, there is a sudden consciousness you feel, the old relationship is gone and she is moving into a new world, a new family. These sensations bring feelings of both joy and sadness.

What brings a father back to the moment and away from his own mixed feelings is the joy and radiant beauty he can see in the eyes and presence of his daughter on that momentous day.

Changing the guard is part of the process of breaking the ties. The new Knight in shining armor is now going to be fully in charge of the well-being and success of your daughter. You have been the guardian of her virtue, and her guide for the development of her values and character up to this moment. From this day forward, for the rest of her life, she is in the hands of the man you both have prayed for, and have decided is the man for her.

**There is a new head and a new covenant family of faith and grace!**

The new Knight is now taking the reigns of a new life together with your daughter, a life in which they hope and pray to be able to raise a wonderful family, realize their personal goals of children, careers, and romantic love and happiness.

The statistical odds are not in their favor. Well over fifty percent of all first time marriages end in a tragic divorce. Divorce is the evidence of changed minds and attitudes. Once where there was a decision to love and to commit, now in divorce, there is a decision to hate and to cast off. The wounds inflicted leave deep scars which are never completely healed. The family is broken apart, and the children suffer a loss the likes of which no human being should ever be asked to endure.

As a father you cannot ignore the dangers that threaten your daughter and her new Knight, as they embark upon this new and exciting adventure. Yet, in your role as a real father of faith and grace you will have done all you can, and you will have given her a great advantage over what is normally experienced, in our present world of uncommitted relationships. You can trust, first of all, in God, to help the new couple and their new family, and secondly, you can trust in the wisdom you taught your daughter and new son- in-law. You will have touched the most central of all of their natural desires and motivations, for quality and excellence in their relationship. You will have given them the very foundation of their efforts and commitment, to overcome all the obstacles this life can throw at them. There is only one thing left to do. Relax! Enjoy the wedding! After all, you are paying for it!

Giving the bride away should be more than just a near- inaudible grunt! In every wedding I have attended, except the last two, when I was giving away my own daughters, all I have ever heard from the father was this nearly inaudible grunt, which acknowledged he was giving his daughter away. Even I was guilty of this on my own first occasion, when I gave away my daughter, Jennifer, to Paul O'Neill.

Weddings are more than just ceremony. The process of having a wedding, of inviting the guests who are the couples' witnesses to their vows of commitment, and all the activities of the day, are very important. The events of such a day will forever be inscribed on the hearts and minds of your daughter and new son-in-law. The new husband may be thinking more of the upcoming wedding night and what he hopes will be a new experience of sexual bliss; this is not so for the bride. Although she is not oblivious to the up-coming sexual discoveries, she is more focused on who is at the wedding and what is being said, both in song and in the words of the pastor or priest officiating.

**Fathers parting words ring forever in the mind of a bride of faith and grace:**

However, no pastor, priest or rabbi can say anything as memorable for your daughter and her new husband as the words you can say to them. You are the one who has been in the forefront of this growing relationship and romance. You are the love and marriage team captain who has shepherded this couple to this successful moment, joining their lives together for evermore. What you say is important. It doesn't have to be long, but it should leave them with a feeling of your complete approval—approval of each of them, of their love—coupled with your undying support for the success and happiness of their new life together.

As the moment grew near to give Melissa away on the day of her wedding, I found a quiet place where I could think. I was unsatisfied with the traditional role a father usually plays in a wedding, saying little or nothing. I felt a need to express how I was feeling and how much I approved of my daughter and her new husband-to-be. I was determined to break with tradition, and to say something to illustrate, in as few words as possible, the depth and importance of their love and courtship and of my complete approval and support.

I wrote down in a few lines what I thought would best express my feelings and desires of the moment. I placed them between the pages of my Bible, and when I was standing with Melissa in front of the pastor, and he asked the traditional question: "Who gives this bride away?" I responded by looking: first at Jay, and I read the following words:

- "Jay, in November of 1986, you asked for the privilege of marrying Melissa and of becoming her husband, to be her protector, her provider and her lover.

- "Knowing of your love for her, her mother and I agreed and the two of you became engaged

- "Jay, at that time, as her father, I asked you to be obedient to me and to follow my instructions until I could give her to you to be your bride.

- "1 delegated to you the headship and authority over her, which God had given to me as her father, so that she could look to you as her new headship and authority and cultivate a spirit of understanding and commitment for you, as her future husband.

- "You kept your promise, and her mother and I are very proud and honored this day to have you as our new son!"

Then I looked at Melissa. (I tried not to look directly into her eyes; she was crying and I was struggling not to cry myself.) I read to her the following words:

- "Melissa, when you were only a young child, I promised, as your father, to give to you my complete support, to lead you, protect you and be everything I could be for you, until God would provide a young man for you, to be your wonderful new head and leader, and to be, for you, all things in personal care, provision and romantic fulfillment.

- "You agreed to work with me and to follow my instructions. You kept your promise and God answered your prayers and has given to you the man of your dreams!

- "Your mother and I love you and we are very proud to give you this day to Jay, to be his beautiful bride forever!"

**Stephanie's dream comes true:**
A month later, I felt the same emotions for Stephanie and Keith. The past relationship was over, and only the future, their new family, lay ahead.

Stephanie's dream had come true. Her most ardent prayers for a real man of faith and grace, who would commit to love her forever, had been answered. In addition to all the other victories she was celebrating on that day, she was also privileged to be having her wedding on those very steps, on the campus of Eastern College, in Saint David, Pennsylvania.

We walked together down the long winding steps, reached the landing where she had asked me to promise to have her wedding, on this very hillside. We paused a moment and I asked her if she remembered this spot. She squeezed my arm and we walked on down to the bottom of the hill, where Keith and the pastor were waiting.

Once again: when I was asked the question, "Who gives this bride away?" I looked first at Keith and read the following words:

- "Keith, in September of 1986, you discovered a young lady on this college campus, who was destined to capture your love and devotion; her name is Stephanie.

- "In April of 1987, you accepted the challenge of receiving Stephanie as your fiancée and the challenge of protecting her above all others, so that one day you could stand on this very spot and receive her as your wonderful and beautiful bride forever.

- "Keith, her mother and I are proud to give Stephanie to you this day and to receive you as our new son.

- "May God bless you and give you great wisdom and courage all the days of your life!"

Then I looked at Stephanie. (I was getting stronger at this, since it had only been four weeks previously that I had given Melissa away to Jay. So, I was in a little more control, and was not quite so close to crying. Maybe it was—Spring and the outdoor fresh air—that helped keep me a little more composed. Believe me, it is not easy for a father to speak at such moments as these, but it is worth the effort!) I read to her the following words:

- "Stephanie, as a little girl, I promised to be your guide and to champion your personal development and your dreams for the perfect man, who would capture your love and devotion forever.
- "In August of 1986, when we first visited this campus, you took me to the top of these magnificent steps and told me that when you found the man of your dreams, you wanted to be married here on these steps.
- "Stephanie, you have found that man in Keith, and today your mother and I are proud to give you to Keith, to be his beautiful bride forever!"

Be creative—you can do better than I did—I know because I have heard and participated in better presentations by others. I'm sure that when the moment comes for you to give your daughter away, you too will want to say more than just the traditional; "Her mother and I," or something else hardly audible. You will want to mark the occasion with the best words of love and support for this new love and new family possible. It will not be easy for you to speak but if you write it down, as I did, and muster up the courage, you can do it. Remember, you are doing it for her and her new husband.

# Epilog
# DADDY'S LITTLE GIRL & MOMMY'S LITTLE BOY

## Chapter Two
## The Rest of the Story

**Many children make for a variety of experiences:**

The more children we have the more we realize how each one is so different. When it comes to daughters we have had five wonderful and very different experiences. You have already been introduced to Jennifer, Stephanie and Melissa. There are two more daughters, Robin and Lorena, who are very special and very different in their own personal ways.

**Slow is sometimes the only way:**

Robin is our fourth daughter and only fourteen calendar months younger than her older sister Melissa, but her emotional and academic develop lagged more than three years behind that of Melissa. At first there was no noticeable difference in the speed of her development, in fact her physical development seemed faster. She was very physically active and into everything. One difference could have warned us of what to expect with other things—but at the time—it didn't. This was her inability to digest anything but Marilyn's breast milk and cooked carrots.

Some readers might remember when the first simulated breast milk formulas came on the market. This happened the year Robin was born and it was what saved her life. Robin being the fourth child and only fourteen months after Marilyn gave birth to Melissa, had weakened Marilyn's milk producing capabilities. Instead of having more than enough milk—which was usual for Marilyn—she found her milk running low and Robin still asking for more. To make a long story short—we tried everything from goat's milk to the latest formulas. Then a Pediatrician told us that he thought that a new product: Pregestamil might actually be what she needed. We bought some that same day and Robin took it down without throwing it back up—Wow—what a victory. A wet nurse might have also served our needs, but in those days and where we were on the mission field, none were available.

Robin was three years old before she could start assimilating regular food, except for the one food that had served as her only other source besides the Pregestamil—cooked carrots. This became a pattern for her.

As a young student was so distracted and uninterested in studying that Marilyn had to spend a lot of personal time with her and—even that was not enough—so we hired a young high school girl from our local church that came to the house every night and worked with Robin. In her delayed way, Robin started college two years later than her sisters and yet, after her first year she received a full scholarship to attend the Oral Robert's School of Nursing in Tulsa, Oklahoma. Robin—the slow one—is our only daughter to have received a full scholarship! She graduated in the spring of 1996 and received her Bachelor of Science in Nursing.

**Robin's dream comes true at last:**

Robin—true to her way—married at twenty seven to another person who also had a history of being slow to develop but also very brilliant and very mature. She was introduced to Rick Osborn of Springfield, Virginia, by a fellow student from their old Christian high school in Alexandria, Virginia and it was love at first sight for both of them. Rick is a computer programmer and computer securities expert with a major defense contractor in Manassas, Virginia. Robin continues to keep up with her nursing profession on a very part-time basis—like only one day every two weeks: pediatric nurses are in such high demand she can tell them when she can work and when she can't.

Robin and Rick went through almost exactly the same process as did the other daughters—just a little older—when it all took place. They were married on March 6, 1999 and are now the proud parents of two boys and one girl—you guessed it—their children are developing at about the same pace they did. Funny—isn't it—how life is like that?

**Some daughters choose their parents:**

In 1991, when Robin first began her university studies at UTEP—University of Texas at El Paso—she met, Lorena, a lovely young blond girl from Mexico who had immigrated, with her mother, to the USA when she was twelve years old.

The people of Mexico are not all dark skinned with dark hair. Mexico, like the USA has many different ethnic groups. One of the principle ethnic groups is that of the, Spaniards, who conquered the Aztec Indians and took over the country under the leadership of Cortez. I'm sure you remember that many Spaniards are very light complexioned and often with blond or red hair. For you history buffs, you will remember that El Cid, a famous Spanish General, had blond hair.

Lorena's biological father is a light complexioned Mexican with red hair and her mother is from Parral, Chihuahua, Mexico and of light complexion and dark hair. Lorena has two sisters, one fair and blond like her and one like her mother, her three brothers also have very light complexions.

This friendship; became as close—as any two sisters—have ever had. First: as just two young ladies going to the same school. Then Robin invited Lorena to attend a retreat organized by InterVarsity Christian Fellowship. This Christian group along with Robin's love and care for Lorena, served as God's catalyst to reveal His gift of faith to Lorena. Robin is three years older than Lorena and she became Lorena's "older sister" and her closest confidant. Within just two years Lorena would choose to become our fifth and youngest daughter.

**A surprising proposal is made:**

Robin brought Lorena home with her several times—they studied together—and went to Christian youth meetings together. Marilyn and I knew Lorena only as Robin's friend from school. According to Lorena, Robin would often mention her relationship with me as a father of faith and grace and as her champion for love and marriage. This was something very new for Lorena. Her own father had abandoned her mother and their children when Lorena was only eighteen months old. She never really knew a functioning father of any kind. The whole idea of a real father—one who would love her and be a champion of love and marriage—was more like a miracle for.

One Sunday afternoon, Marilyn and I had just returned from church when the two girls popped in—full of energy and excitement—something was up! It went something like this:

> "Oh, Daddy I've got something very important I want to ask you and mother. You know how that I am going to go to Oral Robert's University this coming fall and I won't need my room anymore. Well—what I want to know is—what we want to know is—will you and Mom let Lorena stay here and live with you while I'm at Oral Roberts?"

**Some background:**

Robin and Lorena then began to explain to us how her mother did not understand Lorena's new faith in Christ and that she also was against her boy friend, Bobby Maddox—a young man she met at the Intervarsity meetings—also a Christian. The abandonment of Lorena's dad from her mother had deeply embittered her to the point of losing all confidence in men—any man—of any kind. As a result of this lost confidence, Lorena's mother had spent much of her time—disparaging Lorena's two older sisters in their marriages—to the point that their families and children were extremely impacted. Her sister, just older than she, had already been divorced once and was currently in a very bad relationship. Her oldest sister was having serious moral problems of her own and her husband was openly living with another woman on the side. The whole scene was one of family dysfunction and moral collapse on all sides.

Lorena's mother—as with the majority of Mexicans, is a traditional Catholic who does not believe in Christ through faith—but holds a hope that the Catholic church will somehow protect her and ultimately save her. However, in stark contrast to this centuries old apostasy, the gospel message of salvation through faith and that not of ourselves—but a gift from God—is permeating the post modern Catholic Church at record rates. This has been especially true under the reign of the late Pope, John Paul II, a man who personally testified of his salvation through faith in Christ. However, there is a great gulf between the traditional doctrines of the Catholic Church and God's revealed Law-Word.[164]

The point of complete despair for Lorena came when her mother had begun to accuse her of immoral conduct with Bobby. Lorena is a very attractive young lady, well groomed with good poise. Her life as a young girl, before we ever met her, was one that had been—very providentially—blessed by God. Although she had been exposed to young Mexican men from well-to-do families she had never allowed any of them to be more than just the kind of friends you talk to and no more. If a woman is a natural blond in Mexico or in the Southwest of the US where the Latin community is very large—she is a great attraction—to any and all Mexican males. She was later able to tell me that even at a very early age she had a sense that God was preparing her for a special man who would be her husband and that she was supposed to be a virgin when she married.

**Taking a big step:**

Our first reaction was to look at each other and take a deep breath. We had counseled other young girls and we had even accepted four other young girls—all of whom were Mexican girls—to live with us as daughters. We knew that our home could never be just a place for Lorena to sleep—it would have to be her home as a daughter—or she could not stay.

We agreed to pray about the matter and that on the next Sunday we would have our answer for them. The girls accepted this and again presented themselves on the following Sunday afternoon to get our answer.

Marilyn and I had talked it over and indeed we had taken the matter to the Lord in prayer to ask for assurances, that this was—our place to be and the right thing to do—at this time in our lives. By week's end we both felt that we were to offer Lorena the covering of real parents of faith and grace and that if she were to be a part of our family she could not come as anything less than as a daughter in every sense of the word—love, support, team player in a love and marriage

---

164 "The next pope may discover his calling is to demonstrate tellingly that, in man's affairs, man doesn't come first, God does. A truly daunting task. But if it could be brought off, well, for one thing, we'd need no binocular-toting journalists to spread the news." Bill Murchison, in a post John Paul II article posted on Townhall.com, April 5, 2005.

covenant with me as father and Marilyn as her supportive mother. She would also be required to agree to be a daughter worthy of discipline—when such was necessary. These thoughts were the main part of our confirmation; the other part would be that her mother must voluntarily allow her to make such a decision. At eighteen, she could make it without her mother, but we purposed that it could only be with her mother's blessing—this was a test!

**Facing the challenge:**

The two girls sat down and waited for our response to this challenging—and potentially life changing proposal—things got a little quiet. We all held hands and joined our minds together in a short prayer to ask our Lord for wisdom and understanding and for confirmation of what our actions should be.

I then presented a question to Lorena that embodied all of our conditions for accepting the responsibility to serve as adopted parents for her, except the part about her mothers blessing. Lorena was so moved she could not hold back the tears and she said that to be in our family as a daughter exceeded her greatest expectations. She also agreed that to be a daughter would require that she submit to correction and discipline.

Then came the moment of truth; a moment that was to prove—both the most challenging as well as the greatest victory—over the whole process. I took Lorena's hands in mine and as I looked her in the eyes I said:

"Lorena there is one thing that must happen before we can do this."

I could see a moment of doubt and fear in her eyes as she waited for me to clarify just what it was that would have to happen, to transform her hope of a new father and mother of faith and grace, into a reality. I continued and said:

"Lorena I must talk with your mother and somehow, by God's grace gain her support and blessing in this new relationship between you and our family."

All of the pent up emotion and expectant hope that a young girl could possibly have just burst forth in one flowing motion of her tears and her arms coming up to hug me and her broken sobbing words:

"Oh no—my mother will never give her permission—this is impossible!"

I could only hold her and whisper in her ear that I understood how she felt but that with God all things are possible and that we had no choice but to call her mother, set up an appointment and meet with her—if possible—that very afternoon. I remember so well how she drew back and looked at me with eyes that seemed to say:

"I want to believe but this is beyond anything I can imagine!"

She gathered her composure and said:

"I'm not sure if she is home this afternoon, sometimes she visits my sister on Sunday afternoons, but I'll try."

**Making the move:**

Lorena picked up the phone and called her mother. To the great relief of us all her mother was home and readily accepted an appointment for that afternoon to speak with Marilyn and me. So the three of us went to visit Lorena's mother—who had never met us before—and who had not the slightest idea why we wanted to speak to her. Personally, I was overjoyed at the prospects; I had a sense of great peace about the whole thing. Her mother being home, her acceptance of our meeting, Lorena's whole hearted willingness to be a daughter of faith and grace, under covenant love and discipline—all witnessed to me—that our meeting was going to be very successful.

We arrived and after short introductions I presented to Lorena's mother the principles of God's revealed Law-Word regarding a daughter's great need for a father to direct her in matters of romance, sex, love and marriage in order to insure her greatest possible success for a happy life-long relationship with her future husband. I pointed out how I suspected that she already had some important insights into this matter—given the facts surrounding the failure of her two other daughters—to realize any success in their attempts at marriage. I assured her that this was more the fault of her husband who had abandoned her and her daughters than it was her own. I encouraged her to believe that although she could not understand the—details of the process—one thing was for sure. Not only would Lorena develop into a successful candidate for marriage but that they would both become more successful in their relationship as mother and daughter. I told her that although it appeared that she was giving up her daughter, she was actually setting in motion the process of regaining her daughter.

**God's gift of a new daughter:**

Somewhere in the midst of my short presentation to Lorena's mother, she began to cry. I believed then and still maintain that her tears were mixed: they were tears of hope that what I was saying was true; relief that somehow, someway she was going to receive help in a matter that she intuitively knew was beyond her. Her reaction to all that I said was more emotional than I expected but the outcome was never in doubt. When I finished she looked at me and said:

> "Yes, you have my permission for Lorena to live with your family. I pray that what you say is true and that you will be able to return her to me."

As we drove back to our home to give the good news to Robin—Lorena could not stop saying how she could not believe that her mother had just agreed to let her leave and to live with us as a daughter in our family.

**A daughter by choice:**

Of our five daughters, only one chose to be our daughter, and she is treasured for that and more importantly for her whole hearted commitment to the process. She submitted to discipline, she was attentive to all my instructions and she grew to understand and appreciate her biological mother as never before. They are still distant in faith but they are friends and of all her children, Lorena is the only one who has a marriage and family of faith and grace.

Lorena and Bobby were engaged the next year, and after three years crammed to the brim with daily attention to her development in romance, sex, love and marriage I was honored to give her away to Bobby Maddox as his beautiful bride forever. You guessed it—her mother was there, rejoicing in a daughter regained—and honored to join me in giving her away.

Lorena and Bobby now have two lovely boys, Ben and Sam, two of our twenty grandchildren—gifts from God and part of our hope—for tomorrow.

# Epilog

# DADDY'S LITTLE GIRL & MOMMY'S LITTLE BOY

## Chapter Three

## As Life Goes On

**Unspeakable joy:**

The joy of being a real father of faith and grace is not easy to convey in words alone. It is a lot like trying to tell your friends how you felt when your team won its first National title, or how you felt when you made your first solo flight. Fatherhood offers men an experience of joy and satisfaction of the highest order!

We men will never know what a mother feels when she first holds her new born child in her arms and caresses it to her breast for the first time. She is powerless to tell us how it feels, although she would do all she could to make us understand. We could let our desire to know and to have such an experience lead us into all kinds of frustration and abnormal activity. We could march on Washington, demand that we be taken more seriously, and pass laws that would give us the right to be mothers, and to have children, and it would all be to no avail. We have been born with God-given physical characteristics and emotional aspirations which do not include the role of mother or the birthing experience.

On the other hand, women cannot know the unspeakable joy of being a real father of faith and grace. The joy of seeing our children grow up with the self-discipline, moral values and principles which bring success in personal and family goals, can be shared by the mother, but only the father has the secret to make it happen. On the surface a real father of faith and grace looks like any other man you might meet on the street. However, underneath the surface there beats a heart filled with commitment and determination—animated and enabled to succeed by and through the presence of Christ who ordained him to the position—to not allow circumstance and bad breaks to destroy his children or the love he has for them and his wife.

**No higher calling:**

Things, positions and friends have their place in life, but in the heart of a real father of faith and grace, none of these is a priority to be held above the successful development of his family. When he walks into his house, he has the sense and presence of true love, warmth and respect. There is no place on the face of the earth where he can go or be present, where he can get such a feeling. The arms of his wife are more precious and desirable than all the other female arms in the world. There are no sexual joys or heights of intimate ecstasy to be compared with or achieved like those he has with her, the Queen of his world! None other can give to him what she can give him. In addition to the sexual intimacies and feminine tenderness, she gives him his honor in his role as family leader. She honors and respects him before their children. He is indeed a Knight in shining armor, a King in his own castle.

A man can be elected to political office or enrolled in the hall of fame for some sport, given the medal of honor for service to his country, made president of his company, or even enter the ministry of his church, but he can rise no higher in this life than to be a real father of faith and grace and family leader for his wife and children!

**The transgenerational victory:**

Honoring the new family structure created by the marriage of your daughter to her Knight in shining armor is not only wise and necessary for their success as a new family. It also brings great satisfaction to the father and mother of the bride. The new family is now established and the success of this family depends on the opportunity and ability of the new husband to take the reigns and lead this family into the future.

Fathers and mothers alike, beware! It is so easy to think that—your maturity, increased experience and age—gives you the right to tell your son or daughter how you feel about what they or their spouse should do or not do. This is the typical "mother-in-law" trap which so many mothers have fallen into. Since most mothers of today have taken the family reigns and have been the primary parents involved in their son's and daughters' love and romantic development—or the lack there of—they feel the need to keep giving their opinions after the sons and daughters marry . This is a formula for marital disaster and unhappiness!

You, the father, must set the standards of communication with the new husband and his new wife, whether it be your son or daughter. This is especially true in the case of a daughter. Our little princess is no longer first a daughter. She is now first a wife and secondly a daughter. She no longer is under our roof or under our authority as family head and leader, disciplinarian, and counselor. She is now the wife, Queen of the Universe, of her Knight in shining armor, and future mother of their children.

The mother of faith and grace must likewise understand the results of all of her labors and prayers that she and her husband have invested in their son, their little prince—will now have blossomed into a full grown head of family, Knight in Shining Armor for his Queen of the Universe—and must be respected as such!

**New family structures and honor:**

I cannot stress enough the importance of honoring the new family structure, whether of your son or daughter. The relationship which you began with your son-in-law—when he and your daughter were involved in personal discovery dating and then when they were engaged—should serve as a foundation upon which to build your continuing relationship. You passed the role of family leadership to your daughter's new husband. Now he needs your support, even when you think he is wrong. He will never develop into an accomplished family leader for your daughter and their children if he is not given the freedom to make mistakes. He doesn't need to feel as though someone were breathing down his neck. Parents become negative influences in the lives of their children when they attempt to meddle in their problems after marriage.

The support your daughter and her new husband need is your love expressed, first, in your commitment to honor them as the new family they are, and, second, as a counselor when they ask for your advice. Even then, the advice you give must be without any strings or emotional baggage! I feel so strongly about this that when I am asked for counsel on a given subject or problem, I give it with the clearly stated understanding they are under no obligation to do what I say.

In Book I Chapter Two, *Recapturing Virtue*, we discovered the importance of understanding the difference between "being" and "function." My love for my wife, my children and their families, is not predicated on the success or failure of their functions. I love them because of who they are. My decision to love them and to be committed to them is not affected by how perfectly they master the art of functional behavior. We would all like to be perfect. However, being perfect is something only God has the privilege to claim. As humans, we need grace and understanding and the knowledge of being loved, in spite of our shortcomings.

The wisdom you display in understanding and actually incorporating these values and principles into your daily life and relationship with your loved one's, will give you more opportunity to be a positive influence for them than any other way!

Overcoming life's challenges and problems; is a constant day-by-day processing and development—through which God in His loving discipline and good pleasure—perfects our own moral fiber, character and principles.[165] Without these challenges and the opportunity to overcome, we would become as weak and atrophied as an unused muscle. Yet, in today's world, the normal experience of this day-by-day processing, as a way of life, is rejected by many people. We hear the hue and cry of unrest and dissatisfaction from "leaders" all over the country. Yet, instead of actually leading our society into greener pastures with personal and family commitment for excellence, they keep insisting that we reduce our moral fiber and principles to new lows. Many of our so-called "leaders" even view the aspect of morality as being prudish and unenlightened.[166]

**Admitting the obvious:**

We know that, indeed, as a society, we are already atrophied and wasted, morally bankrupt and with few, if any, real principles? (Remember: principles are values for which you will die, all else are just strongly held opinions.) Are the leaders you respect and look up to telling you to look to government to solve your problems? Are we so weak? Do we need intravenous feeding with government financial and moral substitutes for our own personal involvement and commitment? Is our government, or any government, stronger than the individual adherence to God's revealed Law-Word expressed in the moral fiber, values and principles of its people?

Government is no more than a representation of the collective values of the people, the collective constituency, who make up the individual families in the country being governed. You and I, as individuals, must first learn to acquire moral fiber, values and principles from what we experience as family members. Then we can take the wisdom and power of those values into government. The reverse is never true. Moral fiber, values and principles have never been—are not today, and will never be—acquired from government. They are unique products of a strong family experience, governed under the—ordained leadership—of a father and mother of faith and grace!!

The goal of good government is to provide the protection and opportunity for such families to be successful in this day-to-day experience of processing. However, in reality, there are strong elements in our government who are determined to protect the immoral and unprincipled individuals or groups of individuals who reject God and want nothing to do with His revealed Law-Word. The rights of rapists, drug pushers, pornographers, thieves, murderers and organized crime

---

165 "Therefore, having been justified by faith, we have peace with God through our Lord Jesus Christ, through whom also we have access by faith into this grace in which we stand, and rejoice in hope of the glory of God. And not only that, but we also glory in tribulations, knowing that tribulation produces perseverance; and perseverance, character; and character, hope. Now hope does not disappoint, because the love of God has been poured out in our hearts by the Holy Spirit who was given to us." Romans 5:1-5.

166 "David Brooks argued in Bobos in Paradise that most Americans think they are, or want to be, "bourgeois bohemians" combine the laissez faire morality of the 1960s with the laissez faire economics of the 1980s. For them, the good life is nothing more than one of great prosperity and unlimited personal freedom. Questions of virtue, love, and justice do not inflame their passions-only health and fashion do. They are self-absorbed, politically correct, non-judgmental, apathetic consumer-democrats." Peter-Christian Aigner, comments taken from his posting in a review of, *"The Strange Truth About Our Souls"* By Peter Augustine Lawler, 2004.

members, are more important—to those who would force their form of government without God on us—than are the rights of real men and women of faith and grace to develop strong families. Is this the attitude of government, the priority of values, which we inherited from our forefathers? I think not![167]

**A gauntlet has been laid:**

These unbridled sources of influence for evil, which work against the building of strong families of faith and grace, are interested in only two things—power and money! Such leaders and their followers have proven themselves unfit to govern their own families and—doubly unfit—to govern our great country. These are not just godless men and women; on the contrary, they are gods unto themselves. They have made a religion out of having no moral fiber, values or principles. Their work ethic is to let others work while they play. They are powerless to overcome the great problems of our country because they are—faithless, without God, rebels all—uncommitted to overcome the problems of their own families. Our hope for change is NOT in such would be "leaders" and their ilk—our hope of change is in the working of Christ in us, men and women of faith and grace—to overcome against all odds! We will see "leaders" come and go, but most of what we see, in the way of changes, will only be—window dressing—except where God's families of faith and grace have made their influence felt from the breakfast table to the White House!

How was it possible for our forefathers to bring better moral fiber, values and principles to government than we are able to do today? How was it possible for their society to be able to have so little crime, corruption, and moral decay—as has become so common—in our own society? How could they do without all of the government decrees about what—is moral and immoral—based on the present day interpretation of the "freedom of speech" first amendment and a host of other misinformation? And how were their mothers and wives able to survive the lack of such legal privileges as abortion as a contraceptive, based on the present day interpretation of the "right to privacy" act? How were they able to rear such God-fearing, well-educated children, with what many today would have us believe—was an incorrect understanding—of "Church and State separation?" This of course, notwithstanding they wrote it. Or, how could they manage financially, without all of the government involvement we have in business today? How was it possible for them to develop such a great foundation for personal success, without the redistribution of wealth through taxation?

Could it be, and is it just possible, that they had a much higher percentage of males who were willing to be fathers of true faith and grace? Was it because these were men who were willing to put everything on the line for their wives and children, first in moral fiber, values and principles, and then, by God's grace, economic success as well? Have we—as males—lost the vision of our true calling to be men? What we need is not more government but more REAL MEN of faith and grace, who are willing to accept the high calling of God's Great Commission for fatherhood? Are you willing to be a real man of faith and grace and embark on the greatest experience of all—fulfilling the highest call—God has ever given to men? If you are, then accept God's high calling of fatherhood, and commit yourself to the challenge of building a strong family under God through Christ in you. There are no written guarantees for your success. There is inherent risk in being a real man of faith and grace, but with your commitment, and the grace of God, the odds are heavily weighted in our favor.

---

[167] "Your love of liberty -- your respect for the laws -- your habits of industry -- and your practice of the moral and religious obligations are the strongest claims to national and individual happiness." --George Washington

**Christ and His Great Commission for fatherhood are God's force for change!**

As such men, we are in a unique position to change the world for good. It is often said that a mother's hand rocks the cradle that controls the world. True enough, but it is you, a real man of faith and grace, committed to being a real father of faith and grace, who guides the hand rocking the cradle. It is you, a real man of faith and grace, committed to being a real father of faith and grace, who develops the moral fiber, values and principles of the—baby son or daughter—in that cradle!.

In the near future your little princess will take her place at the side of her Knight in shining armor. They will establish their family and have children of their own. Your little princess will be rocking her own cradles sooner than you think! Your son will become a father and he too will be challenged with the decision to accept God's Great Commission for fatherhood—to assume the responsibility for the moral character, spiritual, sexual and romantic development of his new bride and future mother of their children.

As their father of faith and grace, you have the opportunity and the responsibility to prepare them for a life-time of both the joys and the challenges that lie ahead! The kind of world we leave for our grand children depends more on the kind of sons and daughters we rear than on how many trees we leave standing.

Role models for grandchildren are the most important legacies we can leave our grandchildren. They are much more important than are beautiful buildings or Government projects of grandeur.

We hear much talk today about what kind of legacy we will leave our grandchildren. Will we leave them a ravaged countryside, a large national debt, and a destroyed ecology?

Given the attitude of a majority of our male population, who seems to find it more interesting, more challenging and more worthwhile, to pursue—sexual promiscuity, money and sports—than to commit to God's high calling of fatherhood, I'm convinced that our opportunities for success have never been better! Adversity develops character and values through experiences of gut wrenching challenges—therefore as bad as our environment for success may appear outwardly—there has never been a better opportunity for the development of real men of faith and grace who are willing to—GO FOR IT—to rise to the occasion!

**America is being prepared for a new harvest—will it be Good or Evil?**

The rewards of accepting the challenge of fatherhood, and of committing to be the leader, moral role model, disciplinarian, teacher and counselor of your family, are like harvests garnered from a well-tended orchard. The harvests do not begin the first year the orchard is planted. It takes years to bring a well-tended orchard to harvest. Your family is very much like such an orchard. You will spend many years planting, tending, pruning, and cultivating before you begin to see the harvest.

Rest assured harvest time is coming. In fact, you will reap a harvest whether you plant and tend your orchard well or not. If you have tended it along the lines and principles expressed in this book, your rewards will be in the form of great blessings. If you ignore these discoveries of God's revealed Law-Word and the application of His uncommon common sense which are the tools of His wisdom, and fail to embrace His challenge of fatherhood with all your heart, your harvest will be one of tears and sorrow for many years to come!

Families and nations are inseparable. No nation, no matter how many natural resources it has or how noble its constitution, can rise above the quality of its families. In as much as we dedicate ourselves to the purpose of building families of faith and grace—all with strong moral fiber, values and principles—we will build a strong country. Conversely, in as much as we allow ourselves to be convinced—by the left liberal atheistic humanists—of success and fulfillment through sexual titillation, promiscuity, and perversity, sports, clean air, and Government programs, we will continue to destroy ourselves, our families and our country!

**Let us make a firm stand from which there is no retreat!**

Our challenge to you as one family of faith and grace to another is this: Decide today to answer the true calling of your new heart—not your biological leftover impulses—from the old heart of stone. Commit yourself to the high calling of Christ in His Great Commission for fatherhood. You were born, first and foremost, to be a successful father. Whatever else you are able to accomplish through education, natural ability and opportunity is secondary to your spiritual gift from God to be a real husband and father of faith and grace! Don't allow yourself the luxury of sitting on the sidelines of life while our society's—moral decay and the failure of our political system to properly represent you—chugs along towards a suicidal death in a last plunge into Hell's bottomless pit! Take heart, you have within your hands the opportunity to make a difference in your own personal life—the life of your wife, and the lives of your children—and the future of your country. You come naturally equipped for the job; God has uniquely blessed you for this purpose. Your success with yourself and with your family will be the single largest contribution which you can make in this life for the good of everyone and His Kingdom.

America awaits with anticipation the rise of real men of faith and grace, who will not be distracted by the voices of immoral and Godless leaders, who cry out for your attention and your allegiance! These voices promise you sexual satisfaction, great joy, personal success and a trouble-free future, filled with great excitement. They say if you don't listen to them you will be considered ignorant and prudish. They say you will be forsaking the—greater good—for everyone. However, we men of faith and grace take strong opposition to such a godless and rebellious attitude against our Christ and King! We say they are liars and children of their father Satan the father of lies and deception!

**When and where will you make your stand?**

There is a hunger among men and women of today for an opportunity to throw off the shackles of—no respect, no honor, and no commitment—the lackluster world of promiscuity and moral irresponsibility. If we work together we can encourage others and be encouraged at the same time. We do not have to settle for personal and national defeat; we can choose to make a stand, to make a difference. Christ is Lord of the battle, we are promised—victory over Satan and his minions—the very walls of Hell are doomed to crumble under our onslaught! How is it possible that we would refuse so great an opportunity to experience the joys of victory under His banner of dominion over every power, every authority, every enemy—the last of which—will be death itself? Surely we cannot refuse!!

In the Latin-American culture there is a spectacle which is often criticized as gross and unfair by those who feel it is cruel to animals. I am referring to the sport of bull-fighting. Without taking sides as to the aspects of sportsmanship or animal cruelty in the matter, I want to share a point that gives meaning and depth of understanding, to which a real men and women of faith and grace can relate.

When the bull first comes into the ring, he is all over the arena, charging first one sector, then another. He charges anything that moves. As he tires and—is seriously wounded by the lances thrust into his withers—he begins to perceive that the battle is a serious one of life and death, he makes a stand. He finds a spot in the ring which he decides to defend to the death. He finds what is referred to in Spanish as his "Querencia." Here, in his querencia—his chosen spot for battle to the death—he makes a stand, a place from which he will not retreat. He will either win or die here.

Unlike the bull in the arena, we do not fight alone—we fight side by side with our Commander in Chief, the Lord of Lords and King of Kings, Jesus Christ—He brings fear and trembling into the hearts of our enemies. Not even the gates of Hell themselves will stand against us![168] Our querencia in this life—where ever our Lord should assign us to fight—is a place of guaranteed success, even though our mortal bodies should be killed, we will arise again at the resurrection with all of the saints from Adam until then and rejoice at the destruction of all of our Lord's enemies—the last of which is death itself!

Have you found your "Querencia?" Have you found your place in life from which you will not retreat? Are you ready to make a stand for something so precious, you would rather die than give up your resolve to be successful in its quest? Christ's Great Commission of Fatherhood and Motherhood—Love and Marriage—is such a querencia! My prayer and hope is for this writing and the ministry it represents to assist you in your chosen place of battle. May you find it, and through Christ in you—your hope of glory[169]—may you be outrageously successful in your stand!

**We can do all things through Christ who strengthens us!**

No man or woman who has read this book from cover to cover can believe in the godless advice of secular atheistic humanism. Therefore why should we wait any longer to take decisive action? Let us cast off the mold into which they strive to embed us and let us reach up for the higher ground!

> "I know how to be abased, and I know how to abound. Everywhere and in all things I have learned both to be full and to be hungry, both to abound and to suffer need. I can do all things through Christ who strengthens me." Philippians 4:13

I invite all who will accept the challenge of God's Great Commission of Fatherhood and Motherhood—His way with His power through Christ—to join us in this most noble endeavor! Feel free to write to me, e-mail me—go online and learn more details as they are posted. Attend one of the many conferences we will be holding in areas where you can easily drive or fly. Invite us into your congregation, company or organization; we will be honored to respond. I'm sure that many of you have questions you feel were not covered in this book. You are absolutely correct in that assumption. So, for responses to your personal situation or for more in-depth responses to those areas already covered, please feel free to contact me. (See the Contact Information, page 327)

---

168 "For though we walk in the flesh; we do not war according to the flesh. For the weapons of our warfare are not carnal but mighty in God for pulling down strongholds, casting down arguments and every high thing that exalts itself against the knowledge of God, bringing every thought into captivity to the obedience of Christ, and being ready to punish all disobedience when your obedience is fulfilled." II Corinthians 10:3-6.

169 "To them God willed to make known what are the riches of the glory of this mystery among the Gentiles: which is Christ in you, the hope of glory." Colossians 1:27.

[illegible]

[illegible] should be killed, we will [illegible] at the [illegible]

[illegible] which you will [illegible] ready to make a stand for something so [illegible] to be successful in its [illegible] Great Commission of [illegible] and [illegible] prayer and hope [illegible] and the ministry [illegible] your stand.

[illegible]

[illegible]

[illegible]

# Special Use Privileges

The following material, in all the appendices, is all copyrighted in its present form or any other form, plastic, paper, graphic, etc. for the exclusive use of the author and his assigns.

The author extends the limited opportunity for all those who purchase the book: "Daddy's Little Girl & Mommy's Little Boy" to copy these teaching aids and lesson handouts for themselves and their families. The author also extends the limited opportunity for all of those who wish to use this book for group teaching to quote from the book and to copy these teaching aids and lesson handouts for their class. Each student or family represented in such classes is expected to purchase a copy of the book. Copies of the book: photo, digital or by any other means for class or personal use is strictly forbidden. For any other use please refer to the copyright reprinting and use limitations listed in the beginning pages.

# Appendix I

# BOOK I—LOVE AND MARRIAGE

## Teaching Aids & Lesson Handouts:

## Chapter One

### The Victories of Love versus The Problems of Love

**Redefining roles and responsibilities for husbands and wives:**

1. V. 25: "Husbands love your wives, even as Christ also loved the church..."

2. V. 28: "So ought men to love their wives as their own bodies..."

3. V. 33: "Nevertheless let every one of you in particular so love his wife even as himself..."

### Christ's worldview on husbands

Husbands must be willing to believe and to act on Christ's revealed truth that we are responsible for our wife's spiritual, moral, character and romantic success—yes we—her husband of faith and grace, are Christ's revelation—by His grace and for His glory—of what is true, love and romance for our wife.

1. The husband can no longer point the finger of blame at his wife nor can he seek answers for the discord in their relationship through changes that he thinks she should make.

2. The husband must look to God to strengthen himself and give him the wisdom and understanding to seek change within himself and victory for his family.

3. The husband must first change his perspective about himself—how and with what—he will now love his wife. Before it was all about his needs and his carnal love through masculinity and being right for him—now it must all be about asking God for His perfect love to overflow in the husband so that the love the husband gives her will be from Christ, through Him and by His power, to fulfill His good pleasure in him and in them together as one flesh.

## Chapter Two
## Recapturing Virtue

### Christ's worldview on recapturing virtue

"Come now, and let us reason together," Says the LORD,
'Though your sins are like scarlet,
They shall be as white as snow;
Though they are red like crimson,
They shall be as wool.
If you are willing and obedient,
You shall eat the good of the land;
But if you refuse and rebel,
You shall be devoured by the sword;'
For the mouth of the LORD has spoken." Isaiah 1:18-20.

1. Men and women of faith and grace are all sinners.

2. Men and women of faith and grace all have the option to repent and to renew their virtue through Christ and His promise of forgiveness and renewal.

## Chapter Three
## Breaking Old Habits

### Christ worldview on standards

It is this law which is written in our hearts that also confirms the revealed law of the ten commandments, which guides us and also which chastises us immediately with our bruised conscience—our guilt—when we rebel against it. God's revealed Law-Word is absolute truth!

1. We men and women of faith and grace must no longer "Do our own thing," which is obviously not a good recommendation where Right and Wrong are concerned.

2. We men and women of faith and grace are also brought face-to-face with the fact that when we rationalize our behavior, trying to seek "easier" ways of living or what we might think to be more "exciting" ways to live, we violate our conscience which firmly believes in the correctness of the Real Morality and tells us we are wrong.

3. It is—Wrong—for men and women of faith and grace to seek help for their feelings of guilt, save through repentance and submission to the sovereignty of God and His Christ.

4. We men and women of faith and grace have been given a new heart—a heart of flesh to replace the heart of stone that is the old man of our old natures. Paul confirms this in eloquent and clear terms in his message in Romans 2:1-16. It is this law which is written in our hearts that also confirms the revealed law of the ten commandments, which guides us and also which chastises us immediately with our bruised conscience—our guilt—when we rebel against it.

5. We men and women of faith and grace have the promise of God's gift of wisdom, understanding and overcoming because we now are resurrected in Him. Romans 6:1-23 is crystal clear on who we are and why we are no longer servants of sin and rebellion against God. It is because of His work in us. To say or to do otherwise is to deny Him and the grace of His salvation!

6. We men and women of faith and grace must reject the secular atheistic concept of—your truth or my truth—when in fact the only truth is God's truth, His gospel of Christ crucified and Christ resurrected and living in us. Christ is God's absolute truth.

## Chapter Four
## Navigation

### Christ's worldview on navigation
### He is the way the truth and the light

1. We men and women of faith and grace know the way; we know the course that God has set for us—for we have the mind of Christ. Philippians 2:5, "Let this mind be in you which was also in Christ Jesus." We have the choice to choose to have the mind of Christ.
2. Our journey of life is assured for we do not navigate alone: Philippians 3:12-15, he reveals a most astounding factor of our life and being: vs. 13, "For it is God in you who works both to will and to do His good pleasure."
3. Men and women of faith and grace are thankful to God for His gift of the mind of Christ!
4. Men and women of faith and grace are thankful to God for working His good pleasure in us.

### Christ's worldview on great sex:

1. A young man cannot look back on his present wife as a wife of his youth, they are both young. The promise is for the young son when he is old. The secret is to focus all of his amorous attentions onto his wife. This will bring sexual satisfaction and success for them both now while young and also later when they are both old.
2. We men of faith and grace reject the amorous attentions of any woman other than our wife, although such a woman might have the appearance as one who could give—delight and joy—we know that to embrace her is to embrace death, for her paths lead to death. Such a woman can offer us no satisfaction.
3. We men of faith and grace are committed to God's revealed truth that our amorous focus must be the wife of our youth and that her breasts will satisfy us all the days of our lives, and that she will be beautiful for us and we will be ravished by her love all our life!

## Chapter Five
## Communication between the Sexes

### Christ's worldview on our communication

His worldview is the *vowel and alphabet system* of our new language in Christ.

1. Men and women of faith and grace do NOT accept the watered down pabulum of secular academia's drool as a truth they can live by, they understand that to do so reduces them to victim status.
2. We Men and women of faith and grace do NOT waste time seeking after dates and times of our Lord's return but rather we believe in His promises of victory for His Church and His Kingdom in time and in history according to His sovereign will.
3. Love and marriage are the crown jewels of his richest blessings for all men and women of faith and grace—now in this time—not later—NOW in our history—in our time. It has been so for all who came before us, it is so for us and it will be so for our children and for all who follow after us!

## Chapter Six
## Reigning With Christ

### Christ's worldview of men of faith and grace

### The woman was deceived:

"Then the serpent said to the woman, 'You will not surely die. For God knows that in the day you eat of it your eyes will be opened and you will be like God, knowing good and evil.'

"So when the woman saw that the tree was good for food, that it was pleasant to the eyes, and a tree desirable to make one wise, she took of its fruit and ate. She also gave to her husband with her, and he ate. Then the eyes of both of them were opened, and they knew that they were naked; and they sewed fig leaves together and made themselves coverings.

"And they heard the sound of the LORD God walking in the garden in the cool of the day, and Adam and his wife hid themselves from the presence of the LORD God among the trees of the garden. Genesis 3:4-8.

### The first man Adam disobeyed and accepted his wife's role as his leader and ate:

"Then the man said, 'The woman whom you gave to be with me, she gave me of the tree, and I ate.'

"And the LORD God said to the woman, 'What is this you have done?' Genesis 3:11-13.

### The first woman Eve had her desire focused in her husband to lead her:

"To the woman He said: 'I will greatly multiply your sorrow and your conception; in pain you shall bring forth children; your desire shall be for your husband, and he shall rule over you.'

### Five Important Changes

- **The first change you will notice;** is that you feel so much more free and cleaner inside. All of those—JUDGE ROLES—you have had cluttering your mind was like barnacles on the bottom of a ship. No matter how much effort you put into your attempts to move forward you could never get up any real speed.

- **The second change you will notice;** is that you can talk to each other without having to justify your position through accusations of the each others failures or inconsistencies.

- **The third change you will notice;** is that there will be flashbacks of the old ways—you will be tempted—but with your new perspective of reality and because of Christs' blessing you with new wisdom and understanding you will successfully recognize it for what it is and chose not to go there.

- **The fourth change you will notice;** is that over time your mind will refuse to catalog the old or the new mistakes of your spouse. You will notice that although neither of you have reached any new level of perfection—the old tendency to catalog each others mistakes and misdeeds will fade away. Husbands and wives of faith and grace will learn to deal with their mistakes and misdeeds as they happen—transparently, without malice—and then move on, never looking back!

- **The fifth and most important of all changes that you will notice;** is the way your prayer life will change.[170] You will soon discover that you have many more things for which to be thankful than you ever had before. Your list of needs and wants will diminish and your list of things for which you are grateful, appreciative and thankful will increase! One of these will be your spouse!!

## Chapter Seven
## Structuring our Love and Sexual Relationship
## The Great Commission for Husbands

## The Confession and Vows of a Husband of Faith and Grace

1. As a man of faith and grace I hereby solemnly vow before God, my wife and my family that I embrace as His greatest commission and commandment of God—given to husbands—is to be the head of my wife and my family. To be charged with her spiritual, moral, emotional and personal development to the point of returning her to God as one without spot—just like the queen was cared for by her king in the Song of Solomon. To be charged with the responsibility to rear our children in the Lord and to not be a discouragement to them for so long as I shall live.

2. I believe that the Church as expressed through me, has failed in the GREAT commission and commandment of God to teach—by word and by example—that a man of faith and grace is the head of his wife and his family and that he is charged by God to minister to them and to deliver them all to God through Christ; and I vow to commit myself to victory over such failure.

3. I believe that by putting second things first the Church leadership as expressed through me and those who have gone before me, have for decades—if not centuries—sinned against God—weakening and in many cases alienating—the effectiveness of his greatest tool for the Kingdom here on earth, second only to the Holy Spirit; and I vow to commit myself to victory over such failure.

4. I believe and will support that the tool God—through Christ—has placed here on earth to sojourn and serve Him as head of all of His daughters of faith and grace and His family units until he returns is—THE HUSBAND—of one wife and the ordained father of the Lord's institution The Family.

5. I believe and will support that God has ordained only three institutions on the earth: His *Family Institution*, His *Church Institution*[171] and His *State Institution.*

6. I believe and will support that all three of these institutions are part of His Kingdom here on earth and are dependent upon His theocratic rule; The Lord of Lords and King of Kings—His Son Jesus Christ.

7. I believe and will support that the quality of all the leaders of the State Institution and all the leaders of the Church Institution come from the—success or failure—of the quality of His Family Institution.

8. I believe and will defend that God's Family Institution is the—number one target—of Satan and all his minions in secular atheistic humanism?

9. I understand and accept the responsibility that my failure to complete this commission and commandment guarantees the Church's failure—as represented in me—in its commandment to go into all the world and disciple the nations and baptize the believers.

10. By God's grace and enablement through Christ in me—I vow to commit my walk to the steps He has foreordained for me and to trust in Him for the victory—now in our time and in history, Amen.

**The Confession and Vows of a Wife of Faith and Grace**

1. As a woman of faith and grace I hereby solemnly vow before God, my husband and my family that I embrace as His greatest commission and commandment of God—given to wives—is to honor and obey my husband in the Lord; to be charged with being a help meet for him and to be his focus of femininity, romance, love and sexual fulfillment—just like the king we discovered in the Song of Solomon was fulfilled by his queen. To be charged with the responsibility to rear our children in the Lord and to not be a discouragement to them, for so long as I shall live.

2. I believe that the Church as expressed through me, has failed in the GREAT commission and commandment of God to teach—by word and by example—that a woman of faith and grace is to honor her husband and that the man of faith and grace is the head of his wife and his family and that he is charged by God to minister to them and to deliver them all to God through Christ; and I vow to commit myself to victory over such failure.

3. I believe that by putting second things first the Church leadership as expressed through me and those who have gone before me, have for decades—if not centuries—sinned against God—weakening and in many cases alienating—the effectiveness of his greatest tool for the Kingdom here on earth, second only to the Holy Spirit; and I vow to commit myself to victory over such failure.

4. I believe and will support that the tool God—through Christ—has placed here on earth to sojourn and serve Him as head of all of His daughters of faith and grace and His family units until he returns is—THE HUSBAND—of one wife and the ordained father of the Lord's institution The Family.

5. I believe and support that God has ordained only three institutions on the earth: His *Family Institution*, His *Church Institution* and His *State Institution*.

6. I believe and support that all three of these institutions are part of His Kingdom here on earth and are dependent upon His theocratic rule; The Lord of Lords and King of Kings—His Son Jesus Christ.

7. I believe and support that the quality of all the leaders of the State Institution and all the leaders of the Church Institution come from the—success or failure—of the quality of His Family Institution.

8. I believe and will defend that God's Family Institution is the—number one target—of Satan and all his minions in secular atheistic humanism?

9. I understand and accept the responsibility that my failure to complete this commission and commandment guarantees the Church's failure—as represented in me—in its commandment to go into all the world and disciple the nations and baptize the believers.

10. By God's grace and enablement through Christ in me—I vow to commit my walk to the steps He has foreordained for me and to trust in Him for the victory—now in our time and in history, Amen.

## God's Family Charter

1. Do not be unwise, but understand what the will of the Lord is.
2. Be filled with the Spirit.
3. Giving thanks always for all things.
4. Submitting to one another in the fear of God.
5. Wives, submit to your own husbands as unto the Lord.
6. Husbands, live with your wife in understanding and honor her.
7. The husband is head of the wife.
8. Christ is head of the church.
9. Just as the church is subject to Christ, so let the wives be to their own husbands in everything.
10. Children, obey your parents in the Lord.
11. Honor your father and mother; that it may be well with you and you may live long on the earth.
12. Fathers, do not provoke your children to wrath, but bring them up in the training and admonition of the Lord.

**The world looks at men and women—especially at men—and it asks these questions:**

1. Who are his parents?
2. Where did he go to school?
3. How much education does he have?
4. What is his profession?
5. What is his net financial worth?
6. Whom did he marry?
7. Is he famous?

**God looks at men and women—very especially at men—and He asks these questions:**

1. Is he one of Mine?
2. Does he hear My voice?
3. Does he obey My voice?
4. Does he seek My understanding?
5. Does he seek My wisdom?
6. Does he love his wife?
7. Does he execute the leadership role of his wife and family?

**Our goal is His good pleasure in us:**

Men and women of faith and grace, we indeed want to be great and successful—truly great and successful—so let us be in the eyes of Christ, our Lord and King as he wants to see us—clothed in His righteousness—and not in our own righteousness! He is faithful who has called us and he knows our needs for the things of this life—even before—we ask Him!

# Chapter Eight-Part I
# Structuring Our Children's Environment
# The Origins

## The locus of moral fiber, values and principles for the family:

Contrary to a wide segment of popular belief, it is not the mother who should set the standards of how a family measures up to God's revealed Law-Word, the real source—the true locus for Right and wrong within the family—it is the father.

## It's not a matter of color:

In October of 1991, the national Education Goals Panel reported, "Currently, one of every four children in U.S. schools comes from a single-parent family. Among black Americans the number of single-parent families runs over 60 percent." (The latest statistics show this number to now be about 50 %.) ZH

The problem of Hispanic and black men is not their ethnic origin or color; it is the high percentage of their numbers who will not accept the challenges of manhood and fatherhood. There is either a warning or an encouragement here for each one of us. If you are a man, regardless of your color or ethnic origin, embracing or willing to embrace the challenges of God to be a father of faith and grace, then you are to be commended. If you are a man who will not accept the challenge of Christian fatherhood, regardless of ethnic origins or color, then you are part of the problem.

## Chapter Eight-Part II

## Discipline

### Five easy things to remember:

1. Make small inputs.
2. Wait for the effects of your inputs before making more change.
3. Recognize small errors as soon as possible.
4. Make small navigation corrections as often as necessary.
5. Don't wait to make changes until it requires a BIG change.

### Curses on Disobedience

"But it shall come to pass, if you do not obey the voice of the LORD your God, to observe carefully all His commandments and His statutes which I command you today, that all these curses will come upon you and overtake you:

"Cursed shall you be in the city, and cursed shall you be in the country.
"Cursed shall be your basket and your kneading bowl.
"Cursed shall be the fruit of your body and the produce of your land, the increase of your cattle and the offspring of your flocks.
"Cursed shall you be when you come in, and cursed shall you be when you go out.

"The LORD will send on you cursing, confusion, and rebuke in all that you set your hand to do, until you are destroyed and until you perish quickly, because of the wickedness of your doings in which you have forsaken Me. ..."

### Blessings on Obedience:

"Now it shall come to pass, if you diligently obey the voice of the LORD your God, to observe carefully all His commandments which I command you today, that the LORD your God will set you high above all nations of the earth. And all these blessings shall come upon you and overtake you, because you obey the voice of the LORD your God:

'Blessed shall you be in the city, and blessed shall you be in the country.
'Blessed shall be the fruit of your body, the produce of your ground and the increase of your herds, the increase of your cattle and the offspring of your flocks.
'Blessed shall be your basket and your kneading bowl.
'Blessed shall you be when you come in, and blessed shall you be when you go out.
'The LORD will cause your enemies who rise against you to be defeated before your face; they shall come out against you one way and flee before you seven ways.
'The LORD will command the blessing on you in your storehouses and in all to which you set your hand, and He will bless you in the land which the LORD your God is giving you.

'The LORD will establish you as a holy people to Himself, just as He has sworn to you, if you keep the commandments of the LORD your God and walk in His ways. Then all peoples of the earth shall see that you are called by the name of the LORD, and they shall be afraid of you. And the LORD will grant you plenty of goods, in the fruit of your body, in the increase of your livestock, and in the produce of your ground, in the land of which the LORD swore to your fathers to give you. The LORD will open to you His good treasure, the heavens, to give the rain to your land in its season, and to bless all the work of your hand. You shall lend to many nations, but you shall not borrow. And the LORD will make you the head and not the tail; you shall be above only, and not be beneath, if you heed the commandments of the LORD your God, which I command you today, and are careful to observe them. So you shall not turn aside from any of the words which I command you this day, to the right or the left, to go after other gods to serve them." Deuteronomy 28:1-13

## Three basic factors for our recovery:

If, in our roles as fathers, we cannot be serious about our own rules, then discipline is very unlikely to have much of an effect. In fact, almost any kind of discipline with respect to family rules or structure is of little consequence if at least three basic factors are not in strong evidence.

**First:** we as the father must be under our own self discipline. Your rules cannot be just a matter of convenience for keeping your child in order while you allow yourself the privilege of breaking the rules as you please. Your child will see through such shallowness so fast it will make your head swim. Be forewarned, you are human and you will break your own rules. When such a mistake on your part does occur and your child should notice and bring it to your attention.

**Second**: you must be ready to admit very frankly and candidly that you did break the rule. Tell what it has cost or will cost you, and promise to do all you can not to break it again. This is exactly what you expect from him or her and anything less from you will only give reason to your child to disrespect you.

**Third:** you must be the main guardian and disciplinarian. Mothers can and should be involved in the disciplining and teaching of the children, absolutely they should! Authority comes from the head, and she needs your delegated authority to perform this role successfully. However, if you as father do not supply the main support for this structure, that is, outline the structure and methods for discipline—teach by example in the family for her support and use—the mother's influence is limited. Without the husband's support and example the children very quickly learn to play both of you against each other. This can reach advanced levels, and they will play you like a fine instrument.

## In order to fly again we must do what logic tells us not to do:

**First:** we decide that we are not going to keep doing the same thing. We are going to STOP what we were doing and we are going to take DECISIVE STEPS to correct this death dealing problem.

**Second:** we are going to slam our foot down on the rudder pedal that is opposite to the direction in which we are spiraling and at the same we are going to—PUSH—forward on the controls and point our nose even more directly toward the ground than before.

Trust me men and women, husbands and wives of faith and grace, when I say that this is an act of FAITH and COURAGE. Faith because it is against what appears to be normal and courage because if you are wrong you are going to die.

**Third:** we are going to pull the throttle all the way back and let the engine only idle.

### The Confession of Transparency for a Father of Faith and Grace

1. Father is responsible for the structure and discipline of the family and its moral role model.

2. Father is still learning, but even so, he is the best the family has and what he learns he will always share with the family.

3. Father has bad days in spite of his desire for more perfection.

4. Father has bad habits that he is still working on.

5. You my children will genetically image your father and will have a tendency toward my same bad habits.

6. Father is committed to change and to grow together with mommy and you children, as a team player.

7. Our family is our most important institution and personal responsibility in the world!

**The Confession of Transparency for a Mother of Faith and Grace**

1. Mother is responsible for supporting father in the structure and discipline of the family and its moral role model.

2. Mother is still learning, but even so, she is God's gift to daddy and the family and what she learns she will always share with the family.

3. Mother has bad days in spite of her desire for more perfection.

4. Mother has bad habits that I am still working on.

5. You my children will genetically image your mother and will have a tendency toward my same bad habits.

6. Mother is committed to change and to grow together with daddy and you children as a team player.

7. Our family is our most important institution and personal responsibility in the world!

## Discipline priorities

The following is a list of discipline priorities. Adopting a plan along these lines will greatly reduce stress and disorder in the home.

1. Establish an atmosphere of respect and control with openness and joy—lots of hugging and kissing.

2. Hold regular family meetings to discuss the do's and don'ts of family functions, activities and duties as a whole, and for each member. This atmosphere eliminates the need to get mad or speak unkindly in order to get your point across. It also establishes you in the role of leader and teacher of the family.

3. In this teaching atmosphere you have an opportunity to express your deeper thoughts, concerns and experiences about life and love. You are able to teach the basics of moral fiber, values and principles. You can ask and answer questions to make sure they understand. Mother can also have her meetings, more often when you are not present. However, father should always be given the respect as the main teacher, counselor and disciplinarian for the family.

4. Have several questions in mind that will help the children get into the theme of what you want to discuss. Be as creative as possible. Learning is easier when it is fun.

# Appendix II

# BOOK II—DADDY'S LITTLE GIRL

## Teaching Aids & Lesson Handouts:

## Chapter Six, Seven & Ten

### Daddy's Little Princess and Her Virtue

**Virginity Is:**

1. Mental
2. Psychological
3. Spiritual
4. Sexual

A young daughter intuitively desires to share the first three aspects of her virginity, her innocence of mental, psychological, and spiritual make-up with her father. It is natural for her to open her mind, her emotions and her spiritual make-up to him first.

1. Mentally, she will submit her mind to his teaching.
2. Emotionally, she will condition her emotional responses to life based on what she learns from him, in word and by example.
3. Spiritually, she will respond quickly to his spiritual leadership. In essence the sum total of all her expressions of moral character and sexual conduct as a woman will be what she has learned or not learned from her father.
4. Her physical sexual expressions are reserved and protected for her future intimacies with her husband.

**Actions must follow the words of a sincere man or woman:**

Follow this up by including regular church attendance in your family's activities. Visit several churches and be sensitive to getting the answer to your prayer. You will get answers. You will get insight as to where you should go to church and what you should do. Only consider churches offering at least three spiritual growth basics:

1. One that consistently teaches salvation by faith only in Jesus Christ and that as a gift and act of God: Read: John 1:12-14; Eph. 2:8-10; and II Cor. 2:14-16
2. One that teaches personal responsibility for one's actions and for repentance and submission to the sovereign will of God for one's life. Read: Acts 20:22-24; Gal. 2:17-21; and Mk. 5:36, 10:30
3. One that teaches strong support for parents as the primary family leaders, and for fathers as the heads of the family leadership. Read: I Pet. 3:7; Col. 3:18-21; I Tim. 3:4-5; and Eph. 6:1-4

# Book II

## Daddy's Little Girl
## Chapter Seven
## A Daughter's Dream Come True

**A most important proposal; second only to the one you gave your wife:**

Sit down with your daughter somewhere quiet and private. Tell her as straight-forwardly as you can about your desire to propose a plan and a life-time commitment to her. For this to work you must be committed all the way. This is not a "pick and choose" list of possibilities; you must be committed to tell her that you are committing to be her personal champion, coach and cheerleader for her success in love and marriage. She does not need your half-hearted attempts at this. Such an approach would only hurt her and leave her frustrated. Tell her in your own words, the following points of this plan:

1. You want to be the champion of her cause and her desire to know all about men and boys and you will answer all of her questions.

2. You are committed to sharing with her all that you now know or will learn about men. You will tell her the good and the bad.

3. Tell her how important her virginity is to her for her overall development as a woman and for the most successful and satisfying sexual relation with her future husband. (This portion will vary depending on how well you have prepared her.) This is a good time to share with her the three deeper and more complex aspects of her virginity. Book II, Chapter Six, *Daddy's Little Princess and Her Virtue*

4. You are the guardian and protector of her virginity, and as she learns more about men and boys, she will understand why it is so important

5. You are committed to her in her development as a woman; you are committed to prepare her and to support her in her desire of someday finding the man of her romantic dreams.

6. Your counsel and guidance in these matters will prepare her for the most exciting, romantic and sexual satisfaction that any woman can have.

7. You believe in her and in return you only ask one thing from her. You want her complete trust. You want her to demonstrate this by telling you, about all the boys that she finds interesting.

8. She can ask you any questions she wants to and you will do your best to give her the answers.

9. Ask her if she likes this plan, and will she promise to trust you and to be transparent with you! (You might have to explain the concept of "transparency" to her with different words.) Transparency can be taught at a very early age.

## Book II
## Daddy's Little Girl
## Chapter Ten
## The Engagement

**Personal experience:**

By now the reader has learned many of our personal experiences and there are more to come—but our experience with NOT divorcing—is most important at this time. Engagement leads to only one of three things:

1. Broken engagement

2. Marriage for life

3. Divorce

# Appendix III

# BOOK III—MOMMY'S LITTLE BOY

## Teaching Aids & Lesson Handouts:

## Introduction – Chapter Three

**We report on Barna's 2001 poll with the following comments:**

1. Thirty three percent of all adults have lived with a member of the opposite sex without being married. Among these "Christians" the rate is twenty five percent for born-again individuals.

2. John C. Green, a Christian political scientist and director of the Ray C. Bliss Institute of Applied Politics at the University of Akron. Green has discovered that:

3. Twenty six percent of traditional evangelicals—do not think premarital sex is wrong—and forty six percent of nontraditional evangelicals—read liberal—see nothing morally wrong with it.

4. Thirteen percent of traditional evangelicals say it is okay for married persons to have sex with someone other than one's own spouse.

5. Nineteen percent of nontraditional evangelicals say adultery is morally acceptable.

### Book III
### Mommy's Little Boy
### Chapter One
### Haloed Queens

**Great commissions bring great responsibilities:**

There are seven examples of woman's special and highly valued relationship with man. Four of the seven are juxtaposed against—the potential volatility of woman—therefore in the fourth one you will notice that a—good wife—is said to obtain favor from God for her husband:

1. "For a man indeed ought not to cover his head, since he is the image and glory of God; but woman is the glory of man." I Corinthians 11:7.

2. "An excellent wife is the crown of her husband, but she who causes shame is like rottenness in his bones." Proverbs 12:4.

3. "The wise woman builds her house, but the foolish pulls it down with her hands." Proverbs 14:1.

4. "He who finds a wife finds a good thing, and obtains favor from the LORD." Proverbs 18:22.

5. "A foolish son is the ruin of his father, and the contentions of a wife are a continual dripping." Proverbs 19:13.

6. "Houses and riches are an inheritance from fathers, but a prudent wife is from the LORD." Proverbs 19:14.

7. "Better to dwell in the wilderness, than with a contentious and angry woman." Proverbs 21:19.

**The true covering of a virtuous woman:**

It has been said many ways and from many different points of reference since we first started our journey of discoveries in this book—the husband/father of faith and grace—is God's true covering for Woman.

1. The husband of faith and grace is God's true delegated covering for his wife—whom the Lord has given him.

2. The father of faith and grace is God's true delegated covering for his daughter—whom the Lord has given him.

3. When neither husband nor father is available, then God's institution the Church is God's delegated authority to serve as the provisional head for the woman who has lost all her other options for covering.

## Book III
## Mommy's Little Boy
## Chapter Two-Part I
## Introducing The Male World
## The Status Quo

**Serious questions we must consider:**

1. Who is in control of your family as a wife/mother of faith and grace?

2. Do you take part in supporting your husband in this control?

3. Who is the moral role model, teacher, counselor, disciplinarian and leader of your family?

4. As a wife/mother of faith and grace do you receive delegated authority from your husband to support his role?

5. Have you accepted the challenge of being the champion and coach for your son's emotional and sexual development, for his possible future relationship with a wife? If not, would you like to?

## Book III
## Mommy's Little Boy
## Chapter Two Part II
## Introducing the Male World
## Normal Male Sexuality

**Moralists are forced to superimpose their own fears and opinions:**

1. Sperm or issue on the ground: Genesis 38:8-10
2. Issue of sperm in bed alone: Leviticus 15:16-17
3. Issue of sperm in bed with a woman: Leviticus 15:18
4. Issue of sperm in bed alone: Deuteronomy 23:10

## Book III
## Mommy's Little Boy
## Chapter Two Part III
## Introducing the Male World - A Real Man Of Faith And Grace

**Personal Moral Values and Principles of a Real man of Faith and Grace**

1. By the grace of God he will remain a virgin until marriage and will be faithful to his wife for the rest of his life. He will focus his attentions and energies before marriage on preparing himself to be a husband and father of the highest quality.

2. He will desire and seek a life-time partner and lover in a marital relationship. He will choose such a woman from among those women he knows to be virtuous, preferably a biological virgin, but a restored virgin of faith and grace could be God's choice as well. Also, a virtuous

widow is not out of the question. His respect and compassion, not passion, for all women, allow him to exercise self-discipline and self-respect in his pursuit of the right woman for him. Once he finds the right woman for him, he will make his decision to love her, and will obligate himself to allow nothing to change that decision!

3. All of his sexual desires and passions will be focused on this one woman whom he has chosen to be his wife and lover for life! Mutual communication of these desires and needs will be a high priority. See: I Cor.7:3-5 and I Peter 3:7

4. He avoids the slippery slope of the double standard and considers all women to be worthy of his respect and compassion. He has compassion for women who have elected to participate in the pursuit of male titillation, the topless dancers, prostitutes, porno stars and the sexually promiscuous. He understands that they are the legacy of men who would not accept the high calling of a father of faith and grace, or even the common grace fatherhood of an unbeliever. He is painfully aware of the many dangers such women present. Pursuit of such women only leads to the death of his self-respect and of his dedication to his own husbandry/fatherhood and in effect, the death of his own personal life as a husband/father of faith and grace.

5. He is not out to "conquer" everything wearing a skirt or a tight pair of pants. His self-control and self-respect are not—just tempered—by his knowledge of the evil they represent, but by the sustaining power of Christ through grace to enable him to do so. Such a man of faith and grace knows that he cannot hope to focus his complete sexual needs and desires on just one woman if, his lifestyle were to demonstrate, that in fact his—true attitude toward women—is one that considers them as mere sex objects and sex trinkets.

6. He is not confused concerning the difference between erotic sexual arousal and love. Biological sexual arousal is not to be confused with love; it's a natural drive given by God, intended for the fulfillment of God's blessings in love and marriage and by itself, is not love. Whereas love is a decision, which, when once made never has to be changed. He knows one does not "fall" in love, one decides to love. Thus, he decides anew, everyday, to love this woman which he has chosen to be his wife, and which he sees as a gift from God. Likewise one cannot "fall" out of love; it requires a selfish, faithless decision to stop loving.

7. He accepts the responsibility of providing the commitment and leadership necessary to establish a successful family structure and the high calling of fatherhood based on God's gift of faith and grace. He accepts the challenge of creating a love relationship with his chosen mate, one which includes her fulfillment in all areas. He puts a top priority on her continued spiritual, emotional development, her need and desire for motherhood, her educational and vocational development. He is not threatened by his wife's potential or realized education or vocation. He understands both of them will experience their greatest romantic and sexual satisfaction as a result of this complete understanding and commitment.

8. He protects the bonds of their relationship and intimacy from all intrusions, especially from his or her immediate family members who might be tempted to criticize them or their relationship.

9. He does not abuse his wife or his children, verbally or physically.

10. He wants to pursue the best possible approach to realizing his full potential and destiny in life. He accepts his own creation with humility and seeks a personal relationship with God.

11. He will not reject the inner stirrings within his heart and soul to reach out and ask God for help and guidance in this, the most complex of all challenges, the challenge of fatherhood! He walks in faith, knowing that alone—without God—he cannot hope to fulfill the blueprint for husbands, as stated in Eph. 5:23-33. He refuses to be controlled and manipulated by disoriented male counterparts, who use intellectual pride, secularist mentality, selfish ego, machismo, and so-called "male virility" as a substitute for God's revealed Law-Word. He does not delegate his spiritual development to others, such as Rabbis, Priests, Pastors or Sunday school teachers. He has the courage to read the Bible for himself. He is a man of prayer, both alone, deep and personal and also with his wife—daily seeking—God's grace, wisdom and mercy in their lives. He makes his own decisions regarding what God is saying to him and about his role in this life. He is open-minded and therefore accessible to counsel from his wife, pastors and others—but more importantly—more importantly his greatest source of wisdom is from his continual reading of God's Law-Word. Thus armed for life's battles, he makes his own final decisions!

12. He is committed to seeking His answers for the proper worldview from Christ and to—search

**His Law-Word in the pursuit of all the answers to the demands of day to day living routines, vocational excellence, child rearing challenges, spousal romance and sexual satisfaction with and for the benefit of his wife—encouraging and including her in all his pursuits through wise counsel and prayer.**

## Book III
## Mommy's Little Boy
## Chapter Three
## The First Personal Discovery Date

**Walking the walk with God's uncommon common sense:**
The following is a list of questions which will help prepare your son or daughter to understand what kind of young lady or young man they are meeting or considering for a personal discovery date. Any potential prospect for their life-time commitment of love and devotion in marriage should be able to respond properly to the following questions. These questions are stated as from our Princess—Our Prince however must also qualify for his prospect with or without any questions! From the perspective of his parents of faith and grace his character and moral lifestyle founded and lived in Christ must be a given at this point!

### Qualifying Questions and Answers for Candidates

1. **What do you think of your father?**
   **Wrong Answer:**
   Any response that shows a young man does not respect his father and is openly hostile to his father, is a wrong answer. Such a response is demonstrating that he has not been successfully prepared for leadership by his father. This is a very poor candidate.
   **Correct Answer:**
   A young man should respond with a strong response of respect and admiration for his father. He should be proud of the things his father has taught him and be able give details. Score one point

2. **What do you think of your mother?**
   **Wrong Answer:**
   A young man who does not respect and speak highly of his mother will not be able to maintain a high level of respect and honor for any woman. Obviously, this is not a good candidate.
   **Correct Answer:**
   The response to this question should be one of obvious tenderness and great respect for his mother. It should be natural for him to talk about her qualities and about her love and marriage with his father. Score one point.

3. **What major are you planning to study in college?**
   **Wrong Answer:**
   Any response not expressing a strong commitment to further education is evidence that this young man lives in a dream world, and is not a good candidate.
   **Correct Answer:**
   Any young man who has serious plans for his life and his future wife and family will have definite educational objectives. College is preferred, but is not the only form of higher education. Score one point.

4. **What is love?**
   **Wrong Answer:**
   Any indication showing the young man in question equates sex with love is a wrong answer. Any serious candidate should be able to articulate the difference between love and sex, and should know that it is a decision based on a commitment and not an emotion. A wrong answer here indicates the young man has parents who don't know either, or they would have told him.
   **Correct Answer:**
   The ideal response is one showing good understanding of and strong attachment to the principle of love as a decision, based on commitment. Score one point.

5. **What is your opinion about virginity?**
   **Wrong Answer:**
   Look for an expression of surprise on his face, like: "You've got to be kidding me." The eyes will tell you what he really thinks. If a young man thinks a girl is a virgin, he is likely to say that he is for virginity. The next question should be: Are you a virgin? This will get the truth out in the open, even if he lies. Your daughter will be able to pick up a lie most of the time. There are mitigating circumstances which sometimes may allow for past mistakes, but there should be no doubt about the level of understanding or commitment to virtue and protection of the state of virginity until marriage.

**Correct answer:**
The best response to this question is a strong and sincere commitment to virginity, both for the man as well as the young Princess. Score one point.

6. **What plans do you have for being a father?**
**Wrong Answer:**
Any response not showing a strong desire to be a family leader is an automatic wrong answer! There is absolutely no room for error in this response. Any doubt on the part of a male regarding his future role as a father and family leader, spells disaster for unsuspecting woman unfortunate enough to end up with him.
**Correct Answer:**
A young man who has been reared by a father, who taught him the joys of fatherhood and the basics of moral role modeling and principles, will answer this with strong feelings of commitment to the role of father and family leader. Score one point.

7. **What kind of discipline structure do your parents have?**
**Wrong Answer:**
Any response showing anger and deep frustration with the discipline structure or lack there of in a family setting, is a sign that there is not much understanding or experience with good discipline. Also, a person with such reactions to discipline will usually show signs of his own lack of personal discipline. This is not a good candidate.
**Correct Answer:**
Expressions of appreciation for the discipline that he has received and a willingness to talk about the need for discipline in our lives, are a good sign that a young man will develop into a responsible disciplinarian. The honesty and sincerity of this response should also be measured by the individual's demonstration of his own self- discipline. Score one point.

8. **Does your father show his affection for your mother?**
**Wrong Answer:**
If the response to question number one is negative, then the honesty of any response to this question is in serious doubt. However, assuming the response to question number one is positive, you could still get a wrong answer to this question. Any response indicating embarrassment or surprise usually indicates that a father does not show affection for his wife in the presence of the children. This could also indicate the presence of some physical abuse. A tendency for physical abuse is one of the easiest character faults to hide. Even when there is open affection there can sometimes be severe abuse behind the scenes. It will take some time and persistence to really know the truth. This could be an undesirable candidate.
**Correct Answer:**
There should be a genuine joy and appreciation for the affection that a son sees his father show for his mother. No marriage is without its disagreements, but the overwhelming impression that a son receives about his father's love and tenderness for his mother should come through loud and clear. Score one point.

9. **Has your father or mother ever been divorced?**

**Wrong Answer:**
An affirmative response to this question is undoubtedly all too common in our present state of family decay. However, divorce, in and of itself, is not the deciding factor in such cases. There is a need for further questioning and understanding of the circumstances really to have a feel for how much it should count against a young man. More than one divorce on the part of the father or mother, or recent divorce, or evidence of extreme bitterness over a divorce, are all signs that permanent damage has probably taken place. Once children witness their parents' use of divorce as a solution to their relationship problems, the same option remains open as a possibility for them in solving their own future relationship problems. Not a good candidate.
**Correct Answer:**
The best answer is not only a negative response, but one that indicates a strong commitment to solving mutual problems, with divorce as an unacceptable alternative. The truth is—ALL—marital problems can be solved without divorce when both parties are pledged to reject divorce as an alternative, no matter what! Divorce never solves the problem; it only moves the problem forward to another place and time, for solution. On the contrary the damage caused by the divorce itself far outweighs the alternative costs or sacrifices, which could be implemented to deal directly with the problem and achieve a victory. Score one point.

# Contact Information

## Reformation Ministries International, Corp.

**421 Ridge Pike**
**Lafayette Hill, PA 19444**

**Internet:**

**Blogging**
**Book Purchases**
**Family and Group Teaching Aids**
**Free email subscriptions**
**Web Casting subscription for members**
**Web links**
**Downloads..................................www.ReformationInAction.com**

**Personal Speaking Engagements:**

**Phone-Cell: 610-809-2336**
**Phone-Cell: 915-588-7874**
**Phone--Off: 610-828-1216**
**Phone-Fax: 610-619-3517**
**Email:.......................................zester@reformationinacton.com**

**Media:**

**Conferences**
**Publications**
**Radio**
**Television**
**See our Webpage:........................www.ReformationInAction.com**

# Bibliography

I wish to acknowledge my deepest respect and appreciation for all of the men that God has used to minister into my life and who have been His instruments to exercise His will and to do His good pleasure in me. I list the Holy Bible as the first and keystone source for God's instruction, (my twentieth complete reading of the Bible was completed 03-05) but we must all recognize that God uses others of faith and grace in His preparation and molding activities of one's life. Those men who have already departed and are now with the Lord are listed first; the others are listed in relative importance to their impact and effective witness into my life and ministry. I have read and studied all the works listed, many more than once.

The more contemporary are by nature the least impacting on my personal life, but they are the most relevant for many readers to serve as confirmation of the on going problems and our need to effect change in our Christian culture now in our times. For this reason I have quoted more from them than from others, except for God's revealed Law-Word. These and other quoted sources are listed in the footnotes.

**The Holy Bible:**

**Aurelius Augustine:**
1. Confession
2. City of God
3. Christian Doctrine

**Martin Luther:**
1. The Bondage of The Will (Translation by J. I. Packer & O. R. Johnston)

**Dolina MacCuish:**
Luther and his Katie—The Influence of Luther's Wife on His Ministry

**Roland H. Bainton:**
Here I Stand—A Life of Martin Luther

**John Calvin:**
1. Calvin's Institutes of the Christian Religion (2Vols)

**Sam Wellman:**
John Calvin—Father of Reformed Theology

**Cornelius Van Til:**
1. Foundations of Christian Education: Addresses to Christian Teachers

**C. S. Lewis:**
1. Mere Christianity
2. The Screwtape Letters
3. The Abolition of Man
4. Miracles

**Greg. L. Bahnsen:**
1. By This Standard: The Authority of God's Law Today,
2. House Divided: The Break-Up of Dispensational
3. Theology, (With Kenneth L. Gentry, Jr.
4. No Other Standard: Theonomy And Its Critics
5. Foundations of Christian Scholarship: Essays In The Van Til Perspective, (With North, Rushdooney, Singer, Blake, Pratt, Poythress and Frame.)

**David Chilton:**
1. Paradise Restored: A Biblical Theology of Dominion
2. The Days of Vengeance: An Exposition of Revelation,
3. The Great Tribulation,
4. Productive Christians In An Age of Guilt-Manipulators

**Rousas John Rushdoony:**
1. Institutes of Biblical Law,
2. Foundations of Social Order: Studies in the Creeds and Councils of the Early Church,
3. Thy Kingdom Come: Studies in Daniel and Revelation
4. The One and The Many: Studies in the Philosophy of Order And Ultimacy,
5. Politics of Guilt and Pity,
6. The Messianic character of American Education,
7. This Independent Republic,
8. By What Standard?
9. Foundations of Christian Scholarship: Essays In The Van Til Perspective, (With North, Bahnsen, Singer, Blake, Pratt, Poythress and Frame.)

**Louis Berkhof:**
1. Systematic Theology
2. Foundations of Christian Education: Addresses to Christian Teachers

**Gary DeMar:**
1. God and Government: Issues in Biblical Perspc.
2. The Legacy of Hatred Continues: A Response to Hal Lindsey's "The Road to Holocaust," (With Leithart)
3. The Reduction of Christianity: A Biblical Response to Dave Hunt, (With Peter J. Leithart)
4. Christian Reconstruction, (With Gary North)

**Kenneth L. Gentry:**
1. The Beast of Revelation,
2. Before Jerusalem Fell: Dating the Book of

Revelation,
3. House Divided: the Break-up of Dispensational theology, (With Greg L. Bahnsen)
4. The Greatness of the Great Commission: The Christian
Enterprise in a Fallen World,
5. God's Law in the Modern World,
6. The Great Tribulation: Past or Future? (With Thomas D. Ice.)
7. He Shall Have Dominion: A Postmillennial Eschatology

**James Jordan:**
1. All the articles published in ICE newsletter since Dec. 1994

**Gary North:**
1. Marx's Religion of Revolution,
2. Puritan Economic Experiments,
3. Unconditional Surrender,
4. The Dominion Covenant: Genesis,
5. Backward, Christian Soldiers?
6. 75 Bible Questions Your Instructors Pray You Won't Ask,
7. Moses and Pharaoh,
8. The Sinai Strategy,
9. Conspiracy: A Biblical View,
10. Unholy Spirits: Occultism & New Age Humanism,
11. Dominion and Common Grace,
12. Inherit the Earth,
13. Liberating Planet Earth,
14. Is the World Running Down?
15. Political Polytheism,
16. Tools of Dominion: The Case Laws of Exodus,
17. Victim's Rights,
18. Judeo-Christian Tradition,
19. Westminster's Confession,
20. Christian Reconstruction, (With Gary DeMar)
21. The Coase Theorem,
22. Salvation through Inflation,
23. Rapture Fever,
24. Tithing and the Church,
25. Leviticus: An Economic Commentary,
26. Lone Gunners For Jesus,
27. Crossed Fingers: How the Liberals Captured the Presbyterian Church,
28. Sanctions and Dominion: An Economic Commentary on Numbers

**Karl Duff:**
1. Restoration of Men
2. Teen Sex and Happiness
3. Restoration of Marriage

**Dennis Peacock:**
1. Almighty and Sons: Doing Business God's Way
2. The Battle for The Mind of Men

**Ray R. Sutton:**
1. That You May Prosper

**Douglas Wilson:**
1. Recovering The Lost Tools of Teaching
2. The Paideia of God
3. Fidelity-What It Means To Be a One-Woman Man
4. Future Man

**Dwight Wilson:**
1. Armageddon Now! (Maybe the only honest premillenarian author, at least the bravest.)

**R. C. Sproul:**
1. Free Will,
2. Grace Unknown: The Heart of Reformed Theology,

**Starr Parker:**
1. Uncle Sam's Plantation-How Big Government Enslaves America's Poor and What We Can Do About It

**Douglas Giles:**
1. Political Twerps, Cultural Jerks, Church Quirks
2. Ruling Babylon

**Cal Thomas & Ed Dobson:**
1. Blinded By Might

**Gary Smalley & John Trent:**
1. Love is a decision

**John Leo:**
1. Incorrect Thoughts

**Vicki Courtney:**
1. Your Girl

**Kenneth Cain, Heidi Postlewait, and Andrew Thomson**
2. Emergency Sex and other Desperate Measures—A True Story From Hell On Earth

# Word Index

## E